# Deviant
# Life-Styles

# Deviant Life-Styles

## Edited by
## James M. Henslin

Transaction Books
New Brunswick, New Jersey

Library of Congress Catalog Number: 76-1765.
ISBN: 0-87855-101-8.
Printed in the United States of America.

Library of Congress Cataloging in Publication Data
Main entry under title:

Deviant life-styles.

Includes index.
1. Subculture—Addresses, essays, lectures. 2. Deviant behavior—Addresses, essays, lectures. 3. Sexual deviation—Addresses, essays, lectures. 4. Minorities—United States—Addresses, essays, lectures. I. Henslin, James M. II. Title.
HN65.D48      301.2'2     76-1765
ISBN 0-87855-101-8

FOR THE ONE WITH WHOM
I SHARE A LIFE-STYLE

# Contents

# Contributors

# Index

# Introduction

## James M. Henslin

Perhaps the most basic fact of human life is that no one faces solely by himself the rugged demands of living. Our birth signals the beginning of a series of voluntary and involuntary memberships by which each of us becomes a member of various human groups. Each of these groups that we join has already worked out its own forms of adjustment to the multifaceted and conflicting crosscurrents of social life. With at least the minimum degree of success required for survival, each has adapted to the complicated interplay of demanding circumstances that confront it. This reactive and creative process continues as groups confront changing demands due to changing situations.

As we participate in a group we learn the group's way of responding to the intricate contingencies of social life. We acquire specific ways and approaches for coming to terms with the exigencies that surround us, press down upon us, and continually demand reaction, adjustment, adaptation. Our group participation imparts to us far more than merely practical solutions to the problems of living, however, for as they jointly work out solutions to the circumstances they face, the members of a group are also developing mutual understandings on many aspects of social life. These shared understandings are of the utmost significance for the members of a group because these understandings serve as the basic frameworks by which reality is interpreted.

As we participate in group life, sharing in its activities, solutions to problems, and the basic approaches to the array of circumstances confronting the group, we are also participating in the group's orientational framework for interpreting the events of life. We not only learn fundamental, generally agreed-upon expectations of what to do under a myriad of circumstances, but we also learn ways of conceptualizing and giving order to the objects and events in our social and material environments. We acquire approved ways for reacting to the world around us, including a group-based orientation for sifting out the significant from the nonsignificant. The basic approach to life imparted by our group membership becomes a part of the self-identity with which we face the world and by which we evaluate that which surrounds us. Our group memberships even modify that finely honed instrument of cognition, the mind, including our feeling-sentiments, that complex of inter- and innerworkings of emotional evaluations and reactions. From our participation in groups we gain not only guides for our actions but also perspectives on life that color what we see and help determine the meaning we give to what happens to us.

In this reactive, creative process of adapting to the contingencies they confront, people around the world have worked out a fascinating variety of contrasting approaches to life. Consequently, societies radically differ from one another regarding both their expectations of overt behaviors and the fundamental orientations and frameworks by which they interpret the world. Within a given society, however, there can be high agreement on the basic ways of approaching and evaluating the world, as is the case with traditional societies in which there exists little competition for ideas and behaviors.

Though life in traditional societies has historically been the common human situation, such groups are fading from the social scene. Becoming more common are extensive, pluralistic social arrangements, societies composed of diverse groups that often conflict with one another as they vie for adherents and attempt to competitively demonstrate the supremacy of their form of behaviors and orientations to life. Each pluralistic society, however, contains dominant frameworks for interpreting the events of life. For example, overarching the fascinating diversity that characterizes our society are the major orientational themes of the possession and disposal of private property as a fundamental human right, a predominant future orientation, and the verification of knowledge through empirical means.

On the one hand, the competing groups of a pluralistic society can be oriented primarily toward the dominant cultural framework. In such cases they represent a varying stress on particular orientational themes. For example, this is the case with The National Academy of Sciences with its strictly empirical orientation to knowledge, as well as the garden varieties of the local chambers of commerce with their fierce defense of private capital. On the other hand, competing groups of a pluralistic society can be oriented away from the dominant cultural framework. Where this is the case, the orientational and behavioral differences can represent an appositional approach to life that brings the group into sharp conflict with representatives of the dominant moral order. Appositional approaches to social life can center around essential disagreement with basic cultural orientations, as with a group that once created a furor in American society, "hippies," with their fundamental focus on the present, their rejection of consumerism, and their concentrated search for metaphysical reality. Appositional approaches, however, need not present such broadly based challenges to dominant understandings of social reality. They can, on the contrary, be limited to more segmented portions of life, as evidenced by swingers and homosexuals who may well be in solid agreement with most basic cultural expectations but who differ fundamentally in their approach to achieving sexual satisfaction.

This book focuses on groups in American society that have worked out orientations to life that differ from life-styles commonly expected in our culture. The range of the differences covered is broad, from life-styles centering around variation in body type to appositional styles of life that are perceived as menacing threats and reacted to accordingly. Throughout these chapters run the dual emphases of group support in departing from dominant norms and the profound effects that deviant life-styles have on members who lead them.

The goal of this book is to share with the reader a "sympathetic understanding" of deviant life-styles, that is, an appreciation of the diversity of living arrangements that people in our pluralistic society have worked out as they have made their various adaptations to the contingencies they have faced. In striving for this goal, I have selected papers in which the authors use their pen and paper as a form of brush and canvas, painting in broad, descriptive strokes the characteristics of the groups they studied. Foremost in my mind in choosing a chapter was that as little as possible be lost in the difficult process of rendering the complexities and varieties of human behavior onto the otherwise cold communication form of an analytical article. These authors are remarkably successful in remaining true to their subject while subjecting human behavior to sociological analysis.

In order to gain a sympathetic understanding of any life-style, whether deviant or not, it is first necessary to gain the perspective of individuals who are participating in that life-style. If one wants to understand any group, to the degree that it is possible one must see the world as it is viewed by members who are participating in that group. Because the meanings people construct are major guides to their behavior, grasping those meanings is essential to sociological understanding. As people actively participate in the ongoing, highly complicated, and involving process of social living, they make both behavioral and orientational adaptations to the particular problems they face. As they overcome the obstacles they confront and as they experience the joys and sorrows of living human lives in an imperfect and frequently repressive society, people develop social constructs by which they define their unique worlds of social reality. By gaining the meanings of the participants in a deviant life-style, we are able to see the world at least somewhat as they see it and thus to at least partially grasp why they lead their particular style of life.

A variety of avenues are available that can open a sympathetic understanding to nonmembers of a life-style. The best is that of directly participating in these unique worlds oneself. But few of us possess either the time that such participation would require in removing us from our own routines or the contacts necessary for entry into such groups. If we did have the time and the contacts, most of us would probably lack the inclination to participate in life-styles that differ radically from our own—for our basic assumptions of what is "normal" in the world would undergo a profound and deeply upsetting challenge. Even granting that we have these requisites, very few of us possess the highly developed perceptual and analytical talents that are sine qua non for understanding through direct participation. Lacking access to this direct avenue, the next best route is to engage in detailed and extended discussions with knowledgeable representatives of deviant life-styles. But similar limitations apply that also close to most of us this means to understanding. The viable alternative is to gain this perspective by reading a thorough, penetrating account of worlds that fundamentally depart from dominant expectations, such as the detailed descriptions the authors of these selections provide of the world as seen and experienced by individuals living deviant life-styles.

As people live out their lives, they are limited to some small corner of existence. Consequently, their understandings of their own situations are necessarily limited by their limiting experiences. If an author were only to describe a deviant life-style from the point of view of group members experiencing that life, one would be left with an understanding that does not go beyond that of the participants. A sociological understanding, however, must surpass this, moving beyond simple description to include much more than the participants' view of their behavior. This is where sociological analysis comes into play. The observed human behavior is subjected by the sociological researcher to both an objective analysis within the framework of current sociological concepts and to a comparison with related research findings. The researched behavior, consequently, does not remain an isolated fragment of knowledge, but the social analyst develops a comparative understanding of the behaviors that he has observed and described.

Constructing an integrated book of readings while meeting these goals of detailed description and sociological analysis involves much pain, as well as pleasure. Fortunately, there was more pleasure than pain in working on this anthology because of the fascinating array of material available from *Transaction/Society*. Rather than having to search for papers that might be of suitable quality, I found myself in the enjoyable but difficult position of having available more selections of quality than I could use. Consequently, I was able to select articles that met the double criteria of presenting both excellent detailed descriptive materials and a rich conceptual analysis of the observed behaviors, chapters that can aid the reader in gaining an appreciative understanding of deviant life-styles.

From what I have written so far in this overview it should be apparent to the reader that my use of the word *deviant* to modify life-style does not mean *bad*, *sick*, *perverse*, or even *undesirable*. Indeed, I mean to imply no negative connotation by the terms *deviant* or *deviance*. These terms simply mean *nonnormative* or *departing from generalized expectations*, often in such a way that negative sanctions are the typical result. Because deviant is meant to be non-pejorative and nonevaluative, it is perhaps best equated with words having fewer negative connotations in the public mind such as non-dominant or differing from major expectations.

The opening selections analyze deviant life-styles located within the Japanese-American and the black-American communities and demonstrate some of the far-ranging, profound effects that socialization into an organized subgroup of society has on the individuals who become members of these subgroups. These particular chapters especially illustrate how subgroup membership directly affects social interaction. As the authors indicate, the self is presented in interaction with others in highly stylized ways commensurate with the values of the group. Styles of communication, both linguistic and nonverbal, are profoundly influenced by the expectations of fellow group members. But life-styles, of course, represent far more than readily observable external behaviors. Because they also represent basic approaches to the world, we find that subgroup memberships also shape world views. They provide evaluative screens through which members of these groups view major aspects of life, evaluating through their unique conceptual frameworks both the behaviors of others and of themselves. A major emphasis in these opening papers is that participation in a life-style greatly determines how people construct the moral order; that is, how they evaluate behavior as being right or wrong.

Each life-style, whether matching dominant expectations of society or whether deviating from them, is an adaptive mechanism for dealing with the expectations of others and the resulting manifold pleasures, challenges, and frustrations of social life. A number of alternative life-styles are open to the members of a pluralistic society, although only a highly limited number are usually possible for any individual given the primary mediating mechanisms of membership in geographical, social class, age, sex, racial, and ethnic groupings. A major life-style developed by many people in their adaptations to the contingencies of life centers around religious participation, the focus of the second part of this anthology.

In this second grouping of selections, the authors analyze persons who are dissatisfied with major orientations of contemporary American society and are searching for a more satisfying approach to life. The first example is persons whose search for alternatives leads them to traverse the exotic avenue of trying to remove themselves as much as possible from the insecurities of social life by placing themselves into what they consider to be the securities of God's will in handling poisonous snakes. The next selection focuses on persons who have been disillusioned by their withdrawal into a subcultural world characterized by drugs, sex, and the search for true meaning in life, and who have then turned to a form of "turned on" religion catering to the youth culture—now sans drugs, sans sex, but with the search for meaning and perfection relentlessly continuing. The third offering examines a group made up of persons who have met with severe frustration because of the typical ways in which others have reacted to their obesity. They are consequently following a series of "secular religious" rites as they relentlessly search for the illusive perfection of appearance. As we focus in this second part on deviant life-styles centering around religious participation, the major emphasis is on religious rites as an adaptive mechanism for dealing with the pressing problems of social life.

In the third part we turn to an analysis of people who develop deviant life-styles in their search for sexual satisfaction. The focus is both on people who seek culturally disapproved forms of sexual relations and individuals who supply these sexual outlets. The initial chapters analyze aspects of homosexual activities, namely, fellatio in public rest rooms and the social organization of a house of prostitution staffed by call boys. The following selection is a study on persons who have come through highly individuated learning experiences, including participation in the homosexual subculture, to the point that their major goal in life is to undergo an operation to change their sex so they can lead the life of a female. The concluding articles in this part, in contrast, focus on people who pursue deviant life-styles in their search for heterosexual relationships; namely, the behaviors of strippers and their customers, the females who sexually satisfy the clients of massage parlors, and married couples who seek both sexual relationships and long-term friendships with other married couples. Highly emphasized in this section are the twin themes of learning the norms adhering to a deviant life-style and learning how to manage a deviant identity, that is, coming to terms with the fact that one is heavily involved in activities that are culturally disapproved.

When deviant life-styles come into sharp conflict with dominant expectations, especially involving illegal acts, arrest and incarceration are frequently the result. In the fourth grouping of readings we focus on the social context of activities that frequently stimulate the judicial system to employ its heavy armor and weaponry against offenders of cultural expectations. The first two chapters deal with law-breaking activities of juveniles, whose reputations feed back into the authority system and, by shaping others' images and expectations, set into motion mechanisms that profoundly effect conformity and deviance. The moral career of a bum concludes this part with a soul-searching and depressing analysis of the never-ending fight with drunkenness, jail, forced relocation, and the continuing cycle of the same—until death provides release. Especially emphasized in these selections are how self-fulfilling prophecies lead to commitment to or away from deviant life-styles and how societal reaction affects the self-concepts and activities of deviants.

A number of major types of societal reaction to deviant life-styles is possible, ranging from the extreme of completely ignoring them to the extreme of organizing society's resources in a fierce attempt to combat and perhaps extinguish those people who are different. In the final part we focus on two major societal reactions. From the city of San Francisco an example of accommodation is examined, where straights and deviants have worked out a form of fairly peaceful toleration of one another resulting in a number of competing life-styles coexisting within the same small geographic region.

Also from the United States is provided a study of organized repression and persecution directed against hippies. The analytical emphasis in this final part is on the social processes that result in different forms of societal reaction being directed toward people who are living deviant life-styles.

In concluding this introduction, I would like to warn the reader that the class bias of contemporary sociology also shows up in this book. Sociologists who study deviance concentrate on those people who are on the receiving end of the impact of the law. It is primarily members of the upper class who are in the favorable power position of influencing and formulating the legislation that determines what behaviors will be formally disapproved by law. With their privileged influence on the judiciary, they are usually able to make certain that the enforcement of the law is directed away from themselves. The judicial system, consequently, moves a heavy hand against members of the lower class, whose behaviors frequently become outlawed because they differ from the ideas of morality held by people in power. Because contemporary sociology reflects this differential power of the social classes, there is, unfortunately, in this collection not a single offering on deviant life-styles among the rich.

This class bias also reflects the differential power of the wealthy in insuring their own privacy, in evading the scrutiny of social-science analysis of their own behaviors, while directing social-science research toward people who occupy the less privileged end of the economic spectrum. Among the many deprivations of the lower class, we must also number their inability to maintain distance from the probes of social-science researchers.

# Deviant
# Life-Styles

# I

# Deviant Life-Styles
# and Minority Membership

# Introduction

In this first section of the book we deal with deviant life-styles characterizing two contemporary racial groups in our multiethnic United States. The characteristics detailed in these chapters are not racially based. That is, they are behavioral characteristics that are learned as part of culture, not behaviors that originate geneologically. Like the chapters in the succeeding sections, these opening selections analyze contrasting *behavior styles*, learned ways of interacting with others. As the members of minority groups have made adjustments to their unique life experiences, they have learned highly specific ways of presenting the self to others. Over a period of generations, they have developed adaptations to the various contingencies of living with which they have been confronted. Unique life-styles are the result. Elaborately developed expectations of self-presentation have become part of their common culture, part of the basic ways of life that those individuals being socialized into the culture are expected to master.

Each subculture frees the individual to some extent by providing a degree of emotional security, a way of developing predictability in a world that so often seems unpredictable. Each subculture also provides some degree of protection or insulation from the outer world that so frequently appears threatening and insecure. While subculturally based protection, security, and predictability free their members for comfortable, ongoing interaction with others, subcultures also constrain their members. They both make highly insistent demands for conformance and provide harsh penalties for failure to comply with their constraints.

21

The far-reaching effects of subcultures on the lives of their members become apparent when we note from these articles that subcultures regularize activities, guide interaction, influence perceptions of time, provide interpretations of life's events, and direct evaluations of both others and the self. In short, highly developed subcultures such as those of American blacks and Japanese provide the basic framework from which the world is viewed. To remain a member in good standing in the subculture, indeed perhaps to survive within it, one must successfully meet these demands and expectations which exert such a remarkable degree of influence over the individual, guiding not only his overt behavior but also providing the basic evaluative screen from which he views and judges both his own performances and those of others.

In the first selection, Lyman analyzes the primary emphases in the current Japanese-American subculture. The paramount orientation of this subculture upon which basic interactions depend is emotional management. The ideal is provided by the samurai model, that of emotional equanimity based on reserves of inner psychic strength. In striving for this ideal of emotional equanimity even in the face of misfortune and disaster, fundamental expectations of requisite social distance must be constantly maintained. Control over body language, especially facial disclosure, along with careful concealment of feelings, opinions, and activities become primary means by which interactional relationships are kept formal in order to vigilently maintain social distance. Language is similarly crucial in this exacting process of maintaining distance in interpersonal relationships. Conversational propriety is highly valued, characterized by a marked deemphasis of the individual. Speaking style centers around the subject and predicate being only indirectly related in sentences, together with the maintenance of a high degree of tonal control, passivity, and the use of euphemisms. Go-betweens are also frequently used to express one's personal needs and desires, a form of "indirect speech" that avoids directly confronting others with one's personal problems and needs. Through these and similar techniques the interactional style in the Japanese-American subculture maintains a high degree of aloofness and formality in interpersonal relationships.

A fascinating contrast with these subcultural expectations of communication style is provided by Kochman's analysis of speech patterns in the black ghetto. Black idiom is almost at the opposite end of the interactional spectrum. It is fluent, lively, and highly colorful. It is marked by heavy emphasis on personal persuasiveness in the goal of creating favorable impressions of the self. Black idiom greatly emphasizes the personality of the speaker, whose utterances are expected to demonstrate a highly individuated personal style. By animated verbal and gestural communications, the speaker expresses his emotional involvement in the interaction. In doing this, he attempts to systematically break down interpersonal distance, frequently with the goal of directly securing personal gains from others.

As a group of people develop a distinctive style of life, their life-style exerts fascinating and far-ranging influences on people's lives. Not only are outward forms of communication affected, along with fashions in dress, hair style, and other aspects of appearance, but as Horton analyzes in the last chapter in this section, subcultural membership also influences perception of time, something that we frequently take for granted as being a part of nature.

In the realities of day-to-day living, people form attitudes and develop a behavioral repertoire similar to others in their subculture. These may be at sharp variance with the expected behaviors and attitudes of the dominant culture. Sometimes the differences are primarily limited to an external style that can be fairly easily accepted by nonmembers of the subculture. Frequently, however, these contrasting expectations of behavior also differ in the moral sphere, that is, in ideas of right and wrong. When this is the case, those people following a deviant life-style can be brought into direct conflict with the enforcement agents of the dominant culture. So it is with the *hustling* that has developed in black-ghetto culture as an adaptation to deprivating life circumstances. Hustling involves activities that are seen by these street-corner men as normal and expected, but are commonly viewed by others as illegal, immoral, and justifiably punishable. Yet hustling is integral to their lives, being an adaptive technique so central to their life-style that it not only sets the rhythm of their social activities but it also greatly contributes to their perception of the structure of time.

In each of these three opening chapters the authors do an excellent job of describing the world as it is perceived by persons living life-styles that sharply contrast with dominant cultural expectations. The authors painstakingly attempt to avoid imputing their own value judgments on the behavior they are describing. They attempt, instead, to be dispassionate sociological observers of the subcultural scene, communicating what the world looks like from that particular perspective. The life-styles characterizing these groups, which frequently seem so strange to those people who have been socialized into contrasting and sometimes conflicting standards of

behavior, thus take on new meaning. From these contributions we
can see, for example, how and why the middle-class world appears
so threatening to street-corner blacks, as well as how the communication style common to the middle-class world appears so
strange to those individuals raised in Japanese-American and black-
American subcultures.

# 1

# Japanese-American Generation Gap

## Stanford M. Lyman

When the first Japanese embassy arrived in the United States in 1860, the *Daily Alta Californian* reported with mingled approval and astonishment that:

> every beholder was struck with the self-possessed demeanor of the Japanese. Though the scenes which now met their gaze must have been of the most intense interest for novelty, they seemed to consider this display as due the august position they held under their Emperor, and not one of them, by sign or word, evinced either surprise or admiration.

Thus, with their first major debarkation in the New World, the Japanese appeared to Americans to lack emotional expression. Indeed, San Francisco's perceptive journalist went on to observe: "This stoicism, however, is a distinguishing feature with the Japanese. It is part of their creed never to appear astonished at anything, and it must be a rare sight indeed which betrays in them any expression of wonder." In the eighty-five years between Japan's first embassy and the end of World War II, this "distinguishing feature" of the Japanese became the cardinal element of the anti-Japanese stereotype. Characterized by journalists, politicians, novelists, and filmmakers as a dangerous, hostile people, the Japanese were also pictured as mysterious and inscrutable.

When World War II broke out, Japanese-Americans in the United States were automatically presumed to be loyal to Japan, and incarcerated for the duration of hostilities—a violation of their fundamental civil rights justified in the minds of many ordinary Americans by the perfidious character they imputed to all Japanese.

The Japanese stereotype was so widespread that it affected the judgments of some sociologists about the possibilities of Japanese assimilation. In 1913 sociologist Robert E. Park predicted their permanent consignment to minority status, and although he later reversed this prediction, his observations on Japanese characteristics emphasized their uncommunicative features, stolid faces, and apparently vacuous personality. "The American who is flattered at first by the politeness of his Japanese servant will later on, perhaps, cite as a reproach against the race the fact that 'we can never tell what a Japanese is thinking about.' "

Others were quick to recognize the remarkable record of achievement by Japanese-Americans. As early as 1909 Chester Rowell pointed to their refusal to accept unprofitable contracts, their commercial advancement beyond the confines of the ghetto, and their geniality and politeness. More recently, Rose Hum Lee vividly contrasted Chinese-Americans with their Japanese counterparts, noting that the *nisei* (American-born Japanese) "exhibit greater degrees of integration into American society than has been the case with the Chinese whose settlement is twice as long." Others have declared that the record of the Japanese in America is an achievement perhaps rarely equaled in the history of human migration. Careful statistical measures indicate that present-day Japanese in America have outstripped all other "colored" groups in America in occupational achievement and education.

It is interesting that analyses of Japanese-American achievement lay stress on those very same character traits that once made up the notorious stereotype. During World War II personnel managers and fellow workers in California and Chicago admired the nisei working in their factories as an alternative to detention. "What has happened here," wrote William Caudill and George de Vos, "is that the peers, teachers, employers, and fellow workers of the nisei have projected their own values onto the neat, well-dressed, and efficient nisei in whom they saw mirrored many of their own ideals." What were these ideals? They included patience, cleanliness, courtesy, and minding one's own business—the same ideals that could be distorted into the negative characteristics of unwarranted aloofness.

## Time-Person Perspectives

Both time and person are perceived in terms of geographic and generational distance from Japan. Japanese-Americans are the only immigrant group in America who specify by a linguistic term and characterize with a unique personality each generation of descendants from the original immigrants. They do not merely distinguish native-born from foreign-born but rather count geogenerationally forward or backward with each new generational grouping. Each generation removed from Japan is assumed to have its own characteristics, qualities that are derived at the outset from its spatiotemporal position, and are thus not subject to voluntary adoption or obviation.

Immigrants from Japan are called *issei*, literally *first generation*, a term referring to all those who were born and nurtured in Japan and who later migrated to the United States. The children of at least one issei parent are called *nisei*, literally *second generation*, a term that encompasses all those born in the United States of immigrant parentage. The grandchildren of issei are called *sansei*, literally *third generation*, and include all those born of nisei parentage. The great-grandchildren of issei are called *yonsei*, literally *fourth generation*, and include all those born of sansei parentage. The great-great grandchildren of issei are called *gosei* and include all those born of yonsei parentage. In addition, those who were born in the United States of issei parentage, were educated in Japan, and then returned to the United States are called *kibei*, literally *returned to America*, and their children are considered sansei.

The Japanese in America lay great emphasis on contemporaries. This does not mean that they have no sense of predecessors (those who lived in the past), successors (those who will live in the future), and consociates (those contemporaries with close personal relationships). Rather their ideas about these categories are vague and diffuse, or in the case of consociates, deemphasized and deprecated.

The basic conception of the nisei phenomenon depends ultimately on the objective existence of their own generational group. The Japanese community in general and the nisei group in particular provide a nisei with emotional security and a haven from the turbulence and unpredictable elements of the outer world. But the nisei group is threatened by both centripetal and centrifugal forces, by individual withdrawal and acculturative transcendence. Should individuals withdraw into dyadic relationships or small cliques or transcend the generational group by moving out into the world of their non-Japanese contemporaries, both the objective and subjective senses of nisei identity would lose their compelling force and the group's collective identity would be dissolved.

Thus, the nisei must worry on two fronts about the risks of intimate association. On the one hand the very close contacts inherent in the segregated yet secure Japanese community allow for intimate association below the level of the generational group; on the other hand the breakdown of prejudice and discrimination threatens to seduce the nisei individual away from the confines of his racial group. It follows that, for the nisei, social and interpersonal relations are governed by a permanent interest in maintaining an appropriate social distance, so that individuals do not escape into integration or withdraw themselves from group solidarity.

For the nisei to preserve the objective identity of their own generational group, interpersonal relations must be kept formal. The Japanese language itself is one of social forms, indicative politeness, and status identifiers. It is also one of indirection, removing the subject (speaker) in a sentence from direct relation to the predicate, and utilizing stylistic circumlocutions so that the intended object of the particular speech is reached by a circular rather than linear route. The result is that individuals are held at arm's length: potential consociates remain simply contemporaries—quasi-strangers and quasi-friends.

The issei were able to transmit the basic ideas of this culture to their offspring; however, not all of its conventions remain viable. Although the bow, whose rigid rules the Japanese imposed upon themselves while exempting all foreigners, did not survive the generational passage except in vestigial form of the quick jerk of the head offered by nisei to elders, issei, and visitors from Japan, other forms, especially verbal ones, could be translated into English. Japanese-Americans are likely to pay careful attention to titles, to employ the terms of genteel propriety, to avoid obscenity, and to use the passive voice. Further, they attempt to employ tonal control, euphemisms, and circumlocutive forms in speaking English. Europeans who speak English and most native-born Americans employ tonal change for emphasis and object indication. The nisei strive for flatness of tone and equality of meter, which make it difficult for the uninitiated to distinguish between important and insignificant items in any verbal encounter. For the nisei this style of speaking provides a continuous demonstration to self and comprehending others of the proper state of emotional equanimity; for the "foreigner" it induces wonder about what is really being said and in some instances nurtures suspicion of ulterior motives.

Nisei employ euphemisms whenever the more direct form might indicate a state of emotional involvement or evoke an undesirable emotional response and especially when the precise term could be insulting or otherwise provocative. Where no English euphemism is available, a Japanese term may be employed. For example, nisei understand that race is a touchy subject in America so they substitute more neutral terms derived from Japanese—and this despite the fact that nisei tend not to speak Japanese to their peers. The term *Caucasian* is sometimes used, but one is more likely to hear *hakujin*, which means, literally, *white man*, and occasionally one might overhear the pejorative *keto*, literally, a *hairy person* but freely translated as *barbarian*. For *Negro*, the nisei, who combine a culturally derived, mild antipathy to blackness of skin with an unevenly experienced and ambivalent form of the American Negrophobia, use the denotatively pejorative *kuron-bo*, literally, *black boy*, usually in a neutral and unpejorative sense, at least on the conscious level. For *Chinese*, another people toward whom nisei are ambivalent, the mildly pejorative Hawaiian term, *pake*, is quite commonly used.

Indirect speech is also affected by the use of go-betweens to mediate delicate matters. An intermediary may be employed to inform one friend that another wishes to borrow money from him and to sound out the former on his willingness to lend it. This saves the would-be borrower from a direct face-losing refusal should his friend decide not to lend the money, and the borrowee escapes the mutually embarrassing situation that would arise if he had to refuse to oblige his friend. An intermediary is also employed, occasionally, to warn someone that he will receive a social invitation or to inform him that a "surprise party" is planned for him.

One difficulty in using indirect speech is that it is the listener's duty to ascertain the context of what he hears and to glean from it and from his knowledge of the speaker and the context just what the important point is. Violations of this tacit, ritual speech relationship occur fairly often, sometimes among nisei themselves, but more often in encounters with outsiders. If a nonnisei, frustrated by the apparent pointlessness of a conversation, asks a specific, pointed question, the nisei is troubled. He may refuse to answer, change the subject, or more subtly redirect the conversation back to its concentric form. To maintain the appropriate ritual and calm state of speaker and audience, important items are buried beneath an avalanche of trivia, and in the most perfected of conversations, they are never brought to the surface at all, but are silently apprehended by the listener.

This emphasis on composure lends itself to unstated but widely held norms of conversational propriety appropriate to different social occasions. Because it is at informal parties, dinners, and tête-à-têtes that one's speech partners and oneself are vulnerable to conversion from contemporaries to consociates, it is precisely such occasions that require careful monitoring. Nisei "rules" for social gatherings include: 1) an emphasis on "democratic participation" in speech, that is, no one should speak too long or too much and everyone should have an opportunity to speak; 2) circulation—small clusters of people conversing are permissible but these should regularly decompose and reform with new elements, while lengthy dyadic conversations at a gathering of ten or twenty people are actively discouraged; 3) and unimportance—the content of conversations should be restricted to trivial matters. The most fruitful items for conversation, consequently, are sports, stocks and bonds, and technical subjects.

Nisei emotional management is also seen in their emphasis on form over function. Nisei golfers and bowlers who are performing poorly, or who believe they will do so, may justify their bad scores by pointing out that they are working on their stance, body form, follow-through. Because it is widely accepted that form and content are analytically separable but related aspects of a variety of activities, the claim to be emphasizing the former irrespective of the latter is perfectly acceptable, and prevents any attribution of the poor scores to the inner or actual state of the performer. Nisei behavior at pornographic movies shows a similar use of the emphasis of form to mask emotional discomfiture. For example, a nisei may comment on the physical anatomy, aesthetic quality, or gymnastic innovation of the nude bodies copulating on the movie screen, thus neutralizing stimulation.

Another response is to tease a member of the group about his excessive interest in the films, alleged similarities or dissimilarities between his behavior and that depicted on the screen, or his remarkable quietness in the presence of an obviously stimulating event.

To communicate their perfect control of body, mind, and feelings, nisei strive to set their faces at the expressionless level. Some nisei are so disturbed at the possibility of facial disclosure that they avoid facing others for any length of time or employ newspapers and magazines as a means of reducing eye contact during a conversation. The fact that they share a common concern over face management facilitates a mutual avoidance of staring.

Dissimulation is a regular feature of nisei life. Its most elementary form is the self-imposed limitation on disclosure. Nisei tend not to volunteer any more information about themselves than they have to. Thus, a nisei will sometimes not tell about an important event or will casually dismiss it with a denial or only a partial admission, suggesting by style and tone that it was not important at all. Direct questions are usually answered with vague or mildly meretricious replies. Still another element of dissimulation is concealment of feelings, opinions, or activities, especially in the presence of employers, colleagues, and guests. Colleagues and superiors of middle-management nisei have sometimes been astonished at their silence during conferences or executive meetings. But the nisei do not feel the need to justify these omissions, "white lies," or evasions; rather the burden would appear to be on the listener to demonstrate why such tact and tactics should not be employed.

Nisei avoid persons and situations likely to evoke embarrassment, personal disorganization, or loss of self-control. When a nisei takes on a new line of endeavor, especially one that requires learning a new skill or taking a risk, he does so in secret or with people he does not know well. After the skill has been mastered or the risk evaluated as worthwhile, he will casually tell close associates that he might be about to undertake the line of action in question. Fellow nisei will understand that all preparations, rehearsals, and calculations have already been made and if they later see a performance of the new skill, they remain silently aware that it is in fact an exhibition of an already perfected ability.

When a nisei recognizes a close associate's excessive *amae* (*dependence*) toward him, he may become upset by this fact, retreat even further behind a formal facade of etiquette, and attempt to establish greater social distance. Or he might clandestinely request that a third party tactfully urge the friend to be less demanding. An alternative is to gently but firmly tease the offending party until he realizes that he has overstepped the bounds of propriety. Still another tactic is to make sure that all contacts with the offending party will take place with other friends present, so that his excessive affection will be diffused among the whole body of friends rather than centered on just one person.

### Building Nisei Character

The fundamental source of nisei character is to be found in the samurai ethic. *Chambara* (*samurai*) stories always emphasize the stoic character of the solitary and often tragic warrior, who though beset by personal or clan enemies, political misfortunes, and natural disasters, nevertheless retains inner psychic strength and emotional equanimity. These heroes, familiar to non-Japanese-Americans by the poignant screen portrayals of such actors as Toshiro Mifune and Tatsuya Nakadai, serve the nisei as ideal character models and reminders of the appropriate presentation of self.

The patterns of hierarchical society were predominant in the early life of the issei, who grew up in a time of great technological and political but little ethical or interpersonal change in Japan. The mod-

ernization of the country was achieved not by overturning the old
cultural order but by adapting Western industrial, educational, and
military forms to its framework. The educational system fostered
the study of classics and, later, the more technical subjects; it also,
and more important, directed its major attention to the development of virtue, humble modesty before superiors, self-control, and
etiquette. Consequently, though few of the issei were of samurai
rank, they bore the cultural marks that had been part of the Japanese tradition for at least two centuries.

In addition to the samurai ethic, elements of the rural farmer's
outlook helped forge the orientation with which the issei reared their
children. The *ie* system, by which Japanese farmers represented
both the contemporary physical house and the permanent family
household, operated through the notion of preservation and continuity to forestall the development of individualism. In Japan's rural
villages the *honke-bunke* (*stem-branch family system*) allowed nu-
clear families to split off from one another in a partial sense, so that
nothing like the extended Chinese clan system developed, but atomi-
zation below the *ie*, or household, level was strongly discouraged.
The *ie* was far more important than the individuals who comprised
it, and village people would speak of the *iegara* or *kakaku*, that is,
the reputation or standing of a family, rather than the *hitogara* or
*jinkaku*, the personality or social standing of individual members.

In America the issei men, often married by proxy to women
whom they had only seen in pictures and who were sometimes quite
a bit younger than they were, applied traditional principles of child
rearing to the nisei offspring. In certain respects, perhaps because
the issei fathers lacked the outlet of Japan's bath houses and geisha,
child rearing was harsher than in Japan; the nisei offspring in turn
lacked the presence of an indulgent grandmother to counterbalance
the severity of parental authority. Physical punishments were rarely
used, although in one known instance an Okinawan nisei reported
that his father purposely cut his ears when giving him a haircut.
When the boy screamed in pain, his father would slap him across the
face with the stern admonition: "You don't scream. Japanese boys
do not scream." However, physical punishment is unusual in issei-
nisei families. Much more likely is the use of ridicule and teasing, a
common theme being to tease a recalcitrant, noisy, emotionally
upset, or otherwise obstreperous boy about behaving like a little
girl.

Emphasis was placed on individual superiority, achievement, and
education as criteria for both individual and group maturity. Nisei
children would not be invited to discuss family matters at the dinner

table until age and achievement had demonstrated their worth. Children and adolescents would be admonished with the statement *nisei wa mada tsumaranai*, that is, they were told that the nisei generation was still worthless. Until manhood had been demonstrated, the nisei were treated as immature but developing children.

Central to this demonstration of maturity was self-control. Emotional management, even in childhood, was always worthy of exhibition and constantly tested. A line of family authority extended downward from the issei father through the mother to the first-born, second-born, third-born, and so on, while a line of obligation extended upward from the youngest to the eldest. This authority system was not infrequently tested by an elder brother harshly rebuking a younger, sometimes for no apparent reason. Younger brothers learned that if they could take these rebukes with outward calm they would ultimately be rewarded with a recognition of maturity. First-born sons received similar treatment from their fathers, and daughters sometimes found that they had to live up to both the precepts of manhood maturity and of womanliness.

Among the nisei, peer-group teasing and ridicule function to monitor behavior. Cuts, digs, put-downs, and embarrassing stories are the stuff of verbal life in the clubs, cliques, and gangs of nisei teenagers. The didactic purpose of this teasing is widely accepted and regular "victims" have on occasion reported to me their heartfelt gratitude for it.

Two rules appear to govern nisei teasing. First, the relative status position of any particular nisei may render him either ineligible or preferable for teasing. There is a tendency, for instance, for nisei whose parents hail from peasant and poor prefectures not to tease those who parents are from urban and socioeconomically better-off areas; for nisei from rural parts of California to be somewhat awed by those from San Francisco or Los Angeles; and for clique leaders to be less eligible for cuts than ordinary members.

Second, nisei ridicule and joking must steer a careful course between the Scylla of ineffectiveness and the Charybdis of associative breakup. If jokes and cuts are too mild, too obscure, or always mitigated by apologies and explanations, then the straying party is not brought to heel. If, on the other hand, the jokes are too pointed, if they cut to the very heart of a person and leave him no room for maneuver or retreat, then he may withdraw from the group in shame or anger and be lost, perhaps permanently, to its benefits and protections.

To indicate that a teasing person has gone too far, a nisei "target" may warn his persecutor by directing a telling remark at a third party within earshot. Once I was watching two youthful nisei friends of mine escalate their reciprocal cuts when the offended party turned to me and said, "Man, he's a chilly dude, isn't he?" The other recognized the rebuke for what it was and began to deescalate his humorous assaults. And so the appropriate relationship—not too close, not too distant— was maintained.

The nisei ideal character is not unfamiliar. It was once thought to be peculiar to aristocrats, Orientals, and urbanites, but today's industrial societies seem to require of everyone that they be blasé, sophisticated, and, in more recent times, cool. For the nisei this means, ideally, combining courage, that is, willingness to proceed on an anticipated dangerous course of action without any manifestation of fearfulness; gameness, that is, sticking to a line of action and expending energy on it despite setbacks, injury, fatigue, and even impending failure; and integrity, that is, the resistance to temptations that would reduce the actor's moral stance. The greatest emphasis is on composure, which includes all its ramifications of physical and mental poise, calmness in the face of disruptions and embarrassing situations, presence of mind and the avoidance of "blocking" under pressure, emotional control during sudden changes of situation, and stage confidence during performances before audiences.

In everyday discussions with nisei, any nonnisei listener would be impressed by their pointed perceptions and shrewd observations of others. These observations are made about absent third parties and are never uttered in the presence of the person under discussion. Many people would be surprised at how keenly quite ordinary nisei have paid attention to the minute details of interpersonal situations, placed brackets around particular sets of events, and interpreted words and gestures in light of the general theory of nisei character.

Parlor psychoanalysis is quite common. One nisei may speak of another in terms of the latter's essential inability to mask his "inferiority complex," "fear of failure," or "feelings of inadequacy." These perceptions may in fact be projections. Nisei tend to function as one another's mirrors, showing up the defects in each other's character. This is possible because the wall that the nisei have built to prevent others from seeing their own emotions is really only a set of personal blinders that keep the individual from introspection. In attempting to separate personal feeling from particular action the nisei have alienated their emotional from their behaving selves. Thus they see their fellow men from an angle not shared by those with less self-detachment.

Witty repartee is a well-developed and highly prized art among the nisei, but precisely because skill at it is differentially distributed, no nisei feels quite comfortable about it. They often have trouble deciding whether a joke is didactic or destructive. Beyond adolescence, nisei occasionally confess discomfiture about being permanently locked into a system of competitive relations with their fellows. Social visits are occasions for the reciprocal giving of humorous remarks calling attention to invidious distinctions. Birth, sex, and growth of children, richness and style of furniture, occupational advancement, skill at leisure-time activities, and many other everyday things may become grist for the wit's mill.

Nisei encounters with friends and colleagues tend to be episodic rather than developmental, as is normal in nonnisei interactions. Among nisei, there is a limit in expressing feelings that may not be deepened without loss of inner equanimity or outer poise. Hence, nisei tend to treat each encounter almost as if the participants were meeting for the first time. To Americans, who usually assume that each new social encounter will begin at the emotional level or feeling-state reached at the end of the last meeting, the apparent coldness of response may be puzzling.

It does sometimes occur that ceremony and etiquette collapse and nisei find themselves locked in the mutually embarrassing relationship of consociates. This most often happens when one party in an encounter is unable to sustain appropriate emotional equipoise and ceremony collapses. The others present will try to restore the proper social distance—either by studied nonobservation of the other's embarrassment or by a warm but unmistakably triumphant grin signaling simultaneously a victory in the ever-played game of social testing and the social reinstatement of the losing player.

### The Crisis of the Future

The Japanese geogenerational conception of time and person evokes the recognition that each generation with its attendant character structure will eventually decline and pass away. The issei generation is by no means gone, but its influence has been declining since 1942, when the enforced incarceration propelled the nisei into positions of prison camp and community leadership. At the present moment the nisei group is beginning to sense its own decline and eventual disappearance as the sansei generation comes to maturity and establishes its independent existence and special group identity in America.

The census of 1960 reported that 82 percent of all Japanese in 13 Western states were born in the United States, its territories, or its possessions. The manner of taking the census prohibits any further breakdown of these figures into their respective geogenerational groupings; but we can arrive at a crude approximation by looking at age distribution. Out of 159,545 persons of Japanese descent living in California, the 1960 census recorded 68,015 between the ages of zero and 24. Most of these are the children, grandchildren, or occasionally great-grandchildren of nisei. So the nisei can clearly see the end of their generational existence in the not too distant future.

The inevitability of this end has provoked a mild crisis in the *Lebenswelt* of the nisei. They are coming to realize with a mixture of anxiety, discomfort, and disillusion, but primarily with a sense of fatalistic resignation, that the way of life they are used to, the presentation of self they have always taken for granted, the arts of self-preservation and impression management they have so assiduously cultivated and so highly prized, will soon no longer be regular features of everyday existence among the Japanese in America, and what they have accomplished by living this way will no longer be accomplished this way or perhaps at all. The sansei, and for that matter, the other successor generations, will be different from the nisei in certain fundamental respects.

Nisei have always seemed to recognize the sociocultural and psychic differences between themselves and the sansei. Some of these are based on clearly distinguishable generational experiences. Few sansei are old enough to have experienced the terrible effects of imprisonment during World War II; many come from homes in which there is no noticeable cultural division between America and Japan and very often have received support for their educational pursuits from parents who have been materially successful. Finally, very few of the sansei have borne the oppressive burden of racial discrimination or have felt the demoralizing agony of anti-Japanese prejudice with the same intensity as the nisei. In all these respects the nisei recognize that sansei are the beneficiaries of their own and their parents' struggles and acknowledge that if the sansei do behave differently it is only right and proper that they do so.

But there is one aspect of sansei behavior that worries and disappoints the nisei: their lack of appropriate nisei character. Some nisei see this characterological loss as a product of increased urbanization and Americanization; others emphasize the loss of Japanese culture in the third generation. Whatever the explanation, many nisei perceive a definite and irremediable loss of character in their successor generation. To illustrate this point, note that nisei often use the term *sansei* to indicate at one and the same time the existence and the cause of social impropriety. Thus in the face of an individual's continued social errors in my presence, a nisei explained to me, "What can you expect? He's a sansei."

Ironically, nisei child-rearing and parental practices contribute to the creation of the very character that disappoints them, just as their own issei parents helped to lay the groundwork for nisei character. Despite the general respect and personal deference the nisei render their parents, they recall the isolation, the harshness, and the language and communication difficulties that marred their own childhoods, and many of them determined to raise their children differently. As a result nisei parents rarely emphasize the ethics of samurai stoicism, endurance, and discipline, preferring to follow the white, middle-class ethos of love, equality, and companionship.

From the point of view of most nisei, the results have been disappointing. Sansei, they complain, lack the drive and initiative that once was a hallmark of the Japanese; they have no interest in Japanese culture, especially its characterological elements; they are more prone to delinquency and have less respect for authority than the nisei; they are "provincial" and bound to the "provincialisms" of Los Angeles, which has probably the single largest aggregate of sansei. They also deplore the lack of psychological self-sufficiency and independent capacity for decision making among sansei.

A nisei scoutmaster told me how his scout troop, mostly sansei, became homesick and upset when away for a week's camping trip, and how their projected wiener roast would have been ruined if he had not stepped in and directed the planning for food purchases. He attributed these "failings" to their sansei background, but admitted that his own intervention in the scouts' plans was a distinct departure from what his own parents would have done in a similar situation during his childhood. Issei parents would probably have let their children fail in such an endeavor in order to help them cultivate responsibility and initiative. But to many nisei such a seemingly unfeeling response to their own children is anathema.

Sansei indicate an ambivalence and a mild anxiety over their own situation. They do exhibit a desire to recover selected and specific elements of the culture of old Japan, but find that their own Americanization has limited the possibility of very effective recovery. If juvenile delinquency among them is on the rise (in fact the evidence is inconclusive), they attribute it in small part to parental misunderstandings and in larger part to the effects of the great social change taking place in America. They find their parents old-fashioned, often unprepared to understand their hang-ups and unwilling to offer sufficient love and understanding. At times they seem about to claim the right to dissolve their own geogenerational identity and that of their successor generations in order to achieve deeper intimate associations below the level of the generational group and interracial intimacies that transcend it. Yet they also wonder how and in what manner they can or should retain their Japanese identity.

As for the nisei, they have not merely survived the hatred and oppression of America's racism, but they have triumphed over it. In nearly every objective measure they outstrip their minority competitors, and in education they have surpassed the white majority. They have turned almost every adversity into a challenge and met each with courage and cool judgment. In all this their own subcultural character has been an invaluable aid and an ever-present source of pride. Inevitably, their own generation and this character are both coming to an end; they cannot turn back the generational clock, but only wonder what psychic supports will provide mental sustenance for the generations to come. In one sense the nisei are the last of the Japanese Americans; the sansei are American-Japanese.

# 2

# "Rapping" in the Black Ghetto

## Thomas Kochman

"Rapping," "shucking," "jiving," "running it down," "gripping," "copping a plea," "signifying," and "sounding" are all part of the black-ghetto idiom and describe different kinds of talking. Each has its own distinguishing features of form, style, and function; each is influenced by, and influences, the speaker, setting, and audience; and each sheds light on the black perspective and the black condition—on those orienting values and attitudes that will cause a speaker to speak or perform in his own way within the social context of the black community.

I was first introduced to black idiom in New York City, and, as a professional linguist interested in dialects, I began to compile a lexicon of such expressions. My real involvement, however, came in Chicago, while preparing a course on black idiom at the Center for Inner City Studies, the southside branch of Northeastern Illinois State College.

Here I began to explore the full cultural significance of this kind of verbal behavior. My students and informants within black Chicago, through their knowledge of these terms, and their ability to recognize and categorize the techniques, and to give examples, gave me much reliable data. When I turned for other or better examples to the literature—such as the writings of Malcolm X, Robert Conot, and Iceberg Slim—my students and informants were able to recognize and confirm their authenticity.

While often used to mean ordinary conversation, *rapping* is distinctively a fluent and a lively way of talking, always characterized

by a high degree of personal style. To one's own group, rapping may
be descriptive of an interesting narration, a colorful rundown of
some past event. An example of this kind of rap is the answer from a
Chicago gang member to a youth worker who asked how his group
became organized:

> Now I'm goin' tell you how the jive really started. I'm goin'
> to tell you how the club got this big. 'Bout 1956 there used to be
> a time when the Jackson Park show was open and the Stony
> show was open. Sixty-six street, Jeff, Gene, all of 'em, little
> bitty dudes, little bitty . . . Gene wasn't with 'em then. Gene
> was cribbin' [living] over here. Jeff, all of 'em, real little bitty
> dudes, you dig? All of us were little.
> Sixty-six [the gang on sixty-sixth street], they wouldn't allow
> us in the Jackson Park show. That was when the parky [?] was
> headin' it. Everybody say, "If we want to go to the show, we
> go!" One day, who was it? Carol Robinson. He went up to the
> show . . . and Jeff fired on him. He came back and all this was
> swelled up 'bout yay big, you know. He come back over to the
> hood [neighborhood]. He told [name unclear] and them dudes
> went up there. That was when mostly all the main sixty-six
> boys was over here like Bett 'Riley. All of 'em was over here.
> People that quit gang-bangin' [fighting, especially as a group],
> Marvell Gates, people like that.
> They went on up there, John, Roy, and Skeeter went in
> there. And they start humbuggin' [fighting] in there. That's
> how it all started. Sixty-six found out they couldn't beat us, at
> *that* time. They couldn't *whup* seven-o. Am I right Leroy? You
> was cribbin' over here then. Am I right? We were dynamite!
> Used to be a time, you ain't have a passport, Man, you couldn't
> walk through here. And if didn't nobody know you it was worse
> than that. . . .

Rapping to a woman is a colorful way of "asking for some
pussy." "One needs to throw a lively rap when he is 'putting the
make' on a broad." (See the following chapter by John Horton.)

According to one informant, the woman is usually someone he
has just seen or met, looks good, and might be willing to have sexual
intercourse with him. My informant says the term would not be
descriptive of talk between a couple "who have had a relationship
over any length of time." Rapping, then, is used at the beginning of
a relationship to create a favorable impression and be persuasive at
the same time. The man who has the reputation for excelling at this
is the pimp or mack man. Both terms describe a person of considerable status in the street hierarchy, who, by his lively and persuasive

rapping ("macking" is also used in this context) has acquired a stable of girls to hustle for him and give him money. For most street men and many teenagers he is the model whom they try to emulate. Thus, within the community you have a pimp walk, pimp-style boots and clothes, and perhaps most of all "pimp talk." The following is a colorful literary example of a telephone rap. One of my informants regards it as extreme, but agrees that it illustrates the language, style, and technique of rapping. "Blood" is rapping to an ex-whore named Christine in an effort to trap her into his stable:

> Now try to control yourself baby. I'm the tall stud with the dreamy bedroom eyes across the hall in four-twenty. I'm the guy with the pretty towel wrapped around his sexy hips. I got the same hips on now that you X-rayed. Remember that hump of sugar your peepers feasted on?
> She said, "Maybe, but you shouldn't call me. I don't want an incident. What do you want? A lady doesn't accept phone calls from strangers."
> I said, "A million dollars and a trip to the moon with a bored, trapped, beautiful bitch, you dig? I'm no stranger. I've been popping the elastic on your panties ever since you saw me in the hall. . . ."

Rapping between men and women often is competitive and leads to a lively repartee with the women becoming as adept as the men. An example follows:

> A man coming from the bathroom forgot to zip his pants. An unescorted party of women kept watching him and laughing among themselves. The man's friends "hip" [inform] him to what's going on. He approaches one woman—"Hey baby, did you see that big black Cadillac with the full tires? ready to roll in action just for you." She answers—"No mother-fucker, but I saw a little gray Volkswagen with two flat tires." Everybody laughs. His rap was "capped" [excelled, topped].

When "whupping the game" on a "trick" or "lame" (trying to get goods or services from someone who looks like he can be swindled), rapping is often descriptive of the highly stylized verbal part of the maneuver. In well-established "con games" the rap is carefully prepared and used with great skill in directing the course of the transaction. An excellent illustration came from an adept hustler who was playing the "murphy" game on a white trick. The "murphy" game is designed to get the *trick* to give his money to the hustler, who in this instance poses as a "steerer" (one who directs or steers customers to a brothel), to keep the whore from stealing it. The hustler then skips with the money.

> Look Buddy, I know a fabulous house not more than two blocks away. Brother you ain't never seen more beautiful, freakier broads than are in that house. One of them, the prettiest one, can do more with a swipe than a monkey can with a banana. She's like a rubber doll; she can take a hundred positions."
>
> At this point the sucker is wild to get to this place of pure joy. He entreats the con player to take him there, not just direct him to it.
>
> The "murphy" player will prat him [pretend rejection] to enhance his desire. He will say, "Man, don't be offended, but Aunt Kate, that runs the house, don't have nothing but high-class white men coming to her place. . . . You know, doctors, lawyers, big-shot politicians. You look like a clean-cut white man, but you ain't in that league are you? (Iceberg Slim, *Pimp: The Story of My Life*)

After a few more exchanges of the "murphy" dialogue, "the mark is separated from his scratch."

An analysis of rapping indicates a number of things.

For instance, it is revealing that one raps *to* rather than *with* a person supporting the impression that rapping is to be regarded more as a performance than verbal exchange. As with other performances, rapping projects the personality, physical appearance, and style of the performer. In each of the examples given, the intrusive "I" of the speaker was instrumental in contributing to the total impression of the rap.

The combination of personality and style is usually best when "asking for some pussy." It is less when "whupping the game" on someone or "running something down."

In "asking for some pussy," for example, where personality and style might be projected through nonverbal means—stance, clothing, walking, looking—one can speak of a "silent rap." The woman is won here without the use of words, or rather, with words being implied that would generally accompany the nonverbal components.

As a lively way of "running it down," the verbal element consists of personality and style plus information. To someone *reading* my example of the gang member's narration, the impression might be that the information would be more influential in directing the listener's response. The youth worker might be expected to say, "So that's how the gang got so big," instead of, "Man, that gang member is *bad* [strong, brave]" in which instance he would be responding to the personality and style of the rapper. However, if the reader would *listen* to the gang member on tape or could have been present when the gang member spoke, he more likely would have reacted more to personality and style as my informants did.

Remember that in attendance with the youth worker were members of the gang who *already knew* how the gang got started (for example, "Am I right Leroy? You was cribbin' over here then") and for whom the information itself would have little interest. Their attention was held by the *way* the information was presented.

The verbal element in "whupping the game" on someone, in the preceding example, was an integral part of an overall deception in which information and personality style were skillfully manipulated for the purpose of controlling the "trick's" response. But again, greater weight must be given to personality style. In the "murphy game," for example, it was this element that got the trick to trust the hustler and leave his money with him for "safekeeping."

The function of rapping in each of these forms is *expressive*. By this I mean that the speaker raps to project his personality onto the scene or to evoke a generally favorable response. When rapping is used to "ask for some pussy" or to "whup the game" on someone, its function is *directive*. By this I mean that rapping becomes an instrument to manipulate and control people to get them to give up or to do something. The difference between rapping to a "fox" (pretty girl) for the purpose of "getting inside her pants" and rapping to a "lame" to get something from him is operational rather than functional. The latter rap contains a concealed motivation where the former does not.

"Shucking," "shucking it," "shucking and jiving," "S-ing" and "J-ing," or just "jiving," are terms that refer to language behavior practiced by the black when confronting "the Man" (the white man, the establishment, or *any* authority figure), and to another form of language behavior practiced by blacks with each other on the peer-group level.

In the South, and later in the North, the black man learned that American society had assigned to him a restrictive role and status. Among whites his behavior had to conform to this imposed station and he was constantly reminded to "keep his place." He learned that it was not acceptable in the presence of white people to show feelings of indignation, frustration, discontent, pride, ambition, or desire; that real feelings had to be concealed behind a mask of in-

nocence, ignorance, childishness, obedience, humility, and deference. The terms used by the black to describe the role he played
before white folks in the South was "tomming" or "jeffing." Failure
to accommodate the white Southerner in this respect was almost
certain to invite psychological and often physical brutality. A description related by a black psychiatrist, Alvin F. Poussaint, is typical and revealing:

> Once last year as I was leaving my office in Jackson, Missis-
> sippi, with my Negro secretary, a white policeman yelled,
> "Hey, boy! Come here!" Somewhat bothered, I retorted: "I'm
> no boy!" He then rushed at me, inflamed, and stood towering
> over me, snorting "What d'ja say, boy?" Quickly he frisked me
> and demanded, "What's your name boy?" Frightened, I re-
> plied, "Dr. Poussaint. I'm a physician." He angrily chuckled
> and hissed, "What's your first name, boy?" When I hesitated
> he assumed a threatening stance and clenched his fists. As my
> heart palpitated, I muttered in profound humiliation, "Alvin."
> He continued his psychological brutality, bellowing, "Alvin,
> the next time I call you, you come right away, you hear? You
> hear?" I hesitated. "You hear me, boy?" My voice trembling
> with helplessness, but *following my instincts of self-preserva-
> tion*, I murmured, "Yes, sir." *Now fully satisfied that I had
> performed and acquiesced to my "boy" status*, he dismissed me
> with, "Now, boy, go on and get out of here or next time we'll
> take you for a little ride down to the station house! ("A Negro
> Psychiatrist Explains the Negro Psyche," *The New York
> Times Magazine*, 20 August 1967, emphasis added)

In the Northern cities the black encountered authority figures
equivalent to Southern "crackers"—policemen, judges, probation
officers, truant officers, teachers, and "Mr. Charlies" (bosses)—
and soon learned that the way to get by and avoid difficulty was to
shuck. Thus, he learned to accommodate "the Man," to use the
total orchestration of speech, intonation, gesture, and facial expression for the purpose of producing whatever appearance would be acceptable. It was a technique and ability that was developed from
fear, a respect for power, and a will to survive. This type of accommodation is exemplified by the Uncle Tom with his, "Yes sir, Mr.
Charlie," or, "Anything you say, Mr. Charlie."
Through accommodation, many blacks became adept at concealing and controlling their emotions and at assuming a variety of
postures. They become competent actors. Many developed a keen
perception of what affected, motivated, appeased, or satisfied the

authority figures with whom they came into contact. Shucking became an effective way for many blacks to stay out of trouble, and for others it was a useful artifice for avoiding arrest or getting out of trouble when apprehended. Shucking it with a judge, for example, would be to feign repentance in the hope of receiving a lighter or suspended sentence. Robert Conot reports an example of shucking in his book, *Rivers of Blood, Years of Darkness:* Joe was found guilty of possession of narcotics. But he did an excellent job of shucking it with the probation officer.

The probation officer interceded for Joe with the judge: "His own attitude toward the present offense appears to be serious and responsible and it is believed that the defendant is an excellent subject for probation."

Some field illustrations of shucking to get out of trouble came from some seventh-grade children from an inner-city school in Chicago. The children were asked to talk their way out of a troublesome situation.

You are cursing at this old man and your mother comes walking down the stairs. She hears you.

To "talk your way out of this":

"I'd tell her that I was studying a scene in school for a play."

What if you were in a store stealing something and the manager caught you?

"I would start stuttering. Then I would say, 'Oh, oh, I forgot. Here the money is.' "

A literary example of shucking comes from Iceberg Slim's autobiography. Iceberg, a pimp, shucks before "two red-faced Swede rollers [detectives]" who catch him in a motel room with his whore. My italics identify which elements of the passage constitute the shuck.

> I put my shaking hands into the pajama pockets. . . .
> *I hoped I was keeping the fear out of my face. I gave them a wide toothy smile.* They came in and stood in the middle of the room. Their eyes were racing about the room. Stacy was open mouthed in the bed.
> I said, *"Yes gentlemen, what can I do for you?"*
> Lanky said, "We wanta see your I.D."
> I went to the closet and got the phony John Cato Fredrickson I.D. I put it in his palm. I felt cold sweat running down my back. They looked at it, then looked at each other.
> Lanky said, "You are in violation of the law. You signed the motel register improperly. Why didn't you sign your full name?

What are you trying to hide? What are you doing here in town? It says here you're a dancer. We don't have a club in town that books entertainers."

I said, *"Officer, my professional name is Johnny Cato. I've got nothing to hide. My full name had always been too long for the marquees. I've fallen into the habit of using the shorter version."*

*"My legs went out last year. I don't dance anymore. My wife and I decided to go into business. We are making a tour of this part of the country. We think that in your town we've found the ideal site for a Southern fried chicken shack. My wife has a secret recipe that should make us rich up here."* (Iceberg Slim, *Pimp: The Story of My Life*)

Another example of shucking was related to me by a colleague. A black gang member was coming down the stairway from the club room with seven guns on him and encountered some policemen and detectives coming up the same stairs. If they stopped and frisked him, he and others would have been arrested. A paraphrase of his shuck follows: "Man, I gotta get away from up there. There's gonna be some trouble and I don't want no part of it." This shuck worked on the minds of the policemen. It anticipated their questions as to why he was leaving the club room, and why he would be in a hurry. He also gave *them* a reason for wanting to get up to the room fast.

It ought to be mentioned at this point that there was not uniform agreement among my informants in characterizing the above examples as shucking. One informant used shucking only in the sense in which it is used among peers, for example, bullshitting, and characterized the above examples as jiving or whupping game. Others, however, identified the above examples as shucking, and reserved jiving and whupping game for more offensive maneuvers. In fact, one of the apparent features of shucking is that the posture of the black when acting with members of the establishment be a *defensive* one.

Frederick Douglass, in telling of how he taught himself to read, would challenge a white boy with whom he was playing, by saying that he could write as well as the white boy. Whereupon he would write down all the letters he knew. The white boy would then write down more letters than Douglass did. In this way, Douglass eventually learned all the letters of the alphabet. Some of my informants regarded the example as whupping game. Others regarded it as shucking. The former were perhaps focusing on the maneuver rather than the language used. The latter may have felt that any maneuvers

designed to learn to read were justifiably defensive. One of my informants said Douglass was "shucking *in order to* whup the game."
This latter response seems to be the most revealing. Just as one can
rap to whup the game on someone, so one can shuck or jive for the
same purpose; that is, assume a guise or posture or perform some
action in a certain way that is designed to work on someone's mind
to get him to give up something.

### Whupping Game to Con Whitey

The following examples from Malcolm X illustrate the shucking
and jiving in this context, though jive is the term used. Today, whupping game might also be the term used to describe the operation.
Whites who came to Harlem at night got a better reception than in
the daylight; the several Harlem nightclubs they patronized were
geared to entertain and jive (flatter, cajole) the night white crowd to
get their money.

The maneuvers involved here are clearly designed to obtain some
benefit or advantage.

> Freddie got on the stand and went to work on his own shoes.
> Brush, liquid polish, brush, paste wax, shine rag, lacquer sole
> dressing. . .step by step, Freddie showed me what to do.
> "But you got to get a whole lot faster. You can't waste
> time!" Freddie showed me how fast on my own shoes. Then be-
> cause business was tapering off, he had time to give me a dem-
> onstration of how to make the shine rag pop like a firecracker.
> "Dig the action?" he asked. He did it in slow motion. I got
> down and tried it on his shoes. I had the principle of it. "Just
> got to do it, faster," Freddie said. *"It's a jive noise, that's all.*
> *Cats tip better, they figure you're knocking yourself out!"* (*The*
> *Autobiography of Malcom X*)

An eight-year-old boy whupped the game on me one day this way:

> My colleague and I were sitting in a room listening to a tape.
> The door to the room was open and outside was a soda ma-
> chine. Two boys came up in the elevator, stopped at the soda
> machine, and then came into the room.
> "Do you have a dime for two nickels?" Presumably the soda
> machine would not accept nickels. I took out the change in my
> pocket, found a dime, and gave it to the boy for two nickels.
> After accepting the dime, he looked at the change in my
> hand and asked, "Can I have two cents? I need carfare to get
> home." I gave him the two cents.

At first I assumed the verbal component of the maneuver was the rather weak, transparently false reason for wanting the two cents. Actually, as was pointed out to me later, the maneuver began with the first question which was designed to get me to show my money. He could then ask me for something that he knew I had, making my refusal more difficult. He apparently felt that the reason need not be more than plausible because the amount he wanted was small. Were the amount larger, he would no doubt have elaborated on the verbal element of the game. The form of the verbal element could be in the direction of rapping or shucking and jiving. If he were to rap, the eight-year-old might say, "Man, you know a cat needs to have a little bread to keep the girls in line." Were he to shuck and jive, he might make the reason for needing the money more compelling, look hungry, and so on.

The function of shucking and jiving as it refers to blacks and "the Man" is designed to work on the mind and emotions of the authority figure for the purpose of getting him to feel a certain way or give up something that will be to the other's advantage. Iceberg showed a "toothy smile" that said to the detective, "I'm glad to see you," and, "Would I be glad to see you if I had something to hide?" When the maneuvers seem to be *defensive*, most of my informants regarded the language behavior as shucking. When the maneuvers were *offensive* my informants tended to regard the behavior as "whupping the game."

Also significant is that the first form of shucking described, which developed out of accommodation, is becoming less frequently used today by many blacks, because of a new found self-assertiveness and pride, challenging the system. The willingness on the part of many blacks to accept the psychological and physical brutality and general social consequences of not "keeping one's place" is indicative of the changing self-concept of the black man. Ironically, the shocked reaction of some whites to the present militancy of the black is partly due to the fact that the black was so successful at "putting Whitey on" via shucking in the past. This new attitude can be seen from a conversation I recently had with a shoe-shine attendant at O'Hare airport in Chicago.

I was having my shoes shined and the black attendant was using a polishing machine instead of the rag that was generally used in the past. I asked whether the machine made his work any easier. He did not answer me until about ten seconds had passed and then responded in a loud voice that he "never had a job that was easy," that he would give me "one hundred dollars for any *easy* job" I could offer him, that the machine made his job "faster" but not "easier." I was startled at the response because it was so unexpected and I realized that here was a new "breed of cat" who was not going to shuck for a big tip or ingratiate himself with "Whitey" anymore. A few years ago his response probably would have been different.

The contrast between this "shoe-shine" scene and the one illustrated earlier from Malcolm X's autobiography, when "shucking Whitey" was the common practice, is striking.

Shucking, jiving, shucking and jiving, or S-ing and J-ing, when referring to language behavior practiced by blacks, is descriptive of the talk and gestures that are appropriate to "putting someone on" by creating a false impression. The terms seem to cover a range from simply telling a lie, to bullshitting, to subtly playing with someone's mind. An important difference between this form of shucking and that described earlier is that the same talk and gestures that are deceptive to the "the Man" are often transparent to those members of one's own group who are able practitioners at shucking themselves. As Robert Conot has pointed out, "The Negro who often fools the white officer by 'shucking it' is much less likely to be successful with another Negro. . . ." Also, S-ing and J-ing within the group often has play overtones in which the person being "put on" is aware of the attempts being made and goes along with it for enjoyment or in appreciation of the style.

*Running it down* is the term used by speakers in the ghetto when it is their intention to give information, either by explanation, narrative, or giving advice. In the following literary example, Sweet Mac is "running this Edith broad down" to his friends:

> Edith is the "saved" broad who can't marry out of her religion . . . or do anything else out of her religion for that matter, especially what I wanted her to do. A bogue religion, man! So dig, for the last couple weeks I been quoting the Good Book and all that stuff to her; telling her I am now saved myself, you dig. (Woodie King, Jr., "The Game," *Liberator*, August 1965)

The following citation from Claude Brown uses the term with the additional sense of giving advice:

> If I saw him [Claude's brother] hanging out with cats I knew were weak, who might be using drugs sooner or later, I'd run it down to him.

It seems clear that running it down has simply an informative function, that of telling somebody something that he does not already know.

"Gripping" is of fairly recent vintage, used by black high-school students in Chicago to refer to the talk and facial expression that accompanies a *partial* loss of face or self-possession, or showing of fear. Its appearance alongside "copping a plea," which refers to a total loss of face, in which one begs one's adversary for mercy, is a significant new perception. In linking it with the street code that acclaims the ability to "look tough and inviolate, fearless, secure, 'cool,' " it suggests that even the slightest weakening of this posture will be held up to ridicule and contempt. There are always contemptuous overtones attached to the use of the term when applied to the others' behavior. One is tempted to link it with the violence and toughness required to survive on the street. The intensity of both seems to be increasing. As one of my informants noted, "Today, you're *lucky* if you end up in the hospital"—that is, are not killed.

**Reaction to Fear and Superior Power**

Both gripping and copping a plea refer to behavior produced from fear and a respect for superior power. An example of gripping comes from the record *Street and Gangland Rhythms* (Band 4, "Dumb Boy"). Lennie meets Calvin and asks him what happened to his lip. Calvin says that a boy named Pierre hit him for copying off him in school. Lennie, pretending to be Calvin's brother, goes to confront Pierre. Their dialogue follows:

> Lennie: "Hey you! What you hit my little brother for?"
> Pierre: "Did he tell you what happen man?"
> Lennie: "Yeah, he told me what happened."
> Pierre: "But you. . . but you. . . but you should tell your people to teach him to go to school, man." (Pause) "I, I know, I know I didn't have a right to hit him."

Pierre, anticipating a fight with Lennie if he continued to justify his hitting of Calvin, tried to avoid it by "gripping" with the last line.

Copping a plea, originally meant, "To plead guilty to a lesser charge to save the state the cost of a trial," (with the hope of receiving a lesser or suspended sentence), but is now generally used to mean "to beg," "plead for mercy," as seen in the example, "Please cop, don't hit me. I give" (*Street and Gangland Rhythms*, Band 1, "Gang Fight"). This change of meaning can be seen from its use by Piri Thomas in *Down These Mean Streets*.

> The night before my hearing, I decided to make a prayer. It had to be on my knees, 'cause if I was gonna cop a plea to God, I couldn't play it cheap.

The function of gripping and copping a plea is obviously to induce pity or to acknowledge the presence of superior strength. In so doing, one evinces noticeable feelings of fear and insecurity that also result in a loss of status among one's peers.

*Signifying* is the term used to describe the language behavior that, as Abrahams has defined it, attempts to "imply, goad, beg, boast by indirect verbal or gestural means" (Roger D. Abrahams, *Deep Down in the Jungle*). In Chicago it is also used as a synonym to describe language behavior more generally known as *sounding* elsewhere.

Some excellent examples of signifying as well as of other forms of language behavior come from the well-known "toast" (narrative form) "The Signifying Monkey and the Lion," which was collected by Abrahams from Negro street-corner bards in Philadelphia. In the above toast the monkey is trying to get the lion involved in a fight with the elephant:

> Now the lion came through the jungle one peaceful day,
> When the signifying monkey stopped him, and that is what he started to say:
> He said, "Mr. Lion," he said, "A bad-assed mother-fucker down you way,"
> He said, "Yeah! The way he talks about your folks is a certain shame.
> I even heard him curse when he mentioned your grandmother's name."
> The lion's tail shot back like a forty-four
> When he went down that jungle in all uproar.

Thus the monkey has goaded the lion into a fight with the elephant by "signifying," that is, indicating that the elephant has been "sounding on" (insulting) the lion. When the lion comes back, thoroughly beaten up, the monkey again "signifies" by making fun of the lion:

> . . . lion came back through the jungle more dead than alive,
> When the monkey started some more of that signifying jive.
> He said, "Damn, Mr. Lion, you went through here yesterday, the jungle rung.
> Now you come back today, damn near hung."

The monkey, of course, is delivering this taunt from a safe distance away on the limb of a tree when his foot slips and he falls to the ground, at which point,

> Like a bolt of lightning, a stripe of white heat,
> The lion was on the monkey with all four feet.

In desperation the monkey quickly resorts to "copping a plea":

> The monkey looked up with a tear in his eyes,
> He said, "Please, Mr. Lion, I apologize."

His "plea," however, fails to move the lion to show any mercy so the monkey tries another verbal ruse, "shucking":

> He said, "You lemme get my head out of the sand, ass out the grass, I'll fight you like a natural man."

In this he is more successful as,

> The lion jumped back and squared for a fight.
> The mother-fucking monkey jumped clear out of sight.

A safe distance away again, the monkey returns to "signifying":

> He said, "Yeah, you had me down, you had me at last,
> But you left me free, now you can still kiss my ass."

This example illustrates the methods of provocation, goading, and taunting artfully practiced by a signifier.

It is interesting that, when the *function* of signifying is *directive*, the *tactic* employed is *indirection*, that is, the signifier reports or repeats what someone else has said about the listener; the "report" is couched in plausible language designed to compel belief and arouse feelings of anger and hostility. There is also the implication that if the listener fails to do anything about it—what has to be "done" is usually quite clear—his status will be seriously compromised. Thus the lion is compelled to vindicate the honor of his family by fighting or else leave the impression that he is afraid, and that he is not "king" of the jungle. When used for the purpose of directing action, signifying is like shucking in also being deceptive and subtle in approach and depending for success on the naivete or gullibility of the person being "put on."

When the function of signifying is to arouse feelings of embarrassment, shame, frustration, or futility, to diminish someone's status, the tactic employed is direct in the form of a taunt, as it is in the example where the monkey is making fun of the lion.

## Sounding to Relieve Tensions

*Sounding* is the term that is today most widely known for the game of verbal insult known in the past as *playing the dozens, the dirty dozens,* or just *the dozens.* Other current names for the game have regional distribution: signifying or "sigging" (Chicago), joning (Washington, D.C.), screaming (Harrisburg), and so forth. In Chicago, the term *sounding* would be descriptive of the initial remarks that are designed to sound out the other person to see whether he will play the game. The verbal insult is also subdivided, the term *signifying* applying to insults that are hurled directly at the person and the dozens applying to results hurled at your opponent's family, especially, the mother.

Sounding is often catalyzed by signifying remarks referred to earlier such as, "Are you going to let him say that about your mama," to spur an exchange between members of the group. It is begun on a relatively low key and built up by verbal exchanges. The game goes like this:

> One insults a member of another's family; others in the group make disapproving sounds to spur on the coming exchange. The one who has been insulted feels at this point that he must reply with a slur on the protagonist's family which is clever enough to defend his honor (and therefore that of his family). This, of course, leads the other (once again, more due to pressure from the crowd than actual insult) to make further jabs. This can proceed until everyone is bored with the whole affair, until one hits the other (fairly rare), or until some other subject comes up that interrupts the proceedings (the usual state of affairs). (Roger D. Abrahams, "Playing the Dozens," *Journal of American Folklore,* July-September 1962)

Mack McCormick describes the dozens as a verbal contest

> in which the players strive to bury one another with vituperation. In the play, the opponent's mother is especially slandered. . . . Then, in turn fathers are identified as queer and syphilitic. Sisters are whores, brothers are defective, cousins are "funny," and the opponent is himself diseased. (Mack Mc-Cormick, "The Dirty Doyens," book jacket in the record album *The Unexpurgated Folksongs of Men,* Arhoolie Records)

An example of the "game" collected by one of my students goes:

> Frank looked up and saw Leroy enter the Outpost.

Leroy walked past the room where Quinton, "Nap," "Pretty Black," "Cunny," Richard, Haywood, "Bull," and Reese sat playing cards. As Leroy neared the TV room, Frank shouted at him.

*Frank:* "Hey Leroy, you mama—calling you man."

Leroy turned and walked toward the room where the sound came from. He stood in the door and looked at Frank.

*Leroy:* "Look mother-fuckers, I don't play that shit."

*Frank* (signifying): "Man, I told you cats 'bout that mama jive" (as if he were concerned about how Leroy felt).

*Leroy:* "That's all right, Frank; you don't have to tell these funky mother-fuckers nothing; I'll fuck me up somebody yet."

Frank's face lit up as if he were ready to burst his side laughing. Cunny became pissed at Leroy.

*Cunny:* "Leroy, you stupid bastard, you let Frank make a fool of you. He said that 'bout your mama."

*Pretty Black:* "Aw, fat ass head Cunny shut up."

*Cunny:* "Ain't that some shit. This black slick head motor flicker got nerve 'nough to call somebody 'fat head.' Boy, you so black, you sweat Permalube Oil."

This eased the tension of the group as they burst into loud laughter.

*Pretty Black:* "What 'chu laughing 'bout Nap, with your funky mouth smelling like dog shit."

Even Leroy laughed at this.

*Nap:* "Your mama mother-fucker."

*Pretty Black:* "Your funky mama, too."

*Nap* (strongly): "It takes twelve barrels of water to make a steamboat run; it takes an elephant's dick to make your Grandmammy come; she been elephant fucked, camel fucked and hit side the head with your Grandpappy's nuts."

*Reese:* "Godorr-damn; go on and rap mother-fucker."

Reese began slapping each boy in his hand, giving his positive approval of Nap's comment. Pretty Black in an effort not to be outdone, but directing his verbal play elsewhere stated:

*Pretty Black:* "Reese, what you laughing 'bout? You so square, you shit bricked shit."

*Frank:* "Whoooowee!"

*Reese* (sounded back): "Square, huh, what about your nappy ass hair before it was stewed; that shit was so bad till, when you went to bed at night, it would leave your head and go on the corner and meddle."

The boys slapped each other in the hand and cracked up.

> *Pretty Black:* "On the streets meddling, bet Dinky didn't offer me no pussy and I turned it down."
> *Frank:* "Reese scared of pussy."
> *Pretty Black:* "Hell yeah; the greasy mother rather fuck old ugly, funky cock Sue Willie than get a piece of ass from a decent broad."
> *Frank:* "Godorr-damn! Not Sue Willie."
> *Pretty Black:* "Yeah ol' meat-beating Reese rather screw that cross-eyed, clapsy bitch, who when she cry, tears rip down her ass."
> *Haywood:* "Don't be so mean, black"
> *Reese:* "Aw shut up, you half-white bastard."
> *Frank:* "Wait man, Haywood ain't gonna hear much more of that half-white shit; he's a brother, too."
> *Reese:* "Brother, my black ass; that white-ass landlord gotta be his mother-fucker's paw."
> *Cunny:* "Man, you better stop foolin' with Haywood; he's turning red."
> *Haywood:* "Fuck yall" (as he withdrew from the "sig" game).
> *Frank:* "Yeah, fuck yall; let's go to the stick hall."
> The group left enroute to the billiard hall. (James Maryland, "Signifying at the Outpost," unpublished term paper for the course *Idiom of the Negro Ghettos*, January 1967)

The above example of sounding is an excellent illustration of the "game" as played by fifteen-seventeen-year-old Negro boys, some of whom have already acquired the verbal skill that for them is often the basis for having a high "rep." Ability with words is apparently as highly valued as physical strength. In the sense that the status of one of the participants in the game is diminished if he has to resort to fighting to answer a verbal attack, verbal ability may be even more highly regarded than physical ability.

The relatively high value placed on verbal ability must be clear to most black boys at an early age. Most boys begin their activity in sounding by compiling a repertoire of "one liners." When the game is played, the one who has the greatest number of such remarks wins. Here are some examples of "one liners" collected from fifth- and sixth- grade black boys in Chicago:

> Yo mama is so bowlegged, she looks like the bite out of a donut.
> You mama sent her picture to the lonely hearts club, and they sent it back and said, "We ain't that lonely!"

Your family is so poor the rats and roaches eat lunch out.
Your house is so small the roaches walk single file.
I walked in your house and your family was running around
the table. I said, "Why you doin' that?" Your mama say,
"First one drops, we eat."

Real proficiency in the game comes to only a small percentage of
those who play it. These players have the special skill in being able
to turn around what their opponents have said and attack them with
it. Thus, when someone indifferently said "fuck you" to Concho, his
retort was immediate and devastating: "Man, you haven't even
kissed me yet."

The "best talkers" from this group often become the successful
street-corner, barber-shop, and pool-hall storytellers who deliver
the long, rhymed, witty, narrative stories called *toasts*. They are, as
Roger D. Abrahams has described, the traditional "men of words"
and have become on occasion entertainers such as Dick Gregory
and Redd Foxx, who are virtuosos at repartee, and preachers, whose
verbal power has been traditionally esteemed.

The function of the dozens or sounding is to borrow status from
an opponent through an exercise of verbal power. The opponent
feels compelled to regain his status by sounding back on the speaker
or other group member whom he regards as more vulnerable.

The presence of a group seems to be especially important in controlling the game. First of all, one does not "play" with just anyone
since the subject matter is concerned with things that in reality one
is quite sensitive about. It is precisely *because* "Pretty Black" has a
"black slick head" that makes him vulnerable to "Cunny's" barb,
especially now when the Afro-American "natural" hair style is in
vogue. Without the control of the group, sounding will frequently
lead to a fight. This was illustrated by a tragic epilogue concerning
Haywood. When Haywood was being sounded on in the presence of
two girls by his best friend (other members of the group were absent), he refused to tolerate it. He went home, got a rifle, came
back, and shot and killed his friend. In the classroom from about
the fourth grade on fights among black boys invariably are caused
by someone sounding on the other person's mother.

Significantly, the subject matter of sounding is changing with the
changing self-concept of the black with regard to those physical
characteristics that are characteristically Negro, and that in the past
were vulnerable points in the black psyche: blackness and "nappy"
hair. It ought to be said that for many blacks, blackness was always
highly esteemed and it might be more accurate to regard the present

sentiment of the black community toward skin color as reflecting a shifted attitude for only a *portion* of the black community. This suggests that sounding on someone's light skin color is not new. Nevertheless, one can regard the previously favorable attitude toward light skin color and "good hair" as the prevailing one. "Other things being equal, the more closely a woman approached her white counterpart, the more attractive she was considered to be, by both men and women alike. "Good hair" (hair that is long and soft) and light skin were the chief criteria" (Elliot Liebow, *Tally's Corner*).

The dozens has been linked to the overall psychosocial growth of the black male. McCormick has stated that a "single round of a dozen or so exchanges frees more pent-up aggressions than will a dose of sodium pentothal." The fact that one permits a kind of abuse within the rules of the game and within the confines of the group that would otherwise not be tolerated is filled with psychological import. It seems also important to view its function from the perspective of the nonparticipating members of the group. Its function for them may be to incite and prod individual members of the group to combat for the purpose of energizing the elements, or simply relieving the boredom of just "hanging around," and the malaise of living in a static and restrictive environment.

A summary analysis of the different forms of language behavior that have been discussed above permit the following generalizations:

The prestige norms that influence black speech behavior are those which have been successful in manipulating and controlling people and situations. The function of all of the forms of language behavior discussed above, with the exception of running it down, was to project personality, assert oneself, or arouse emotion, frequently with the additional purpose of getting the person to give up or do something that will be of some benefit to the speaker. Only running it down has as its primary function to communicate information and often here, too, the personality and style of the speaker in the form of rapping is projected along with the information.

The purpose for which language is used suggests that the speaker views the social situations into which he moves as consisting of a series of transactions that require that he be continually ready to take advantage of a person or situation or defend himself against being victimized. He has absorbed what Horton has called *street rationality*. As one of Horton's respondents put it: "The good hustler . . . conditions his mind and must never put his guard too far down, to relax, or he'll be taken."

I have carefully avoided limiting the group within the black community of whom the language behavior and perspective of their environment is characteristic. While I have no doubt that it is true of those who are generally called *street people*, I am uncertain of the extent to which it is true of a much larger portion of the black community, especially the male segment. My informants consisted of street people, high-school students, and blacks, who by their occupation as community and youth workers, possess what has been described as a "sharp sense of the streets." Yet it is difficult to find a black male in the community who has *not* witnessed or participated in the dozens or heard of signifying, or rapping, or shucking and jiving at some time during his growing up. It would be equally difficult to imagine a high-school student in a Chicago inner-city school not being touched by what is generally regarded as "street culture."

In conclusion, by blending style and verbal power, through rapping, sounding, and running it down, the black in the ghetto establishes his personality; through shucking, gripping, and copping a plea, he shows his respect for power; through jiving and signifying he stirs up excitement. With all of the above, he hopes to manipulate and control people and situations to give himself a winning edge.

# 3

# Time and Cool People

John Horton

## The Variety of Time

Time in industrial society is clock time. It seems to be an external, objective regulator of human activities. But for the sociologist, time is not an object existing independent of man, dividing his day into precise units. Time is diverse; it is always social and subjective. A man's sense of time derives from his place in the social structure and his lived experience.

The diversity of time perspectives can be understood intellectually—but it is rarely tolerated socially. A dominant group reifies and objectifies its time; it views all other conceptions of time as subversive—as indeed they are.

Thus, today in the dominant middle-class stereotype, standard American time is directed to the future; it is rational and impersonal. In contrast, time for the lower class is directed to the present, irrational, and personal. Peasants, Mexican Americans, Negroes, Indians, workers are "lazy"; they do not possess the American virtues of ambition and striving for success. Viewed solely from the dominant class norm of rationality, their presumed orientation to present time is seen only as an irrational deviation, something to be controlled and changed. It is at best an epiphenomenon produced in reaction to the "real, objective" phenomenon of middle-class time.

Sociologists have not been completely exempt from this kind of reified thinking. When they universalize the middle-class value of rational action and future time and turn it into a "neutral" social fact, they reinforce a negative stereotype: Lower classes are un-

dependable in organized work situations (they seek immediate rewards and cannot defer gratification); in their political action, they
are prone to accept immediate, violent, and extreme solutions to
personal problems; their sense of time is dysfunctional to the stability of the economic and political orders. For example, Seymour
Martin Lipset writes in a paper significantly entitled "Working
Class Authoritarianism":

> This emphasis on the immediately perceivable and concern
> with the personal and concrete is part and parcel of the short
> time perspective and the inability to perceive the complex pos-
> sibilities and consequences of action which often results in a
> general readiness to support extremist political and religious
> movements, and generally lower level of liberalism on non-
> economic questions.

To examine time in relation to the maintenance or destruction of
the dominant social order is an interesting political problem, but it
is not a sociology of time; it is a middle-class sociology of order or
change in its time aspect. Surely, a meaningful sociology of time
should take into account the social situation in which time operates
and the actor's as well as the observer's perspective. The sociologist
must at least entertain the idea that lower-class time may be a phenomenon in and of itself, and quite functional to the life problems of
that class.

Of course, there are dangers in seeking the viewpoint of a minority: The majority stereotypes might be reversed. For example, we
might find out that no stereotype is more incorrect than that which
depicts the lower classes as having no sense of future time. As Max
Weber has observed, it is the powerful and not the powerless who
are present oriented. Dominant groups live by maintaining and ex-
panding their present. Minority groups survive in this present, but
their survival is nourished by a dream of the future. In "Ethnic
Segregation and Caste" Weber says:

> The sense of dignity that characterizes positively privileged
> status groups is natural to their "being" which does not tran-
> scend itself, that is, to their beauty and excellence. Their king-
> dom is of this world. They live for the present by exploiting the
> great past. The sense of dignity of the negatively privileged
> strata naturally refers to a future lying beyond the present
> whether it is of this life or another. In other words it must be
> nurtured by a belief in a providential "mission" and by a belief
> in a specific honor before God.

It is time to reexamine the meaning of time, the reality of the middle-class stereotype of itself, as well as the middle-class stereotype of the lower class. In this chapter I explore the latter: the meaning of time among a group most often stereotyped as having an irrational, present sense of time—the sporadically unemployed young Negro street-corner population. I choose the unemployed because they live outside of the constraints of industrial work time; Negroes because they speak some of the liveliest street language, including that of time; young males because the street culture of the unemployed and the hustler is young and masculine.

To understand the meaning of street time was to discover "what's happening" in the day-to-day and week-to-week activities of my respondents. Using the middle-class stereotype of lower-class time as a point of departure, I asked myself the following questions:

In what sense is street time personal (not run by the clock) and present oriented?

What kind of future orientation, if any, exists?

Are street activities really irrational in the sense that individuals do not use time efficiently in the business of living? I have attempted to answer the questions in the language and from the experience of my respondents.

**Time and Cool People**

Street culture exists in every low-income ghetto. It is shared by the hustling elements of the poor, whatever their nationality or color. In Los Angeles, members of such street groups sometimes call themselves *street people, cool people,* or simply *regulars.* Whatever the label, they are known the world over by outsiders as *hoods* or *hoodlums,* persons who live on and off the street. They are recognizable by their own fashions in dress, hair, gestures, and speech. The particular fashion varies with time, place, and nationality. For example, in 1963 a really sharp Los Angeles street Negro would be "conked to the bone" (have processed hair) and "togged-out" in "continentals." Today "natural" hair and variations of mod clothes are coming into style.

Street people are known also by their activities—"duking" (fighting or at least looking tough), "hustling" (any way of making money outside the "legitimate" world of work), "gigging" (partying)—and by their apparent nonactivity, "hanging" on the corner. Their individual roles are defined concretely by their success or failure in these activities. One either knows "what's happening" on the street, or he is a "lame," "out of it," "not ready" (lacks his diploma in street knowledge), a square.

There are, of course, many variations. Negroes, in particular, have contributed much to the street tongue that has diffused into both the more hip areas of the middle class and the broader society. Such expressions as "a lame," "taking care of righteous business," "getting down to the nitty-gritty," and "soul" can be retraced to Negro street life.

The more or less organized center of street life is the "set"— meaning both the peer group and the places where it hangs out. It is the stage and central marketplace for activity, where to find out what's happening. My set of Negro street types contained a revolving and sometimes disappearing (when the "heat," or police pressure, was on) population of about forty-five members ranging in age from eighteen to twenty-five. These were the local "dudes," their term meaning not the fancy city slickers but simply "the boys," "fellas," the "cool people." They represented the hard core of street culture, the role models for younger teenagers. The dudes could be found when they were "laying dead"—hanging on the corner, or shooting pool and "jiving" ("goofing" or kidding around) in a local community project. Isolated from "the Man" (in this context the man in power—the police, and by extension, the white man), they lived in a small section of Venice outside the central Los Angeles ghetto and were surrounded by a predominantly Mexican and Anglo population. They called their black "turf" "Ghost-town"— home of the "Ghostmen," their former gang. Whatever the origin of the word, Ghost-town was certainly the home of socially "invisible" men.

## The Street Set

In 1965 and 1966 I had intensive interviews with twenty-five set members. My methods emerged in day-to-day observations. Identified as white, a lame, and square, I had to build up an image of being at least "legit" (not working for police). Without actually living in the area, this would have been impossible without the aid of a key field-worker, in this case an outsider who could be accepted inside. This field-worker, "Cowboy," was a white dude of twenty-five. He had run with "Paddy" (white), "Chicano" (Mexican), and "Blood" (Negro) sets since the age of twelve and was highly respected for having been president of a tough gang. He knew the street, how to duke, move with style, and speak the tongue. He made my entry possible. I was the underprivileged child who had to be taught slowly and sympathetically the common-sense features of street life.

Cowboy had the respect and I the toleration of several set leaders. After that, we simply waited for the opportunity to "rap." Although sometimes used synonymously with street conversation, "rap" is really a special way of talking—repartee. Street repartee at its best is a lively way of "running it down," or of "jiving" (attempting to put someone on), of trying "to blow another person's mind," forcing him "to lose his cool," to give in or give up something. For example, one needs to throw a lively rap when he is "putting the make on a broad."

Sometimes we taped individuals, sometimes "soul sessions." We asked for life histories, especially their stories about school, job, and family. We watched and asked about the details of daily surviving and attempted to construct street-time schedules. We probed beyond the past and present into the future in two directions—individual plans for tomorrow and a lifetime, and individual dreams of a more decent world for whites and Negroes.

The set can be described by the social and attitudinal characteristics of its members. To the observer, these are expressed in certain realities of day-to-day living: not enough skill for good jobs, and the inevitable trouble brought by the problem of surviving. Of the twenty-five interviewed, only four had graduated from high school. Except for a younger set member who was still in school, all were dropouts, or perhaps more accurately kicked-outs. None was really able to use or write formal language. However, many were highly verbal, both facile and effective in their use of the street tongue. Perhaps the art of conversation is most highly developed here where there is much time to talk, perhaps too much—an advantage of the lumpen-leisure class.

Their incomes were difficult to estimate, as "bread" or "coins" (money) came in on a very irregular basis. Of the seventeen for whom I have figures, half reported that they made less than $1,400 in the last year, and the rest claimed income from $2,000–4,000 annually. Two-thirds were living with and partially dependent on their parents, often a mother. The financial strain was intensified by the fact that although fifteen of seventeen were single, eight had one or more children living in the area. (Having children, legitimate or not, was not a stigma but proof of masculinity.)

At the time of the interview, two-thirds of them had some full- or part-time employment—unskilled and low-paid jobs. The overall pattern was one of sporadic and—from their viewpoint—often unsatisfactory work, followed by a period of unemployment compensation, and petty hustling whenever possible and whenever necessary.

When I asked the question, "When a dude needs bread, how does he get it?", the universal response was "the hustle." Hustling is, of course, illegitimate from society's viewpoint. Street people know it is illegal, but they view it in no way as immoral or wrong. It is justified by the necessity of surviving. As might be expected, the unemployed admitted that they hustled and went so far as to say that a dude could make it better on the street than on the job: "There is a lot of money on the street, and there are many ways of getting it," or simply, "This has always been my way of life." On the other hand, the employed, the part-time hustlers, usually said, "A dude could make it better on the job than on the street." Their reasons for disapproving of hustling were not moral. Hustling meant trouble. "I don't hustle because there's no security. You eventually get busted." Others said there was not enough money on the street or that it was too difficult to "run a game" on people.

Nevertheless, hustling is the central street activity. It is the economic foundation for everyday life. Hustling and the fruit of hustling set the rhythm of social activities.

What are the major forms of hustling in Ghost-town? The best hustles were conning, stealing, gambling, and selling dope. By gambling, these street people meant dice; by dope, peddling "pills" and "pot." Pills are "reds" and "whites"—barbiturates and benzedrine or dexedrine. Pot is, of course, marijuana—"grass" or "weed." To "con" means to put "the bump" on a "cat," to "run a game" on somebody, to work on his mind for goods and services.

The "woman game" was common. As one dude put it, "If I have a good lady and she's on county, there's always some money to get." In fact, there is a local expression for getting county money. When the checks come in for child support, it's "mother's day." So the hustler "burns" people for money, but he also "rips off" goods for money; he thieves, and petty thieving is always a familiar hustle. Pimping is often the hustler's dream of the good life, but it was almost unknown here among the small-time hustlers. That was the game of the real professional and required a higher level of organization and wealth.

Hustling means bread and security but also trouble, and trouble is a major theme in street life. The dudes had a "world of trouble" (a popular song about a hustler is "I'm in a World of Trouble")—with school, jobs, women, and the police. The intensity of street life could be gauged in part by the intensity of the "heat" (police trouble). The hotter the street, the fewer the people visible on the street. On some days the set was empty. One would soon learn that there had been a "bust" (an arrest). Freddy had run amok and thrown rocks at a police car. There had been a leadership struggle; "Big Moe" had been cut up, and the "fuzz" had descended. Life was a succession of being picked up on suspicion of assault, theft, possession, "suspicion of suspicion" (an expression used by a respondent in describing his life). This was an ordinary experience for the street dude and often did lead to serious trouble. Over half of those interviewed claimed they had felony convictions.

## The Structure of Street Time

Keeping cool and out of trouble, hustling bread, and looking for something interesting and exciting to do created the structure of time on the street. The rhythm of time is expressed in the high and low points in the day and week of an unemployed dude. I stress the pattern of the unemployed and full-time hustler because he is on the street all day and night and is the prototype in my interviews. The sometimes employed will also know the pattern, and he will be able to hit the street whenever released from the bondage of jail, work, and the clock. Here I describe a typical time schedule gleaned through interviews and field observation.

Characteristically the street person gets up late, hits the street in the late morning or early afternoon, and works his way to the set. This is a place for relaxed social activity. Hanging on the set with the boys is the major way of passing time and waiting until some necessary or desirable action occurs. Nevertheless, things do happen on the set. The dudes "rap" and "jive" (talk), gamble, and drink their "pluck" (usually a cheap, sweet wine). They find out what happened yesterday, what is happening today, and what will hopefully happen on the weekend—the perpetual search for the "gig," the party. Here peer socialization and reinforcement also take place. The younger dude feels a sense of pride when he can be on the set and throw a rap to an older dude. He is learning how to handle himself, show respect, take care of business, and establish his own "rep."

On the set, yesterday merges into today, and tomorrow is an emptiness to be filled in through the pursuit of bread and excitement. Bread makes possible the excitement—the high (getting loaded with wine, pills, or pot), the sharp clothes, the "broad," the fight, and all those good things that show that one knows what's happening and has "something going" for himself. The rhythm of time—of the day and of the week—is patterned by the flow of money and people.

Time is "dead" when money is tight, when people are occupied elsewhere—working or in school. Time is dead when one is in jail. One is "doing dead time" when nothing is happening, and he has got nothing going for himself.

Time is alive when and where there is action. It picks up in the
evening when everyone moves on the street. During the regular
school year it may pick up for an hour in the afternoon when the
"broads" leave school and meet with the set at a corner taco joint.
Time may pick up when a familiar car cruises by and a few dudes
drive down to Johnny's for a "process" (hair straightening and
styling). Time is low on Monday (as described in the popular song,
"Stormy Monday"), Tuesday, Wednesday, when money is tight.
Time is high on Friday nights when the "eagle flies" and the "gig"
begins. On the street, time has a personal meaning only when something is happening, and something is most likely to happen at night—
especially on Friday and Saturday nights. Then people are together,
and there may be bread—bread to take and bread to use.

Human behavior is rational if it helps the individual to get what
he wants whether it is success in school or happiness in the street.
Street people sometimes get what they want. They act rationally in
those situations where they are able to plan and choose because they
have control, knowledge, and concern, irrationally where there are
barriers to their wants and desires.

When the street dude lacks knowledge and power to manipulate
time, he is indeed irrational. For the most part, he lacks the skills
and power to plan a move up and out of the ghetto. He is "a lame"
in the middle-class world of school and work; he is not ready to
operate effectively in unfamiliar organizations where his street
strengths are his visible weaknesses. Though irrational in moving up
and out of the street, he can be rational in day-to-day survival in the
street. No one survives there unless he knows what's happening
(that is, unless he knows what is available, where to get what he can
without being burned or busted). More euphemistically, this is "taking advantage of opportunities," exactly what the rational member
of the middle class does in his own setting.

To know what's happening is to know the goods and the bads, the
securities, the opportunities, and the dangers of the street. Survival
requires that a hustling dude know who is cool and uncool (who can
be trusted); who is in power (the people who control narcotics, are
fences, and so on); who is the "duker" or the fighter (someone to be
avoided or someone who can provide protection). When one knows
what's happening he can operate in many scenes, providing that he
can "hold his mud," keep cool, and out of trouble.

With his diploma in street knowledge, a dude can use time efficiently and with cunning in the pursuit of goods and services—in
hustling to eat and yet have enough bread left over for the pleasures

of pot, the chicks, and the gig. As one respondent put it, "The good hustler has the know-how, the ambition to better himself. He conditions his mind and must never put his guard too far down, to relax, or he'll be taken." This is street rationality. The problem is not a deficient sense of time but deficient knowledge and control to make a fantasy future and a really better life possible.

The petty hustler more fully realizes the middle-class ideal of individualistic rationality than does the middle class itself. When rationality operates in hustling, it is often on an individual basis. In a world of complex organization, the hustler defines himself as an entrepreneur; and, indeed, he is the last of the competitive entrepreneurs.

The degree of organization in hustling depends frequently on the kind of hustling. Regular pimping and pushing require many trusted contacts and organization. Regular stealing requires regular fences for hot goods. But in Ghost-town when the hustler moved, he usually moved alone and on a small scale. His success rested solely on him. He could not depend on the support on some benevolent organization. Alone, without a sure way of running the same game twice, he must continually recalculate conditions and people and find new ways of taking or be taken himself. The phrase "free enterprise for the poor and socialism for the rich" applies only too well in the streets. The political conservative should applaud all that individual initiative.

### Clock Time vs Personal Time

Negro street time is built around the irrelevance of clock time, white man's time, and the relevance of street values and activities. Like anyone else, a street dude is on time by the standard clock whenever he wants to be, not on time when he does not want to be and does not have to be.

When the women in school hit the street at the lunch hour and he wants to throw them a rap, he will be there then and not one hour after they have left. But he may be kicked out of high school for truancy or lose his job for being late and unreliable. He learned at an early age that school and job were neither interesting nor salient to his way of life. A regular on the set will readily admit being crippled by a lack of formal education. Yet school was a "bum kick." It was not his school. The teachers put him down for his dress, hair, and manners. As a human being he has feelings of pride and autonomy, the very things most threatened in those institutional situations where he was or is the underdeveloped, unrespected, illiterate, and undeserving outsider. Thus whatever "respectable" society says will help him, he knows oppresses him, and he retreats to the streets for security and a larger degree of personal freedom. Here his control reaches a maximum, and he has the kind of autonomy that many middle-class males might envy.

In the street, watches have a special and specific meaning. Watches are for pawning and not for telling time. When they are worn, they are decorations and ornaments of status. The street clock is informal, personal, and relaxed. It is not standardized nor easily synchronized to other clocks. In fact, a street dude may have almost infinite toleration for individual time schedules. To be on time is often meaningless, to be late an unconsciously accepted way of life. "I'll catch you later," or simply "later," are the street phrases that mean business will be taken care of, but not necessarily now.

Large areas of street life run on late time. For example, parties are not cut off by some built-in alarm clock of appointments and schedules. At least for the unemployed, standard time neither precedes nor follows the gig. Consequently, the action can take its course. It can last as long as interest is sustained and die by exhaustion or by the intrusion of some more interesting event. A gig may endure all night and well into another day. One of the reasons for the party assuming such time dimensions is purely economic. There are not enough cars and enough money for individual dates, so everyone converges in one place and takes care of as much business as possible there, that is, doing whatever is important at the time—sex, presentation of self, hustling.

## Colored People's Time

Events starting late and lasting indefinitely are clearly street and class phenomena, not some special trait of Afro-Americans. Middle-class Negroes who must deal with the organization and coordination of activities in church and elsewhere will jokingly and critically refer to a lack of standard time sense when they say that Mr. Jones arrived "C.P.T." (colored people's time). They have a word for it because being late is a problem for people caught between two worlds and confronted with the task of meshing standard and street time. In contrast, the street dudes had no self-consciousness about being late; with few exceptions they had not heard the expression CPT. (When I questioned members of a middle-class Negro fraternity, a sample matched by age to the street set, only three of the twenty-five interviewed could not define CPT. Some argued vehemently that CPT was the problem to be overcome.)

Personal time as expressed in parties and other street activities is not simply deficient knowledge and use of standard time. It is a positive adaptation to generations of living whenever and wherever possible outside of the sound and control of the white man's clock. The personal clock is an adaptation to the chance and accidental character of events on the street and to the very positive value placed on emotion and feeling.*

Chance reinforces personal time. A dude must be ready on short notice to move "where the action is." His internal clock may not be running at all when he is hanging on the corner and waiting for something to do. It may suddenly speed up by chance: Someone cruises by in a car and brings a nice "stash" of "weed," a gig is organized and he looks forward to being well togged-out and throwing a rap to some "boss chick," or a lame appears and opens himself to a quick "con." Chance as a determinant of personal time can be called more accurately *uncertain predictability.* Street life is an aggregate of relatively independent events. A dude may not know exactly what or when something will happen, but from past experience he can predict a range of possibilities, and he will be ready, in position, and waiting.

In white, middle-class stereotypes and fears—and in reality—street action is highly expressive. A forthright yet stylized expression of emotion is positively evaluated and most useful. Street control and communication are based on personal power and the direct impingement of one individual on another. Where there is little property, status in the set is determined by personal qualities of mind and brawn.

The importance of emotion and expression appears again and again in street tongue and ideology. When asked, "How does a dude make a rep on the set?", over half of the sample mentioned "style," and all could discuss the concept. Style is difficult to define because it has so many referents. It means to carry one's self well, dress well, to show class. In the ideology of the street, it may be a way of behaving. One has style if he is able to dig people as they are. He does not put them down for what they do. He shows toleration. But a person with style must also show respect. That means respect for a person as he is, and since there is power in the street, respect for another's superior power. Yet one must show respect in such a way that he is able to look tough and inviolate, fearless, secure, cool.

---

*For a discussion of CPT that is close to some of the ideas presented here, see Jules Henry, "White People's Time, Colored People's Time," *Transaction/Society* 2, no. 3: 31-34.

Style may also refer to the use of gestures in conversation or in dance. It may be expressed in the loose walk, the jivey or dancing walk, the slow cool walk, the way one "chops" or "makes it" down the street. It may be the loose, relaxed hand rap or hand slap, the swinger's greeting that is used also in the hip middle-class teen sets. There are many refined variations of the hand rap. As a greeting, one may simply extend his hand, palm up. Another slaps it loosely with his finger. Or, one person may be standing with his hand behind and palm up. Another taps the hand in passing, and also pays his respect verbally with the conventional greeting, "What's happening, Brother." Or, in conversation, the hand may be slapped when an individual has "scored," has been "digging," has made a point, has got through to the person.

Style is a comparatively neutral value compared to soul. Soul can be many things—a type of food (good food is "soul food," a "bowl of soul"), music, a quality of mind, a total way of acting (in eating, drinking, dancing, walking, talking, relating to others, and the like). The person who acts with soul acts directly and honestly from his heart. He feels it and tells it "like it is." One respondent identified soul with ambition and drive. He said the person with soul, once he makes up his mind, goes directly to the goal, does not change his mind, does not wait and worry about messing up a little. Another said soul was getting down to the nitty-gritty, that is, moving directly to what is basic without guise and disguise. Thus soul is the opposite of hypocrisy, deceit, and phoniness, the opposite of "affective neutrality," and "instrumentality." Soul is simply whatever is considered beautiful, honest, and virtuous in men.

Most definitions tied soul directly to Negro experience. As one hustler put it, "It is the ability to survive. We've made it with so much less. Soul is the Negro who has the spirit to sing in slavery to overcome the monotony." With very few exceptions, the men interviewed argued that soul was what Negroes had and whites did not. Negroes were "soul brothers," warm and emotional—whites cold as ice. Like other oppressed minorities these street Negroes believed they had nothing except their soul and their humanity, and that this made them better than their oppressors.

### The Personal Dream

Soul is anchored in a past and present of exploitation and deprivation, but are there any street values and activities that relate to the future? The regular in the street set has no providential mission; he lives personally and instrumentally in the present, yet he dreams about the day when he will get himself together and move ahead to the rewards of a good job, money, and a family. Moreover, the personal dream coexists with a nascent political nationalism, the belief that Negroes can and will make it as Negroes. His present-future time is a combination of contradictions and developing possibilities. Here I shall be content to document without weighing two aspects of his orientation: *fantasy-personal future* and *fantasy-collective future*. I used the word *fantasy* because street people have not yet the knowledge and means and perhaps the will to fulfill their dreams. It is difficult enough to survive by the day.

When the members of the set were asked, "What do you really want out of life?", their responses were conventional, concrete, seemingly realistic, and—given their skills—rather hopeless. Two-thirds of the sample mentioned material aspirations—the finer things in life, a home, security, a family. For example, one said, in honest street language, "I want to get things for my kids and to make sure they have a father." Another said, jokingly, "a good future, a home, two or three girls living with me." Only one person did not know, and the others deviated a little from the material response. They said such things as "for everyone to be on friendly terms—a better world . . . then I could get all I wish," "to be free," "to help people."

But if most of the set wanted money and security, they wanted it on their own terms. As one put it, "I don't want to be in a middle-class bag, but I would like a nice car, home, and food in the icebox." He wanted the things and the comforts of middle-class life, but not the hypocrisy, the venality, the coldness, the being forced to do what one does not want to do. All that was in the middle-class bag. Thus the home and the money may be ends in themselves, but also fronts, security for carrying on the usual street values. Street people believed that they already had something that was valuable and looked down upon the person who made it and moved away in the middle-class world. For the observer, the myths are difficult to separate from the truths—here where the truths are so bitter. One can only say safely that street people dream of a high status, and they really do not know how to get it.

### The Collective Future

The Negro dudes are political outsiders by the usual poll questions. They do not vote. They do not seek out civil-rights demonstrations. They have very rudimentary knowledge of political organization. However, about the age of eighteen, when fighting and being tough are less important than before, street people begin to discuss their position in society. Verbally they care very much about the politics of race and the future of the Negro. The topic is always a ready catalyst for a soul session.

The political consciousness of the street can be summarized by noting those interview questions which attracted at least a seventy-five percent rate of agreement. The typical respondent was angry. He approves of the Watts incident, although from his isolated corner of the city he did not actively participate. He knows something about the history of discrimination and believes that if something is not done soon America can expect violence: "What this country needs is a revolutionary change." He was more likely to praise the leadership of Malcolm X than Lyndon Johnson, and he definitely was opposed to the Vietnam War. The reason for his opposition was clear: Why fight for a country that is not mine, when the fight is here?

Thus his racial consciousness looks to the future and a world where he will not have to stand in the shadow of the white man. But his consciousness has neither clear plan nor political commitment. He has listened to the Muslims, and he is not a black nationalist. True, the Negro generally has more soul than the white. He thinks differently, his women may be different, yet integration is preferable to separatism. Or, more accurately, he does not quite understand what all these terms mean. His nationalism is real as a folk nationalism based on experience with other Negroes and isolation from whites.

The significance of a racial future in the day-to-day consciousness of street people cannot be assessed. It is a developing possibility dependent on unforeseen conditions beyond the scope of their skill and imagination. But bring up the topic of race and tomorrow, and the dreams come rushing in—dreams of superiority, dreams of destruction, dreams of human equality. These dreams of the future are salient. They are not the imagination of authoritarian personalities, except from the viewpoint of those who see spite lurking behind every demand for social change. They are certainly not the fantasies of the hipster living philosophically in the present without hope and ambition. One hustler summarized the Negro street concept of ambition and future time when he said:

> The Negro has more ambition than the whites. He's got farther to go. "The Man" is already there. But we're on your trail, daddy. You still have smoke in our eyes, but we're catching up.

# II

# Deviant Life-Styles
# and the Pursuit of Perfection

# Introduction

In the last chapter we examined the life-style that some lower-class black urbanites have developed in adaptive response to their oppressive social conditions. Taking the "view from within" of the hustler subculture provided a different context for understanding these behaviors. In the first selection in this part, we move to a presentation of the life-style that some lower-class Appalachian whites have developed as an adaptive reaction to their oppressed status in the American economic spectrum. The focus in this opening article is on their participation in deviant religion. As with hustling behavior, when we view snake-handling from the context in which snake-handlers see it and combine this with an analysis of their general life situation, the behaviors take on new meaning and become much more readily understandable.

Members of the Scrabble Creek Church face a trying existence They are rural in a historical period in which cities dominate the culture; they have little education in an age where education is a major key to unlocking the door of material success; and they have learned to make their livelihood from mining coal at a time in which other sources of energy have become preferable. Being shunted aside from the mainstream of culture can lead to a number of different reactions, including agonizing despair, withdrawal into alcohol or drugs, blindly striking out at authority figures, and the nurturance of revolutionary hopes. These rejected of our society, however, have chosen a different life-style for dealing with their frustrations in life. They have turned to religion, developing and participating in a religious form that provides a large part of their identity and the security they are seeking.

The future appears unpredictable and uncontrollable to these people, coming upon them in unanticipated ways regardless of the actions they take in the present. Insecurity has become a taken-for-granted part of their lives. Handling poisonous snakes in religious services matches this outlook since the danger of death by snakebite is constantly present. But at the same time snake-handling provides great security. The watershed difference is that in these activities they feel that God is revealing himself to them. If a snake bites, it is a sign of the great danger inherent in following the Lord's commandments and a public testimony to unbelievers, while if they participate unscathed it is a sign of God's favor in their behalf, the revealing of their own saintliness in a corrupt society. They may be out of the mainstream of American life, but they are solidly in the mainstream of God's will. Though success as commonly measured in American society is out of their reach, holiness with God becomes attainable. Saintliness and God's approval become intricately bound up with the willingness to risk one's life for strongly held religious beliefs.

While the dominant culture has bypassed many groups of people and relegated them to oblivion in the small corners that they occupy in life and in which they work out their unique life-styles, others develop deviant life-styles because *they* reject the dominant culture. These persons, coming in contrast from the white middle class, have decided that the values of the dominant culture are not worth the price that the game of conformance demands. They have chosen not to strive for the American ideal of success via conformity to cultural dictates, but have, instead, joined those who "turn on, tune in, and drop out." But these persons described by Adams and Fox have also found severe disappointment with what they turned onto, with what they tuned into, and with what they dropped out for. Neither life-style alternative represented by conformance with the middle-class world of respectability or the rejection of this world by withdrawal into the drug subculture holds the promise of personal fulfillment.

But where dreams are shattered, religion is sometimes able to pick up the pieces. And this is their pursuit as they turn on to a "turned on" religion. Among a group of fellow seekers, they attempt to reconstruct their lives by bringing their actions into conformity with God's will. The religion of this youth subculture, with its rock music, antiestablishment orientation, rituals of healing and testimonies, and ecstaticism of speaking in tongues, provides guidance they feel is of supernatural origin, giving them a highly desired direction and purpose in life. They searchingly exchange their deviant life-style of the drug subculture for the deviant life-style of the religious commune. Here they seek not only peer approval for their orientation to life, but also a "rush" not dissimilar to the drug experience. From libertine to ascetic, from physically sensate to spiritually sensate, along with a sharp ideological swing from Left to Right, they are in the process of ritual reentry into active participation in their previously rejected social system with its central emphasis on work ethics.

Participation in this alternative deviant life-style symbolizes for themselves and for many others a radical conversion to morality. But *morality* is an extremely tenuous term. It means quite contrasting and even conflicting behaviors to different people. Morality can mean keeping blacks out of your restaurant by force of axe handles. Or it can mean pushing your aged relatives off on an ice floe, bidding them a sad but loving farewell as they depart for a certain death by starvation. Or it can mean systematically slaughtering peasant populations in the name of freedom and peace. Morality can be whatever happens to be defined as a moral act at that particular historical-cultural moment.

Morality is so inclusive of human behavior that it can also incorporate external appearance into its broad sweep. If, for example, a culture exhibits marked preference for one body type over another, constantly rewarding the one while denigrating the other, one particular type of body style can eventually come to be seen as moral, while another can come to represent the sin of departing from cultural norms. So it is with thinness and fatness in contemporary American life. Thinness is so highly valued and emphasized that thin people frequently come to think of themselves as morally superior to fat people, while the fat ones also internalize these same normative values and frequently think of themselves as less virtuous than the thin group. Consequently, thinness has come to represent beauty, happiness, health, and hope, while ugliness, misery, sickness, and despair personify fatness.

Where the first two chapters of this section deal with deviant religious life-styles developed by those people who are rejected by the culture and who reject the culture, the concluding selection analyzes a group of people who are "solid members" of the dominant culture. But these are people who feel left out of many of the desirable aspects of society because they "look different." They consequently seek perfection of body appearance in order to be even more integrated into the cultural mainstream. People who find themselves on the negative end of the cultural dictum of thinness have lately taken to organizing themselves in groups to combat their imperfection. In these groups, which Allon analyzes in terms of religious participation, they mutually support one another in the apparently unending struggle to achieve the virtue of thinness. With participation primarily by middle-class females, they gain a sense of unified sisterhood, of solace from cohorts they feel understand their plight. Banding together, they relentlessly strive for the socially acceptable but mythical ideal of a single body style for all. With their confessions of sins of eating, public affirmations of the goodness of thinness, evangelical sermons by individuals who have already experienced the healing of body change, and public testimonials of conversion to the new way of life, they are participating in religious rites of release from their "deviant" body style.

# 4

# The Serpent-Handling Religions of West Virginia

Nathan L. Gerrard

> And these signs shall follow them that believe; In my name shall they cast out devils; they shall speak with new tongues; They shall take up serpents; and if they drink any deadly thing, it shall not hurt them; they shall lay hands on the sick, and they shall recover. *Mark* 16:17-18

In southern Appalachia, two dozen or three dozen fundamentalist congregations take this passage literally and "take up serpents." They use copperheads, water moccasins, and rattlesnakes in their religious services.

The serpent-handling ritual was inaugurated between 1900 and 1910, probably by George Went Hensley. Hensley began evangelizing in rural Grasshopper Valley, Tennessee, then traveled widely throughout the South, particularly in Kentucky, spreading his religion. He died in Florida at 70—of snakebite. To date [1968], the press has reported about 20 such deaths among the serpent-handlers. One other death was recorded last year in Kentucky.

For seven years, my wife and I had been studying a number of West Virginia serpent-handlers, primarily in order to discover what effect this unusual form of religious practice has on their lives. Although serpent-handling is outlawed by the state legislatures of Kentucky, Virginia, and Tennessee and by municipal ordinances in North Carolina, it is still legal in West Virginia. One center is the Scrabble Creek Church of All Nations in Fayette County, about thirty-seven miles from Charleston. Another center is the Church of Jesus in Jolo, McDowell County, one of the most poverty-stricken

79

areas of the state. Serpent-handling is also practiced sporadically elsewhere in West Virginia, where it is usually led by visitors from Scrabble Creek or Jolo.

The Jolo church attracts people from both Virginia and Kentucky, in addition to those from West Virginia. Members of the Scrabble Creek Church speak with awe of the Jolo services, where people pick up large handfuls of poisonous snakes, fling them to the ground, pick them up again, and thrust them to the ground, pick them up again, and thrust them under their shirts or blouses, dancing ecstatically. We attended one church service in Scrabble Creek where visitors from Jolo covered their heads with clusters of snakes and wore them as crowns.

Serpent-handling was introduced to Scrabble Creek in 1941 by a coal miner from Harlan, Kentucky. The practice really began to take hold in 1946, when the present leader of the Scrabble Creek Church, then a member of the Church of God, first took up serpents. The four or five original serpent-handlers in Fayette County met at one another's homes until given the use of an abandoned one-room schoolhouse in Big Creek. In 1959, when their number had swelled several times over, they moved to a larger church in Scrabble Creek.

**Snakebites, Saints, and Scoffers**

During the course of our seven-year study, about a dozen members of the church received snakebites. (My wife and I were present on two of these occasions.) Although there were no deaths, each incident was widely and unfavorably publicized in the area. For their part, the serpent-handlers say the Lord causes a snake to strike in order to refute scoffers' claims that the snakes' fangs have been pulled. They see each recovery from snakebite as a miracle wrought by the Lord—and each death as a sign that the Lord "really had to show the scoffers how dangerous it is to obey His commandments." Since adherents believe that death brings one to the throne of God, some express an eagerness to die when He decides they are ready. Those who have been bitten and who have recovered seem to receive special deference from other members of the church.

The ritual of serpent-handling takes only fifteen or twenty minutes in religious sessions that are seldom shorter than four hours. The rest of the service includes singing Christian hymns, ecstatic dancing, testifying, extemporaneous and impassioned sermons, faith-healing, "speaking in tongues," and foot-washing. These latter rituals are a part of the firmly rooted Holiness movement, which encompasses thousands of churches in the southern Appalachian region. The Holiness churches started in the nineteenth century as part of a perfectionist movement.

The social and psychological functions served by the Scrabble Creek Church are probably very much the same as those served by the more coventional Holiness churches. Thus, the extreme danger of the Scrabble Creek rituals probably helps to validate the members' claims to holiness. After all, the claim that one is a living saint is pretentious even in a sacred society—and it is particularly difficult to maintain in a secular society. That the serpent-handler regularly risks his life for his religion is seen as evidence of his saintliness. As the serpent-handler stresses over and over, "I'm afraid of snakes like anybody else, but when God anoints me, I handle them with joy." The fact that he is usually not bitten, or if bitten usually recovers, is cited as further evidence of his claim to holiness.

After we had observed the Scrabble Creek serpent-handlers for some time, we decided to give them psychological tests. We enlisted the aid of Auke Tellegen, department of psychology, University of Minnesota, and three of his clinical associates: James Butcher, William Schofield, and Anne Wirt. They interpreted the Minnesota Multiphasic Personality Inventory that we administered to 50 serpent-handlers (46 were completed)—and also to 90 members of a conventional denomination church 20 miles from Scrabble Creek. What we wanted to find out was how these two groups differed.

What we found were important personality differences not only between the serpent-handlers and the conventional church members, but also between the older and the younger generations within the conventional group. We believe that these differences are due, ultimately, to differences in social class: The serpent-handlers come from the nonmobile working class (average annual income: $3,000), whereas members of the conventional church are upwardly mobile working-class people (average annual income: $5,000) with their eyes on the future.

But first, let us consider the similarities between the two groups. Most of the people who live in the southcentral part of West Virginia, serpent-handlers or not, have similar backgrounds. The area is rural, nonfarm, with only about one-tenth of the population living in settlements of more than 2,500. Until recently, the dominant industry was coal mining, but in the last fifteen years mining operations have been drastically curtailed. The result has been widespread unemployment. Scrabble Creek is in that part of Appalachia that has been officially declared a "depressed area"—which means that current unemployment rates there often equal those of the Depression.

There are few foreign born in this part of West Virginia. Most of
the residents are of Scotch-Irish or Pennsylvania Dutch descent,
and their ancestors came to the New World so long ago that there
are no memories of an Old World past.

Generally, public schools in the area are below national standards. Few people over fifty have had more than six or seven years
of elementary education.

Religion has always been important here. One or two generations
ago, the immediate ancestors of both serpent-handlers and conventional church members lived in the same mining communities and
followed roughly the same religious practices. Today there is much
"backsliding," and the majority seldom attend church regularly.
But there is still a great deal of talk about religion, and there are few
professed atheists.


**Hypochondria and the Holy Spirit**

Though the people of both churches are native-born Protestants
with fundamentalist religious beliefs, little education, and precarious employment, the two groups seem to handle their common
problems in very different ways. One of the first differences we noticed was in the way the older members of both churches responded
to illness and old age. Because the members of both churches had
been impoverished and medically neglected during childhood and
young adulthood, and because they had earned their livelihoods in
hazardous and health-destroying ways, they were old before their
time. They suffered from a wide variety of physical ailments. Yet
while the older members of the conventional church seemed to dwell
morbidly on their physical disabilities, the aged serpent-handlers
seemed able to cheerfully ignore their ailments.

The serpent-handlers, in fact, went to the opposite extreme. Far
from being pessimistic hypochondriacs like the conventional church
members, the serpent-handlers were so intent on placing their fate in
God's benevolent hands that they usually failed to take even the normal precautions in caring for their health. Three old serpent-
handlers we knew in Scrabble Creek were suffering from serious
cardiac conditions. But when the Holy Spirit moved them, they
danced ecstatically and violently. And they did this without any apparent harm.

No matter how ill the old serpent-handlers are, unless they are actually prostrate in their beds, they manage to attend and enjoy
church services lasting four to six hours, two or three times a week.
Some have to travel long distances over the mountains to get to

church. When the long sessions are over, they appear refreshed rather than weary.

One evening an elderly woman was carried into the serpent-handling church in a wheelchair. She had had a severe stroke and was almost completely paralyzed. Wheeled to the front of the church, she watched everything throughout the long services. During one particularly frenzied singing and dancing session, the fingers of her right hand tapped lightly against the arm of the chair. This was the only movement she was able to make, but obviously she was enjoying the service. When friends leaned over and offered to take her home, she made it clear she was not ready to go. She stayed until the end, and gave the impression of smiling when she was finally wheeled out. Others in the church apparently felt pleased rather than depressed by her presence.

Both old members of the conventional denomination and old serpent-handlers undoubtedly are frequently visited by the thought of death. Both rely on religion for solace, but the serpent-handlers evidently are more successful. The old serpent-handlers are not frightened by the prospect of death. This is true not only of those members who handle poisonous snakes in religious services, but also of the minority who do *not* handle serpents.

One eighty-year-old member of the Scrabble Creek Church—who did not handle serpents—testified in our presence: "I am not afraid to meet my Maker in Heaven. I am ready. If somebody was to wave a gun in my face, I would not turn away. I am in God's hands."

Another old church member, a serpent-handler, was dying from silicosis. When we visited him in the hospital he appeared serene, although he must have known that he would not live out the week.

The assertion of some modern theologians that whatever meaning and relevance God once may have had has been lost for modern man does not apply to the old serpent-handlers. To them, God is real. In fact, they often see Him during vivid hallucinations. He watches over the faithful. Misfortune and even death do not shake their faith, for misfortune is interpreted, in accordance with God's inscrutable will, as a hidden good.

Surprisingly, the contrast between the optimistic old serpent-handlers and the pessimistic elders of the conventional church all but disappeared when we shifted to the younger members of the two groups. Both groups of young people, on the psychological tests, came out as remarkably well adjusted. They showed none of the neurotic and depressive tendencies of the older conventional church members. And this cheerful attitude prevailed despite the fact that many of them, at least among the young serpent-handlers, had much to be depressed about.

The young members of the conventional church are much better off, socially and economically, than the young serpent-handlers. The parents of the young conventional church members can usually provide the luxuries that most young Americans regarded as necessities. Many conventional church youths are active in extracurricular activities in high school or are attending college. The young serpent-handlers, in contrast, are shunned and stigmatized as "snakes." Most young members of the conventional denomination who are in high school intend to go on to college, and they will undoubtedly attain a higher socioeconomic status than their parents have attained. But most of the young serpent-handlers are not attending school. Many are unemployed. None attend or plan to attend college, and they often appear quite depressed about their economic prospects.

The young serpent-handlers spend a great deal of time wandering aimlessly up and down the roads of the hollows, and undoubtedly are bored when not attending church. Their conversation is sometimes marked by humor, with undertones of cynicism and bitterness. We are convinced that what prevents many of them from becoming delinquent or demoralized is their wholehearted participation in religious practices that provide an acceptable outlet for their excess energy, and strengthen their self-esteem by giving them the opportunity to achieve "holiness."

Now, how does all this relate to the class differences between the serpent-handlers and the conventional church group? The answer is that what allows the serpent-handlers to cope so well with their problems—what allows the older members to rise above the worries of illness and approaching death, and the younger members to remain relatively well adjusted despite their grim economic prospects—is a certain approach to life that is typical of them as members of the stationary working class. The key to this approach is hedonism.

### Hopelessness and Hedonism

The psychological tests showed that the young serpent-handlers, like their elders, were more impulsive and spontaneous than the members of the conventional church. This may account for the strong appeal of the Holiness churches to those members of the stationary working class who prefer religious hedonism to reckless hedonism, with its high incidence of drunkenness and illegitimacy. Religious hedonism is compatible with a Puritan morality—and it compensates for its constraints.

The feeling that one cannot plan for the future, expressed in religious terms as "being in God's hands," fosters the widespread conviction among members of the stationary working class that opportunities for pleasure must be exploited immediately. After all, they may never occur again. This attitude is markedly different from that of the upwardly mobile working class, whose members are willing to postpone immediate pleasures for the sake of long-term goals.

Hedonism in the stationary working class is fostered in childhood by parental practices that, while demanding obedience in the home, permit the child license outside the home. Later, during adulthood, this orientation toward enjoying the present and ignoring the future is reinforced by irregular employment and the other insecurities of stationary working-class life. In terms of middle-class values, hedonism is self-defeating. But from a psychiatric point of view, for those individuals who actually have little control of their position in the social and economic structure of modern society, it may very well aid acceptance of the situation. This is particularly true when it takes a religious form of expression. Certainly, hedonism and the associated trait of spontaneity seen in the old serpent-handlers form a very appropriate attitude toward life among old people who can no longer plan for the future.

In addition to being more hedonistic than members of the conventional church, the serpent-handlers are also more exhibitionistic. This exhibitionism and the related need for self-revelation are, of course, directly related to the religious practices of the serpent-handling church. But frankness, both about others and themselves, is typical of stationary working-class people in general. To a large extent, this explains the appeal of the Holiness churches. Ordinarily, their members have little to lose from frankness, since their status pretensions are less than those of the upwardly mobile working class, who are continually trying to present favorable images of themselves.

Because the young members of the conventional denomination are upwardly mobile, they tend to regard their elders as "old-fashioned," "stick-in-the-muds," and "ignorant." Naturally, this lack of respect from their children and grandchildren further depresses the sagging morale of the older conventional church members. They respond resentfully to the tendency of the young "to think they know more than their elders." The result is a vicious circle of increasing alienation and depression among the older members of the conventional denomination.

### Respect for Age

There appears to be much less psychological incompatibility between the old and the young serpent-handlers. This is partly because the old serpent-handlers manage to retain a youthful spontaneity in their approach to life. Then, too, the young serpent-handlers do not take a superior attitude toward their elders. They admire their elders for their greater knowledge of the Bible, which both old and young accept as literally true. And they also admire their elders for their handling of serpents. The younger church members, who handle snakes much less often than the older members do, are much more likely to confess an ordinary, everyday fear of snakes—a fear that persists until overcome by strong religious emotion.

Furthermore, the young serpent-handlers do not expect to achieve higher socioeconomic status than their elders. In fact, several young men said they would be satisfied if they could accomplish as much. From the point of view of the stationary working class, many of the older serpent-handlers are quite well off. They sometimes draw two pensions, one from Social Security and one from the United Mine Workers.

Religious serpent-handling, then—and all the other emotionalism of the Holiness churches that goes with it—serves a definite function in the lives of its adherents. It is a safety valve for many of the frustrations of life in present-day Appalachia. For the old, the serpent-handling religion helps soften the inevitability of poor health, illness, and death. For the young, with their poor educations and even poorer hopes of finding sound jobs, its promise of holiness is one of the few meaningful goals in a future dominated by the apparent inevitability of lifelong poverty and idleness.

# 5

# Mainlining Jesus: The New Trip

Robert Lynn Adams
and Robert Jon Fox

"It's the greatest rush I've ever had," commented one hip young man describing his experience in turning on to Jesus. Similar drug-culture metaphors are used by other former drug users who have joined the spreading movement of evangelical religion among the young—a movement that originated largely in southern California. The ranks of the "Jesus people" or "Jesus freaks," as some call them, have grown considerably during the early seventies. Thousands have been baptized off the beaches of southern California, and the movement has spread across the country trailing colorful publicity in its wake.

"We made *Time*!" exulted a young prophet of the movement recently. Bumper stickers substitute, "Have a Nice Forever," for the familiar California expression, "Have a Nice Day"; the Jesus-oriented *Free Paper* is sent to fifty states and eleven foreign countries—a biweekly, it claims a circulation of 260,000. In new recordings featuring "Jesus rock" the composers search for spiritual guidance and direction. Musical groups such as the J. C. Power Outlet and The Love Song proliferate. A new social system blends the hip style of dress, music, and speech into the "Jesus culture"—something new, yet something old indeed! The Jesus trip is the Great Awakening of 1740 (Jonathan Edwards) revisited; it is American frontier religion revisited with Volkswagens and amplifiers supplanting the horses, wagons, and saddlebacks of Cane Ridge, Kentucky, 1801.

The young whites of middle-class background turning toward

87

revivalist religion come from two rather distinct groups. From observations of crowds at religious services, one of these groups consists largely of teenagers whom we call *Jesus-boppers*. In them, rock groups turned on to Jesus have a ready-made audience from the large ranks of rock-music fans. Free concerts followed by an invitation to accept Jesus Christ attract large youth audiences.

The other element in the Jesus movement is a smaller and more intense group of young adults (usually in their twenties) who have opted out of the drug culture. Many are former peace-movement activists who have dropped out of society over the past four or five years. For them, the Jesus movement constitutes a ritual of reentry into the system.

In our investigation of the Jesus movement we used both observations and interviews. We attended many religious services, interviewing the ministers of the church in Orange County, where the movement is largely centered, visited religious communes, using a formal questionnaire to interview eighty-nine young people. Although the sample is small, it served to add validity to the observations and unstructured interviews, the latter being taped for analysis. We encountered great resistance in the communes to the questionnaire; some attributed their reluctance to an unwillingness to mull over the past. One respondent mentioned that talking about one's past was actually forbidden in the San Francisco commune where he had formerly lived.

### A Trip to the Chapel

As an institution, Gethsemane Chapel is three years old [1972]. It is an independent, nondenominational congregation whose basically conservative Baptist theology is a blend of holiness and pentecostalism. Its ministry is antiestablishment in its rejection of the theology and social positions of the major Protestant denominations. The main minister was a hawk on the Vietnam War, decrying the no-win policy that has been pursued by the government.

Sunday morning and evening as well as several week nights are Bible-study sessions, attended mainly by older persons. Some weeknight meetings find Gethsemane Chapel jammed with youth, but the big youth night is Wednesday, when a number of musical groups are featured. The church is packed two hours prior to the service—crowd estimates range from 1,300 to 1,400 persons; about one-third are outside listening to loudspeakers and participating visually through the chapel's walls. Approximately eighty percent of the audience is female; and less than five percent are what could be called *hippies*. Yet the style of dress is informal—jeans and hip garb and long hair abounds. Over half the crowd consists of early teens and less than fifteen percent are over twenty.

A twenty-two-year-old lay minister—a former drug user, with flowing robe, long hair, and beard—leads this service. Later, in an "afterglow" he leads a smaller group in receiving the baptism of the Holy Spirit—speaking in tongues. The interaction style in the worship and in the entire movement is intensely personal, a kind of "Gospel Anonymous," with pastors and members first-naming each other.

Gethsemane's services are more holiness than pentecostal in that they follow a definite order, eschewing the freewheeling "do your thing" style of the latter. The young minister mentioned above, whom we shall call Rennie, has been known to silence persons who interrupt to speak in tongues during the service. Informal songs are sung by the congregation, mostly centering around the person of Jesus and his imminent return to earth. Prayers for the sick are offered and testimonies are heard. The ubiquitous "one-way" sign (extended index finger with clenched fist) shows the congregation's approval of various elements of the services. Rennie affirms that God desires to heal anything from "warts to cancer." The "flashes" from previous LSD trips can also be cured. One woman (older than most present) testifies that she has been cured of dandruff. "Praise the Lord!" says Rennie. An examination of her head reveals no trace of dandruff.

Following the singing, testimonies, and music groups, Rennie reads from the Bible and gives a sermon—often a defense of speaking in tongues. At the close, an invitation is given to accept Jesus. On an average Wednesday night, about 100 young persons come forward, affirm their faith in unison, and are then led to another part of the church to be presented with a Bible. When there were fewer converts, individual counseling was also conducted. Many of the converts are later baptized in the ocean, although apparently no set plan is announced for doing so immediately.

In the afterglow, another Bible study is conducted, after which Rennie invites individuals who want the baptism of the Spirit to come forward. A flute player provides an eerie background (he "plays by the Spirit") while Rennie assists those who wish to receive the Spirit, with such blandishments as, "you may kneel, if you wish," or "you may extend your arms toward heaven, if you wish."

Rennie moves in and out among those standing on the platform, touching and speaking to them. Eventually a cadence of people speaking in a babble and singing in tongues intertwines with the mystic tones of the flute. (Many Jesus-boppers report receiving this baptism.) For this part of the service the church is full, but the aisles and the grounds are empty of people; some teenage girls attempt to sit in the aisle to get close to the platform where Rennie is leading the service. Following the afterglow, which is terminated at Rennie's command, certain individuals remain fixed in apparent hysterical stupor. "Counselors" help them to "give in" to the Spirit, some of whom are unable to pull out of their babbling and hysteria.

On Friday nights there are no music groups, although the service is supposedly programmed for youth. Another young lay minister—more square than Rennie—leads this service. The attendance is about one-third of the Wednesday night assemblage, with fewer teenagers present. This difference is likely due to the drawing power of the professional gospel-rock groups on Wednesday plus the charisma of Rennie.

### The Jesus Commune

The leaders of Gethsemane Chapel, being interested in reaching young people in the drug culture for Jesus, developed the idea of adopting the commune as a service-oriented institution. And the movement appears to be very successful. Scores of Jesus-oriented houses have sprung up along the entire West Coast under the sponsorship of Gethsemane Chapel.

Visits to these communes reveal a rigid separation of male and female living quarters, with a strict affirmation of asceticism. Many of the occupants have been members of drug-oriented communes, where sexual relations were available. The same individuals appear to move toward early marriage after being saved. Their frequently idealistic conception of marriage is exemplified by the response of one young man, who when asked if he thought sex could be misused in marriage, said, "Certainly not." (He believed that he had misused it out of marriage.)

The communes visited had approximately twenty to thirty permanent residents, although their turnover appears high. When one commune becomes fairly large, another is established; when one is overpopulated, members move to another that has space. The commune also serves as a type of crash pad where anyone is welcome to eat and/or sleep.

Money earned by members is given to a central treasury, although one's worldly wealth is not demanded (as was the case in the traditional monastery movement). Yard and gardening work is done for local residents to earn money to support the house as well as to learn to work and live together. Several deacons are in charge of finances plus the physical and spiritual nurture of the house. The leaders deny that there are rules, saying everyone is to follow God's will. Emphasis on cooperation rather than rules appears to be effective in accomplishing the day's tasks. There is a minimum of scheduling, although a list of those preparing breakfast is posted. The diet, which has a heavy starch content, is augmented by fruit and vegetable discards donated by local grocery stores. The direction of the Spirit is sought in all matters, including remodeling and obtaining materials for a new roof, for example.

Persons visiting a commune receive an open and friendly welcome. Such was the case at Mansion Messiah. A tour of the premises may reveal a young man speaking in tongues in the garden, a modest "prayer house" in the back yard, with another young man just leaving it to return to the main building. Just recently the "family" had added the eating room. There were no contractors hired to build the addition, and the plywood and materials for the roof were all donated. "The Lord just showed us where to lay the beams," and the members built the roof. The garage was converted into a bedroom by the members also and holes in the walls were left for the windows. "The Lord provided us with windows to fit the holes." In this bedroom at least nine men sleep, in three bunk-beds, three high, that the men had made themselves.

The girls (about ten in number) do all the cooking, mending, serving, washing, and other housework and hold no outside jobs. The men do the yard work, gardening, repairs around the house, building of furniture, and some hold outside jobs. It costs about $2,000 per month to run the house. Donations and contributions help to pay the expenses that are not covered by the men's pay.

Many individuals in the commune appear for the first time in their lives to be learning how to work and live with others. The leaders do not deny that conflicts arise in the house; such conflicts, they emphasize, are a creative opportunity for individuals to learn to live together. The nightly Bible-study time is used to deal with such problems; leaders of the evening frequently pick a New Testament passage dealing with mutual sharing and responsibility.

Life in the Jesus movement is ruled by two norms: the Bible and the direct guidance of the Holy Spirit. As their former lives have been physically sensate in relation to drugs and sex, so their "born-again" lives tend to be spiritually sensate. Thus it is difficult to gather information on such mundane topics as finances either at Gethsemane Chapel or in the communes. "The Lord provides" and "right on!" are the expressions one elicits upon bringing up the problem of money. Since all problems are dealt with by the direct guidance of the Spirit (unless explicit Biblical instructions can be found), it is not surprising to find commune members and ministers of the church extremely spiritually sensate in regard to budgets.

During the study of the communes, it became evident that the wide publicity given the movement in the press and on television was affecting the communes' image. These problems and others were observed by a student researcher during her visit to what we term *Christus House:*

I went to the Christus House on a Friday night. Everyone was sitting around talking and drinking either coffee or tea, waiting for the meeting to start. At about 7 P.M. every night the house has a meeting with people who live outside. These are carefully screened by the leader, a deacon named John. The meeting lasts between two and three hours.

While I was waiting for the meeting to begin I talked with several people who were very open to introduce themselves, but very hesitant to carry on a conversation. The first question they asked was, "Have you been saved?" I overheard a conversation between two members of the house, one male and one female. The female, Jane, was expressing her previous concern (before being saved) and anxiety about getting married. She said she was glad she did not have to worry about that any more because it was now in God's hands. The meeting began with guitar music and singing by everyone present. John led the meeting, but everyone was given a chance to talk. This they referred to as "sharing."

At first they shared different encounters they had had during the day. The main topic of discussion was a program on television that afternoon in which John, a girl name June, and several people from another commune participated. They had spent the time talking about God and Christ. John had cut his hair for the program and had suffered "trials" throughout the week because he was afraid the devil was making him do it. They both expressed how upset they had been because they might misrepresent the Lord. However, they were both at ease when they discovered, while on the air, that they did not really even speak but "it was the Lord speaking through them." They expressed concern with changing their image from that of long-haired, former drug users to conservative, clean-cut citizens. In fact, they showed hostility at the image they thought the public had of them. Others mentioned having individual problems and the Lord leading them to a specific chapter in the Bible that solved the problem. They discussed what the phrase, "I love someone but I don't like them," means, that John had just found out from a minister at Gethsemane that afternoon. One member expressed how thrilled he was because it was his first day working for Jesus.

Experience in the communes is dichotomous: one is led either by the Lord or the devil. It was thus very difficult to get very detailed answers to questions. The public (that is, the "world") is likewise viewed in authoritarian, either/or terms: like "darkness" and "searching for the light." After the meeting, members left for a theater to witness to people waiting in line. John tends to use scare tactics in a gentle way, illustrated by the fact that he very calmly asked me [that] if I died on the way home, which I might, would I go to heaven? He had also mentioned in the meeting that in the studio that day he had asked someone else the same question.

## The Jesus-boppers

Most of the members of the Jesus movement in Orange County seem to be teenage youth—the Jesus-boppers. Their motivation for being in the movement is apparently twofold, stemming both from a desire for peer-group approval and a need for resolving the identity crisis. According to Erik Erikson's analysis of the teenage years as a period of identity versus role confusion, puberty marks the beginning of the developmental stage crisis. The physiological revolution within and the tangible adult tasks ahead of them cause youth to be primarily concerned with how they appear to others rather than with what they feel they are. Erikson writes:

> The adolescent mind is essentially a mind of *moratorium*, a psychosexual stage between childhood and adulthood, and between the morality learned by the child, and the ethics to be developed by the adult. It is an ideological mind—and, indeed, it is the ideological outlook of a society that speaks most clearly to the adolescent who is eager to be affirmed by his peers and is ready to be confirmed by rituals, creeds, and programs which at the same time define what is evil, uncanny, and inimical.

The Jesus trip seems tailor-made for adolescents. Not only does commitment to Jesus preserve childhood morality with its absolutistic definitions of right and wrong, but it also provides an ideology based on personal, internal, and, for the most part, unexplainable experience rather than on critical, rational, or realistic analysis. Indeed, the ideology is unchallengeable and thereby not available for analysis by the uninitiated.

The Jesus trip also provides adolescents with the necessary peers, rituals, creeds, and programs—brothers, baptisms, speaking in tongues, and a source for the ideology, the Bible. Approval and affirmation by peers are guaranteed within the movement. To the droves of young teens who fill Gethsemane Chapel on the nights that the professional music groups perform, Rennie issues the invitation in these words, "Accept Jesus Christ. Don't get left out. Come right now."

The Jesus trip can be seen as an attempt to resolve the crisis of the onset of sexuality by denying sexual feelings. Previous to puberty, the individual has developed to some degree an identity based upon his or her experiences and needs. With the onset of the physiological revolution within and with the growing awareness of adult roles, this identity is threatened; suddenly he must accept a new aspect of identity—sexuality. Successful growth depends on the individual's ability to meet his new needs and expand his identity without threatening the self. Rather than risk the trauma of this adjustment, the individual may resolve the crisis in neurotic fashion: by establishing an ideal by which to deny his feelings. Adolescent idealism represents one such attempt to keep oneself separate from one's real feelings. An example of such denial is this statement by a sixteen-year old who had been on drugs and sexually active prior to his conversion:

> I am free, free from the garbage of the world—the kind of stuff that you're a slave to. Jesus said, "Whoever commits sin is a servant of sin." I've quit taking drugs, I've quit getting it on the girls—I've changed, man! Don't you understand? I'm free, free, free—all the time and not just for six to eight hours—all the time. I still have problems, but I don't hassle with them, because I'm free!

We believe that religion as represented in this movement is a step backward. The Jesus trip, like drugs, appears to be used in such a way as to avoid coming to terms with the anxieties related to the identity crisis. In normal development the new dimensions of identity are added to the previously established identity, modifying it to some degree; some parts of one's previous identity will be discarded, submerged, or eradicated by new behavior. Instead of progressing toward adult ethics, the Jesus person clutches tenaciously to childhood morality, with its simplistic black-and-white, right-and-wrong judgments. Rather than developing behavior oriented toward reality, he flies into ideational, ideological abstractions to numb his awareness of his newly arisen needs. Spurning a reality that begins with individual feelings, he subordinates himself to peer approval. For these reasons we term the Jesus trip a *pseudosolution* to the identity versus role-confusion crisis.

## Comparing Drug and Jesus Cultures

Members of the Jesus movement have a high incidence of past drug use, with 62 percent of those over 18 and 44 percent of those under 18 having used dope. Only a few individuals were extremely light users, usually of marijuana.

Continuities between the drug and Jesus experiences are as follows: 1) Both are outside the modal American life-style, in fact, both are antiestablishment in their attempts to create alternatives to the American middle-class life-style. Middle-class denominational religion, in the words of one pastor, "is as phony as it can be." 2) Both are subjective and experientially oriented, as opposed to the dominant cultural style, which is objective, scientific, and rationally oriented. 3) The nature of the religious experience at Gethsemane Chapel and other holiness-type congregations is wholly consonant with previously experienced drug highs. A common description of the conversion experienced is: "It's a rush like speed."

We found a number of discontinuities between the dope and Jesus trips. As compared with the drug culture, the Jesus trip offers an extremely limited repertoire for action. For the Jesus person, life revolves entirely around Jesus, his acceptance, and mission. All events are either of the Lord or of the devil. Brothers and sisters of the faith meet each other with religiously infused greetings, and, "God bless," substitutes for "good-bye." The drug culture as a whole exhibits a much greater variety. Certainly there are drug users whose lives center solely around dope, its procurement, and use, but drug use has become quite generalized among a wide variety of people, many of whom have a broader range of action alternatives in dealing with reality than the Jesus people.

The Jesus trip represents an almost violent ideological swing from far Left to far Right, a type of "reaction formation." A shift toward a conservative position in solving world problems is reported by seventy-six percent of those interviewed. Only two persons have changed toward the Left. Of those who reported no change in position, none were dropouts in the usual sense of the word. They represent a more consistent ideological history—no rebellion against parents, a continuity between their childhood religious faith and the adult Jesus movement. Their feelings toward American society, for example, are that it is "pagan like the Roman Empire at the time of Christ" or it is "too complex" for an opinion to have been formed. A slightly more liberal outlook was articulated by one respondent who observed that "the system is great, but people pervert justice." The focus here is still typically on the individual rather than on system change.

Four out of five of those reporting a shift in outlook state that the change coincided with their religious conversion. World problems, they now believe, "can only be solved through finding Christ"; "We can't have peace on the outside if we don't on the inside"; "If everyone was a Christian, there wouldn't be any world problems."

However, certain Jesus publications in the area encourage a more worldly approach to political and social problems, indeed a very conservative one. For example, the *Hollywood Free Paper* routinely attacks the peace movement. *For Real* made the following comments in the May 1971 edition in an article entitled, "The Real Lesson of the Calley Trial":

> The fact is, too many people are bad. Because people are bad, they must be restrained by force. Because they must be restrained by force, police are necessary. Armies, navies, and air forces are necessary. Wars are inevitable. Killing is necessary. That's the real lesson of the William Calley trial.

For Jesus people, sexual behavior also undergoes profound alternation when they leave the drug culture. Although sixty-two percent of the Jesus people in the sample report premarital sex prior to conversion, in most cases asceticism has become the dominant rule since being saved. A few slips are reported "once after conversion," but these can hardly be classified as libertine. Less then five percent openly differ with the sexual ethics of the movement and continue to practice premarital sex after their conversion. Another divergency is that the Jesus culture entails reentering the system, returning to a middle-class work ethic, and closing the generation gap. After coming from middle-class backgrounds (seventy-two percent of those reporting father's occupation are from white-collar homes and over two-thirds of these are clearly upper-middle-class occupations), dropping out represents downward mobility; these youth are now reentering the system, preparing to participate in the work force.

The movement's strong antiintellectualism, however, is prompting some young people to drop out of college at a time when their reentry into the system requires additional training. Many Jesus people, however, are still involved in routine educational programs while at the same time they hold antiintellectual views. Of the 89 young people who answered the questionnaire, 17 had completed high school, 19 were still in college, three had some college, two were college graduates, and many were young high-school students.

Several in the sample, who had dropped out of college, cite their religious experience as the motivating force in this decision. A songwriter-itinerant singer for gospel causes asserts that, "The more education one has, the less likely one is to join (the) Jesus movement . . . (the) less one becomes childlike . . . becomes hardened." He elaborates that school teaches that science is God, that truth is relative, and that there can be good and evil at the same time, but this is not true.

College graduates are included among the ranks of commune dwellers who tend gardens as a livelihood. Generally, though, the older persons in the movement had dropped out during or after high school and now represent a most interesting sociological phenomenon: downward mobility and movement from church to sect (many come from church-affiliated families). Thus in closing the gap between themselves and their parents by rejoining the system, they have created fresh conflict over their education and religion. However, many parents are so pleased with their return to the system that they are financing their offspring's stay in the commune. One youth mentioned the possibility of going to Europe to an evangelical convention, explaining that his father would pay his expenses.

Preachers at Gethsemane Chapel admonish the audience to "honor thy father and thy mother." Many youth noted their conscious attempts to help them rebuild relationships with their families. Prayers in communes often concern members of the family who have problems and "need to be saved."

Whereas the drug trip represents a quest, the Jesus trip is a panacea. Despite its attendant problems, the drug culture is admirable in its affirmation of the individual's quest for experience and discovery of truth; in this it is not unlike the basis of modern liberal education. The Jesus trip, however, is a cure-all. No problem is too great to be answered easily; the believer desists from solving problems, "leaves it up to the Lord."

Another difference between the two cultures relates to authoritarianism. The free-lance drug culture is by definition nonauthoritarian. The Jesus culture, on the other hand, sees the world in either/or terms. No experience is free from being of God or of the devil. This unequivocal embracing of authoritarianism may be a byproduct of the scanty education of many young believers combined with a background of family conflict.

The Jesus culture escapes the leadership problem posed by the individualism of the drug culture. Lewis Yablonski observes how the individualism of the drug scene often leads to a lack of leadership—a vacuum that sometimes allows "deviants" from the scene to wreak havoc on the peace and tranquillity desired by the majority. Although leadership in the Jesus movement is attributed to God, there is no want of self-anointed human leaders around to make suggestions: the hierarchy ranges from the deacons in the commune (often young Christians with less than one year's experience of being saved) to the ministers of Gethsemane Church. The ministers are consulted on biblical and other problems that the deacons in the commune cannot solve.

Before undertaking this study, the writers had theorized that Jesus people who are ex-dopers had participated in a succession of social movements: they began in the peace movement, had dropped out into the drug scene, and finally joined the religious revival. The data, however, refute this assumption about the sequence of membership in the various movements, for the use of drugs almost always had preceded participation in the peace movement. We find the mean age of 25 former drug-and-peace people to be 20.3, while the mean age of nondrug-nonpeace participants (Jesus-boppers) is 17.4. Another segment in the sample consists of ex-dopers who were not in the peace movement (16 individuals with a mean age of 20.2, similar to the drug-and-peace group). Only four persons participated in the peace movement, but not in drugs; their mean age is 18.2.

Since the mean ages of the two ex-dope groups is similar, a contrast between them is fruitful. The drug-peace contingent is more likely to report (79 percent) dropping out of society than the nonpeace group (55 percent). However, contrary to popular opinion, their dropping out did not mean total absorption in the quest for individual experience; it did not interfere with New Left political participation by 32 Jesus people in the survey.

If the movements are so dissimilar, why the switch from dope to Jesus? One possibility is the faddishness of the Jesus trip; the same quest for novelty had motivated some to join the drug scene. The hippie faddist finds that drugs and sex are not "where it's at." Those of middle-class background may be torn between their former values and those of the drug scene; they may welcome the Jesus trip as an expedient means of returning to middle-class values, while retaining peer approval. The religious fervor of the Jesus movement provides a more socially acceptable way for them to resolve their conflict; its life-style is as much a drop in as a drop out. One can gradually become reoriented to the larger segments of the population without really going too straight. In fact, few changes in life-style are required in the move from dope to Jesus.

**Criticisms of the Movement**

The Jesus culture bears watching in the future because of several ironic twists: It is a victim of area right-wing politics, and we foresee its steadily increasing exploitation by reactionary political forces. Pamphlets distributed by the Jesus people are beginning to contain familiar attacks on one-world government, the ecumenical movement among liberal denominations, and other favorite targets of local conservative politicians. Disaffection of the movement's adherents (who generally interpret the teachings of Jesus as condemning all wars) may be expected when they discover that their leaders are militarists. The "true believer" psyche in the Jesus people, however, may well make it possible to rationalize their loyalty to their leaders.

The movement is insular—a cop-out from the realities of social change that face America. A basically white movement, it has no program for reaching the members of another race or less affluent economic groups than those in its area. The attempt to equate denominational religion with the establishment is presently successful; however, when the youth see that the denominational church has stood against racism, war, and poverty, the Jesus movement may well fade. As one liberal, establishment, campus minister put it:

> I think the kind of world in which we live leads to some kind of escape. And some of the same kids who were escaping through heroin are now mainlining Jesus, and confusing Jesus with a way of withdrawing from the world and its problems. I can sympathize with them. There are times when I would like to withdraw, too.
>
> Jesus to them is a kind of spirit that they have a union with. Whereas Jesus, for the early Christians, was a man of flesh and blood who took history seriously, and whose concern [was] about the whole man, not just his spirit, not just his soul. Jesus will push someone back into those problems, back into the world, only if they stay with him.

The movement denies the complexity of human nature. It abrogates the psychosociosexual nature of man by dividing the self into physical and spiritual entities; the individual is indoctrinated to anticipate "rapture" when the soul is delivered from the body. Many Judeo-Christian theologians would label this as heresy, citing that the Bible teaches the unity of man's nature.

The movement's faithful show a rapid turnover. This may be related to their return to middle-class society. Some young teens who were in the movement have lessened in religious fervor considerably as they approach the middle teen years.

The movement denies the future by turning its back on the temporal world. The apocalyptic feature of the movement dissuades young people from rejoining society because they are led to believe that the second coming of Christ is imminent. They need not concern themselves with improving our decaying cities, solving the problems of poverty, war, and disease—all can be left up to God. A new pamphlet says the ecology movement is irrelevant because Jesus is coming soon anyway. Similarly the individual has no need for long-range plans; his exclusive concern is with the immediacy of his personal needs. Such myopia will certainly obstruct attempts to bridge the generation gap. (The movement's dropouts will undoubtedly become more oriented toward the future.)

Among the potential trouble spots uncovered in our data was the gap between the ministers' beliefs and those of their followers. For example, the ministers interviewed saw nothing contradictory in being both Christian and economically successful; the young people, particularly the commune members, take the antimaterialism of Jesus seriously.

The communes are the most impressive part of the Jesus movement. The contribution made by their members lies in the simplicity of their life-style, their easy acceptance of themselves, their genuine attempts at learning to get along with others and participate in communal tasks. Although they have kicked the drug habit, their abstinence has been too brief to predict how successful they will be at giving up drugs permanently. We may wonder what will happen if and when they are no longer high on Jesus. The potential psychological difficulties could be enormous, for in large measure they have channeled their anxieties about their problems into displays of religious fervor rather than coming to terms with the realities of the identity crisis.

# 6

# Group-Dieting Rituals

Natalie Allon

"Lose those extra pounds!" "Get rid of unsightly flab!" "Re-move those unwanted inches in just seven days!"

Messages like these bombard us daily from newspapers, maga-zines, radio, and television. Thin is in, fat is out. The ideal of thinness is commonly regarded as a good in itself, while overweight—any deviation from the "norm"—is considered a sin. Americans are obsessed with slimming down to the point that dieting is rapidly becoming the national pastime. And group dieting is one of the most popular of all methods.

Group dieting on a large-scale, national basis is a relatively new phenomenon, only about ten-years old. I studied one weight-losing organization in the Northeast that sponsored about 100 weekly group meetings and reached over 3,000 "patients" a week. There were about 125 "healers" working for this organization, consisting of executives, group leaders, clerks, and secretaries.

My basic role was that of participant-observer—after experi-menting with a variety of diets for 14 years I have somewhat of an inside viewpoint. I sat in on 90 group-diet meetings sponsored by an organization under the pseudonym of *Trim-Down*. Altogether I saw over 1,400 healers and patients—about 95 percent were women and 5 percent were men. In many meetings there were 20 to 40 members; many were wives and mothers between 25- and 55-years old. Most members were middle-class women of various ethnic and religious backgrounds. Many had between 20 and 45 pounds to lose—

quite a few had lost at least 5 to 10 pounds on the Trim-Down diet and intended to lose more.

It has been estimated that at least 52 million Americans are calorie conscious. They express their devotion to the Ideal of Thinness in various ways, ranging from restriction of food intake, specialized foods and drugs, and exercise, to prayer, hypnosis, psychotherapy, and health spas. Weight-losing groups offer an attractive alternative healing system for the "disease" or "sin" of overweight. Many dieters find comfort in submission to the external authority of the group. The group pressure in this case emphasizes not the final thinness-cure, but the process of healing-thinner. The morally good Trim-Downer is one who attempts to perfect a better and better body. To be such a supreme good, the final cure of a thin body must evolve from a fat body. The holiness is in the act of cleansing. To be a saint, one must start as a sinner.

Not coincidentally, these saints-in-the-making were good-paying customers of this profit-making organization. Having arrived at thinness is not such a noble fait accompli, for the cured thin need no longer pay to be healed. Indeed, I noted a constant tension between the missionary fervor of commitment and conversion to group weight-losing and the profit-prestige orientation of recruiting more members.

Almost seventy-five percent of all Trim-Downers studied were involved in continual dieting cycling and recycling patterns throughout much of their lives. They were on a perpetual merry-go-round of reducing diets, and the Trim-Down cure was just another one of these reducing methods:

> So this month it is Trim-Down. Last month I tried one of those exercise spas, and last year I went on a kick of magazine diets. I guess I am just hooked on dieting for life and I am always looking for the magical cure—the final end to my dieting mania when I will be thin forever. I am willing to give everyone a fair chance to cure me and make some money off me. I am very egalitarian. Some of the diets work for a while, and then they peter out. On some of them, like here, you get to meet a lot of interesting people. You just keep looking for the right medicine.

This sentiment is common to many Trim-Downers—many came to the groups at least in part to engage in sociability for its own sake. These dieters look for mutual support from others in the group, who understand them and know dieting doldrums from an inside viewpoint.

Many dieters tried Trim-Down because it was one of the cheapest cures they could find. Other methods, such as spas, were too costly in terms of money, time, and energy. Some Trim-Downers had tried medical doctors and were sorely disappointed. Some alternated between the group and medical doctors. As they lost faith in one route, they recaptured faith in the other. Still others went to both simultaneously, feeling that everything and anything helps. Medical doctors presented physiological and nutritional know-how, while group leader-healers provided emotional support.

Many Trim-Downers acknowledged their dependence upon individual healers, whether they were in the persons of medical doctors or Trim-Down leaders. Many said that they needed an authority figure to watch over them—they could not trust their own willpower to heal themselves. "Depending on your own conscience never pays off—you need a policeman."

Other members stated that they enjoyed the Trim-Down route to thinness because the group was a close-knit, familial gemeinschaft. Trim-Downers did not have cold and aloof secondary relationships with each other, as did traditional medical healers with their patients. Many appeared to transpose their gossipy morning coffee sessions with the girls to the different time and place setting of the Trim-Down group.

Trim-Down healers were self-styled experts whose basic qualification to lead weight-losing groups was the fact that they had been healed from their own fatness by the Trim-Down diet plan. Most Trim-Down healers offered one uniform diet plan to be followed by their patients, which was based upon an obesity clinic diet. Beside this diet, the quasi-religious service of group dieting was the primary method of operation of the Trim-Down healing system.

Trim-Downers made territorial processions inside the doors of the meetings as rites of entrance. This initiation rite might be viewed as a rite of separation from the healees' previous world, in which they were unclean and unhealed. Once a member had one foot in the door, she became "sacred" because she was on the road to becoming healed from her fatness. The group participation and weight loss which occurred inside the door can be seen as an initiation rite into the culturally preferred thin American way of life. Participants sought out entrance-partners in this initial walk. Such entrance-partners exchanged professions of their goodness and confessions of their badness in regard to their healing progress.

The second processional march of the meeting took place as the Trim-Downers waited in line to offer their standardized and required alms to lecturers or clerks. As continuing members, they paid $2. The initial registration fee was $5. Individuals who missed meetings paid one dollar for each meeting missed, never to exceed the initial $5 fee. Trim-Downers thus made a monetary payment for their healing, but there was a noncontractual element to their healing contract.

The dieters appeared to speak with their bodies in pay-in lines. Some were embarassed by their bodies and snuggled in their coats to hide. Others announced their mixed feelings about their bodies by throwing open their coats and exhibiting tightly fitting clothing. Many engaged in double conversations—eyes sizing up one another while chattering about the diet and social activities.

The third processional march occurred in weigh-in lines. The scale became the totemic representation of the Ideal of Thinness. Some seemed to pray in the presence of the scale. They cried out in joy or sorrow about their weight-losing progress; they stared straight in front of them in devout silence. In their moment of judgment some felt cleansed from their sins of cheating, while others felt exalted in their holiness of good eating. Indeed, Trim-Downers labeled themselves good or bad according to the scale's decree of a two- and three-digit number.

### The Devil

Trim-Downers anthropomorphized the scale, calling it a "kind friend" or a "mean monster." Many asked the scale to be "fair," "have a heart," or not be a "devil." As they begged the scale to be good to them, some disrobed toward a naked innocence. Shoes and heavy jewelry were taken off; sometimes woolen skirts and pants, slips, and girdles were removed.

In a very concrete, quantitative manner, the scale made the final judgment of the degree to which each Trim-Downer was healed each week. The leader-healer read this absolute sentence to each patient. Pounds shed indicated that healing was taking place.

In the social chattertime that followed, healees "responsively read" each other, verbally and visually. Ego and alter ego questioned and answered each other about their dieting efforts; they offered each other pep talks. Some seemed to pray with each other at this time as they asked the Ideal of Thinness to bestow Its omnipotent blessings on them. Many believed that thinness did mean beauty, happiness, and health.

Believers discussed their faith in the Trim-Down diet creed. Some offered testimonies to the Ideal of Thinness as they lauded its miraculous healing powers. They asserted that since their conversion to the Trim-Down diet they were "born again," or were "really living" for the first time in their lives. Others offered choral refrains in agreement with the marvels of thinness and the Trim-Down diet.

In contrast, others challenged the Trim-Down creed—they did not like the food on the diet, or there was too much or too little food on the diet. Some devil's advocates even questioned the need to be healed from their fatness plight at all—perhaps the Thin Power advocates required healing from their "warped fetish." Nevertheless, all such atheists, agnostics, and believers often forgot their differences and indulged in sociable gossip for its own sake.

Next, lecturer-healers were on center stage for the "lecture-sermon." These healers exalted the Ideal of Thinness and the Trim-Down diet plan as the best means to reach the Ideal. Many lecturers told humorous and sad anecdotes about their own weight-losing careers. Some revealed how their lives had been saved by the Trim-Down healing method.

### The Straight and Narrow

Other prophetic healers told of the horrors of fatness and the evil fortunes that befell those who resisted Trim-Down healing. They warned that members must not be tempted to stray from the straight and narrow of the diet and eat taboo foods. Some lecturers gave elaborate rationales for parts of the Trim-Down creed. They emphasized how and why the Trim-Down healing system was the best of all healing systems for dealing with being overweight, including pills, doctors' diets, exercising, and other group methods. Lecturers got their points across through jesting, storytelling, and solemn admonitions.

The detailed and technical question-and-answer period followed the lecture-sermon. Member-healees and lecturer-healers seemed to engage in responsive readings with each other, with members doing most of the asking, and lecturers doing most of the answering. The ideology of thinness was stressed in the lecture; the question-and-answer period concentrated upon tactics—the "how to do it." There was an elaborate exchange of information about the kinds and amounts of food on the diet. Some clarified and elaborated upon the creed for others. Some affirmed and lauded the Trim-Down creed; others challenged it.

One specific healing procedure was articulated in each weekly meeting as the lecturer read the "recipe-scripture" passage. This presentation was similar to the reading of a sacred text—many listened devoutly to each and every word, carefully writing down and memorizing every last detail. Healees responded to the healer's prescriptions of the recipe-medicine as they became involved in an exegesis of the text. The dieters spent much time and energy on the particulars of ingredients of recipes that were seductive in their mouth-watering names. For example, there were Trim-Down recipes for lasagna, eggplant kebab, pink-cloud chiffon pie, and lemon custard. But healers and healees did not worship the recipe-scriptures as perfect. Worship of the recipes per se would be idolatry—it was the Ideal of Thinness that was revered. Diet recipes were the significant medium through which this Ideal spoke to Trim-Downers by calling them to respond in faith and obedience.

Again, healees and healers responsively read each other verbally and visually as the healers announced their individual patient's weight losses and gains. With these public announcements of individual and group weight-loss averages, the worthiness of the Trim-Down healing method was confirmed. Most lecturers mumbled weight gains quickly—if they did not completely ignore them. They preferred to minimize the fact that the Trim-Down cure was not working for all. In terms of pounds shed in a total group, the Trim-Down healing method seemed quite effective.

As leader-healers read off weight losses and gains, they offered "individualized benedictions" to members as they wished them well on the diet. That is, they blessed them in their dieting efforts and wished that the members would approach nearer and nearer to the Ideal of Thinness in their bodies. Cheating sins were errors of the past, and holy dieting was the order of the day.

**Physical Worship**

In some meetings, Trim-Downers seemed to worship the Ideal of Thinness in a direct physical way when they exercised. The exercises seemed to show parallels with religious genuflections and more vigorous body movements, as well as with the recitation of Pater Nosters with rosary beads. During this period, Trim-Downers revered thinness with their bodies as well as with their words.

The meeting was finished. Trim-Downers then partook of their last processional march from inside to outside the door in their rite of exit. Lecturer-healers appeared to be coaches who offered short pep-talk farewell phrases, like, "Bye, I'll see you back here next week with a good weight loss," or, "You can do it—take it meal by meal."

"Exit-partner" healees wished each other good luck and happy eating. They did not look over each other's bodies in bidding each other farewell as much as they did at other times during the meeting. Verbal good-byes seemed to symbolize the end of body-readings. Jackets or coats defended or protected many from further body perusals. These actions signified the end of the meeting, just as their verbal farewells did. Many looked each other straight in the eye when they said good-bye. They seemed to have arrived at a certain quality of honesty in tackling a common problem by the end of the meeting. There was a sense of unified sisterhood.

Some remained after the end of the meeting. Healers asked first-timers to stay so that they could explain the diet in detail to them. Others lingered to seek out more verbal and visual encouragement from lecturer-healers and sister-healees. Some stayed to challenge the Trim-Down healing method or to question whether the cure from fatness was necessary or even legitimate.

For some, the end of the meeting meant that the time had come to practice the preachings of the Trim-Down healers. Others chose to reject the Religion of Thinness outside the context of the Trim-Down healing sessions—they were purely "Sunday worshippers."

**"I have seen the way"**

Many of the healees were profoundly affected by the Trim-Down experience. Some believers had such strong faith that they would proselytize to any and all who would listen (and even some who would not). Sometimes these believers interrupted others' conversations just to declare the goodness of the Ideal of Thinness and the Trim-Down healing system:

> Excuse me, but what you are gossiping about can't be as important as what I must say. This diet has changed me into a different person—I don't hide in my shifts, and I have come out of my shell. I have got energy to do everything, and my husband is proud to show me off to his friends. The Trim-Down desserts are delicious. I must rant and rave as much as I can—I thank the heavenly stars that led me here. Just stick with it, and you will be 100 feet above the ground like I am.

Others were not as fanatical about airing their views but asked to speak. Still others seemed to believe in the Ideal of Thinness in spirit, but the flesh would just not follow.

The healers of the organization attempted to perpetuate a self-fulfilling prophecy—that the Trim-Down healee who lost weight was a better and happier person. Many believers seemed to buy this party line. The major themes of the confessional, the testimonial, and redemption for one's "sins of cheating" were integral parts of believers' routes to the Cure of Thinness. In confessing to others throughout the meeting, these believers made known to others their past and present errors of their ways in terms of eating patterns. In the believers' testimonials, they solemnly declared their belief in the goodness of thinness; they offered personal evidence in support of the Ideal of Thinness and the Trim-Down diet plan.

In their redemption, they sought out salvation from their eating sins through the atonement of the earthly representatives of the Ideal of Thinness, the group leader and the scale. In redeeming themselves they sought to compensate for their fatness and gain possession of thinness by paying money that acknowledged their state of sin. Believers evidenced such major themes throughout each Trim-Down meeting; my data have suggested that such orientations were also a microcosm of their attitudes toward eating and dieting shown outside of the group as well.

Healers are also proselytizers—but for a very different reason. Whatever else it may be, Trim-Down is a business; it is concerned with making a profit. Trim-Down healers here attempted to legitimize their brand of cure to the general public at large, beyond the healees reached in Trim-Down meetings. Executives and lecturers have written articles and advertisements in newspapers and magazines that praise the benefits of thinness and the Trim-Down diet. Common slogans that open such advertisements include: "Tired of being loads of fun? Perhaps you are not at home with your large jolly self," and, "Inside every fat man is a thin man trying to get out."

The Trim-Down organization itself has also printed an abundance of fliers and leaflets that are full of autobiographical details of healers and healees and of the specifics of the Trim-Down cure. Such advertisements were distributed to food and dress stores by healers and healees, these latter being effective "walking advertisements."

### Faith, Hope, and Charity

Newspaper and magazine reporters wrote short articles about annual luncheons that were held for Trim-Downers. These luncheons stressed the philanthropic aspects of the Trim-Down organization; they were advertised in part as charity benefits, with much of the proceeds going to service organizations such as the Army Emergency Relief Fund and the Heart Association. The organization was advertised as extending itself beyond its own vested interests in order to help the needy—what more legitimate mission could it accomplish! It was a business concerned for the human welfare of the fat as well as of the poor and sick.

The organization has also tried to legitimize itself to the potential and actual dieting population at large. Italian, Chinese, and American restaurants had menus that stamped certain dishes as "Trim-Down approved." Breads and low-calorie canned fruits in supermarkets were also labeled "Trim-Down approved." When there were public demonstrations of cooking and women's interests, Trim-Down staff members operated a booth. The organization was always reaching out to sell its healing system.

One significant salespitch was the appearance of Trim-Down healers and healees on a television talk show. Participants discussed their overweight problems and the diet. They received telephone calls on the air from distraught overweight people. Some demonstrated Trim-Down exercises; others ate Trim-Down recipes. On the basis of this single television appearance there were over 7,000 written communications to the Trim-Down organization. Extra clerical staff was hired to deal with the onslaught of mail. One healer remarked, "This was the single most successful piece of publicity that we ever had."

Indeed, Trim-Down healers viewed their mass-media appearance as a legitimation of the Trim-Down cure. Some hoped for an interview on a late night nationwide television talk show. Executive-healers asked nutritional experts to write books with them. They advertised the Trim-Down cure at some national group psychotherapy conferences. They were thrilled to secure the services of a famous nutritional specialist as a permanent medical consultant to the Trim-Down organization.

**Blessed Be the Dieter**

Healers tried to convince medical doctors and religious leaders to publicly endorse the Trim-Down cure. Often clergymen made the best sponsors—they wanted to help people as well as make money. These sponsors could make a few hundred dollars a month with little effort by offering time and space for the group-dieting meetings. One priest even went so far as to bless the Trim-Downers before their meeting in his church. This priest also announced individuals' weight losses at masses.

Many healers agreed that one of the most important ways to legitimize the Trim-Down diet plan was to prove that it was the best of all reducing methods. This proof came in the form of verbal arguments to Trim-Down healees and outsiders as well. The Trim-Down cure was superior. Intensive exercising only increased your appetite, and you needed to do a lot of exercising to burn up a few calories. Fad diets could be tolerated for only a short time; the

Trim-Down diet was a lifetime way of eating. Health spas were expensive, and most people gained back the weight that they lost at such places. Shots and medications had harmful physiological and psychological effects. Intensive psychiatric therapy only frustrated you and permitted you to wallow in your overeating.

When a healer affirmed the superiority of the Trim-Down diet method over other group methods, she needed to do more rationalizing and elaborating. The Pound-Shedders' brand was cheaper than the Trim-Down brand, and allowed for individual preferences in dieting—there was not one standardized diet. Some Trim-Down meetings were dull and boring, compared with the lively zest and fun that pervaded many Pound-Shedders' meetings. Nevertheless, Trim-Down healers did find ways to criticize Pound-Shedders:

> We stress the positive approach. We offer help to you who are having a hard time. Pound-Shedders' lecturers use a negative approach; they scold their bad little girls who gain. The bad dieters are teased. It is a humiliating experience to be ridiculed. Pound-Shedders who gain a little weight are really degraded when they wear pig and hippopotamus signs. We don't whip you like little babies. Our diet is a plan for mature adults. The negative approach is demoralizing—it does not put you in a positive frame of mind to lose your weight.

Trim-Down healers had more difficulty in proving the greater legitimacy of the Trim-Down diet plan over the Anti-Fat Vigilantes' plan. The basic diet plans and group methods were much the same in the Anti-Fat Vigilantes' and the Trim-Down programs. And, the Anti-Fat Vigilantes' brand had some hard-to-beat legitimizing credentials—it was the original, oldest, and largest international group-dieting program. This organization published a cookbook and monthly magazines. It had its own brands of frozen foods, ran its own restaurants, and sponsored summer camps for overweight teenagers.

**Impious Language**
One Trim-Down healer criticized the Anti-Fat Vigilantes' healers for resorting to the language of drug and alcoholic addiction. They talked about "getting your weekly fix" at meetings and "getting high on diet foods." This Trim-Down healer insisted that overeating was not necessarily a compulsive addiction for everybody. And members who did have drug and alcoholic problems resented the use of such language in relation to their weight, since overweight people were not always "carboholics."

Another way to deflate the Anti-Fat Vigilantes' organization was to call it too impersonal and too commercialized because of its large size. "Our groups are smaller in size, and we have a more personal touch. We offer more individual attention than do Anti-Fat Vigilantes' lecturers," Another Trim-Down healer criticized the Anti-Fat Vigilantes' lecturers:

> They treat their members like robots. They say "snap to" and expect their members to become automatic dieters at once. We allow for human error. We are more understanding of the complexities of the overweight problem than those Anti-Fat Vigilantes' promoters who have the simple-minded idea that everybody just sticks to a diet and loses weight. And we are more optimistic than they are. We talk about the pleasures of greater beauty, happiness, and health as an inducement for weight reduction. Their lecturers frighten their members when they emphasize the dire consequences of a future of fatness.

Executive Trim-Down healers seemed convinced that Trim-Down healers would feel less threatened by Anti-Fat Vigilantes' power once the Trim-Down cure became more nationally known and respected. The sale of an increasing number of Trim-Down franchises throughout the country indicated that the Trim-Down cure was taking hold. The organization was beginning to legitimize itself more by publishing articles and books. The Trim-Down cure did have a long way to go before it became as commonly used a household word as was the Anti-Fat Vigilantes' organization. Yet the Trim-Down enterprise was still in the running for top legitimacy each day that it expanded itself and opened more groups and attracted more customer-patients.

### Saintly Approval

Many Trim-Down healers felt that the true key to the legitimacy of the Trim-Down cure was its approval and endorsement by medical doctors. "The medical stamp of approval means a triple-A rating for us. If the doctors like us, we must be doing something right." In the contemporary American society, medical doctors often seem to be viewed as gods or saints—doctors are deified cultural heroes. Some Trim-Down healers were no different from others in believing that "a doctor's OK was one of the highest forms of praise available."

Many Trim-Down healers were proud to use the basic diet plan of many state obesity clinics as their fundamental "medicine." They felt safe about having a medical doctor as the nutritional consultant to the organization. They believed firmly in the first formal rule of the Trim-Down cure—that the doctor's advice must always take precedence.

It appears that Trim-Down as well as other group-dieting healers are taking some curing business away from traditional Western medical doctors. Some doctors have enthusiastically supported the group-healing systems and have urged family members and friends to go to the groups: "It is a good way to get a lot of lonely, hysterical, chubby women off my back." Other doctors have not been so certain about the physiological and psychological benefits of the group-dieting cure—they are "waiting for more evidence to come in." Other medical men seem cynical: "The groups don't do much good or harm—they are just gossip sessions for frustrated women. It is a sad fact that eighty percent or more of the people who lose weight gain it back fairly quickly." Some doctors appear hostile and defensive about Trim-Down types of healers. "They really don't know what they are doing or why they are doing it—they simply do not have the medical know-how."

Many Trim-Downers desired to achieve the goal that is so revered by doctors—"Doctors know best, and they say you are healthiest if you are thin." But many Trim-Downers also felt that it took a fatty or at the least an ex-fatty to know a fatty—the empathic understanding of overweight in the groups was more significant than all the doctors' pills for weight reduction. For some Trim-Downers, the significantly smaller fee for group-dieting treatment than for doctors' prescriptions also made a difference.

That many medical doctors are personally and professionally dedicated to dieting and thinness is clear. It also seems certain that these self-help groups of dieters led by "lay" healers are here to stay as long as medical doctors continue to exalt the Ideal of Thinness.

There is however a Fat Power movement rebelling against this Ideal. Curiously, the movement seems to be recruiting a growing number of ex- as well as continuing group dieters. Some seem to want the best of both worlds. Perhaps they defensively feel that if they cannot make it in the world of thins, the fats will welcome them with open arms. However, many Fat Power advocates have grown disillusioned with their desperate dieting attempts and have begun to question why fat people are denied their civil rights. The President's Council on Physical Fitness has declared war on fatness. Fat people habitually are subjected to ridicule, negative self-image, guilt feelings, discrimination in education and employment, and exploitation by commercial interests. The Fat Power advocates do not want to get fat people to reduce, but want to change social values and institutions that persecute the fat. They do not say that all people must be fat, but that, "Fat Can Be Beautiful"

**Plump Power**

A few doctors, especially psychiatrists, have begun to question whether thinness was such supreme goodness even before the Fat Power movement became as manifest as it is now. Hilde Bruch found that some overweight people were much more competent and creative in their daily tasks when they ate in their preferred patterns than when they forced themselves to diet. There seem to be an increasing number of doctors who are in sympathy with Plump Power, if not out-and-out Fat Power. Some have suggested that plumpness may be a help and not a hindrance to sexual activity. Dieting, rather than excess pounds, makes some people unhappy and neurotic. Fat victims of heart attacks who live tend to survive longer than thin heart-attack victims. Fat people rarely get tuberculosis and rarely commit suicide. And on-again and off-again dieting may be more harmful to the body than staying at a somewhat elevated weight.

The Fat Power option seems to ask all people, including thins, fats, and traditional medical doctors of whatever size, to be themselves and interact with each other as human beings, not based upon what the absolutistic scale decrees. "Lay" Fat Power sympathizers as well as some medical doctors are becoming increasingly aware that body style is intrinsically bound up with life-style, and that weight reduction requires a total actor-environmental change that some people resist. Eating patterns are intrinsically bound up with styles of living: many people do not want to change their way of life.

It is important, however, not to substitute one arbitrary and autocratic ideal for another. The Ideal of Fatness should not wipe out and replace the Ideal of Thinness. Fat Power must open people's eyes to the legitimacy of multiple body styles in the society. Some might find satisfaction in group dieting. Others, however, might choose to reject weight-reduction attempts and may resist Trim-Down healers or medical doctors trying to browbeat them down to a certain arbitrary body image.

**You Are What You Eat**

It seems appropriate here to include a quote from Llewellyn Louderback, the author of *Fat Power: Whatever You Weigh Is Right:*

We have been brainwashed into accepting the notion that obesity is esthetically displeasing and emotionally disreputable.

This does not mean that everyone should eat like gluttons and become as fat as possible. . . . There are some people . . . whose health demands a reduction in weight. There are others who, for various nonhealth reasons (jobs, social prestige, emotional well-being) are willing to accept a lifetime of sacrifice in exchange for a socially acceptable figure. In cases where such diets are successful, it would be pointless—perhaps even dangerous—to end them. . . . The great majority of overweight adults who have dieted and failed—sometimes repeatedly, year after year—are doing themselves a distinct disservice by persevering. If these people are otherwise healthy, with normal blood pressure, low cholesterol readings, and no diabetic symptoms, they should stop making themselves miserable trying to attain some mythical weight ideal that is completely wrong for their body build.

Instead, they should maintain the weight at which they feel and function best—and the insurance companies' height-weight tables be damned. So long as they get a certain amount of daily exercise and continue to have regular medical checkups, there is no reason on earth (aside from blind prejudice) why these people should not be forty, sixty, or even more pounds over what our society considers ideal. The fat person's major problem is not his obesity but the view that society takes of it.

It is important that medical men and laymen alike not condemn people simply because of body style. Perhaps medical doctors and group-dieting healers should support such an acceptance of different body shapes and sizes. Perhaps more people would recognize the legitimacy of various sizes of body styles. The Fat Power option may restore balance and sanity to a thinness-crazed society.

# III

# Deviant Life-Styles
# and the Search
# for Sexual Satisfaction

# Introduction

Satisfying the sex drive is a major concern for most people. The drive is strong, and the avenues that are traversed in seeking its satisfaction are many and varied. As sizable numbers of our population seek outlets for their sexual drive in ways that are culturally disapproved, they correspondingly develop deviant life-styles centering around their relentless pursuit for sexual satisfaction. The focus in this section of the book is on both those individuals who are involved in this search and those people who cater to these varied demands by providing desired sexual services.

In the opening chapter Humphreys analyzes a little-known sexual service available in some public rest rooms. Fellatio takes place quickly, in silence, and is both impersonal and without monetary cost. Men who patronize the "tearooms" located in all our major cities come from a wide variety of social backgrounds, but their life-styles momentarily intermesh at the critical point of participating in "tearoom sex." Most tearoom participants have a heterosexual identification, and the majority are married to wives who do not even possess an inkling of their husbands' clandestine sexual activities. Following their fleeting sexual encounters, the men return to their "other lives," to what in most cases involve life-styles that are mainly in keeping with conventional societal norms.

Participating in tearoom sex, however, is a risky endeavor. Laws sharply circumscribe fellatio in public places, and members of the vice squad are regularly assigned the task of "protecting the public morality" by vigilantly curtailing tearoom encounters. A much safer place for impersonal homoerotic activities is the bordello that supplies male prostitutes. Here the customer must pay for his sexual orgasm, but his cash payment enables him to freely select among available call boys, to choose which sexual services he desires, and to gratify his sexual desires in relative privacy and security.

In the second selection in this part Pittman focuses on the life-style and career of male prostitutes. The call boys are chosen from the ranks of the homosexual subculture. They are recommended by other male prostitutes, they respond to ads for male models, or they are recruited from the personal acquaintances of the so-called madam of the house. They undergo a detailed, formal interview, are informed of the highly developed rules surrounding their employment, and are given a medical examination. Their career is short as they wage the uphill battle to maintain their youth and good looks in the face of irregular hours and high sexual demands. Stigmatized within their own homosexual subculture for putting a price on that which is thought better to be given free, forbidden emotional attachments with both fellow call boys and customers, and with the heavy demands of their occupation, the call boys quickly go through both psychological and physical decline. Losing the capacity either to attract or to satisfy customers, they are eventually rejected from this highly demanding and specialized life-style.

How does someone become involved in life-styles that so greatly depart from conventional norms? What is the socialization process that leads to deviant orientations and activities? Although the first two articles give some indication of the intricate process of socialization into deviance, the third chapter focuses specifically on the why and the how of deviant sexual involvement and identity. In explaining how someone comes to the point of wanting to change his sex and organizing a life-style around this all-consuming desire, Driscoll does not depend on a psychological or psychiatric explanation. Rather, he presents a learning or developmental model of the process of commitment to deviance. His model of transsexuality includes an analysis of early home life in which the mother was dominant and the male child was treated as a female; the resulting highly pitched conflict with entrance into the public school system; homosexual activities, followed by discovery of the homosexual subculture; the development of new behaviors and a new self-concept with entrance into transvestite activities, along with homosexual prostitution as a means of support; the developing desire to possess female sexual organs and to play the traditional female role "for real"; and for those few who succeed in procuring sufficient money, full entrance into the world of women following the sex-change operation.

Each of these first three chapters places major emphasis on the management of deviant identity. That is, the authors deal with how individuals participating in deviant life-styles protect the self from the negative judgments of "straight society." Subcultural values do not exist entirely isolated from the dominant culture. Some deviant life-styles are indeed lived out in much more isolation from the larger culture and with much more social support from a highly developed subculture than are others, but they are all affected to some degree by the dominant culture. These effects are especially pronounced in Driscoll's analysis of transsexuals, whose behaviors at the various stages in their development are often reactions to expectations of more conventional morality.

It is similarly the case with strippers, as analyzed by Salutin in the first of the three selections that focus on heterosexual deviance. As strippers feel the pinch of negative reactions of the larger society to their deviant style, they develop legitimizing tactics to counter the pressures for conformance and to acceptably define for themselves their occupational role. These tactics include putting the public down as hypocrites, finding justifications for their occupational activities, and concealing their occupation from others. As they are socialized into their life-style, strippers learn a new definition of sexual morality and become involved in an ongoing destigmatizing process in their critical attempt to work out a satisfactory identity.

Socialization into a deviant life-style also requires that one learn the norms adhering to that life-style. For successful participation in tearoom sex, for example, one must learn to follow the expectations of silence and impersonality. Call boys similarly learn the norm of impersonality, as well as those expectations pertaining to pleasing customers. Transsexuals go through several stages in their developing commitment to a deviant way of life, and they must adjust to the expectations appropriate to each. Strippers learn how to handle verbal abuse, masturbating customers, and the police. Masseuses who are employed in the specialized parlors analyzed by Velarde and Warlick in the fifth chapter must similarly learn the norms pertaining to their deviant life-style. They must learn to cope with the stigma of prostitution that adheres to their occupation, to handle phone calls and problem customers, to uncover undercover agents, and to solicit sexual acts without subjecting themselves to legal recriminations.

Masseuses must also come to terms with their activities and learn how to manage a deviant identity. In the same way that strippers handle the problems associated with revealing their occupation, massage-parlor girls either conceal the real source of their income or develop techniques for dealing with typical responses that arise when someone learns of it. Because they are frequently involved in masturbating their customers for monetary return, they must learn to justify their actions to themselves. But maintaining an adequate self-image is as similarly difficult for these masseuses as it is for those who exhibit their bodies for pay and for those who participate in homosexual activities in our highly heterosexually oriented culture. Masseuses commonly develop negative evaluations of other masseuses, which, in turn, often end up being directed against the self.

Satisfying the sex drive is one of the most difficult of human endeavors. Certainly for most people achieving orgasm is a fairly simple matter, and if that is what sexual satisfaction were all about there would be few persons who would be left sexually unfulfilled. We certainly do not lack variety in the means available for attaining orgasm, as these articles make clear. But sexual satisfaction involves much, much more than reaching orgasm. The sexual drive is a central motivating mechanism in human behavior and a major component in the personality structure of each person. Its satisfaction, accordingly, is intricately complex. But even beyond this, the human sex drive becomes intricately interconnected with the structure of society. Satisfying the sex drive, for example, underlies the form given to the pairing process in the Western world, that form and process upon which so much of our brand of civilization is centered: monogomy, heterosexuality, the aid to capitalistic development by establishing and elaborately furnishing homes separate from the home of either parent, the birth of children within the marital relationship, the responsibility of the parents for nurturing the developing newborn and guiding the development of the embryonic personality, and the passing on of property accumulated during their lifetime to the children born of a marital relationship.

But as is so commonly and accurately observed, marriage is no guarantee whatsoever that the sex drive will be satisfied. As is evident from repeated references in these selections, many married males engage in sexual relations outside their marriage bond in a variety of ways other than the more common form of philandering, that of "cheating" on the wife by engaging in sexual relations with other women. The final chapter in this section deals specifically with married couples who have been unable to find full sexual satisfaction within their marriage, but who love one another and do not feel

that furtive extramarital sex would contribute to their sexual fulfillment. Where the first five selections deal with impersonal sex, the
last selection analyzes persons who attempt to combine sexual relations with both emotional relationships and long-term friendship.
The swingers studied by the Palsons actively sought out emotional
relationships with other couples in order to intensify their own marital relationships. According to this study, they were successful, and
the authors conclude that swinging is conservative because it brings
romance back into marriage and solidifies emotional relationships
between marital partners.

# 7

# Tearoom Trade: Impersonal Sex in Public Places

## Laud Humphreys

### The Sociologist as Voyeur

The methods employed in this study of men who engage in rest-room sex are the outgrowth of three ethical assumptions: First, I do not believe the social scientist should ever ignore or avoid an area of research simply because it is difficult or socially sensitive. Second, the researcher should approach any aspect of human behavior with those means that least distort the observed phenomena. Third, respondents must be protected from harm—regardless of what such protection may cost the researcher.

Because the majority of arrests on homosexual charges in the United States result from encounters in public rest rooms, I felt this form of sexual behavior to provide a legitimate, even essential, topic for sociological investigation. In our society the social-control forces, not the criminologist, determine what the latter shall study.

Following this decision, the question is one of choosing research methods that permit the investigator to achieve maximum fidelity to the world he is studying. I believe ethnographic methods are the only truly empirical ones for the social scientist. When human behavior is being examined, systematic observation is essential; so I had to become a participant-observer of furtive, felonious acts.

Fortunately, the very fear and suspicion of tearoom participants produces a mechanism that makes such observation possible: a third man (generally one who obtains voyeuristic pleasure from his duties) serves as a lookout, moving back and forth from door to windows. Such a "watch queen," as he is labeled in the homosexual argot, coughs when a police car stops nearby or when a stranger approaches. He nods affirmatively when he recognizes a man entering as being a "regular." Having been taught the watch-queen role by a cooperative respondent, I played that part faithfully while observing hundreds of acts of fellatio. After developing a systematic observation sheet, I recorded fifty of these encounters (involving 53 sexual acts) in great detail. These records were compared with another thirty made by a cooperating respondent who was himself a sexual participant. The bulk of information presented results from these observations.

Although primarily interested in the stigmatized behavior, I also wanted to know about the men who take such risks for a few moments of impersonal sex. I was able to engage a number of participants in conversation outside the rest rooms, and, eventually, by revealing the purpose of my study to them, I gained a dozen respondents who contributed hundreds of hours of interview time. This sample I knew to be biased in favor of the more outgoing and better educated of the tearoom population.

To overcome this bias, I cut short a number of my observations of encounters and hurried to my automobile. There, with the help of a tape recorder, I noted a brief description of each participant, his sexual role in the encounter just observed, his license number, and a brief description of his car. I varied such records from park to park to correspond with previously observed changes in volume at various times of the day. This provided me with a time-and-place-representative sample of 134 participants. With attrition, chiefly of those who had changed address or who drove rented cars, and the addition of two persons who walked to the tearooms, I ended up with a sample of 100 men, each of whom I had actually observed engaging in fellatio.

At this stage, my third ethical concern impinged. I already knew that many of my respondents were married and that all were in a highly discreditable position and fearful of discovery. How could I approach these covert deviants for interviews? By passing as deviant, I had observed their sexual behavior without disturbing it. Now, I was faced with interviewing these men (often in the presence of their wives) without destroying them. Fortunately, I held another research job that placed me in the position of preparing the interview schedule for a social-health survey of a random selection of male subjects throughout the community. With permission from the survey's directors, I could add my sample to the larger group (thus enhancing their anonymity) and interview them as part of the social-health survey.

To overcome the danger of having a subject recognize me as a watch queen, I changed my hair style, attire, and automobile. At the risk of losing more transient respondents, I waited a year between the sample gathering and the interviews, during which time I took notes on their homes and neighborhoods and acquired data on them from the city and county directories.

Having randomized the sample, I completed fifty interviews with tearoom participants and added another fifty interviews from the social-health survey sample. The latter control group was matched with the participants on the bases of marital status, race, job classification, and area of residence.

This study, then, results from a confluence of strategies: systematic, first-hand observation, in-depth interviews with available respondents, the use of archival data, and structured interviews of a representative sample and a matched control group. At each level of research, I applied those measures which provided maximum protection for research subjects and the truest measurement of persons and behavior observed.

## Tearoom Trade: Impersonal Sex in Public Places

At shortly after five o'clock on a weekday evening, four men enter a public rest room in the city park. One wears a well-tailored business suit; another wears tennis shoes, shorts, and tee shirt; the third man is still clad in the khaki uniform of his filling station; the last, a salesman, has loosened his tie and left his sports coat in the car. What has caused these men to leave the company of other homeward-bound commuters on the freeway? What common interest brings these men, with their divergent backgrounds, to this public facility?

They have come here not for the obvious reason, but in a search for "instant sex." Many men—married and unmarried, those with heterosexual identities and those whose self-image is a homosexual one—seek such impersonal sex, shunning involvement, desiring kicks without commitment. Whatever reasons—social, physiological, or psychological—might be postulated for this search, the phenomenon of impersonal sex persists as a widespread but rarely studied form of human interaction.

There are several settings for this type of deviant activity—the balconies of movie theaters, automobiles, behind bushes—but few offer the advantages for these men that public rest rooms provide. "Tearooms," as these facilities are called in the language of the homosexual subculture, have several characteristics that make them attractive as locales for sexual encounters without involvement.

Like most other words in the homosexual vocabulary, the origin of *tearoom* is unknown. British slang has used *tea* to denote *urine*. Another British usage is as a verb, meaning *to engage with, encounter, go in against*. According to its most precise meaning in the argot, the only "true" tearoom is one that gains a reputation as a place where homosexual encounters occur. Presumably, any rest room could qualify for this distinction, but comparatively few are singled out at any one time. For instance, I have researched a metropolitan area with more than ninety public toilets in its parks, only twenty of which are in regular use as locales for sexual games. Rest rooms thus designated join the company of automobiles and bathhouses as places for deviant sexual activity second only to private bedrooms in popularity. During certain seasons of the year—roughly, that period from April through October that Midwestern homosexuals call *the hunting season*—tearooms may surpass any other locale of homoerotic enterprise in volume of activity.

Public rest rooms are chosen by those men who want homoerotic activity without commitment for a number of reasons. Tearooms are accessible, easily recognized by the initiate, and provide little public visibility. They thus offer the advantages of both public and private settings. They are available and recognizable enough to attract a large volume of potential sexual partners, providing an opportunity for rapid action with a variety of men. When added to the relative privacy of these settings, such features enhance the impersonality of the sheltered interaction.

In the first place, tearooms are readily accessible to the male population. They may be located in any sort of public gathering place: department stores, bus stations, libraries, hotels, YMCAs, or courthouses. In keeping with the drive-in craze of American society, however, the more popular facilities are those readily accessible to the roadways. The rest rooms of public parks and beaches—and more recently the rest stops set at programmed intervals along superhighways—are now attracting the clientele that, in a more pedestrian age, frequented great buildings of the inner cities. My research is focused on the activity that takes place in the rest rooms of public parks, not only because (with some seasonal variation) they provide the most action but also because of other factors that make them suitable for sociological study.

There is a great deal of difference in the volumes of homosexual activity that these accommodations shelter. In some, one might wait for months before observing a deviant act (unless solitary masturbation is considered deviant). In others, the volume approaches orgiastic dimensions. One summer afternoon, for instance, I witnessed twenty acts of fellatio in the course of an hour while waiting out a thunderstorm in a tearoom. For one who wishes to participate in (or study) such activity, the primary consideration is finding where the action is.

Occasionally, tips about the more active places may be gained from unexpected sources. Early in my research, I was approached by a man (whom I later surmised to be a park partolman in plain clothes) while waiting at the window of a tearoom for some patrons to arrive. After finishing his business at the urinal and exchanging some remarks about the weather (it had been raining), the man came abruptly to the point: "Look, fellow, if you're looking for sex, this isn't the place. We're clamping down on this park because of trouble with the niggers. Try the john at the northeast corner of [Reagan] Park. You'll find plenty of action there." He was right. Some of my best observations were made at the spot he recommended. In most cases, however, I could only enter, wait, and watch—a method that was costly in both time and gasoline. After surveying a couple of dozen such rooms in this way, however, I became able to identify the more popular tearooms by observing certain physical evidence, the most obvious of which is the location of the facility. During the warm seasons, those rest rooms that are isolated from other park facilities, such as administration buildings, shops, tennis courts, playgrounds, and picnic areas, are the more popular for deviant activity. The most active tearooms studied were all isolated from recreational areas, cut off by drives or lakes from baseball diamonds and picnic tables.

I have chosen the term *purlieu* (with its ancient meaning of land severed from a royal forest by perambulation) to describe the immediate environs best suited to the tearoom trade. Drives and walks that separate a public toilet from the rest of the park are almost certain guides to deviant sex. The ideal setting for homosexual activity is a tearoom situated on an island of grass, with roads close by on every side. The getaway car is just a few steps away; children are not apt to wander over from the playground; no one can surprise the participants by walking in from the woods or from over a hill; it is not likely that straight people will stop there. According to my observations, the women's side of these buildings is seldom used at all.

### What They Want, When They Want It

The availability of facilities they can recognize attracts a great number of men who wish, for whatever reason, to engage in impersonal homoerotic activity. Simple observation is enough to guide these participants, the researcher, and, perhaps, the police to active tearooms. It is much more difficult to make an accurate appraisal of the proportion of the male population who engage in such activity over a representative length of time. Even with good sampling procedures, a large staff of assistants would be needed to make the observations necessary for an adequate census of this mobile population. All that may be said with some degree of certainty is that the percentage of the male population who participate in tearoom sex in the United States is somewhat less than the sixteen percent of the adult white-male population Kinsey found to have "at least as much of the homosexual as the heterosexual in their histories."

Participants assure me that it is not uncommon in tearooms for one man to fellate as many as ten others in a day. I have personally watched a fellator take on three men in succession in a half hour of observation. One respondent, who has cooperated with the researcher in a number of taped interviews, claims to average three men each day during the busy season.

I have seen some waiting turn for this type of service. Leaving one such scene on a warm September Saturday, I remarked to a man who left close behind me: "Kind of crowded in there, isn't it?" "Hell, yes," he answered, "It's getting so you have to take a number and wait in line in these places!"

There are many who frequent the same facility repeatedly. Men will come to be known as regular, even daily, participants, stopping off at the same tearoom on the way to or from work. One physician in his late fifties was so punctual in his appearance at a particular rest room that I began to look forward to our daily chats. This robust, affable respondent said he had stopped at this tearoom every evening of the week (except Wednesday, his day off) for years "for a blow job." Another respondent, a salesman whose schedule is flexible, may "make the scene" more than once a day—usually at his favorite men's room. At the time of our formal interview, this man claimed to have had four orgasms in the past twenty-four hours.

According to participants I have interviewed, men who are looking for impersonal sex in tearooms are relatively certain of finding the sort of partner they want...

> You go into the tearoom. You can pick up some really nice things in there. Again, it is a matter of sex real quick; and, if you like this kind, fine—you've got it. You get one and he is done; and, before long, you've got another one.

...and when they want it:

> Well, I go there; and you can always find someone to suck

your cock, morning, noon, or night. I know lots of guys who
stop by there on their way to work—and all during the day.

It is this sort of volume and variety that keeps the tearooms viable
as marketplaces of the one-night-stand variety.

Of the bar crowd in gay (homosexual) society, only a small percentage would be found in park rest rooms. But this more overt,
gay-bar clientele constitutes a minor part of those in any American
city who follow a predominantly homosexual pattern. The so-called
closet queens and other types of covert deviants make up the vast
majority of men who engage in homosexual acts—and these are the
persons most attracted to tearoom encounters.

Tearooms are popular, not because they serve as gathering places
for homosexuals but because they attract a variety of men, a *minority* of whom are active in the homosexual subculture and a large
group of whom have no homosexual self-identity. For various reasons, they do not want to be seen with those who might be identified
as such or to become involved with them on a "social" basis.

### Sheltering Silence

There is another aspect of the tearoom encounters that is crucial.
I refer to the silence of the interaction.

Throughout most homosexual encounters in public rest rooms,
nothing is spoken. One may spend many hours in these buildings
and witness dozens of sexual acts without hearing a word. Of fifty
encounters on which I made extensive notes, only in fifteen was any
word spoken. Two were encounters in which I sought to ease the
strain of legitimizing myself as lookout by saying, "You go ahead—
I'll watch." Four were whispered remarks between sexual partners,
such as, "Not so hard!" or "Thanks." One was an exchange of
greetings between friends.

The other eight verbal exchanges were in full voice and more extensive, but they reflected an attendant circumstance that was exceptional. When a group of us were locked in a rest room and attacked by several youths, we spoke for defense and out of fear. This
event ruptured the reserve among us and resulted in a series of conversations for several days afterward among the members of the
group who shared this adventure. Gradually, this sudden unity sub-
sided, and the encounters drifted back into silence.

Barring such unusual events, an occasionally whispered "thanks"
at the conclusion of the act constitutes the bulk of even whispered
communication. At first, I presumed that speech was avoided for
fear of incrimination. The excuse that intentions have been misun-

derstood is much weaker when those proposals are expressed in words rather than signaled by body movements. As research progressed, however, it became evident that the privacy of silent interaction accomplishes much more than mere defense against exposure to a hostile world. Even when a careful lookout is maintaining the boundaries of an encounter against intrusion, the sexual participants tend to be silent. The mechanism of silence goes beyond satisfying the demand for privacy. Like all other characteristics of the tearoom setting, it serves to guarantee anonymity, to assure the impersonality of the sexual liaison.

Tearoom sex is distinctly less personal than any other form of sexual activity, with the single exception of solitary masturbation. What I mean by "less personal" is simply that there is less emotional and physical involvement in rest-room fellatio—less, even, than in the furtive action that takes place in autos and behind bushes. In those instances, at least, there is generally some verbal involvement. Often, in tearoom stalls, the only portions of the players' bodies that touch are the mouth of the insertee and the penis of the insertor; and the mouths of these partners seldom open for speech.

Only a public place, such as a park rest room, could provide the lack of personal involvement in sex that certain men desire. The setting fosters the necessary turnover in participants by its accessibility and visibility to the "right" men. In these public settings, too, there exists a sort of democracy that is endemic to impersonal sex. Men of all racial, social, educational, and physical characteristics meet in these places for sexual union. With the lack of involvement, personal preferences tend to be minimized.

If a person is going to entagle his body with another's in bed—or allow his mind to become involved with another mind—he will have certain standards of appearance, cleanliness, personality, or age that the prospective partner must meet. Age, looks, and other external variables are germane to the sexual action. As the amount of anticipated contact of body and mind in the sex act decreases, so do the standards expected of the partner. As one respondent told me:

> I go to bed with gay people, too. But if I am going to bed with a gay person, I have certain standards that I prefer them to meet. And in the tearooms you don't have to worry about these things—because it is just a purely one-sided affair.

Participants may develop strong attachments to the settings of their adventures in impersonal sex. I have noted more than once that these men seem to acquire stronger sentimental attachments to the buildings in which they meet for sex than to the persons with whom they engage in it. One respondent tells the following story: We had been discussing the relative merits of various facilities, when I asked him: "Do you remember that old tearoom across from the park garage—the one they tore down last winter?"

> Do I ever! That was the greatest place in the park. Do you know what my roommate did last Christmas, after they tore the place down? He took a wreath, sprayed it with black paint, and laid it on top of the snow—right where that corner stall had stood. . . . He was really broken up!

The walls and fixtures of these public facilities are provided by society at large, but much remains for the participants to provide for themselves. Silence in these settings is the product of years of interaction. It is a normative response to the demand for privacy without involvement, a rule that has been developed and taught. Except for solitary masturbation, sex necessitates joint action; but impersonal sex requires that this interaction be as unrevealing as possible.

**People Next Door**

Tearoom activity attracts a large number of participants—enough to produce the majority of arrests for homosexual offenses in the United States. Now, employing data gained from both formal and informal interviews, we shall consider what these men are like away from the scenes of impersonal sex. "For some people," says Evelyn Hooker, an authority on male homosexuality, "the seeking of sexual contacts with other males is an activity isolated from all other aspects of their lives." Such segregation is apparent with most men who engage in the homosexual activity of public rest rooms; but the degree and manner in which "deviant" is isolated from "normal" behavior in their lives will be seen to vary along social dimensions.

For the man who lives next door, the tearoom participant is just another neighbor—and probably a very good one at that. He may make a little more money than the next man and work a little harder for it. It is likely that he will drive a better car and maintain a neater yard than do other neighbors in the block. Maybe, like some tearoom regulars, he will work with Boy Scouts in the evenings and spend much of his weekend at the church. It way be more surprising for the outsider to discover that most of these men are married.

Indeed, fifty-four percent of my research subjects are married and living with their wives. From the data at hand, there is no evidence that these unions are particularly unstable; nor does it appear that any of the wives are aware of their husbands' secret sexual activity. Indeed, the husbands choose public rest rooms as sexual settings partly to avoid just such exposure. I see no reason to dispute the claim of a number of tearoom respondents that their preference for a form of concerted action that is fast and impersonal is largely predicated on a desire to protect their family relationships.

Superficial analysis of the data indicates that the maintenance of exemplary marriages—at least in appearance—is very important to the subjects of this study. In answering questions such as, "When it comes to making decisions in your household, who generally makes them?", the participants indicate they are more apt to defer to their mates than are those in the control sample. They also indicate that they find it more important to "get along well" with their wives. In the open-ended questions regarding marital relationships, they tend to speak of them in more glowing terms.

### Tom and Myra

This handsome couple live in ranch-style suburbia with their two young children. Tom is in his early thirties—an aggressive, muscular, and virile-looking male. He works "about seventy-five hours a week" at his new job as a chemist. "I am *wild* about my job," he says. "I really love it!" Both of Tom's "really close" friends he met at work.

He is a Methodist and Myra a Roman Catholic, but each goes to his or her own church. Although he claims to have broad interests in life, they boil down to "games—sports like touch football or baseball."

When I asked him to tell me something about his family, Tom replied only in terms of their "good fortune" that things are not worse:

> We've been fortunate that a religious problem has not occurred. We're fortunate in having two healthy children. We're fortunate that we decided to leave my last job. Being married has made me more stable.

They have been married for eleven years, and Myra is the older of the two. When asked who makes what kinds of decisions in his family, he said: "She makes most decisions about the family. She keeps the books. But I make the *major* decisions."

Myra does the household work and takes care of the children. Perceiving his main duties as those of "keeping the yard up" and "bringing home the bacon," Tom sees as his wife's only shortcoming "her lack of discipline in organization." He remarked: "She's very attractive . . . has a fair amount of poise. The best thing is that she gets along well and is able to establish close relationships with other women."

Finally, when asked how he thinks his wife feels about him and his behavior in the family, Tom replied: "She'd like to have me around more—would like for me to have a closer relationship with her and the kids." He believes it is "very important" to have the kind of sex life he needs. Reporting that he and Myra have intercourse about twice a month, he feels that his sexual needs are "adequately met" in his relationships with his wife. I also know that, from time to time, Tom has sex in the rest rooms of a public park.

As an upwardly mobile man, Tom was added to the sample at a point of transition in his career as a tearoom participant. If Tom is like others who share working-class origins, he may have learned of the tearoom as an economical means of achieving orgasm during his navy years. Of late, he has returned to the rest rooms for occasional sexual "relief," since his wife, objecting to the use of birth-control devices, has limited his conjugal outlets.

Tom still perceives his sexual needs in the symbolic terms of the class in which he was socialized: "about twice a month" is the frequency of intercourse generally reported by working-class men; and, although they are reticent in reporting it, they do not perceive this frequency as adequate to meet their sexual needs, which they estimate are about the same as those felt by others of their age. My interviews indicate that such perceptions of sexual drive and satisfaction prevail among respondents of the lower-middle to upper-lower classes, whereas they are uncommon for those of the upper-middle and upper classes. Among the latter, the reported perception is of a much higher frequency of intercourse and they estimate their needs to be greater than those of "most other men."

### Aging Crisis

Not only is Tom moving into a social position that may cause him to reinterpret his sexual drive, he is also approaching a point of major crisis in his career as a tearoom participant. At the time when I observed him in an act of fellatio, he played the insertor role. Still relatively young and handsome, Tom finds himself sought out as *trade*, that is, those men who make themselves available for acts of fellatio but who, regarding themselves as "straight," refuse to reciprocate in the sexual act. Not only is that the role he expects to play in the tearoom encounters, but it is also the role others expect of him.

"I'm not toned up anymore," Tom complains. He is gaining weight around the middle and losing hair. As he moves past thirty-five, Tom will face the aging crisis of the tearooms. Less and less frequently will he find himself the one sought out in these meetings. Presuming that he has been sufficiently reinforced to continue this form of sexual operation, he will be forced to seek other men. As trade he was not expected to reciprocate, but he will soon be increasingly expected to serve as insertee for individuals who have first taken that role for him.

In most cases, fellatio is a service performed by an older man upon a younger. In one encounter, for example, a man appearing to be around 40 was observed as insertee with a man in his twenties as insertor. A few minutes later, the man of 40 was being sucked by one in his fifties. Analyzing the estimated ages of the principal partners in 53 observed acts of fellatio, I arrived at these conclusions: the insertee was judged to be older than the insertor in 40 cases; they were approximately the same age in three; and the insertor was the older in ten instances. The age differences ranged from an insertee estimated to be 25 years older than his partner to an insertee thought to be ten years younger than his insertor.

Strong references to this crisis of aging are found in my interviews with cooperating respondents, one of whom had this to say:

> Well, I started off as the straight young thing. Everyone wanted to suck my cock. I wouldn't have been caught dead with one of the things in my mouth! ... So, here I am at 40—with grown kids—and the biggest cocksucker in [the city]!

Similar experiences were expressed, in more reserved language, by another man, some fifteen years his senior:

> I suppose I was around 35—or 36—when I started giving out blow jobs. It just got so I couldn't operate any other way in the park johns. I'd still rather have a good blow job any day, but I've gotten so I like it the way it is now.

Perhaps by now there is enough real knowledge abroad to have dispelled the idea that men who engage in homosexual acts may be typed by any consistency of performance in one or another sexual role. Undoubtedly, there are preferences: few persons are so adaptable, their conditioning so undifferentiated, that they fail to exercise choice between various sexual roles and positions. Such preferences, however, are learned, and sexual repertories tend to expand with time and experience. This study of rest-room sex indicates that sexual roles within these encounters are far from stable. They are apt to change within an encounter, from one encounter to another, with age, and with the amount of exposure to influences from a sexually deviant subculture.

It is to this last factor that I should like to direct the reader's attention. The degree of contact with a network of friends who share the actor's sexual interests takes a central position in mediating not only his preferences for sex role, but his style of adaptation to—and rationalization of—the deviant activity in which he participates. There are, however, two reasons why I have not classified research subjects in terms of their participation in the homosexual subculture. It is difficult to measure accurately the degree of such involvement; and such subcultural interaction depends upon other social variables, two of which are easily measured.

Family status has a definitive effect on the deviant careers of participants whose concern is with controlling information about their sexual behavior. The married man who engages in homosexual activity must be much more cautious about his involvement in the subculture than his single counterpart. As a determinant of life-style and sexual activity, marital status is also a determinant of the patterns of deviant adaptation and rationalization. Only men in my sample who were divorced or separated from their wives were difficult to categorize as either married or single. Men who had been married, however, showed a tendency to remain in friendship networks with married men. Three of the four were still limited in freedom by responsibilities for their children. For these reasons, I have included all man who were once married in the "married" categories.

The second determining variable is the relative autonomy of the respondent's occupation. A man is "independently" employed when his job allows him freedom of movement and security from being fired; the most obvious example is self-employment. Occupational "dependence" leaves a man little freedom for engaging in disreputable activity. The sales manager or other executive of a business firm has greater freedom than the salesman or attorney who is employed in the lower echelons of a large industry or by the federal government. The sales representative whose territory is far removed from the home office has greater independence, in terms of information control, than the minister of a local congregation. The majority of men placed in both the married and unmarried categories with *dependent* occupations were employed by large industries or the government.

Median education levels and annual family incomes indicate that individuals with dependent occupations rank lower on the socioeconomic scale. Only in the case of married men, however, is this correlation between social class and occupational autonomy strongly supported by the ratings of these respondents on Warner's Index of Status Characteristics. Nearly all the married men with dependent occupations are of the upper-lower or lower-middle classses, whereas men with independent occupations are of the upper-middle or upper classes. For single men, the social class variable is neither so easily identifiable nor so clearly divided. Nearly all single men in the sample can be classified only as "vaguely middle class."

As occupational autonomy and marital status remain the most important dimensions along which participants may be ranked, we shall consider four general types of tearoom customers: 1) married men with dependent occupations; 2) married men with independent occupations; 3) unmarried men with independent occupations; and 4) unmarried men with dependent occupations. As will become evident with the discussion of each type, I have employed labels from the homosexual argot, along with pseudonyms, to designate each class of participants. This is done not only to facilitate reading but to emphasize that we are describing persons rather than merely "typical" constructs.

**Type I: Trade**
The first classification, which includes nineteen of the participants (thirty-eight percent), may be called *trade*, since most would earn that appellation from the gay subculture. All of these men are, or have been, married—one was separated from his wife at the time of interviewing and another was divorced.

Most work as truck drivers, machine operators, or clerical workers. There is a member of the armed forces, a carpenter, and the minister of a pentecostal church. Most of their wives work, at least part time, to help raise their median annual family income to $8,000 [1970]. One in six of these men is black. All are normally masculine in appearance and mannerism. Although fourteen have completed high school, there are only three college graduates among them, and five have had less than twelve years of schooling.

George is representative of this largest group of respondents. Born of second-generation German parentage in an ethnic enclave of the Midwestern city where he still resides, he was raised as a Lutheran. He feels that his father (like George a truck driver) was quite warm in his relationship with him as a child. His mother he describes as a very nervous, asthmatic woman, and he thinks that an older sister suffered a nervous breakdown some years ago, although she was never treated for it. Another sister and a brother have evidenced no emotional problems.

At the age of twenty he married a Roman Catholic girl and has since joined her church, although he classifies himself as "lapsed." In the fourteen years of their marriage, they have had seven children, one of whom is less than a year old. George does not think they should have more children, but his wife objects to using any type of birth control other than the rhythm method. With his wife working part time as a waitress, they have an income of about $5,000.

"How often do you have intercourse with your wife?" I asked. "Not very much the last few years," he replied. "It's up to when she feels like giving it to me—which ain't very often. I never suggest it."

George was cooking hamburgers on an outdoor grill and enjoying a beer as I interviewed him. "Me, I like to come home," he asserted. "I love to take care of the outside of the house. . . . Like to go places with the children—my wife, she doesn't."

With their mother at work, the children were running in and out of the door, revealing a household interior in gross disarray. George stopped to call one of the smaller youngsters out of the street in front of his modest, suburban home. When he resumed his remarks about his wife, there was more feeling in his description:

> My wife doesn't have much outside interest. She doesn't like to go out or take the kids places. But she's an A-1 mother, I'll say that! I guess you'd say she's very nice to get along with— but don't cross her! She gets aggravated with me—I don't know why. . . . Well, you'd have to know my wife. We fight all the time. Anymore, it seems we just don't get along—except when we're apart. Mostly, we argue about the kids. She's afraid of having more. . . . She's afraid to have sex but doesn't believe in birth control. I'd just rather not be around her! I won't suggest having sex anyway—and she just doesn't want it anymore.

While more open than most in his acknowledgment of marital tension, George's appraisal of sexual relations in the marriage is typical of those respondents classified as Trade. In sixty-three percent of these marriages, the wife, husband, or both are Roman Catholic. When answering questions about their sexual lives, a story much like George's emerged: at least since the birth of the last child, conjugal relations have been very rare.

These data suggest that, along with providing an excuse for diminishing intercouse with their wives, the religious teachings to which most of these families adhere may cause the husbands to search for sex in the tearooms. Whatever the causes that turn them unsatisfied from the marriage bed, however, the alternate outlet must be quick, inexpensive, and impersonal. Any personal, ongoing affair—any outlet requiring money or hours away from home—would threaten a marriage that is already shaky and jeopardize the most important thing these men possess, their standing as father of their children.

Around the turn of the century, before the vice squads moved in (in their never-ending process of narrowing the behavioral options of those in the lower classes), the Georges of this study would probably have made regular visits to the two-bit bordellos. With a madam watching a clock to limit the time, these cheap whorehouses provided the same sort of fast, impersonal service as today's public rest rooms. I find no indication that these men seek homosexual contact as such; rather, they want a form of orgasm-producing action that is less lonely than masturbation and less involving than a love relationship. As the forces of social control deprive them of one outlet, they provide another. The newer form, it should be noted, is more stigmatizing than the previous one—thus giving "proof" to the adage that "the sinful are drawn ever deeper into perversity."

George was quite affable when interviewed on his home territory. A year before, when I first observed him in the tearoom of a park about three miles from his home, he was a far more cautious man. Situated at the window of the rest room, I saw him leave his old station wagon and, looking up and down the street, walk to the facility at a very fast pace. Once inside, he paced nervously from door to window until satisfied that I would serve as an adequate lookout. After playing the insertor role with a man who had waited in the stall farthest from the door, he left quickly, without wiping or washing his hands, and drove away toward the nearest exit from the park. In the tearoom he was a frightened man, engaging in furtive sex. In his own backyard, talking with an observer whom he failed to recognize, he was warm, open, and apparently at ease.

Weighing 200 pounds or more, George has a protruding gut and tattoos on both forearms. Although muscular and in his mid-thirties, he would not be described as a handsome person. For him, no doubt, the aging crisis is also an identity crisis. Only with reluctance—and perhaps never—will he turn to the insertee role. The threat of such a role to his masculine self-image is too great. Like others of his class with whom I have had more extensive interviews, George may have learned that sexual game as a teenage hustler, or else when serving in the army during the Korean war. In either case, his socialization into homosexual experience took place in a masculine world where it is permissible to accept money from a "queer" in return for carefully limited sexual favors. But to use one's own mouth as a substitute for the female organ, or even to express enjoyment of the action, is taboo in the Trade code.

Moreover, for men of George's occupational and marital status, there is no network of friends engaged in tearoom activity to help them adapt to the changes aging will bring. I found no evidence of friendship networks among respondents of this type, who enter and leave the rest rooms alone, avoiding conversation while within. Marginal to both the heterosexual and homosexual worlds, these men shun involvement in any form of gay subculture. Type I participants report fewer friends of any sort than do those of other classes. When asked how many close friends he has, George answered: "None. I haven't got time for that."

It is difficult to interview the Trade without becoming depressed over the hopelessness of their situation. They are almost uniformly lonely and isolated: lacking success in either marriage bed or work, unable to discuss their three best friends (because they do not have three); en route from the din of factories to the clamor of children, they slip off the freeways for a few moments of impersonal sex in a toilet stall.

Such unrewarded existence is reflected in the portrait of another marginal man. A jobless Negro, he earns only contempt and sexual rejection from his working wife in return for baby-sitting duties. The paperback books and magazines scattered about his living room supported his comment that he reads a great deal to relieve boredom. (George seldom reads even the newspaper and has no hobbies to report.) No wonder that he urged me to stay for supper when my interview schedule was finished. "I really wish you'd stay awhile," he said. "I haven't talked to anyone about myself in a hell of a long time!"

### Type II: Ambisexuals

A very different picture emerges in the case of Dwight. As sales manager for a small manufacturing concern, he is in a position to hire men who share his sexual and other interests. Not only does he have a business associate or two who share his predilection for tearoom sex, he has been able to stretch chance meetings in the tearoom purlieu into long-lasting friendships. Once, after I had gained his confidence through repeated interviews, I asked him to name all the participants he knew. The names of five other Type II men in my sample were found in the list of nearly two dozen names he gave me.

Dwight, then, has social advantages in the public rest rooms as well as in society at large. His annual income of $16,000 helps in the achievement of these benefits, as does his marriage into a large and distinguished family and his education at a prestigious local college. From his rest-room friends Dwight learns which tearooms in the city are popular and where the police are clamping down. He even knows which officers are looking for payoffs and how much they expect to be paid. It is of even greater importance that his attitudes toward—and perceptions of—the tearoom encounters are shaped and reinforced by the friendship network in which he participates.

It has thus been easier for Dwight to meet the changing demands of the aging crisis. He knows others who lost no self-respect when they began "going down" on their sexual partners, and they have helped him learn to enjoy the involvement of oral membranes in impersonal sex. As Tom, too, moves into this class of participants, he can be expected to learn how to rationalize the switch in sexual roles necessitated by the loss of youthful good looks. He will cease thinking of the insertee role as threatening to his masculinity. His socialization into the Ambisexuals will make the orgasm but one of a number of kicks.

Three-fourths of the married participants with independent occupations were observed, at one time or another, participating as insertees in fellatio, compared to only one-third of the Trade. Not only do the Type II participants tend to switch roles with greater facility, they seem inclined to search beyond the tearooms for more exotic forms of sexual experience. Dwight, along with others in his class, expresses a liking for anal intercourse (both as insertee and insertor), for group activity, and even for mild forms of sadomasochistic sex. A friend of his once invited me to an "orgy" he had planned in an apartment he maintains for sexual purposes. Another friend, a social and commercial leader of the community, told me that he enjoys having men urinate in his mouth between acts of fellatio.

Dwight is in his early forties and has two sons in high school. The school-bound offspring provide him with an excuse to leave his wife at home during frequent business trips across the country. Maintaining a list of gay contacts, Dwight is able to engage wholeheartedly in the life of the homosexual subculture in other cities— the sort of involvement he is careful to avoid at home. In the parks or over cocktails, he amuses his friends with lengthy accounts of these adventures.

Dwight recounts his first sexual relationship with another boy at the age of "nine or ten":

> My parents always sent me off to camp in the summer, and it was there that I had my sexual initiation. This sort of thing usually took the form of rolling around in a bunk together and ended in our jacking each other off. . . . I suppose I started pretty early. God, I was almost in college before I had my first woman! I always had some other guy on the string in prep school—some real romances there! But I made up for lost time with the girls during my college years. . . . During that time, I only slipped back into my old habits a couple of times—and then it was a once-only occurrence with a roommate after we had been drinking.

Culminating an active heterosexual life at the university, Dwight married the girl he had impregnated. He reports having intercourse three or four times a week with her throughout their eighteen married years but also admits to supplementing that activity on occasion: "I had the seven-year-itch and stepped out on her quite a bit then." Dwight also visits the tearooms almost daily:

> I guess you might say I'm pretty highly sexed [he chuckled a little], but I really don't think that's why I go to tearooms. That's really not sex. Sex is something I have with my wife in bed. It's not as if I were committing adultery by getting my rocks off—or going down on some guy—in a tearoom. I get a kick out of it. Some of my friends go out for handball. I'd rather cruise the park. Does that sound perverse to you?

Dwight's openness in dealing with the more sensitive areas of his biography was typical of upper-middle and upper-class respondents of both the participant and control samples. Actual refusals of interviews came almost entirely from lower-class participants; more of the cooperating respondents were of the upper socioeconomic ranks. In the same vein, working-class respondents were most cautious about answering questions pertaining to their income and their social and political views.

Other researchers have encountered a similar response differential along class lines, and I realize that my educational and social characteristics encourage rapport with Dwight more than with George. It may also be assumed that sympathy with survey research increases with education. Two-thirds of the married participants with occupational independence are college graduates.

It has been suggested, however, that another factor may be operative in this instance: although the upper-class deviants may have more to lose from exposure (in the sense that the mighty have farther to fall), they also have more means at their disposal with which to protect their moral histories. Some need only tap their spending money to pay off a member of the vice squad. In other instances, social contacts with police commissioners or newspaper publishers make it possible to squelch either record or publicity of an arrest. One respondent has made substantial contributions to a police charity fund, while another hired private detectives to track down a blackmailer. Not least in their capacity to cover for errors in judgment is the fact that their word has the backing of economic and social influence. Evidence must be strong to prosecute a man who can hire the best attorneys. Lower-class men are rightfully more suspicious, for they have fewer resources with which to defend themselves if exposed.

This **does** not mean that Type II participants are immune to the risks of the game but simply that they are bidding from strength. To them, the risks of arrest, exposure, blackmail, or physical assault contribute to the excitement quotient. It is not unusual for them to speak of cruising as an adventure, in contrast with the Trade, who engage in a furtive search for sexual relief. On the whole, then, the action of Type II respondents is apt to be somewhat bolder and their search for kicks less inhibited than that of most other types of participants.

Dwight is not fleeing from an unhappy home life or sexless marriage to the encounters in the parks. He expresses great devotion to his wife and children: "They're my whole life," he exclaims. All evidence indicates that, as father, citizen, businessman, and church member, Dwight's behavior patterns—as viewed by his peers—are exemplary.

Five of the twelve participants in Dwight's class are members of the Episcopal church. Dwight is one of two who were raised in that church, although he is not as active a churchman as some who became Episcopalians later in life. In spite of his infrequent attendance to worship, he feels his church is "just right" for him and needs no changing. Its tradition and ceremony are intellectually and esthetically pleasing to him. Its liberal outlook on questions of morality round out a religious orientation that he finds generally supportive.

In an interview witnessed by a friend he had brought to meet me, Dwight discussed his relationship with his parents: "Father ignored me. He just never said anything to me. I don't think he ever knew I existed." (His father was an attorney, esteemed beyond the city of

Dwight's birth, who died while his only son was yet in his teens.) "I hope I'm a better father to my boys than he was to me," Dwight added.

"But his mother is a remarkable woman," the friend interjected, "really one of the most fabulous women I've met! Dwight took me back to meet her—years ago, when we were lovers of a sort. I still look forward to her visits."

"She's remarkable just to have put up with me," Dwight added:

> Just to give you an idea, one vacation I brought another boy home from school with me. She walked into the bedroom one morning and caught us bare-assed in a 69 position. She just excused herself and backed out of the room. Later, when we were alone, she just looked at me—over the edge of her glasses—and said: "I'm not going to lecture you, dear, but I hope you don't swallow that stuff!"

Although he has never had a nervous breakdown, Dwight takes "an occasional antidepressant" because of his "moodiness." "I'm really quite moody, and I go to the tearooms more often when my spirits are low." While his periods of depression may result in increased tearoom activity, his deviant behavior does not seem to produce much tension in his life:

> I don't feel guilty about my little sexual games in the park. I'm not some sort of sick queer. . . . You might think I live two lives; but, if I do, I don't feel split in two by them.

Unlike the Trade, Type II participants recognize their homosexual activity as indicative of their own psychosexual orientations. They think of themselves as bisexual or ambisexual and have intellectualized their deviant tendencies in terms of the pseudo-psychology of the popular press. They speak often of the great men of history, as well as of certain movie stars and others of contemporary fame, who are also "AC/DC." Erving Goffman has remarked that stigmatized Americans "tend to live in a literarily defined world." This is nowhere truer than of the subculturally oriented participants of this study. Not only do they read a great deal about homosexuality, but they also discuss it within their network of friends. For the Dwights there is subcultural support that enables them to integrate their deviance with the remainder of their lives, while maintaining control over the information that could discredit their whole being. For these reasons they look upon the gaming encounters in the parks as enjoyable experiences.

**Type III: Gay Guys**

Like the Ambisexuals, unmarried respondents with independent occupations are locked into a strong subculture, a community that provides them with knowledge about the tearooms and reinforcement in their particular brand of deviant activity. This open participation in the gay community distinguishes these single men from the larger group of unmarried with dependent occupations. These men take the homosexual role of our society, and are thus the most truly gay of all participant types. Except for Tim, who was recruited as a decoy in the tearooms by the vice squad of a police department, Type III participants learned the strategies of the tearooms through friends already experienced in this branch of the sexual market.

Typical of this group is Ricky, a twenty-four-year-old university student whose older male lover supports him. Ricky stands at the median age of his type, who range from nineteen to fifty years. Half of them are college graduates and all but one other are at least part-time students, a characteristic that explains their low median income of $3,000. Because Ricky's lover is a good provider, he is comfortably situated in a midtown apartment, a more pleasant residence than most of his friends enjoy.

Ricky is a thin, good-looking young man with certain movements and manners of speech that might be termed effeminate. He is careful of his appearance, dresses well, and keeps an immaculate apartment, furnished with an expensive stereo and some tasteful antique pieces. Seated on a sofa in the midst of the things his lover has provided for their mutual comfort, Ricky is impressively self-assured. He is proud to say that he has found, at least for the time being, what all those participants in his category claim to seek: a "permanent" love relationship.

Having met his lover in a park, Ricky returns there only when his mate is on a business trip or their relationship is strained. Then Ricky becomes, as he puts it, "horny," and he goes to the park to study, cruise, and engage in tearoom sex:

> The bars are ok—but a little too public for a "married" man like me. . . . Tearooms are just another kind of action, and they do quite well when nothing better is available.

Like other Type III respondents, he shows little preference in sexual roles. "It depends on the other guy," Ricky says, "and whether I like his looks or not. Some men I'd crawl across the street on my knees for—others I wouldn't piss on!" His aging crisis will be shared with all others in the gay world. It will take the nightmarish form of waning attractiveness and the search for a permanent lover to fill his later years, but it will have no direct relationship with the tearoom roles. Because of his socialization in the homosexual society, taking the insertee role is neither traumatic for him nor related to aging.

Ricky's life revolves around his sexual deviance in a way that is not true of George or even of Dwight. Most of his friends and social contacts are connected with the homosexual subculture. His attitudes toward and rationalization of his sexual behavior are largely gained from this wide circle of friends. The gay men claim to have more close friends than do any other type of control or participant respondents. As frequency of orgasm is reported, this class also has more sex than any other group sampled, averaging 2.5 acts per week. They seem relatively satisfied with this aspect of their lives and regard their sexual drive as normal—although Ricky perceives his sexual needs as less than most.

One of his tearoom friends has recently married a woman, but Ricky has no intention of following his example. Another of his type, asked about marriage, said: "I prefer men, but I would make a good *wife* for the right *man*."

The vocabulary of heterosexual marriage is commonly used by those of Ricky's type. They speak of "marrying" the men they love and want to "settle down in a nice home." In a surprising number of cases, they take their lovers "home to meet mother." This act, like the exchange of "pinky rings," is intended to provide social strength to the lovers' union.

Three of the seven persons of this type were adopted—Ricky at the age of six months. Ricky told me that his adoptive father, who died three years before our interview, was "very warm and loving. He worked hard for a living, and we moved a lot." He is still close to his adoptive mother, who knows of his sexual deviance and treats his lover "like an older son."

Ricky hopes to be a writer, an occupation that would "allow me the freedom to be myself. I have a religion [Unitarian] which allows me freedom, and I want a career which will do the same." This, again, is typical: all three of the Unitarians in the sample are Type III men, although none was raised in that faith; and their jobs are uniformly of the sort to which their sexual activity, if exposed, would present little threat.

Although these men correspond most closely to society's homosexual stereotype, they are least representative of the tearoom population, constituting only fourteen percent of the participant sample. More than any other type, the Rickys seem at ease with their behavior in the sexual market, and their scarcity in the tearooms is indicative of this. They want personal sex—more permanent relationships — and the public rest rooms are not where this is to be found.

That any of them patronize the tearooms at all is the result of incidental factors: they fear that open cruising in the more common homosexual marketplaces of the baths and bars might disrupt a current love affair; or they drop in at a tearoom while waiting for a friend at one of the "watering places" where homosexuals congregate in the parks. They find the anonymity of the tearooms suitable for their purposes, but not inviting enough to provide the primary setting for sexual activity.

### Type IV: Closet Queens

Another dozen of the fifty participants interviewed may be classified as single deviants with dependent occupations, "closet queens" in homosexual slang. Again, the label may be applied to others who keep their deviance hidden, whether married or single, but the covert, unmarried men are most apt to earn this appellation. With them, we have moved full circle in our classifications, for they parallel the Trade in a number of ways:

1. They have few friends, only a minority of whom are involved in tearoom activity.

2. They tend to play the insertor role, at least until they confront the crisis of aging.

3. Half of them are Roman Catholic in religion.

4. Their median annual income is $6,000 [1970]; and they work as teachers, postmen, salesmen, clerks—usually for large corporations or agencies.

5. Most of them have completed only high school, although there are a few exceptionally well-educated men in this group.

6. One in six is black.

7. Not only are they afraid of becoming involved in other forms of the sexual market, they share with the Trade a relatively furtive involvement in the tearoom encounters.

Arnold will be used as the typical case. Only twenty-two, Arnold is well below the median age of this group; but in most other respects he is quite representative, particularly in regard to the psychological problems common to Type IV.

A routine interview with Arnold stretched to nearly three hours in the suburban apartment he shares with another single man. Currently employed as a hospital attendant, he has had trouble with job stability, usually because he finds the job unsatisfactory. He frequently is unoccupied.

*Arnold:* I hang around the park a lot when I don't have anything else to do. I guess I've always known about the tearooms. . . so I just started going in there to get my rocks off. But I haven't gone since I caught my lover there in September. You get in the habit of going; but I don't think I'll start in again—unless I get too desperate.

*Interviewer:* Do you make the bar scene?

*Arnold:* Very seldom. My roommate and I go out together once in a while, but everybody there seems to think we're lovers. So I don't really operate in the bars. I really don't like gay people. They can be so damned bitchy! I really like women better than men—except for sex. There's a lot of the female in me, and I feel more comfortable with women than with men. I understand women and like to be with them. I'm really very close to my mother. The reason I don't live at home is because there are too many brothers and sisters living there. . . .

*Interviewer:* Is she still a devout Roman Catholic?

*Arnold:* Well, yes and no. She still goes to Mass some, but she and I go to séances together with a friend. I am studying astrology and talk it over with her quite a bit. I also analyze handwriting and read a lot about numerology. Mother knows I am gay and doesn't seem to mind. I don't think she really believes it though.

Arnold has a health problem: "heart attacks," which the doctor says are psychological and which take the form of "palpitations, dizziness, chest pain, shortness of breath, and extreme weakness." These attacks, which began soon after his father's death from a coronary two years ago, make him feel as if he were "dying and turning cold." Tranquilizers were prescribed for him, "but I threw them out, because I don't like to become dependent on such things." He quoted a book on mental control of health that drugs are "unnecessary, if you have proper control."

He also connects these health problems with his resentment of his father, who was mentally ill:

*Arnold:* I don't understand his mental illness and have always blamed him for it. You might say that I have a father complex and, along with that, a security complex. Guess that's why I always run around with older men.

*Interviewer:* Were any of your brothers gay?

*Arnold:* Not that I know of. I used to have sex with the brother closest to my age when we were little kids. But he's married now, and I don't think he is gay at all. It's just that most of the kids I ran around with always jacked each other off or screwed each other in the ass. I just seemed to grow up with it. I can't remember a time when I didn't find men attractive. . . . I used to have terrible crushes on my gym teachers, but nothing sexual ever came of it. I just worshipped them, and wanted to be around them all the time. I had coitus with a woman when I was 16—she was 22. After it was over, she asked me what I thought of it. I told her I would rather masturbate. Boy, was she pissed off! I've always liked older men. If they are under 30, I just couldn't be less interested. . . . Nearly all my lovers have been between 30 and 50. The trouble is that *they* always want sex—and sex isn't really what I want. I just want to be with them—to have them for friends. I guess it's part of my father complex. I just want to be loved by an older man.

Few of the Type IV participants share Arnold's preference for older men, although they report poorer childhood relationships with their fathers than do individuals of any other group. As is the case with Arnold's roommate, many closet queens seem to prefer teenage boys as sexual objects. This is one of the features that distinguishes them from all other participant types. Although scarce in tearooms, teenagers make themselves available for sexual activity in other places frequented by closet queens. A number of these men regularly cruise the streets where boys thumb rides each afternoon when school is over. One closet queen from my sample has been arrested for luring boys in their early teens to his home.

Interaction between these men and the youths they seek frequently results in the sort of scandal feared by the gay community. Newspaper reports of molestations usually contain clues of the closet-queen style of adaptation on the part of such offenders. Those respondents whose lives had been threatened by teenage toughs were generally of this type. One of the standard rules governing one-night-stand operations cautions against becoming involved with such "chicken." The frequent violation of this rule by closet queens may contribute to their general disrepute among the bar set of the homosexual subculture, where closet queen is a pejorative term.

One Type IV respondent, an alcoholic whose intense self-hatred seemed always about to overflow, told me one night over coffee of his loneliness and his endless search for someone to love:

I don't find it in the tearooms—although I go there because it's handy to my work. But I suppose the [hustler's hangout] is really my meat. I just want to love every one of those kids!

Later, this man was murdered by a teenager he had picked up.

Arnold, too, expressed loneliness and the need for someone to talk with. "When I can really sit down and talk to someone else," he said, "I begin to feel real again. I lose that constant fear of mine—that sensation that I'm dying."

## Styles of Deviant Adaptation

Social isolation is characteristic of Type IV participants. Generally, it is more severe even than that encountered among the Trade, most of whom enjoy at least a vestigial family life. Although painfully aware of their homosexual orientations, these men find little solace in association with others who share their deviant interests. Fearing exposure, arrest, the stigmatization that might result from participation in the homosexual subculture, they are driven to a desperate, lone-wolf sort of activity that may prove most dangerous to themselves and the rest of society. Although it is tempting to look for psychological explanations of their apparent preference for chicken, the sociological ones are evident. They resort to the more dangerous game because of a lack of both the normative restraints and adult markets that prevail in the more overt subculture. To them, the costs (financial and otherwise) of operating among street-corner youths are more acceptable than those of active participation in the gay subculture. Only the tearooms provide a less expensive alternative for the closet queens.

I have tried to make it impossible for any close associate to recognize the real people behind the disguised composites portrayed in this article. But I have worked equally hard to enable a number of tearoom players to see themselves in the portrait of George, and others to find their own stories in those of Dwight, Ricky, or Arnold. If I am accurate, the real Tom will wonder whether he is trade or ambisexual; and a few others will be able to identify only partly with Arnold or Ricky.

My one certainty is that there is no single composite with whom all may identify. It should now be evident that, like other next-door neighbors, the participants in tearoom sex are of no one type. They vary along a number of possible continua of social characteristics. They differ widely in terms of sexual career and activity, and even in terms of what that behavior means to them or what sort of needs it may fulfill. Acting in response to a variety of pressures toward deviance (some of which we may never ascertain), their adaptations follow a number of lines of least resistance.

In delineating styles of adaptation, I do not intend to imply that these men are faced with an array of styles from which they may pick one or even a combination. No man's freedom is that great. They have been able to choose only among the limited options offered them by society. These sets of alternatives, which determine the modes of adaptation to deviant pressures, are defined and allocated in accordance with major sociological variables: occupation, marital status, age, race, amount of education. That is one meaning of social probability.

# 8

# The Male House
# of Prostitution

David J. Pittman

Drift, impermanence, ephemerality—such is life for the male hustler. The homosexual market (like many others) craves two things most of all, novelty and youth. Necessarily, then, the hustler drifts from city to city, from 42d Street in New York to Saint Louis's Forest Park, seeking his fortune (he may say) but also running from scenes and people to which he is no longer new, trying to catch the impossible dream of eternal youth and undying virility. Failing that, and he must fail of course, there is, as we shall see, the dream of something much more ordinary—love, shelter, home.

But a house, as Polly Adler observed some time ago, is not a home, and this is as true of male houses of prostitution as it is of more familiar sorts of brothels. The house I am going to describe here, which caters exclusively to homo- or bisexual tastes, is really a composite of several known to me in a large metropolitan center in the United States. I will be no more specific in identification than this, for obvious reasons.

## The Male House of Prostitution

The house stands in a residential area of single-family dwellings, duplexes, and apartment houses. From the outside, one would imagine it to be occupied by the same sort of middle-income people who live in the neighborhood. The inside, needless to say, offers a different prospect. The doorway opens onto a reception room exquisitely decorated with occasional chairs, an overstuffed couch, brightly painted walls, and wall-to-wall carpeting. Off the reception room is the business office of the house, containing a desk, a chair, and two telephones; this is where Jay works. Whether out of irony or deference to a possibly older tradition I do not know, but Jay is known as the *madam*. Officially, Jay runs a modeling agency.

The rest of the house contains four bedrooms, a kitchen, two bathrooms with showers, and a sitting room for the models when they are not involved with the customers. There is a color television set in the sitting room, as well as a stereo set and a bar. The madam supplies the models with drinks free of charge, but he keeps the liquor cabinet locked. Of the four bedrooms, one can be said to be fairly typical. It is furnished with a queen-sized bed, flanked on each side by a nightstand table each of which contains a towel and a tube of K-Y lubricating jelly. The room is lavishly furnished with zebra skins on the floor, linen curtains, and a quilted bedspread. Illumination is provided by lights recessed behind the bed and/or candles. Two straight-back chairs (for the model's and customer's clothes) complete the room's accoutrements.

### The Business Enterprise
Jay is an active homosexual himself, but he manages his business with the same goals as a legitimate enterprise. He wants to make a profit and to have satisfied customers who will return to use his personnel's services. His typical question to a departing customer is, "Did everything go all right?" If the model goes on a call to a customer at a downtown hotel or a private residence, Jay will often telephone the customer later and ask the same question.

The madam prides himself on the fact that his business is no fly-by-night operation, and that his customers are completely protected against being cheated, robbed, assaulted, or blackmailed in the sexual encounter; furthermore, he protects his clients, many of whom are socially prominent, against their homosexuality becoming public knowledge.

As he would in another business, Jay also advertises, discreetly. In the underground press and periodicals that cater to homosexuals Jay will occasionally run an ad announcing that he has models for hire and giving a telephone number. Jay always interviews a caller over the phone to discover his motives; if he has any doubts, he schedules an appointment to interview the man personally. Most customers, however, are referred by other individuals.

Jay's staff is composed of a core group of approximately 15 full-time models and fringe group of 20 models who supplement their income by doing modeling in their off-hours. The ages of the models range from 18 to 26, although there are exceptions. One of the most successful models in the city, for example, is in his mid-thirties, but given the primacy of youth as a value in the homosexual subculture, he is a rarity. In his ads, Jay usually bills his models as being from one to three years younger than they are, but seldom does a model pass more than three birthdays while in Jay's employ. The demands on them are heavy, physically and psychologically. As one former core model stated: "You were never free from the job. Jay would wake me up at 2 A.M. to go on a call, or if business was active, I might have four or five calls in one day."

## Recruitment of Models

A new model can be recruited either through the recommendation of a current employee or through the advertisements Jay runs calling for "young, well-built, and good-looking" men who are needed to pose for photographers. Or Jay might meet a potential recruit at parties or other social gatherings. One model who was recruited in this way stated: "I met Jay at a party. I indicated that I was having a hard time financially and was looking for a new job. Jay asked me if I would like to go to work for him, and I asked him what he did. He stated bluntly, 'I run a male house of prostitution. If you are interested, why don't you drop by.' He gave me his address and telephone number, and several days later I dropped by."

The indication of interest by a young male is only the first step in the recruitment process. Jay must then determine his suitability through an interview that follows a fairly standard format. If Jay has never met the young man personally, he will try to make him feel at ease by stating, "Call me Jay, I'm the madam of the house." The interview begins with Jay's asking the model his name, his level of education, his last employment, and whether he is homosexual. This, or at least bisexuality, is mandatory. If, for example, the potential recruit claims to be heterosexual but wishes to earn some money by indulging in homosexual encounters, he is denied employment. The young man is then queried whether he has any qualms about whom he goes to bed with. To have certain qualms is perfectly acceptable; Jay does not disqualify someone for not desiring to go to bed with a member of another race, a sadist, or a masochist. Jay next establishes whether the applicant is *versatile* or *aggressive,* trade terms as well as code words in the homosexual subculture. Versatile means one will indulge in both active and passive acts of fellatio and anal intercourse. Aggressive refers to the model who will take only the active role in anal intercourse but will engage in active and passive fellatio. Jay prefers that his models be versatile, but he does accept on occasion men who are only aggressive if they are extremely attractive. Furthermore, Jay asks the young man whether he has any qualms about his nude photographs appearing in magazines or movies, under an assumed name of course. He also establishes whether the applicant has any sadistic or masochistic tendencies. This is important to Jay, for he will not turn away a customer desiring such services, and he has special models to accommodate them.

Further questions elicit whether the candidate has ever been arrested on a morals charge. It is Jay's strict policy never to employ a model who has ever been officially labeled "queer" by police officials; the risk is too dangerous for him. The young man is then asked whether he has had venereal disease or hepatitis in the last five years. If he has been cured of these disorders, he is employable, but a physical checkup in any case is required before be begins work.

### The Physical Examination Interview

If, after an hour of questioning, the prospective model has satisfied Jay with respect to his personality and mental stability, the candidate is then asked to go to one of the bedrooms. There the young man is asked to remove all his clothes and to have an erection. If the latter proves impossible, Jay calls in another model and asks him to go down on the applicant. If this does not cause an erection, the candidate is dismissed on the theory that if he could not perform at this point, in all probability he would be unlikely to be able to perform with the customers.

The prospective model is next photographed with a color Polaroid camera in the nude, with his penis both in the flaccid and erect states. Jay then measures the model's erect penis from the dorsal side and makes a note on its thickness. The photographs and measurements go into a book that the customer can view in selecting his model. Other vital statistics are included, such as height, weight, eye color, age, body build, and so forth. Jay does not have sexual intercourse with the prospective model, which stands in contrast to what has been reported in some accounts of female houses of prostitution. The model-to-be is also warned not to have sexual encounters with other models, because this causes conflicts and interpersonal attachments to develop among the business staff. The applicant then is told that once he is dressed (he may take a shower if he desires), he should return to the business office. One model in commenting on this aspect of the interview stated: "I was very nervous throughout the whole thing, but I kept thinking how good the money was."

When the applicant returns to the business office, Jay informs him whether he is acceptable for employment.

## Acceptance for Employment

Since one of the primary motivations for engaging in prostitution is for material gain, Jay then explains in explicit detail the monetary arrangements. Jay makes all appointments for the models with the customers. Business calls fall into three categories: in-calls, out-calls, and overnight calls. An in-call occurs in the house itself, for which the charge is $20 an hour, of which the model retains $14 and Jay takes $6. On out-calls the fee ranges from $25 to $35 per hour, with the model retaining $19 to $25; the customer is required to pay the model's taxicab fare to and from the hotel or place of meeting. An overnight call can take place at the customer's place of choosing for a period of seven or eight hours. The fee ranges from $100 to $150, with the model retaining $70 to $110 and the remainder going to Jay. Thus, the fee split is approximately 70 percent for the model and 30 percent for the madam of the house. The model is allowed to keep all tips, which range from nothing to as high as $50, with the most usual tip being from $5 to $10. Although he is not required to tell the madam of his tips, he is encouraged to do so.

Finally, Jay discusses the question of the new model assuming a new name. A model rarely chooses to use his legal name but takes a new one, as is frequently the case in the entertainment industry. He is billed under his new name, always a first name, in keeping with the mores of the homosexual subculture.

## Socialization of the Model

In a classic article, the sociologist Kingsley Davis stated that prostitution was characterized by emotional indifference to the customer, by barter, and by promiscuity. Basically, these are the same values that Jay attempts to instill in the new models. They are told not to become emotionally involved with their customers or to see them outside the business context; they are forbidden to give customers their real names, addresses, or telephone numbers. Breaking these rules is grounds for dismissal. The barter aspect is simple enough: on in-calls the customer either pays the model or the madam after the sexual liaison; on out-calls the model collects the fee in cash, unless he has been instructed by the madam to accept a check. Finally, a prostitute is by definition promiscuous; he is expected to accept all calls assigned to him unless he can provide an acceptable explanation for refusing.

**Preparing for a Call**

The model is given general instructions about preparing for a call. Since the accent is on "young, well-built, and attractive" males, the models are expected to maintain an excellent physical appearance. Their hair is to be always well groomed and trimmed within acceptable lengths. Facial preparations are used to remove the telltale signs of lines in the face, especially during periods of heavy sexual activity. Models generally trim their pubic hair, and almost all models remove buttocks hair with a cream preparation.

Both versatile and aggressive models prepare for a specific call in almost identical ways. The model showers, using a deodorant and body powder; the versatile model will also douche his rectum. Clothing worn by the model depends upon the occasion, a dinner engagement with the customer before the liaison calling for one kind of attire, a request for a "butch" or masculine model calling for another, usually a formfitting shirt with tight trousers.

**The First Calls**

Since all the models are practicing homosexuals or bisexuals, homosexual experience is scarcely unfamiliar to them. For a number of the models, however, the first call is their initial experience in receiving money for their sexual favors, in being a prostitute. Previous encounters may have brought them gifts of clothing, weekend trips or no-expense vacations, or loans of money, but there had been no explicit understanding that the benefactor had to be satisfied in every way. In other words, the previous experiences, generally with men older than the models, carried with them expectations of reciprocity but no feeling of prostitution.

Many young men enter the house intending to stay only for a short period of time until they are financially on their feet. For example, one model stated:

> When I first started I told myself I would do it for only one week—until I had all my bills paid off and a few dollars saved. However, the money was so good, and the life was exciting and thrilling to begin with, so I continued. But after a few months it became boring and tiresome.

This initial experience of good money and thrills is an entirely predictable outcome, inherent in a career of male prostitition. New faces are always in demand by Jay's customers; and since the models have been carefully screened to obtain young, well-built, attractive, and versatile males, they receive more calls during the first two weeks at the house than do the older models. This means, of course, more money than the man is accustomed to, as well as high status as the new star of the house. The latter should not be underestimated; as one informant put it:

> All my customers treated me good. No one was ever cruel or mean to me. Of course, occasionally some trick did not tip me, but this was the exception, not the rule. And I had a number of them who always asked for me when I was working for Jay.

Another young man made a similar point:

> At first I thought it was so wonderful to have love made to me by so many wealthy and socially elite men. I will never forget my first experience with a trick. We met in the reception room where Jay introduced me to Bill. We then went to the bedroom and took off our clothes and got into bed. I was very nervous. We began to talk, and he told me he was married with a wife and two children. He said that he did not realize that he had strong gay tendencies until after his marriage and now that he was in his early forties that he wanted both his family and also to have homosexual relations. He was very nice—an airline pilot I think. He then asked me what I liked to do in bed, and I told him. I asked him what he liked, and he said he liked to be screwed, so I did it to him. We talked for the rest of the hour, and he gave me a $10 tip.

In this particular case, the model's intitial experience was a financially and psychologically rewarding one. At first the number of calls the models receive is heavy—as many as seven within a twenty-four-hour period of time. However, unless he is exceptional, he is considered one of the regular members of the business staff after approximately two weeks. The term *exceptional* is given to those models who are outstandingly good-looking, well hung, versatile, and have a pleasing personality. His physical assets are the subject of much talk in the homosexual community, and Jay's customers seek the exceptional model's services frequently until his newness, too, finally wears off. After the model becomes an established member of the business staff he will receive an average of three calls a day, although some models may have only one call per day.

Part of the model's socialization to his role involves learning to satisfy the customer. Jay strongly inculcates his models with the necessity of this. The model is to remember that for one hour he exists to gratify the customer's desires. Part of this means being pleasant, talking with the trick but never asking questions about his personal and business affairs, unless such information is volunteered. Conversely, the model is not to discuss his own personal life with the customer except in the most general terms.

According to my informants, the typical customers are financially affluent, white professional or businessmen in their forties or early fifties; a sizable proportion of these men are married, with various models estimating the number as being between one-third or one-half of their customers. (This is in basic agreement with Laud Humphreys's findings that a majority of the known participants in homosexual encounters in public places are married.) Their relatively advanced age makes it difficult for them to compete for youth in the free market of the homosexual subculture, but their financial status makes it possible for them to purchase the youth and physical attractiveness so strongly desired in the homosexual (as in the heterosexual) world. Most of the customers are what would be termed in the homosexual argot as *size queens*, that is, they are fixated on the size of the penis—the larger, the better. The men constantly comment on the size of the call boy's organ. If there is fetishism here, it is rather analogous to the American heterosexual male's alleged fetishism for large breasts. In any case, one call boy, with frankness, stated: "My big peter was the reason I was chosen so frequently—I want to be liked for myself, not my body." It seems clear, too, that the customers are men whose social and political position as well as marital status require them to keep their deviance a secret. Jay is the key figure here, and he apparently merited the trust his customers place in him.

### Progression in the Career of a Model

As previously noted, the typical model does not begin his work with the expectation that he will become committed to the role of a call boy. The career is begun with the rationalization that it will be for only a few days or weeks until pressing financial problems are resolved. In the initial interview Jay, the madam, always explains to the young man the difference between a *whore* and a *prostitute*. According to him, a whore is "one who gives his sexual favors without being rewarded financially," whereas a prostitute is "one who receives money for his sexual favors." Jay, although avoiding the label *prostitute* for his business staff, does try to make the model understand what his role will be. Although in moments of anger the models will refer to each other as "whore," "slut," or "prostitute," Jay and the models refer to their role as that of a call boy—never prostitute. This self-identification, according to one informant, came "about the third week on the job. It was easy money, and I did not desire to trick on the side. I was having more than enough sex at work. I always had nice clothes and money in my pockets." In other words, he is a businessman like anyone else in the society, above all emotionally uninvolved with his customers.

## Sexual Encounters

Whatever the psychological gratification obtained by either call boy or client in the conversations that occur during the hour, the primary purpose of the male prostitute is to provide sexual gratification to the customer. Sexual encounters fall into a typical pattern. This can be best described in the words of the call boys themselves. Bill, in recounting an episode, stated:

> The customer picked me from the book of photos that Jay has of the boys. Jay got me from our room [the models' sitting room] and took me to the reception room where he introduced me to Jack. Jack was about thirty-five years of age with blond hair and was good-looking. We went into one of the bedrooms, and he asked me to undress. He admired my body, especially my cock, and stated that I was really well hung. He then undressed, and we got in the bed and embraced. He asked me if I liked to have sex with the lights on or off. I said I preferred sex in the dark, so he turned off the lights. We talked for a while; he told me he was from Texas and had heard about our house from some of his friends, so he decided to visit it.
>
> He then told me how good-looking I was and that he wanted us to perform "69," which we did. I told him to tell me when he was going to come, as I don't like for tricks to come in my mouth. It makes me sick. He said he would, and he did. I did not come myself.
>
> We conversed after this about Texas, and he told me about his wife and his son. He said he never tricked with a male unless he was out of town on a business trip. He was very nice to me. He then asked me what I liked to do. I told him I liked to fuck, and he said he liked to be fucked, so I got the K-Y out of the drawer and fucked him. He said he enjoyed it. We talked awhile, and he said that he would like to see me again when he was in town again. I said all right—just call the house.
>
> We then got up and took a shower together. He then dressed, and he gave me a $10 tip—Oh, I guess I had him about once a month over the next five months.

The major thing to note about this episode is that the call boy follows the interactional leads of the customer on both sexual and conversational activities. This liaison also illustrates the statement of most informants that most customers prefer to have fellatio performed on them and to be the passive partner in anal intercourse.

The frequent performance of fellatio on customers raises the question for the call boy of what to do with the fluid at ejaculation. Some require the customers to inform them before they ejaculate. One call boy stated:

> I had this trick who did not tell me he was coming. He came in my mouth. It made me so sick that I had to jump out of bed, grab the towel, and vomit in it. I was sick for hours after that. I just can't stand that.

Some call boys, however, accept the swallowing of the semen as part of the job even though they may not enjoy the taste or the sensation. And there are some who do enjoy it.

### Anal Intercourse

Generally speaking, certain physical attributes of the model determine whether he is to be the active or passive partner in anal intercourse. Customers prefer to be the passive partner when the model is of the butch type, with a larger than average penis. Customers who want the active role in anal intercourse seek models who are more slender, with smooth bodies and an average-sized penis. It should be emphasized that there are exceptions to these generalizations, but on the whole they hold up.

One of the call boys, Ben, related the following experience concerning anal intercourse:

> There was this young guy of about thirty years old who came to the house one night. Much to my surprise he was a guy who I had known from the bar. He was always trying to get me to go home with him, but I always refused. I'm sure he did not know I was a model. Well, he picked me from Jay's photo book, and Jay introduced us as usual. Once we were in the bedroom he said to me, "It's funny that we meet this way finally—in bed." The first thing he did was to blow me, and I came in his mouth, as he wanted it that way. Then after some talk about his always wanting to have sex with me and how much of a crush he had on me from seeing me in the bars, he said, "I'm going to fuck you." I said, "All right, but be careful (as he was well built). Don't ram me as I am built small." To be honest, I enjoyed it— especially the sensation of his coming inside me. He said he would be coming back to the house frequently.

In a few days he returned and told me how much he liked me. He asked me what I liked to do. I said I liked to fuck, but he refused to let me do it as he was almost a virgin—he had been screwed only once or twice before. Well, we did "69" that night. He said he would return soon.

About a week later, he returned. I was attracted to him, and he said he really like me. I told him that I wanted to screw him. At first he hesitated and said I was too large, that it would hurt him. In the end he consented if I would be careful. I told him the easiest way would be for him to lean over the bed and that I would use Vaseline as it does not dry as fast as K-Y. Well, I took it easy and was very careful not to hurt him, and it took me about ten minutes to get it in, as he was so tight. He did not really enjoy it, but he did it for me.

One hears in this story a contradiction of Davis's observation that the prostitute shows emotional indifference. And, in fact, this customer desired the call boy to become his lover, but Jay, sensing that the model might reciprocate these feelings, saw to it that Ben was never available to this customer again.

It should be noted that some customers are so oriented to anal intercourse that after the model has performed the active role, the customer will request that the model use a dildo on him for the rest of the hour. One model quoted a married man who was a regular customer of his as stating: "I like to get fucked and suck a cock. These are two things my wife cannot do for me." Call boys, however, generally view this type of customer as a "weirdo."

### Masturbation and Voyeurism

Less frequent than fellatio and anal intercourse are sexual activities that involve masturbation by the model and/or customer. Customers for this sort of service are often *watch queens*, men who receive gratification from watching the sexual activities of others. They may ask the model to walk around the room nude, and he may or may not masturbate. Or the client may request the model to lie in bed with him while he watches him masturbate, or, a variation on this, the model may sit on the customer's chest and masturbate. Or, while the two lie in bed together, the customer masturbates the model and may or may not expect the model to masturbate him.

Less frequently a customer will request to watch the sexual activities of two models as they perform fellatio and/or anal intercourse. Some models think of voyeurism of this classic type as incomprehensibly odd. As one model stated: "He is paying for something he does not participate in."

**Violations of House Regulations**

One of the cardinal rules of the madam is that the models are not to have sex with each other, the reason being that the models, all young, physically healthy, and attractive, might become emotionally involved with each other, which would lead either to their becoming lovers (with the possibility of leaving his employment) or to friction with other models. Given the transitory nature of many homosexual liaisons, Jay is probably more concerned with the bitterness that might develop between two models at the end of the affair. In his mind, emotional attachments among his staff could only lead to business problems, and that would reduce his profit.

As with all group norms, the rule of no sex between models is violated. As one model stated: "What else could you expect to happen when you had so many virile, young homosexuals together? Sex was bound to occur." The madam is realistic about this and does not dismiss a model for an occasional indiscretion with another model unless they become too emotionally involved.

The major prohibition, which the madam states time after time to the models, also concerns emotional involvement, this time with the customers. However, Jay desires to have satisfied customers who return frequently, and some of them are bound to ask for the same model for each sexual encounter. As long as the model and the customer satisfy the madam that no personal attachments are developing, he approves of such an arrangement. If, however, he discovers an emotional relationship, Jay no longer allows the pair to be together. He would rather risk losing the customer than the model. If they met socially outside the house, he would dismiss the model.

Models and customers, nevertheless, do become emotionally attached to one another, given the context of single, wealthy middle-aged men and striving, attractive young males. The natural history of one such attachment is told by the model Joe:

> Aaron selected me from Jay's book of photographs. We hit if off from the first time. In the next month he asked for me seven times. On his eighth visit he asked me to have dinner with him, but I refused. He kept begging me to go out with him and said that he was very attracted to me. On his next visit he again invited me to dinner, and I accepted his invitation to meet him at a gay bar and then go out to dinner. At that time I was living at the house, and I telephoned the madam to tell him that I was not going to work that night as I was tired and was going to spend the night with a friend. Aaron and I met for dinner, and he invited me to stay overnight at his apartment. I accepted, and we went to his home where we had sexual relations, but he

did not give me any money. I was so happy after that night; I felt that at long last I had found someone to love me. We made arrangements to keep meeting outside my business hours.

Several times in the next week the madam intercepted telephone calls to me from Aaron, as I was living in the house. About two weeks after Aaron and I had been meeting outside the house the madam called me to the office. Bluntly Jay asked me, "What in the hell is going on between you and Aaron? He is always telephoning you, and he hasn't been to the house in the last few weeks. What's the score?"

I replied that I thought I loved Aaron and wanted him for a lover. The madam was furious with me and shouted, "No! No! I will not permit it. It's bad for business. I told you when you first started working here not to become emotionally involved with the customers. You must break it off at once." I replied that I was moving out of the house and going to live with Aaron—that nothing he said would change my mind.

At this point Jay had calmed down somewhat. He said, "I'm against it, and it won't work out. Go ahead if that's what you want. You're a good model, and I'll hate to see you leave. But you'll still work with me, won't you?"

Although I really wanted to stop being a model, I replied that I would, but I was still going to move to Aaron's apartment. I discussed the matter with Aaron. I told him I didn't want to work anymore for Jay. Well, I should have known better when Aaron told me that it would be good for me to continue working at the house until I found another job. I guess I was so attached to Aaron at that time that I would have agreed to anything.

Almost immediately I began to have problems with Aaron. He expected me to work and at the same time to have sex every night before I went to work. Then the newness of the affair began to wear off after a few weeks. I was tired all the time—physically and mentally. I began to drink more heavily and became very depressed. That only made my situation worse. I also began to take more and more "bennies" [amphetamines] to keep me going. But I could not keep up with my work at the house; I could not perform for the customers.

Around a month after I originally left the house to live with Aaron, the madam called me to the office and read the riot act to me. He said that my performance with the customers was poor—that either I leave Aaron or he would fire me. He also said that if I left Aaron I could go visit my parents in another state for a two-weeks' vacation and return to work if I pulled myself together. I told him I would leave Aaron, as I was already regretting ever getting involved with him. He was tricking on the side, and he also drank heavily, which did not help my drinking problem.

Aaron did not seem to care about my leaving him, and I went home to visit. I returned to Jay's house a few weeks later, but it was not the same. I just did not have it in me to be a model anymore.

Joe's recollections are presented here in detail to establish the point that the prostitute does, at times, become very emotionally involved with his clients. It is perhaps doubtful whether such relationships as that which developed between Joe and Aaron have much of a chance of developing into long-term relationships. But it is difficult for many models not to see a solution to their life situations in the permanent attachment that a customer may provide them. If one recalls the strong motives of material gain that led the models into their present jobs, it is understandable that they should prefer being "kept" by a wealthy client to the life of a call boy.

### Disenchantment with Modeling

As I said at the outset, a call boy's career is a short one; it generally comes to an end in the mid- or late twenties. We do not have systematic longitudinal data on a significant number of models, but we can discuss some of the reasons why a model might call it quits. Above all, there is disenchantment with the profession, added to this the physical and psychological decline of the model.

Many models, after the initial excitement, become fed up with their lives. They begin to perceive their occupation as being dead-end, a journey to nowhere. As one former model poignantly stated:

> The job was making me depressed. I was young and wanted to go out and have some fun. If I did, it would take me away from the job, and I would lose money. I could not start a romance—who would want a call boy as a lover. I was lonely all the time. I wanted someone to love me for myself, not just my body.

Hustlers and call boys are stigmatized in the homosexual subculture, despite the fact that the group itself is stigmatized by the larger society, and despite the fact that a significant number of homosexuals are almost as promiscuous as the hustler or call boy. Behaviorally there is little difference between the homosexual's one-night-stands and the call boy's activities. The former, however, justify their behavior on the grounds that it does not involve the exchange of money.

Beyond this, the model is always fighting a battle to keep the appearance of youth and good looks, and against odds made impossible by irregular hours and periods of heavy sexual activity. He becomes physically tired and turns to stimulant drugs to keep him vibrant and awake. Or in moments of depression about his work and stigmatized position he drinks heavily and becomes intoxicated. Whether through drugs or alcohol, his sexual performance with the customers is inevitably affected—he becomes irritable, tired, unable to have an erection. His face begins to show the effects of such a lifestyle—"bags" under the eyes that no amount of makeup can hide, bloodshot eyes or weight loss, and so on. His physical desirability decreases, and slowly he loses customers until he arrives at the inevitable day when the madam fires him.

Psychologically, the strain of many short, intensive encounters with his customers threatens his mental stability. He constantly searches for either a lover to provide him with emotional security, such as the case of Aaron and Joe, or a "sugar daddy," a successful business or professional man, sometimes married, who will support him and provide him with an apartment.

# 9

# Transsexuals

## James P. Driscoll

There is a hotel in the Tenderloin district of San Francisco ~~that is inhabited almost entirely by transsexuals~~. It is not much of a place to look at—a tawdry three-story building. A bar occupies the first floor, apart from an outside door that leads upstairs to the hotel, which consists of the top two floors of the building.

The traffic up those stairs usually begins a little after midnight. Two people enter the hotel. They climb the shabby steps and stop at a grilled window on the second floor. A flyblown sign over it reads *Manager.* The middle-aged man and the young girl stop here. There is another sign that says, "Positively no visitors after ten P.M." Yet another one gives the weekly rates for doubles and singles; it also announces that an additional guest may be registered for the night for three dollars.

Inside the office another girl, the manager, sits in an overstuffed chair. From here she can see her television set and still keep an eye on people from the minute they enter the ground floor. Not much escapes the manager. Outside, the girl whispers something to the man, and he hands three dollar bills through the grill. He and the girl climb the stairs to the third floor.

Not too different, one might say, from thousands of other such arrangements that go on every night. But there is a difference. The girl is not a girl. "She" is a young man of twenty dressed not only as a woman, but also in high fashion. The clothes are good and in style. Her wig is piled high on her head, on top of her own long hair. Her build, carriage, and demeanor are entirely feminine. She is a transsexual, a man who dresses as a woman and wants to undergo sex conversion surgery so that she may be a woman physically.

### Entering the Transsexual World

I became aware of and interested in the transsexuals about four years ago. I was working nights at the time, and our building was on the edge of the Tenderloin. My office was the only place open for several blocks. The rest of the newspaper I worked for went on all night, too, but my cubbyhole was adjacent to the street.

I had got used to the variety of people who dropped in there: some for a free paper, some to cadge money, some who were lonely. And some just to get out of the rain. I met my first transsexual on such a rainy night. She came in and asked if she could stand there for a while. It was all right with me. When my shift was over I told her I would have to lock up. It was five in the morning and still raining. She asked me if I could drop her off at Paul's, an afterhours coffeehouse. I said yes, and when we got there she asked me inside for a cup of coffee. I had never been inside one of these places and was curious, so I agreed. We got stools at the bar, and she introduced me to Heather, the girl serving the coffee. The place was crowded with girls and a few men. The jukebox was playing at its loudest.

She told me her name was Angie and said hello to several of the girls at the bar. They did not respond. I was wondering what I had done wrong, when Angie told them that I was a friend and not a trick. Soon some of the other girls started talking to us, and I was quite stunned to notice, even in the dim light, that one of them needed a shave. Now I may be a little slow about some things and accustomed to take others at face value, but this was a little much. I started looking at the others closely, and sure enough, several were men. I introduced this as tactfully as possible to Angie, and she got a good laugh out of it. She admitted to being a man and was quite proud that I had not "read" her.

At this point I would like to indicate a usage that is followed in this paper. It is impossible to be associated with the transsexuals for any length of time, let alone live with them, without thinking of them as women. They always refer to themselves and each other in the feminine gender, and do all they can to reinforce a feminine identity. They call each other *girl* and refer to other transsexuals as *she* and *her*. In order to accurately reflect the feelings of the people involved, and others' perceptions of them, I shall refer to the transsexuals as girls and shall use feminine pronouns.

Transsexuals have a definite subculture, and it is extremely difficult to breach the walls of distrust and dislike of outsiders. There is a good reason for this. First of all, being in drag was against the law at this time [1971]. Second, all the girls I knew were engaged in prostitution. You may purchase any service you want at any time. But it is an entirely different matter to get one of them to sit down and talk to you. In all the conversations and interviews I had with these girls, I have given them my word that I would never do anything to harm them or put them in jeopardy. I have kept that word. The names you read are fictitious. The people, however, are real, and so are the situations.

Obviously what I needed for my research was a place where a number of the girls lived, and a place I could move into. Through a friend in Police Community Relations, I learned of the hotel described earlier, a hotel we shall call *La Toro*, since this was the name suggested to me by the hotel manager who likes the pun on the mixed gender.

I went to La Toro and introduced myself to Carrie, one of the girls known to my friend. I explained to her that I was a student and that I wanted to do my thesis on transsexuals. This seemed a little beyond her, so I settled for saying that I was going to write a book.

Later on, as I met the girls, I explained to them that no one knew much, if anything, about them or their problems. If some knowledge could be spread, things might be a little easier for them, or at least people might understand them. As it turned out, it did not make much difference what I said I was doing. The important thing was to be accepted as a person.

Carrie said that I would have to have the permission of the manager before I could move in. So we went down to see her. She turned out to be Heather, the girl who had served me coffee that night at Paul's. I explained everything to her and asked if I could move into the hotel. I told her what I wanted to do, including the taping of interviews. She wanted a couple of days to think it over and talk to some of the other girls.

A few days later I called her, and she told me it would be all right. So in early May I took a leave from work and moved into the hotel. Carrie and Heather introduced me to a few of the girls, and I settled back for the watching and waiting game I knew would now begin. I tried to be seen and to talk to the girls as much as possible.

But I had to be careful about this. I would not talk to them unless they made some overture. This was true in the hotel, on the street, and in Winston's restaurant, which was a gathering place for them. In this way I never endangered anything they might be working on. Some nights a girl might sit in Winston's and talk to me by the hour. The next night she might ignore me completely. This was because on these nights she was really hustling and did not want to take any time out from work.

In all I spent a year in field research, and a month living at the hotel. During that time there were 28 people occupying the 21 rooms. A few of these were the "husbands" of transsexuals. I interviewed 21 girls and discarded four tapes because their interviews expressed more transvestite than transsexual tendencies and attitudes. This left me with 17 tapes of people whom I regarded as transsexuals. Most of the interview was loosely structured to encourage the individual to talk as much and freely as possible about herself and her past. The interviews were followed up by open-ended discussions.

Now, obviously, these girls did not appear in full drag out of a clear blue sky. There had to be some preliminary stages to this one.

All but one of the girls were from out of town. Why had they left home, and why had they come to San Francisco? What were their aims in life? What did they do and expect to do, and how did they feel about their lives?

Generally I found that the girls had many things in common in their backgrounds. They had all gone through similar stages of development on their path to transsexualism. To delineate these stages and alternatives was the problem I was faced with. There was a way to make sociological sense out of the lives of these girls.

**Effeminate Childhood**

This stage begins when the child is in infancy and continues to about the tenth or twelfth year. The early years of the socialization process were disruptive ones for the girls. From infancy to puberty their gender was treated inappropriately or ambiguously by their parent or parents.

Moreover, every one of the subjects came from a broken home. When asked about their family backgrounds, the girls replied:

> Yes, my mother and father were divorced when I was four.
> My mother and father were alcoholics. I was really raised by my grandmother.
> My parents were divorced when I was five. My father got custody of the children. I was spoiled rotten. I got away with anything I wanted to do.
> Yes, I was raised mainly by my grandmother. My parents were divorced when I was ten.
> Not really. But I stuck with my mother. My father couldn't be bothered.

I tried to get some other information about the childhood of these girls by asking the question, "Was your mother or father the dominant parent?" As might be expected, almost all of the subjects indicated that the mother was the dominant figure in the household.

> My mother. She ran the family and was really mother and father to me.
> Mother. I could always turn to her. I couldn't talk to my father.
> My mother. She was married four times and divorced three.

A very few girls said that their fathers had been the dominant parent, but it was not because of his authority or status in the hierarchy of the family. It was rather out of necessity or opportunity.

> My father, but only because I did not have a mother.
> Well, my father gave me anything I wanted.

In response to the question, "Did your father provide a good masculine image for you?", the answers were preponderantly no.

> I did not look at him as a masculine person. He provided no image for me.
> Definitely not. He was an alcoholic.

Those few who answered yes did not indicate a good or healthy relationship.

> Yes, but it scared me.
> He was good to my mother, but I always wanted to be a girl.

The picture that emerges of these girls in their early years is one of disorientation and confusion. The girls, of course, had no choice in this matter. The choice was made by the parents or parent. The significant other or others in the girl's life showed her how these female roles were to be performed. The child was rewarded for her behavior in various ways. She was given girls' toys and playthings; she was dressed in female clothing; she was encouraged to let her hair grow long and frequently had it set and ribbons put in it; she was taught to avoid the rough activities of boys; and in general all feminine behavior was reinforced positively.

One question put to the group was, "Did you play boy games or girl games?" None of the girls answered that they had played boys' games exclusively. Some played both. But most answers were like these:

> Girl games. Dolls, dollhouses, that sort of thing.

> Girl games. I played jacks and jumped rope.
> Both. But I preferred to play with the girls and mostly did.

In short, these children were taught to be girls. This was the role prescribed for them and was the central theme in their sexual socialization process. When they were asked if they had been raised as a boy or a girl, only two of the seventeen subjects responded that they had been raised as a boy. One of these was ambiguous.

> I guess I was raised as a boy. But I was raised by my mother and sisters. There was no male influence around the house.

More typical responses ran like these:

> I was raised as a girl by my mother and aunts. My sex was discovered by a school nurse when I was six.
> As a girl. I always had long hair to my shoulders, and my mother put ribbons in it for me when I was young.
> As a girl. My grandparents treated me as a little girl. My father was an airline pilot and always brought me girl toys from his trips.

Sociologist Howard Becker points out that the first step in the career of a deviant is usually the commission of a deviant act. In this case, however, the girls did not do anything really deviant. They obeyed their parents or guardians. They responded to the expectations of femininity by behaving like girls. Once this pattern had been established, they made feminine choices in most aspects of their lives. Eventually, they chose to identify sexually with a feminine model.

But what was seen as normal by the parent and child was perceived by others as deviant. Actual conflict began when they got to school. Here great portions of their lives were expected to be lived according to the conventional standards of normal boys. But it was impossible for them to meet these demands. They had been treated as girls and considered themselves to be so. In this way they alienated themselves from the boys in their community.

Many of the girls recall how they hated gym class. They were forced to undress in front of others and were very self-conscious about this. Even at that age they wanted to be like girls. Besides, they were forced to play boy games that were repugnant to them. They went to considerable trouble to develop ploys that would get them out of gym class.

One of the most important steps in the development of a deviant is that of being caught or found out and publicly labeled. This label places the deviant in a new status and in turn results in changes in his self-concept. It also changes the concepts that other people have of him. He now carries a stigma and is expected to behave in ways that people feel are consistent with the label. It is significant that the labeling process for the transsexual began in school and was brought about by the behavior of the girls and the perceptions of their peers. In response to the question, "How did you get along with the other children in school?", some of the answers were:

> The guys gave me a rough time for being feminine. That's why I left school. They called me a sissy and a queer.
> Not very well. I was raised with my three sisters and was a sissy. I got along with the girls but not the boys.
> Not too well. I liked nail polish and lipstick and makeup. I was always considered a sissy. Most of the time I was poked fun at.

Many of them recall being very lonely, since neither boys nor girls would have anything to do with them. It was a time, also, of some anguish. The girls report that they urinated sitting down and that it seemed natural for them to use the girls' rest room at school. Several of them tried this and were punished for it. They continued, however, to sneak unto the girls' room whenever possible.

Even the simple process of names became a perplexing problem for the girls. They never remember being called by their given name around the house. They were called by some ambiguous abbreviation or pet name. Terrance became Terri, Gerald was Jerri, Phillip was Phyl, and James was Snooky. Even to this day one of the things that the girls hate most about a court appearance is the fact that they must stand up and reply to their male name.

It is not my contention that all children who are called sissies will grow up to be transsexuals or even homosexuals. Why some choose one form of sexual gratification and others another is not yet clear. But in my sample group it was evident that the patterning that begins in childhood was a very important variable in the lives of the girls. There is a good deal of evidence to support the notion of sexual socialization being a crucial influence on whether (or how) one defines oneself as a boy or a girl. Biology is not always destiny.

### Homosexual Stage

The girls performed homosexual acts for some time before they perceived themselves to be homosexuals. This is hardly surprising,

of course, since after all they were deeply confused as to what sex
they were. This was part of the anguish, that they had to act normally while fighting an internal battle over who and what they were. It
was only when they became aware that there was a gay world and
that there were many others who acted as they did that they formed
the self-concept of homosexual.

Nevertheless, to formulate a concept of one's self as being a homosexual, a person must perform a homosexual act, and usually a
series of them. Of paramount importance is the first such act, and I
asked the girls how old they were when it took place and what happened.

> I was thirteen or fourteen. I really didn't know anything, and
> this guy went down on me. He tried to screw me, but I wouldn't
> let him. Before that I used to dream of being a woman and giv-
> ing birth to babies.
>
> I was eight. My cousin was six years older, and we started
> fooling around. He knew what was going on; I didn't. He went
> down on me.
>
> Ten or eleven. It happened with a boy my age. We just took
> off our clothes and experimented with each other's bodies.
>
> Eleven. I met a boy of about twenty-two on the bridle path.
> He blew me and I blew him.

Conceivably, at this point the girls could have decided they did
not like homosexual experiences. When I asked them about this,
some answers were:

> I enjoyed them and have stuck to them ever since.
> Scared me at first. Then I got to like them.
> I had wanted it all my life. I wanted to experiment.
> I never had a man to love when I was younger.

It is interesting that they could recall no sexual curiosity about
"real" girls. If they did not know already, the transsexuals wanted
to know how girls were built and what the differences were between
themselves and the real thing. But there was none of the experi-
mentation and "playing house" that is so common among normal
children. The transsexuals mainly wanted to know what was
required of them so that they could be considered to be girls.

While the girls found homosexual acts pleasurable to some extent, this does not mean that they automatically had to continue
them. They could have chosen the heterosexual path. But they did
not. They got older and found that there were other people who per-

formed these acts and identified themselves as homosexuals. In my study almost all the transsexuals reported that they considered themselves to be homosexuals in late adolescence.

> Seventeen or eighteen. When I had accepted it and felt I couldn't be anything else.
> I was eighteen. I realized that it was not a game but a way of life. I came to understand that this was the way I felt. I liked other men.
> Fourteen to fifteen. I wanted to feel like a woman. I knew I was funny all my life. I wanted to go with men.

Here we see, present and at work, many of the factors that make up what has been called a *career contingency*—exposure to an experience, the experience itself, the desire to continue it, the response of significant others, and the eventual identification with it. But the major contingency seems to be the discovery of other homosexuals and of a gay subculture.

The gay world was a strange but pleasurable place for the girls. They began to frequent those parts of town where other homosexuals gathered. The move was an easy one; after all, they had been performing homosexuals acts for some years. During that time they had felt very isolated, however; they felt that they were one of a kind and were very lonely. But now they found others who shared the same sexual preferences and that these people had their own community. The transition to full homosexual status may even have been a relief to the girls.

But what is a homosexual? Taking a test group of sixty homosexuals, Evelyn Hooker put them through several tests, such as the Rorschach, T.A.T., and M.A.P.S. On the basis of the results, it was found that homosexuality as a clinical entity does not exist. That is, it was not possible to identify the members of the test group as homosexuals from their scores. This clearly indicates that in almost all basic areas, the homosexual is not different from other men. What does set him apart is his behavior, and to explain this behavior we would do well to look closely into the sexual socialization of the homosexual. If we cannot find the cause for his behavior within the person, then we must look for patterns of interaction with other people, especially significant others, which will explain his deviation. With respect to the transsexuals I interviewed, it should be plain that this socialization process was an unconventional and misleading one from the beginning.

The period when they were being socialized into the gay world was also, of course, a training in uncoventionality. The girls admit to a high degree of sexuality, and their sexual encounters were many and varied. They cruised the streets looking for pickups, they frequented the Turkish baths, and spent a great amount of time in homosexual bars and other hangouts. It should be pointed out that the girls came from a broad geographic area and from diverse social settings. They were raised in small towns, large cities, and the suburbs. Their origins seem to have made no difference in their activity, however, except that those from the larger cities had a greater degree of freedom and a wider range of activity. Wherever they had come from, their behavior was no different from that of many other homosexuals. And it was from these other homosexuals that the girls learned. They all report that they were swept up into the gay world. They began to associate with one another and to form friendships. In this mutual exchange they found which were the homosexual bars, where pickups could be made, what they were expected to wear, and how they were expected to act. They also learned how to survive: how to recognize the police, how to approach a prospect, how to dress, how to fix their hair, how to apply a little makeup.

During this period of homosexuality, all the girls relate that they were "hair fairies." That is, they would wear their hair long and tease it. They also had what seems to be almost a uniform: a little makeup, a bulky sweater, and tight trousers—as tight as possible.

In short, they were introduced to the gay world, liked it, and learned from it. They had entered the gay world as pretty uncertain people. Now they had a rationale for their behavior. As a result of what they learned, they emerged far more sure of themselves and far wiser. They were also far stronger in their identification of themselves.

It was at this time that most of the girls left home. For some, leaving was not voluntary; they were rousted by the police so often that they were in effect run out of town. Some others were simply made to feel unwelcome at home. During their early years their behavior was allowed and even encouraged by the people who raised them. But later on, usually in high school, this behavior came under public scrutiny and condemnation. Now the girls were expected to change their behavior from feminine to masculine. When they were unable to do this, many had no choice but to leave home. As one of the girls told me: "My mother wanted a little girl, but not a big one."

With their immersion in the homosexual subculture, the girls became contemptuous of the rules of society. Since the homosexual finds that an important part of the moral code does not apply to him, he calls into question all parts of morality. The girls indulged in a great deal of petty theft; all admitted to male prostitution; and many reported that they had had venereal disease at this point.

I have mentioned that the desire to be feminine was very strong in the girls. In order to be as feminine as possible, they preferred the passive role in sexual activity. But even this was not enough for them. There came a time when the role of the hair fairy was no longer enough. They wanted to be more like real women, and the logical way to do this was to dress as one.

### Transvestite Stage

In general, there are two types of transvestites. One type finds that he gets emotional relief from dressing as a woman. Many of these men are married and lead heterosexual lives. They dress in the privacy of their homes, sometimes with the knowledge and active assistance of their wives. The wives do not see this as a healthy situation but go along for the sake of saving the marriage. Frequently the male must wear some article of female attire in order to engage in sexual intercourse, and he usually adopts the under position. This type presents no social problems, for he rarely dresses in public.

The other type consists of people who are very involved with, and attached to, a feminine way of life. It pervades their every hour and effort. They want to wear female attire in the streets and try to wear this clothing as much as possible. These are the people with whom I am now concerned.

Transsexuals, as we have seen, usually begin cross dressing in childhood. They were dressed in girls' attire by their mothers. Or they were given preferential treatment when they performed female roles, so that they sought these roles and wore the clothes of their sisters and mothers. They were protected from the roughness of other boys and were treated as girls. Under these circumstances it is not difficult to imagine how or why the child came to prefer girls' clothes.

During their homosexual stage the girls came into frequent contact with transvestites. They both frequented the same bars, restaurants, and coffeehouses. The girls wanted to be like the transvestites but lacked the courage of their convictions. There was a great deal of talk among themselves about how these other people dressed and got away with it.

The girls also talked a lot to the transvestites and found that they had come from the same kind of background. Gradually the conviction built up that this was the life that they should be leading, and finally they decided to make the move. The question was put to them:

"When and why did you decide that you wanted to live as a woman?" Some answers were:

> I've always wanted to. I used to dress at home when my father was away. Later when I was working as a beautician, I used to dress after work.
> I met another queen in mid-1965 and decided that that was the time to come out. I started dressing and living as a woman then. I had dressed before at home and at parties.
> Two years ago. I felt more comfortable in female attire. I was very feminine anyhow. I found that I could make myself a very attractive woman rather than a feminine boy.
> I never could stand the sight of a feminine man with the hair dyed and eyebrows plucked. I'm more honest this way. I came out last Halloween.

I also asked them: "What made you decide to come out into the open?"

> If I wanted to be a woman, I might as well learn to act like one.
> I looked better this way. I made more friends, felt more at ease, had a better time. I was put on a pedestal.
> The kids down here. If they are free, there is no sense in me being tied down.

When the girls moved into their new status as transvestites, most of them had no idea what they were getting into or the vast changes it would make in their lives. They seem to have given little thought to what effect continual dressing would have on other aspects of their lives.

One of the first things to be affected was their job. Most of them simply quit and hoped somehow to make a living. But this proved to be very difficult. As has been reported, the girls had dabbled in male prostitution in their homosexual stage. Now they found that they had to hustle in earnest in order to make a living. This was an unforeseen consequence of their change in status.

The queens frequently spent a great deal of time together. There was much for them to learn from the older queens. They had much to learn about how to dress, how to fix their hair, wear their makeup, and so forth.

In response to the question, "How did you learn to dress, act, and pass as a woman?", they replied:

> I watched the other kids. I wore the same hair styles and clothes. I found out about pads and gaffs from them. Now I dress to please myself.

You get a lot of helpful hints. But you must do it yourself. You watch other queens and learn from them. People will tell you to try pads and other things.

I watched other queens. Friends showed me how to get arranged. Other girls gave me a hand with makeup and dress.

Note that the girls did not seem to pay much attention to women. When I asked them about this, they told me that there was more to learn from other queens, since they had similar problems. They noticed women but could not get the kind of instruction that they needed. So they turned to the queens.

I was also interested in how they solved some of the other adjustments that had to be made. So I asked, "When and how did you learn to set your hair, walk, and talk like a woman?":

I always did my mother's hair and the other ladies on the block. I wanted to be a beautician. The makeup came from watching the other kids. The walk is mine.

This is my natural voice, and I have always walked like this. I went to beauty school for a while and learned about hairdressing.

I watched other queens, how they moved, acted, and spoke. Don't overdo. I wore my mother's shoes for years and learned to shift my voice down [that is, softened tone].

This is my own voice and walk. I had a little trouble with the high heels at first, but I got used to them. I learned about setting hair from my sisters and other queens.

The girls also had other things to learn about their everyday lives. There was a tacit understanding with the police that they would not be picked up for impersonation as long as they stayed in the Tenderloin. They were also allowed on the north side of Market Street. If they strayed outside of these areas, they were liable to be, and frequently were, arrested.

They also learned a new rationale. They now considered themselves to be a cut above the homosexual and much more feminine. They now regarded the hair fairy as someone to be laughed at. This feeling is reciprocated by the homosexuals, many of whom think the queens are a bunch of nuts dressed in women's clothing. They enjoy pointing out the shortcomings of the girls, ridiculing them.

The girls have told me that at this stage they thought that they had reached the end of the rainbow. It seemed to them to be the realization of a childhood dream. They were free, they were on their own, they dressed as women, they referred to themselves in feminine terms, and they thought they had found the good life. Even prostitution did not bother them at this point. In fact, all reported that they were having a lot of fun. They did not model themselves after the middle-class housewife, or even the upper-class female swinger. Their dress was intended to startle and to attract attention, and it did. Frankly, they could not have looked more like whores if they tried, and they seemed to get some kind of perverse pleasure out of this.

So this period, when the person comes out, seems to be a relatively happy one for the girls. Of course they have their problems, especially with the police, and several of the girls were arrested for impersonation and prostitution. In San Francisco, however, this contingency was not as traumatic as it would be in other places. It is a measure of the sophistication and tolerance of that city that both the city and county jails have a special tank for the queens. In most other cities they are simply thrown in with the male prisoners and left to an uncertain fate.

The transvestite phase of the girls' life is a relatively short one. It usually lasts from three to eight months. Then something else happens. They find out about the conversion operation and discover that it is possible for them to be a woman physically. Now, however, with this new knowledge, they are ready for the next step. When they first regularly dressed as women they had wanted to get rid of some of the secondary male characteristics, especially the beard, and they had also wanted to acquire a bust. But at the transvestite stage these were merely expressed desires, and not much seems actually to have been done about them.

**Transsexual Stage**

Once they have heard of the conversion operation and know that there is such a thing as a transsexual, the self-concepts of the girls seem to change. Now they regard themselves as women in every sense of the word except one. This female identification is very strong in the transsexuals and dominates all other aspects of their lives. It is what sociologist Everett Hughes has called a *master status*.

An interesting and, I think, good example of this is how they regard themselves sexually. Prior to this phase they considered themselves to be homosexuals. Now they deny any such status and claim that they are normally sexed. When asked how they account for this when they admit to performing homosexual acts, the girls have told me that they think of themselves as women. This identification is so strong that to them it would be a perversion to choose a female sex partner.

Harry Benjamin has called the transsexual a *psychic hermaphrodite*. They have the mind of a woman in the body of a man. They can see only one way out of this dilemma: the conversion operation. They set out to attain this goal and keep after it with a tenacity that can only be referred to as fierce. It becomes the driving force in their lives.

They call it simply *the operation*. The penis is excised, and the patient is castrated. Plastic reconstruction of the external genitalia is then performed. Next an artificial vagina is created. This usually consists of a pouch six- to eight-inches deep. The skin of the amputated penis is stripped off, inverted, and inserted into the pouch, the wound surfaces adhering to each other. This tissue from the penis contains sensory nerve ends that are partially preserved and later on may help in achieving orgasm.

There is a follow-up period of about six months during which time the vagina must be frequently dilated and a prosthetic device frequently worn so that the pouch does not seal itself. After this time the transsexual is able to perform normal sexual relations with a man.

What makes these girls want to go through such a rigorous and traumatizing operation? The only answer is that they want to be women—not just to appear as a woman and successfully pass as one but to be able to function as one. It is this drive that is characteristic of the transsexual's life.

I was interested in when this period began and asked the girls when and why they decided they were transsexuals.

> About five months ago when I first understood what a transsexual was. But I have always wanted to dress as a woman. I was arrested and put in C.Y.A. for stealing women's clothing out of houses.
>
> When I first understood what the word was, about a year ago. I want to be able to do all the things a woman does.
>
> I want a vagina, and I knew I wanted the surgery before I heard the term. That was about ten months ago. I've wanted to be a woman for as long as I can remember.
>
> I guess I have known from the first time I knew such a thing was possible. About three years. I have always wished I was a woman.

Even at the time of my field research, when the girls had come to see themselves as transsexuals, they were all still engaged in prostitution. There are some transsexuals who do not enter this activity. I have met two of them and have heard of a few others, but they are the exception rather than the rule. By their insistence on dressing as women, they are denied many kinds of jobs, for there are very few places where they will be allowed to work while dressed as women. Identification, at least a Social Security card, is required for a job today, and they do not have identification as females, only as males. About the only kind of work they can get is in a coffeehouse or bar that caters to the transsexual, and these jobs, obviously, are limited. The pay is also very low; the major inducement is that the girls are able to contact possible customers as prostitutes.

This life of prostitution has a decided effect on their entire life-style. It determines what hours they sleep, when they get up, when they hit the streets, and just about every other aspect of their lives. It also has a decided effect on the self-conceptions of the girls.

Some of the girls will come right out and tell the customer that they are really boys. They feel that this is the safest course and saves them from considerable trouble with the "johns," the customers. They will tell the john what they are prepared to do. If this is not satisfactory, the deal is off.

Others will not tell the customer, or "trick," that they are boys. They will try to pass as women. When the customer wants normal intercourse, many of the girls will tell him that they are on their period. Quite a few of the girls wear sanitary napkins to carry this off. Other excuses are that they just had a miscarriage, are pregnant, or just had an operation. Sometimes they will simply tell him that they prefer to "french" or engage in sodomy.

It is amazing how often the girls can fool the tricks, and to do so gives them a vast amount of pleasure, for they feel they have passed the ultimate test of their deception. I asked the girls: "When you have sex with a trick and he does not know that you are a boy, does this make you feel good and more feminine?" From those who engaged in this practice, the answer was an overwhelming yes.

But there is always the danger of discovery and a possible beating. All of the girls have some kind of protection in their rooms, ranging from baseball bats and whips to knives. They also always have the spiked heels of their shoes. Nevertheless, several of the girls have been severely beaten by tricks who discovered they were being fooled.

Whether to tell or not to tell is a question that none of the girls has a hard-and-fast rule about answering. Some will confess at times and try to pass at other times. This is in large measure determined by the trick; if he is drunk or an older person, they are more likely to try to pass. I asked the question: "What do you do with a man who picks you up and thinks you are a girl?" Some of the answers were:

> I don't tell him I'm a girl, but it's easy to deceive them. Tell them you are on your period or just had an abortion. Many customers are just looking for oral copulation. If they will not settle for this, I call off the date.
> I'll tell them that I'm on my period or pregnant. I'll definitely try to fake it out.
> I tell them I'm a boy. That's the best way to avoid trouble. I might not tell them if I had my own breasts.
> I don't let them pick me up thinking I'm a girl. The first thing I do is to ask them if they are a cop. The second is to tell them I'm a boy.
> It depends on the trick. If he's old or drunk, I won't tell him. If he is young and sober, I always tell them that I'm a boy. You can stay out of trouble that way, and the man will not feel cheated later.
> Sometimes I'll tell, and sometimes I won't. It depends on the trick. If I think I can get away with it, I'll try.

The sexual acts themselves also have an effect on the self-concept of the transsexual. Another question I asked was: "During sodomy, do you see yourself as being a woman?"

> I do it on my back and feel like a woman when a man lies on top of me.
> Yes, very much so.

The other answers were all yes except for one girl. This activity can be viewed as another way in which the transsexual reinforces her feminine role.

They are no longer content to imitate. They want to *be*. And they form a very strong conception of themselves as women. They all know that it is a long and difficult road. Many fantasize that they will meet a sugar daddy tomorrow and the operation will be taken care of. They think about the operation so much that several of the girls reported that from time to time they feel that they have already had it.

At the same time, however, the girls suddenly realize that it is a far cry from dressing as a woman to actually being one. Now they pay much closer attention to real women and model themselves after them rather than the queens. But they still aim at very high fashion.

The exchange of information among the girls remains free and frequent. As soon as one hears of some new tip on how to dress or makeup, she will try it immediately and pass it on to the other girls. Until they go on hormones or until the hormones have a chance to effect bodily changes, the girls pad themselves. There are several makes of girdles with built-in pads, and the girls will use these as well as dancing girdles with pads in them. If the girl cannot afford these things, she is shown how to insert padded towels around her hips and buttocks under a regular girdle.

Another device is the *gaff*, a cradle, usually made of canvas or denim, to which elastic loops are attached. The gaff is pulled up tight at the crotch, the effect being to flatten the genitalia and to a degree force the testicles back into the body cavity. The same effect can be obtained with the use of a tight dancing girdle, and some of the girls will use both.

The masculine appearance of their legs, they have found, can be somewhat softened by wearing two pairs of dark nylon stockings. Nylons are also good for padding their bras. After much experimenting with commercial products, the girls think that wadded nylons in the bra most closely approximate the shape and feel of a breast.

The girls are all very self-conscious about the size of their hands and feet; they think people will notice them and read the boy behind the girl. They feel this way even when there is no reason for it. They frequently wear long-sleeved dresses with a ruffle at the wrist to minimize hand size. They learn to wear long fingernails with an iridescent polish. They also have what almost amounts to a fetish about shoes. The higher the heels, the better.

The dresses themselves are usually low-necked with the bosom pushed up to show as much cleavage as possible. Many of the girls apply tape across the breast from the side to the middle to create the appearance of more bosom.

These are tricks of the trade, and they learn them readily from each other, but the girls are learning from other sources as well. Some of them go to one of the doctors in San Francisco who will treat transsexual patients. Others go to the Center for Special Problems, operated by the city of San Francisco. From these people they learn about hormones, which ones to take, and what can be expected from them. More than this, the medical contacts strengthen the feminine self-concept of the girls. They feel that they now have some positive medical sanction to their claims for womanhood, and this feeling commits them more firmly than ever to their career pattern as a transsexual.

The hormone treatment itself brings about some startling bodily changes in a surprisingly short period of time. After about three months of hormones, the girls begin to develop a bust, and there are visible changes in the distribution of body fat. The shoulders become thinner, and the hips and buttocks fill out. Body hair begins to fall off, and facial hair becomes lighter and sparser. Needless to say, these changes are extremely encouraging to the girls. Once they have gone this far, they begin to live almost entirely for the eventual operation. They refer to themselves exclusively as women. The drag queen is now regarded as some sort of a freak: a homosexual who dresses as a woman. The girls are now inordinately concerned with their appearance. Everything possible that can rid them of male characteristics and mannerisms is done. All the female traits are sought and coveted.

The hair becomes a hallmark of femininity, the longer the better. All the girls in my group had a collection of wigs, wiglets, and falls to supplement their natural hair. The hairdos are quite elaborate and frequently garish. But they are the pride and joy of the girls, and nothing will alter the way they wear their hair. One of the most cutting remarks that one girl can make to another is that her hair does not look natural. They have a positive horror of becoming bald.

The girls' most frequent social activity revolves around hair. They are constantly gathering in someone's room to dress a person's hair or to set a wig. They will consume a good deal of pot on these occasions, but nothing to match the consumption of hair spray—the average girl goes through five cans of hair spray in a week. One can will last my wife more than a month.

Thus a large amount of information is exchanged among the girls. They learn from each other, and the newcomer has a ready-made classroom and teacher. Moreover, there were several close friendships among the girls in La Toro, and the amount of social interchange was quite large. It is vital to note, however, that at this, the transsexual stage, the girls have come full circle in the process of socialization. Now, there is no discontinuity between childhood learning and adult learning. Much of what they are learning as self-defined and self-accepted transsexuals is the creation of new ways of combining old response patterns. What the girls are being taught is not at variance with what they were taught as children.

But the self-concept also includes some unpleasant things. Among these is seeing oneself as a whore. Every one of the girls in my sample was a prostitute. In fact, the hotel we shared was simply a whorehouse. This is an identity that the girls are conscious of and concerned about. All, without exception, wanted to get out of hustling. I asked the girls the questions, "How do you feel about hustling?", and, "Why do you do it?" The responses were so much of a piece that they can be distilled into the answers, "I hate it," and "I have to have money to eat, and have a place to stay, and money for makeup and clothes." The fact that the young, jobless transsexual indulges in prostitution can be seen as almost a foregone conclusion.

They view their customers with a great deal of disdain and confess to getting little if any pleasure out of these acts. They are most anxious to find some way out of their situation. I asked the girls if they would quit hustling if they could get a job in a place where they could work and dress as women. The answer was a unanimous yes. I then asked them why. Some of the answers were:

> I'm not happy as a prostitute. I don't enjoy it, and I'm scared all the time.
> Because this is no life. You get away with so much, but it catches up with you.
> This is no life. I want to make something out of my life.
> I hate this life.

So their self-concept in this sense is a very realistic one. In another sense it is not quite so realistic. They insist that they are women except, as one put it, for the "excess baggage" between their legs. They demand to be treated as women and most certainly treat each other as such. When they meet, the most frequent expression is, "Hello, girl." They do everything they can to reinforce each other and themselves.

The rub, of course, is that transsexuals do not only want to act and dress as women, they want to be able to perform sexually as women. I asked them what kind of a life they thought they would lead after the operation, and sixteen of the seventeen answered that they wanted to get married and adopt children.

One of the girls has made it, and in almost the classical style, the way the girls dream it will happen. Kristi met a wealthy man who became interested in her, and he financed the operation, which was performed in an undisclosed New York hospital. The girl is most reluctant to talk about many aspects of the operation, but I have talked to her by telephone and have been able to get some little information from her. Kristi told me that the operation lasted for about three hours. She also had operations on her nose and Adam's apple. The total cost for the procedures and living expenses was $7,000. She reports that after a period of only three weeks, she was able to have intercourse. This is at variance with the medical evidence cited earlier, but I have no reason to disbelieve her. She reports that she is perfectly happy now, that she is dating steadily and soon expects to become engaged.

## Feminine Stage

Twelve of the girls have gone on from the transsexual to what I would call a *feminine* stage. That is, the girls want to live the lives of normal housewives or working girls. They have given up prostitution and have found jobs of some sort or are looking for them.

A great deal of this change must be attributed to the hormones they have been taking. In the first place, the female hormones have reduced their normal male sex drive, a change that Benjamin refers to as *chemical castration*. They have become softer in manner and actions. I do not mean to imply that they are entirely on the side of the angels. They still smoke pot and have their one-night-stands. But there is much less drinking, and the use of speed drugs and glue has disappeared.

It is at this stage they come out as women, as they have previously done as queens and transsexuals. They are, of course, still transsexuals. But their self-image has changed. They want to live a normal middle-class life. They no longer revel in being able to turn men's heads. They want to live and pass undetected as women, and they have modified their behavior in order to be able to do it.

This was far from easy, even with the hormones. All of the girls, as we have seen, loathed their lives as prostitutes, but few have been offered any other way of making a living. Moreover, at their level of skill and education, few of the girls could hope to earn much more than $1.35 an hour for a thirty-two-hour week. There is not one of them who could not make this in one night of hustling. Nevertheless, when a few jobs opened up at San Francisco's Economic Opportunity Council all the vacancies were filled. Several of the girls worked on a volunteer basis at the Central City Multi-Service Center so that they would be in line for the next jobs when and if they come.

Two girls were employed by the Neighborhood Youth Corps at the same salary. Two others were trained at the John Adams High School under the Manpower Development Retraining Act. For this they received $50 a week and transportation costs, yet the competition to get into this thirty-six-week training course was very keen. So far two of the girls have been graduated. One works as a cashier in the box office of a theater. The other is the manager of a small hotel. Also, one of the girls from the Central City Project has been promoted to a staff position.

In the work atmosphere of the office, the girls have to learn to be in the company of normal women. At first they are quite shy about these contacts. But as time goes by, they begin to ask questions about how they can best get along and get ahead. The answers that the women give to these questions have a lasting effect on the girls. They also watch carefully what rewards and punishments are accorded to the women because of their behavior. They are especially attentive to the transsexual who has made the successful transition to the ordinary world. The girls observe to see what she does to pass successfully.

Beyond the office, too, the girls actively seek out the company of women, something they avoided in the past. Through my wife and myself they have met several of our friends. They keep in very close contact and come to visit us frequently. They are trying to find out how a normal girl lives, and their appetite for learning is very acute.

This is not to say that everything is beer and skittles for the girls, and that they have it made. At the rate they are being paid, they can just about live, to say nothing of putting anything away for the operation. But there is one big difference: hope. And with that hope comes patience and the facing up to the realities of life.

They no longer talk as if they were going to have the operation next week. They realize now that when all costs are considered—the operation itself, transportation and living expenses for the six-month follow-up period—they are talking about $8,000. So they wait in the belief that the operation will soon be openly offered in the San Francisco Bay Area.

They act entirely differently now. They no longer have to slink along the streets, afraid of both police and customers. They now have a stronger sense of identification. They regard themselves as a minority and want the same rights other minority groups want. The girls have formed a club, C.O.G. (Correction of Gender), and have weekly meetings to discuss their problems. The girls realistically do not expect to change the world. But they would like to have some provisions made for people like themselves. And they are making some progress. At a COG meeting in 1968 there were four police captains present, as well as the police commissioner of Saint Louis, and the girls tried to get some sort of dialogue going. They succeeded, and what they also got was an agreement from the police that officers would not use the charge of impersonation anymore. If a criminal charge were being lodged, such as prostitution, the impersonation charge would have to be included, the police said. But at least the girls were free to walk the streets of the city, and not with the former tacit understanding with the police that they stay in the Tenderloin. Another result of this meeting was that the police captains agreed to inform their men that the girls were to be allowed to use the ladies' rooms in public places. All in all, then, the position of the girls vis-à-vis the law has greatly improved. Such a meeting would have been out of the question in any of the previous stages. It is only now that the girls have matured and gained self-respect that they have the self-confidence to meet with the police. This new attitude is indicative of a similar change in their self-concepts. They now see themselves as law-abiding citizens who are entitled to their rights.

# 10

# Stripper Morality

Marilyn Salutin

The corner of Dundas and Spadina, at the center of downtown Toronto's garment district, is one of the dirtiest areas of town: a conglomeration of hot, smoky dress-and-pants factories, wholesale outlets, delicatessens, bargain houses, bookie joints, noise, dust, cigarette stands, and outdoor food markets run by Portuguese, Chinese, Italian, and Jewish shop owners. Showroom models and working women walk past cheap rooming houses and beer parlors. Tempers are apt to explode easily here. In the summertime, soft music flows out of the upper-story apartments on top of the stores.

Dundas and Spadina is just the sort of area where one might expect to find a burlesque show. Conventional standards of middle-class public morality are not always in play here. And, of course, the spectacle of nude women simulating intercourse and orgasm on-stage does not precisely conform to conventional mores either. Thus, there is a nice social symbiosis here between street and theater. On the street the casual passerby is not expected to adhere to any particular standard of dress or behavior, as would be the case, for example, in the highly stratified social landscape of the financial district. On the contrary, Dundas and Spadina is a salad of social identities and personality types. Here the individual can lose himself, so to speak, in the street. He can slip into the burlesque during the afternoon without being given a second glance by other passersby. His presence in the theater will go unnoticed, and for $2.25 he can sit there, if he so desires, from 1:30 in the afternoon until late in the evening [1971].

The theater itself is called the Victory, and it stands across from Switzer's, the most famous delicatessen in Toronto, where the strippers traditionally grab their evening meal before they go onstage and frontstage. For the passerby, the Victory's big neon lights and bold posters promise sexual delights. Huge blowups of famous strippers such as Sexotica, Sintana, Busty Haze, and SintoLation—posed in the traditional floor positions or bumping and grinding with larger-than-life red lips and lunging torsos—entice the audience while it is still on the street. For the linear minded there are captions: "One Hot Woman," "Sexual Delights Never Before Experienced," "Bare-Breasted Beauties," and "We Go All the Way—No Strings Attached." It is the big sex thrill in a world where, as Norman Mailer says, sex is sin and sin is paradise. Sin is also good for business at the Victory.

From the bright marquee to the little old man taking tickets and promising you that you have not missed too much if you come late, the Victory might appear a haunting relic of the days of Broadway and working-class vaudeville. Inside, the stage is flanked by two statuesque cardboard strippers who stand like pillars setting off an altar. Perhaps they are guarding the sacred ritual of the burlesque from contamination or invasion by outsiders, or perhaps they are the fading afterimages of the time when Gypsy Rose Lee might have come down the aisle to wow the audience with her bumps and grinds.

**No Lilies and Roses**

But this is not the scene for Gypsy Rose Lee or even for Lili St. Cyr. It is the scene for some would-be Gypsy Rose Lee who does not have what it takes, or for some Gypsy Rose Lee who made it several years ago and has had it, or for some Gypsy Rose Lee who just never made it at all.

Because this is not Las Vegas with its gorgeous show girls, nor New York and Paris with their Copas and Lidos—it is Toronto, and it is the Victory at Dundas and Spadina, and I call it *poor man's burlesque*. Still, poor man's burlesque is probably better than no burlesque at all, and it certainly is for the thousands of men in Canada and the Midwest who go to hundreds of other Victorys in search of a kind of "satisfaction."

At any rate, the Victory is a fag end of the day gone by, of which some still say "when men were men," because the Victory is rundown and old, with sleazy seats and cigarette smoking, hunched-up, shabbily dressed men waiting, it seems, for equally jaded strippers to come out and turn them on with their make-believe sexuality, learned perhaps in Libby Jones's book on *How to Striptease*.

Burlesque in Toronto today means the nude dramatization of the sex act, including the orgasm. As such, it is of course, considered an affront to the public definition of sexual morality. It is considered obscene.

In our society the spoken or unspoken reference point of all discussions of sexual morality is the animal. Sexually man is not supposed to be an animal—he is expected to attach social meanings and purposes to the sex act. Sex is associated with marriage and procreation, the preservation of the family system and is, in essence, useful for the maintenance of the ritual ordering of our way of life. Sex is usually exchanged by women for the financial security and honorable social status of marriage. Sex is also shrouded in romantic mystique. An aura of sacredness and privacy is associated with it, as are emotion and affection between the two love partners.

Now, obviously, burlesque destroys all that. It is an exhibition of sheer animalistic physical sex for the sake of sex. This is offensive. It is offensive to lovers because they want to feel secure with each other, with the feeling that they are wanted and needed. It is offensive to women because women like to feel that they are usually more admired by men (and by other women) if they do not appear too eager to engage in sex. Many women, as Fred Davis has noted, feign contempt, or really feel contempt for sex, unless the submission of their bodies to their husbands brings them some material rewards. Strippers demand nothing like this from their public. They demand to be accepted as erotic people, sexual experts who can meet the needs of all men, who can excite all men no matter who they are, where they are from or where they are at. The public nudity, the portrayal of orgasm and masturbation, the open and public enjoyment of eroticism is something most people have been trained to condemn, or even to fear. It represents a devaluation of their sex values and a threat to what Herbert Marcuse has called the *repressive nature of Western civilization's sexual order.*

Strippers are viewed as "bad," then, because they strip away all social decorum with their clothes. They taunt the public with their own mores by teasing them and turning them on. The privacy of the sex act disappears as does its personal quality, that is, the physical touching of one another and the sharing of affection. In burlesque theater and in the strip bars, open to the public for the price of admission, the sex act is made a packaged commercial deal, one of a variety of sex deals offered in a large sex market aimed at exploiting the contingencies in our society that make it difficult for some people to get the sex they think they want.

One of the most important aspects of burlesque is that sex is

made impersonal. It has to be impersonal because it has to be available to large numbers of people at the same time, and it has to offer
anonymity to the participants, to the audiences and performers. It
has to be impersonal because, as a salable, exchangeable commodity, it confers some semblance of normalcy and stability to the occasion. And it has to be impersonal because, when the participants
do not know one another and yet understand each other's needs, the
deviant act becomes much easier to perform, more acceptable; it
becomes something that can be engaged in and then forgotten as
soon as it is over.

Burlesque is also made more acceptable by going under the guise
of "entertainment" and "show business." But its function as a sex
outlet is there for all to see who will see. Says one stripper in this
respect, "I am really a professional cockteaser." She would not say
this to a stranger, however, and most of the performers stick (at
least in public) to the show-business definition of burlesque. Audiences do not; they are more likely to see burlesque for what it is and
to treat it as such. This is because the performers have more at stake
in trying to protect their identities and pass themselves off as normal. For they are considered to be the initiators of the deviant act
and are therefore regarded with more social contempt. The audience
is merely the witness.

Moreover, audiences have more protection from social condemnation in that they are fully clothed whereas the strippers are naked.
They can make all kinds of excuses to rationalize their attendance.
Even if they masturbate in their seats, which some do, members of
the audience are not nude and cannot be accused of public exhibitionism, which, of course, the strippers are accused of all the time.
Until very recently, indeed, the accusation was often legal: strippers
were subject to arrest if they showed their pubic hair or "flashed."
Now they "show everything" with "no strings attached," but the
tolerance of the law has scarcely improved their esteem in the eyes
of the public. (For audiences, the rules are clearly defined: they are
not to undress or go onstage with the strippers; if they do, they can
be arrested.)

Ned Polsky would call burlesque *hard-core pornography done to
music and designed to stimulate masturbation in the audience.* It
does this, as well as act as an occasion for public voyeurism. In
keeping with these functions, strippers learn and professionalize
special techniques and skills. They adopt gimmicks such as wearing
a particular costume or do something unusual such as eating fire
while they strip. They learn how to move their bodies so that the act
becomes a kind of visual sexual extravaganza, available to everyone

there. Just to make sure, strippers often ask the audience if they can see what is going on and point to whatever part of the body they want to "feature" for that moment.

The girls, needless to say, show no inhibitions or shyness or modesty about the body or about sex generally. But at the same time, they show no affection or emotional response toward the audience either. Instead, there is either a blank look, a wink, or contempt expressed on the face of the stripper. If strippers choose a face that is shy, it is because they want their "floor work" (crouching or lying on the floor and simulating intercourse) and "dirty work" (flashing and spreading their legs) to remind the audience of demure girls. They feel this is more erotic; it is supposed to be like seeing the girl next door up there stripping.

Burlesque serves a market mainly composed of men from all walks of life. To the strippers they become indistinguishable from one another. They are seen as a collectivity representing all men. Yet they play to lonely men, frustrated men, happy men, and unhappy men. They play to men who go there a lot and to men who may go once a year or once a month. They are businessmen, traveling salesmen, high-school and university students, office clerks, professionals, immigrants, truck drivers, and transients. They are married and unmarried, and sometimes men and women go together.

There are five shows daily at the Victory every day of the week, and almost every performance is filled. Men pour in during the day, some on lunch breaks, some on out-of-town business, and some just come in off the street. Groups of students bring their sandwiches and drinks and eat their lunch while they watch the show. They laugh and heckle the stripper and reach out for her as she comes down the ramp. They never take their eyes off her whether they are laughing at her or with her. Businessmen, well dressed, hurry in and sit either alone or with one or two others. After the show, they rush out and go back to work. Others, such as transients and immigrants, stop and stare at the photographs of strippers in the lobby on their way out. They walk slowly and stand outside for long periods of time, go away and come back for a later show or for the show the next day.

Strippers note the full houses, the cheering and jeering and excitement in the audience. It tells them that no matter what the public says about them, they are needed. This is gratifying to them. Equally so, perhaps, is the knowledge, if they have it, that burlesque today is a take-off and put-down of most people's sexual fantasies, a burlesque in the true sense, in which the conventional sexual imagination is mirrored and mocked in the act.

## Strippers: Frontstage and Backstage

Like all stigmatized people, strippers, offstage, try to negotiate a more favorable self-image. Briefly, they do this in two ways. First of all, they try to upgrade their occupation in a redefinition of stripping that says it is socially useful, constructive, good, and generally all right to do. Second, strippers conceal backstage information about their own personal lives that would label them as sexual deviants if known publicly. Their public face is designed to demonstrate that they are sexually normal and therefore moral, and that they are really entertainers, that stripping and sex shows in general are true forms of entertainment that require an artistic talent and openness and honesty about sexual matters. When strippers claim to be "erotics" or "dancers," they are giving the job a face-lifting. But they are not denying the fact that they are strippers, merely describing what they do and who they are in a more flattering way, in a way to save themselves embarrassment, shame, and degradation. Still, replacing the negative definition of stripping with a positive one does replace the negative definition of themselves with a more positive one. It says they are engaged in a moral enterprise and therefore must be regarded as moral people.

Strippers' self-concepts are integrally tied up with what they do onstage. Their definition of stripping as good, legitimate entertainment is based largely on the fact that they never saw themselves as anything but strippers, that is, they never were or intended to become real singers, dancers, or Broadway stars. They admire famous strippers like Oneida Mann, Babette, and Amber Haze. Offstage, they talk about them—about their acts and the problems they have in their personal lives. Strippers feel complimented and flattered if one tells them they were good onstage and especially if you tell them they remind you of a famous stripper. For example, one girl remarked: "When they see me and say it looks like her [Oneida Mann], I know I'm doing good." They are proud if you refer to them in a flattering way about being part of a good show doing good work, meaning highly sexy, erotic work. Their vested interest is in the job as it stands, and it is this they are trying to protect in their various encounters with members of the public.

Strippers are realistic in their interpretation of their job and admit they are "with it" or "in it," or at least are "trying to make the most of it." Because strippers never envisioned themselves as show-business stars in the normal sense of the word, they naturally do not fall back on lost dreams in the ways, for example, that their fellow troupers, the comics, do. Whatever lost dreams strippers have in their private worlds are not tied up with ambitions in show business but with ambitions in life as normal women. This is why their stress is on the morality of sex shows in the sense that they are justified in doing them because they are "socially useful."

In short, strippers take the stance of a deviant minority forming and adhering to subcultural values of its own. This means, among other things, that they attempt to normalize or neutralize their roles by downgrading the public, condemning them for being hypocrites, ignorant, and dishonest. Strippers blame many of their problems on the repressive nature of the public sexual order, especially as represented by the police. In the strip bars, for example, strippers resent the police coming in and busting hookers. They are afraid they, too, will be arrested, even if they are just stripping, or that the cops will find dope of one kind or another on them. One stripper declared: "I hate these guys. . . . I can smell them whenever they're near, and I hate them. . . . Why don't they just go away and leave us alone. They could never understand the problems of people." How can the public condemn what it has created a need for and that it supports not just privately in ideology but openly with money (admission fees)? Skid rowers and prostitutes also blame the public for their problems in an attempt to normalize their role. Said one stripper: "We just want to be left alone without any hassles with the public. We aren't trying to make them be like us, just understand us and let us go our way . . . leave us alone."

The public face of strippers should be seen as a cooling-out trick. It is a difficult stance to take because it involves the denial of social attitudes that form the basis of real social facts. For example, strippers must negate or deny that sex for the sake of sex is bad or immoral behavior in public. They must also negate the public typification that all strippers are whores. Strippers, consequently, must be seen as very complex personalities, not simply the middle-class stereotypes of them. What they do in their relations with others is difficult; they are constantly engaged in conscious manipulation of behavior, in concealing and revealing what they deem to be situationally proper and what they believe will bring them the most respect. They are always involved in what Erving Goffman calls *strategic interaction*—putting their best foot forward.

To illustrate how complicated these self-cooling-out or "passing" devices are, think of what strippers, in dealing with outsiders, have to conceal about themselves: their often ambivalent sexual activities, the kinds of men they become emotionally involved with and the exact nature of their heterosexual relationships, why they went into stripping in the first place, what other work they do that is directly related to stripping, what they might be getting out of stripping in addition to money.

Strippers can never reveal, offstage or on, if they want to keep their self-esteem, that they are not normal women—very sexy and desirable women to be sure, but normal nonetheless. Any kind of contrary information can be a threat to their posited conception of who they really are. Little things, such as saying who they live with and what their husband does for a living, become obstacles in interaction with others who are not part of their subculture, either because they fully support their husband or lover by stripping and prostitution or because they are living with a girl in a lesbian relationship. Their habits, and their pasts, have to be concealed from strangers because it might incriminate them. Strippers often invent elaborate tales about why they began stripping as an excuse for their participation in the show. One girl said she is using stripping as a means to get to Hollywood where she wants to become a movie star in the style of Jayne Mansfield. The idea is that they are doing it temporarily as a means to an end. Another girl said she was "tricked into it" and really thought she was going to be a "go-go girl to back up the Feature [an out-of-town star]." Others claim to be doing it just "temporarily" until they earn enough money to go into business. One girl said she wants to buy a flower shop in Chicago where she was born. She also says she wants to raise a family with her husband and that she is only killing time and making lots of money until that day. In reality, the girl is a lesbian who is constantly searching for a female lover in every city she visits, claiming: "I'm just not satisfied with my husband. . . . I need a girl, one who is nice . . .anyone can satisfy you sexually, but I need somebody I can talk to and have a deep emotional relationship with, just like most women want from men." All this came out after a long talk in which, for the first hour or so, she tried to create the impression that, "like every other girl," she loved her husband and desired no other kind of sexual or emotional relationship. Another girl claimed she was stripping only until she saved enough money to go into the rooming-house business. She asserted that her husband loved her to strip "because he knows he can really have me when all those other guys want me but can't get me."

Strippers place a high value on money and believe it should be made in the easiest way possible—their way. But they do not hold on to it for very long. One reason is that they usually are totally supporting the men they live with. Some are also supporting children. They feel a sense of power handing over money to their men because

they enjoy the financial dependency, but at the same time they are
being exploited because the men usually spend most of the money
on themselves. One night I listened for hours as a stripper and her
husband argued over how he had spent her paycheck. He claimed he
had bought a radio and some liquor. The girl was upset because she
told me she was broke and that she could not control the way he
spent the money. She wanted to buy a new costume but would not
be able to now, and she also owed her agent some money but could
not pay him. Her husband tried to joke about it to cool her off. He
asked her what she would do without him. She laughed and smiled
and explained that they were both bad with money, that they could
not save a dime, owed money all over town, and lived from day to
day never knowing what tomorrow would bring. She also told me
she spends some of her money on pills she takes to "keep her going"
and that the main reason she dislikes being so broke all the time is
that it prevents them from taking off whenever they like (traveling)
and that money is a constant source of argument between them.

And so they say that stripping is fun and that they are sexy "artistic" performers who are better than most women because they are
more honest and direct about sex. They also take the following
lines, in general—that they are happily married and look forward to
the day when they can quit and "settle down with a family," or that
the kind of men they go with admire them because they are sexy and
actually prefer them to other women. That they are financially or
emotionally exploited in their personal relationships with men, or
that men go with them for any reasons other than their being sexually desirable, these facts are hidden. Like most other people, they
also try to create the impression in public that their living arrangements are normal. They are apt to say, for example, that they are
married rather than that they are "living common-law," which is
usually the truth. Such are the pressures of conventional morality
on these women.

Strippers do not end up stripping because they have skidded
downward in their careers as have the burlesque comics. They chose
stripping as an occupation, and their decision was based upon what
they knew of the world. The experiences they have had in the world
formulate themselves into a common-sense rationality of how best
to put their bodies to use, how best to live their lives. In their own
view, they have not fallen in status. After all, one alternative would
have been full-time prostitution, which has neither the social status
nor the economic payoff (the prostitutes they know only get $5 to
$10 a trick in Toronto).

To strippers, stripping is a good thing, and they do it as naturally as stenographers type. It earns them a minimum of $165 a week and offers what they call an "easy life." They can sleep late each day, watch soap operas on television, get dressed, go to the theater, get into their costumes, sit around backstage until it is time to work, work, repeat the same process four or five times a day, and pick up their pay at the end of the week. If they work steadily, they earn a fair amount of money.

What strippers do not mention, initially, is that stripping also facilitates lesbian relationships. This is backstage information, the kind that would label them as "unnatural." Backstage, however, they joke around a lot about sex and show a playful affection for each other by touching each others' bodies. One stripper explained that the constant exposure and manipulation of the body and the body contact backstage are often the beginning of lesbian experiences for strippers. They maintain it is very easy for a stripper to become a lesbian because it is "all around." If you add to this a contemptuous feeling for the public, especially the "johns" and "marks" in the audience, lesbianism, as an occupational contingency, is quite understandable. Contempt for men is expressed in terms like this: "All they need is a cute ass and a pair of tits wiggling." Strippers themselves say that more than seventy-five percent of their colleagues are lesbians and that often their first experiences came as a direct result of stripping—which is not to deny that some lesbian strippers are also married to men and continue to have sex with them. One stripper explained this situation like this: "It's quite simple, you see . . . I'll go out and meet a girl and go home with her—that's all—and he'll do whatever he likes . . . he knows I'll come back again . . . he doesn't mind if I pick up a girl . . . he knows what I am . . . he sometimes picks up women . . . but we have a companionship, a kind of love." Nevertheless, it is common for strippers to be bisexual or lesbian, but not straight.

Another occupational contingency of stripping is prostitution. And yet, strippers very carefully, in public, differentiate themselves from full-time prostitutes, whom they perceive to be of a lower social status. They stress the fact that they strip and do not hook for a living, whereas prostitutes just hook. If they do hook, they make sure one understands that it is "just once in a while" and for a very good reason, like "eating and putting a roof over my head."

**Once You Start . . .**

Nevertheless, and for all that they take pains to deny it, prostitution is almost an inevitable consequence of stripping. One woman remarked, for example: "My girl friend just hooks because she is afraid to do what I do in public, and if I was afraid to strip, I'd be doing it all the time, too [hooking]." In my sample, most of the strippers hooked part time to supplement their income. They also performed at stags. They often get their customers in strip bars. Having a career in commercial sex makes prostitution easy to do, even if one does not really want to do it. For one thing, the general public regards all strippers as prostitutes anyway, and for another, strippers are always being propositioned. One stripper recalled: It's so easy to start hooking for some guy. . . . You think, well I really could use the extra money . . . but once you start, you never stop. And most of them never even save any of this money." Nevertheless, strippers much resent being labeled a prostitute. One woman said: "I hate clubs, especially small ones in northern Ontario. They'll treat you like a prostitute whether you are one or not just because most of them have been who were here before you. . . . When you finish the show, you never know what drunk is going to be waiting for you at the top of the stairs."

The strippers in my sample are poorly educated. The average level of education of twenty strippers in this sample was grade seven or eight. They have no office skills or any other kind of talent suitable for an urban labor market. They cannot sing, dance, or act nor could they ever. They do not have bodies suitable for modeling; they are too large, in all dimensions. (Amber Haze, a current favorite, measures fifty-two inches around the bust.) Nearly all said they left home at an early age—by the time they were fourteen- or fifteen-years old. They learned early that they had to support themselves. Most had what they described as unhappy home lives, either because they did not get along with their parents or because they had too much work to do at home or because their sexual experiences upset their parents. For example, one girl said she had to leave home because she was a lesbian and her mother wanted to have her committed to a mental hospital because of it.

Most developed early, that is, their bodies matured early. Sexuality (their own and others') came early, too, often in a violent form such as being beaten or raped; and for as long as they can remember, their bodies were objects of talk, staring, and sexual passes. They were used to being cheered and jeered as they walked down the street. They were used to being whistled at and pawed over. Yet even as they were often humiliated by the nature of some of their sexual experiences, most strippers, by the time they reached their late teens, had come to the conclusion that the body, because it attracts men, can bring in money. This knowledge, plus the desire for attention, plus the exhibitionist tendencies they acknowledge, led them to stripping. One girl claimed, for example: "I like it because to me it seems glamorous, and I like attention. I'm an exhibitionist really." They were also encouraged by people they knew—other girls who were doing it and boyfriends who urged them to do it.

Strippers like stripping because it makes them feel important, especially when the audience claps and cheers. They feel exhilarated. They also like the money. By the time they are "in the life," they have developed an exploitative attitude to men and people in general. They become harder and tougher in their attitudes to men, money, and sex. However, they do not feel badly about this, merely smart, one-up on the world. Said one girl, "If I don't exploit them, they'll do it to me." Stripping becomes easy to do with this kind of attitude.

Being paid to display their bodies in public means they are beating the world at its own game. It is no more immoral in their eyes than getting a man to marry them in exchange for intercourse. Indeed, in their own eyes or at least in the face they turn to the public, they are no different from other women with regard to sex, just more blunt, honest, open, and direct. Other women are hypocrites; they may not strip for money, but they ask a price just the same. It is usually marriage, but it could be just a dinner. Strippers also claim all women are exhibitionists. Said one stripper, "All women are in spirit exhibitionists and prostitutes." Said another, "All women are exhibitionists . . . haven't you ever seen a woman wearing an extra-tight sweater?"

Both onstage and off, strippers like to be referred to as erotic, sexy people, professional sex experts, skilled in ways others are not. They pride themselves on their knowledge of eroticism, and unlike the average woman, they are not ashamed of their sexual knowledge and expertise. In fact, strippers often say that one of their special roles is to teach people about sex, for most people, especially women and most men in their audiences, do not know anything about it. For example, they say college students come to the Victory to learn about sex in a sort of initiation ritual. One stripper told me: "They're still set behind the ears and embarrassed. We have to show them a few things."

The line they take is that society needs strippers in the same way it needs teachers or doctors. Without sex shows, men would be lonely and frustrated and lacking a sex outlet. Thus, their work is actually as good and helpful and socially constructive as any other kind of work, and because the work is useful, they are moral. This, of course, is a "passing" device and a cooling-out trick. Another line is their claim that strip shows are really good entertainment, as are all sex shows from live stag exhibitions to stag movies. One stripper performs at stags with her husband. He encourages it, and they both maintain it is good entertainment as well as a good way to make money.

The line that "anybody will do anything for a buck anyway" is perhaps their principal legitimizing tactic. They feel generally that any dealings they have with members of the public should be of a contractual nature—and that they should be paid for whatever they do. One girl said, "I'm being stared at anyway, so why not be paid for it?" Said another, "I don't care what they say or do to me as long as they pay." They should be paid, then, for just being around, for being sexy. They should be paid also for showing people the "truth" when they strip, which is doing everybody a favor. The "truth" here means the truth about sex—actually, the truth about life.

## Who Profits

At the same time, however, strippers also maintain that they really are not being so terribly exploitative, especially if one remembers that "all men are sexually frustrated and in need of their services," as one of them put it. They claim that if they did not exploit the public's need for a sex outlet, that is, making a profit on it, men would be making a profit on them—that is, they, as women, would be taken advantage of by men. They would be touched, screwed, and not paid.

Strippers, offstage, also argue that stripping is just a job like any other and that what they do is done in a routinized way (this despite their open acknowledgment that they are exhibitionists). One stripper told me:

> I don't think anything about stripping. . . . I don't stand nude. . . . I always wear a G-string even though it looks like I don't. I do my act as a routine, automatically . . . sometimes I don't even see the audience. . . . I can black them out . . . lots of girls do that. . . . We just do our act and do it again the next night . . . but other girls get orgasms right on the stage. . . . They get a charge out of turning the guys on right there in the club or in the theater. . . . I saw a guy finish once right in this girl's face, and she thought it was cute.

Needless to say, if a stripper does get a sexual thrill out of performing, she would not say so in public; it would make her seem unnatural, and that would be to contradict all the legitimizing lines she

may have developed. By the same token, strippers never admit that
their boyfriends are often pimps or addicts who would push them
onto the street if they did not strip.

Backstage, however, these facts do emerge. They also reveal that
they are constantly broke, their money being spent mainly on
liquor, debts, drugs, traveling expenses, costumes, props, as well as
the usual rent and food. Other backstage information would include
the fact that in certain centers, strippers are controlled by the
Mafia, and they must turn tricks in the bars in order to keep their
jobs. Strippers complain about insults from drunk customers, unwanted propositions, depression due to fights with theater owners,
club managers, and other strippers, being lied to, cheated and stolen
from. Bosses are divided into categories of "nice guys" and "bad
guys" according to how they treat them. By the same token, audiences are divided into "nice squares" and "bad squares" according
to how they react to their performances—as one girl put it, "according to how hypocritical they are about their need for us." Loneliness
is also a constant problem, whether traveling the circuit including
New York, Chicago, Montreal, Toronto, Los Angeles, and San
Francisco or traveling from one small town in Ontario to another
(Peterborough, Timmins, Sudbury). One girl claims she "carries
her husband with her everywhere she goes" just to avoid this loneliness. Sometimes they make friends when they visit a town, but they
become depressed because they know the chances of ever seeing the
person again are slim. So they talk of writing leters to one another
and express the hope they will meet again sometime.

But it is what happens to old strippers, or, more precisely, what
the aging process does to them, that is perhaps their worst problem.
They fear getting old, and if they are getting old, they will work desperately to create the illusion that their bodies are firm and still
sexy. Growing old is an incontrovertible denial of a future in terms
of the lines they adhere to, and even the youngest stripper is aware
of this. What happens to older strippers is that they cannot get by
anymore with the "sex is fun and I am very sexy" line, and as a
result, they have to "spread themselves" more and act as the butt of
the MC's dirty jokes. In fact, they become the joke itself, the source
of all the dirty humor. They are no longer very persuasive sexually,
but they are still usable, and perhaps this is the biggest difference
between them and the younger women. Their usability is what keeps
them working, not their desirability, and this is a difficult thing to
rationalize to anybody, especially to themselves.

Often older strippers become alcoholics and do what they do
drunk. Younger strippers know about this, too, but they do not

seem to have any way of stopping it from happening to them. They have no plans for the future. They live from day to day and plan only far enough ahead for tomorrow.

As suggested earlier, life to a stripper is a game of one-upmanship where everyone has the potential to be had. To be a winner, one must be on top of the situation at all times, whether onstage or off. If one lets one's defenses down, she becomes vulnerable to attack and shame.

When audiences clap for them at the end of performances at the Victory, strippers really feel they have put one over. They are being paid and applauded, but they have given nothing of themselves in return. Even their nudity is neutralized by becoming just a part of the job. Winning at the end of a performance lets them see themselves as successful not only as strippers but also in life itself.

Strippers expect one another to adhere to the same line in normal interaction with the public. They attempt to reinforce their definition of the situation within the ranks of their own group. They need solidarity in order for the definition of their situation to have any kind of social reality. For this reason, strippers rarely downgrade each other in the presence of strangers. Only if a stripper disobeys norms does she come under public attack. A stripper who flashes too easily, who does not demand a higher price for doing it, is immensely disliked by the others and is not considered to be a "good stripper," meaning a loyal member of the group. They also avoid and dislike strippers who act superior, who are snobs. One stripper commented about another: "She'll just have to learn she's no better than we are."

Newcomers are initiated into the business by being handed down practical advice. They are taught how to handle verbal insults while they perform. They are taught what to say if they spot a man masturbating and they do not dig it too much: "Put it away and save it for later," and, "Do up your pants; I'm being paid, and you're not" are common methods of turning the guy off. Other tricks they learn are how to handle police by lying to them or "being nice to them when they're around"; the same holds true for any outsider. These protective tricks are taken for granted and are part of their normal daily behavior. It is normal to offer the following kind of advice to one another or a novice: "Think with your head, not with your pants ... keep a cool head, or you'll get sucked under and never get out. They'll own you." Only most of them are in it for life regardless.

Sexual standards are not generally imposed on one another. A person's sexual status is regarded as a private matter, nobody's concern but that particular individual's. As one girl put it: "Each to his own . . . they leave me alone, so I leave them alone. . . . They know it if you're really straight, so they leave you alone usually . . . that's the way it is." Another girl said: "I only initiate a girl if she approaches me first, and most of them like it after, especially after doing a show." However, there are, of course, exceptions. For example, some straight strippers resent playing the same bill as a well-known lesbian and will try to get out of the job or else ask for a separate dressing room. Also, some lesbians disobey the norm and try to initiate an affair with a novice.

When strippers do make friends, they put themselves out for them because friends are not easy to find in this world. If they hit it off, they will try to get each other jobs, teach each other routines, loan props and costumes, sometimes loan money for drinks, socialize in bars after work, go to parties together, protect each other from the police and other outsiders, visit each other at home, introduce each other to their men, and go out in mixed groups. But perhaps most important, they will sit and listen to each other's problems with sympathy, because after all, one girl's troubles are those of every other.

Strippers do not downgrade comics but accept them as part of the show, though not too important a part. They joke around with them after work and go out for drinks with them. They also treat them as confidants, telling them all their troubles, hopes, and dreams.

With respect to the master of ceremonies, strippers like to have him on their side, especially if they are having a fight with another girl. But the MC can also be the cause of friction. If he shows more attention to one stripper than another, the rejected one will feel jealous and malicious. For example, in one of the strip bars in Toronto, the MC always gave a more elaborate introduction to one stripper than to the other. He also joked more with her offstage. His favorite was black, the other white. One evening, the white stripper whispered across the table: "He always spends more time with her than me. . . . I don't know. I guess he just prefers niggers. . . . Oh, I guess that isn't nice, is it? Well, it's the truth anyway, isn't it?" She then began to laugh about her whispered confession of jealousy.

In essence, their everyday world is one of what to do next, after the show, before the next show, what to drink, where to drink it, when to go home, writing to one another, when they might see each other again—about the "old days of burlesque," how good they are onstage, about "14-year-old boys" (college students) who are still wet behind the ears, about owing the agent, a "bum," a fin, about an old friend accused by the police of this or that, in one case murder—

and teasing each other about picking up other men or women and about who will pay for the drinks this time.

A stripper's persona can be thought of as a sexual extravaganza—a way of being and living in the world as a sexual creature, larger than life. It is for this reason they often appear onstage and off as caricatures of female sexuality. Perhaps the silicone injections most of them have had done to their breasts best illustrate this point. Their breasts are made so large that whether they want to be "inplay" offstage or not, it would be difficult to disguise the nature of their work. This might be an additional reason for playing up, offstage, the artfulness of stripping until it takes on a socially significant meaning. However, the attention they pay to the body, to their costumes, facial expressions, makeup, and so forth is all a part of a ritual they go through every day to help make the performance more of a show. It also makes it more unreal and impersonal. It is a kind of sexual circus.

This almost parodic quality in the face they turn to the world perhaps explains why only one woman in my sample tried to deny what she did, and she said she was really a model. It also explains why they do not distance themselves from the occupation itself but rather try to redefine it so that it suits their bodies, so to speak. By endowing their overblown bodies with a useful social function, a sex extravaganza, they are saying they are moral bodies inhabited by moral people. Their "passing" technique, then, involves a new definition of sexual morality rather than an attempt to live up to the existing one.

All the skills they learn as strippers can be seen, in a sense, as working up to this new definition of sexual morality and sexual worth. It is the only stance they can take, which is why it is so strictly enforced among members of their own group.

**Corporeal Ideology**

What I am saying is that as their work is expressed in their bodies, so, too, is their ideology. The body becomes an object that every member of the audience is supposed to identify with and use in his own way. If it stimulates masturbation, that is perhaps not in keeping with the official norms governing the occasion, but it is still in line with the expressed function the strippers declare as being theirs.

Because strippers manifest a certain sameness in their self-presentations, they become almost indistinguishable from one another in the same ways that members of the audience become indistinguishable from one another to the strippers.

Their coping device, then, is to make the body moral in the same
way they make the show and themselves moral, all being part of the
same phenomenon and sharing in stigma. At the same time, it is to
state that, other than having this extravagant body and sexual presence, they are normal, that is, no different than any other woman.
To state this, as I discussed, is to conceal any kind of information
about themselves that would give the lie to their self-presentation.
Strippers are constantly playing this kind of show in a conscious
way; it illustrates the complicated nature of the destigmatizing processes and the complexities of those people who have to work out a
suitable identity.

# 11

# Massage Parlors:
# The Sensuality Business

Albert J. Velarde
and Mark Warlick

The nationwide massage parlor business is booming. Into a world formerly populated by physical therapists and affluent health enthusiasts have come the prostitute, the pimp, and a bevy of innocent young girls looking for any kind of employment. The personality of a masseuse, her working conditions, society's reaction to her occupation, and her problems with owners, customers, and the police were the targets of our investigation.

We concentrated our study on a suburban West Coast community that is supporting one parlor for every 5,000 people. We interviewed fifteen masseuses, four owners, several customers, and the husbands of two masseuses. Our subjects were drawn from nine different parlors within the community.

## The Masseuse

Why does a young woman choose to enter an occupation that carries the stigma of prostitution? In this particular town, the massage boom hit over two years ago [1973]. Word got around slowly at first—friends told friends of friends—then snowballed as the ads in underground newspapers became more blatant. More parlors opened to meet the increasing demand of curious customers. The high rate of unemployment for young, unskilled women in this community has been the major factor in obtaining a work force for massage parlors. "Why did I get into it? Very simple! I needed a job and no other work was available at the time."

Did these girls know what they were getting into? Were they

aware of the prostitute image? To answer this question a time element must be considered. For a full year after the boom began, the straight press was virtually ignorant of any illicit activities taking place in the parlors. Many established newspapers (not to mention the underground and campus papers) carried very respectable advertisements for masseuses: "Masseuses needed—part time or full time—training included. An equal opportunity employer." To all outward appearances and to the public, this smacked more of physical therapy than prostitution. Girls who answered these early ads were almost unanimous in expressing naivete toward the finer points of their new occupation.

Advertisements drew hundreds of women to apply for the few available jobs in the profession. We asked one owner, "How did the job applicants react when you told them about locals (massaging the penis)?" "The first 15 or 20 girls I interviewed I was too ashamed to talk to them about it, I just couldn't do it. I was completely amazed at the girls. I figured maybe one out of 20 would do it (give a local). Well, like 99 out of 100 would! Not all of them would go beyond that, but almost any girl that came in would give a local without even batting an eye!"

Most owners simply said nothing about locals and left informing the new masseuse of her duties to the customer. We found that a sizable percentage of women quit at this point. One masseuse told us, "I lasted three days at my first place, leaving there at night just totally mindblown. I couldn't even think about giving a man a local because to me it was a personal sexual involvement which I just couldn't do for money. Here I was, a trained masseuse and these guys were coming in, laying 20 bucks on the table, and expecting me to jump up there."

Most masseuses would give the first local. "If you think about it, you probably won't do it. It's the same with nude modeling or working in topless bars. If you just do it, it's not so bad. You don't have time to feel guilty."

Training to be a masseuse is as varied as the parlors and bosses themselves. An owner may have the prospective employee read a book on massage, then have her perform a massage on him. Others do just the opposite—training girls by giving *them* a massage or by having them witness someone else receiving a massage. Other owners rely on schools to train their employees. One student complained that "the book was really shitty. All kinds of physical detail and nothing at all about the aesthetic side of massage." Others hold a different view: "I learned so much! I got to meet others girls in my profession and learned everything from the names of muscles to the whole nervous system. They even taught us how to operate a fire extinguisher."

Some owners use the training to check out more than a girl's ability to massage. "Jack puts the make on every girl he hires. It's kind of aggravating 'cause he's a real pimp-type, very smooth and slimy. But it's not true that you have to ball him to get hired. He just checks you out real good to see how loose you are. Sure, he gets his kicks out of it but it's more for his own protection. Anybody he hires is in a position to get him in a lot of trouble."

Other owners are more demanding. "I couldn't stand pumping gas anymore so I applied for a job as a masseuse. I had read horrible stories of what went on in there, but I was curious. The sign said I would be a trained masseuse and that interested me also." What kind of training was involved? "Just reading the book he gave me. He also asked me to give him a massage to see if I could do it right. . . . What an ugly, fat ass he had. I massaged him and he told me to jerk him off in the end. I knew that I would be doing this, so I jerked him off until he came all over my hands. There were some paper towels near the table and I wiped my hands off. It wasn't so bad!"

**Working Conditions**

The first obstacle a prospective masseuse encounters is the law. The local ordinances require eight steps for a masseuse to become licensed: (1) She must present a note from her future employer of his intention to hire her. (2) She must appear at city hall and pay the $15 application fee and fill out a two-page questionnaire on her job and legal and personal background. (3) She must proceed to the police department to be fingerprinted and photographed. (4) The police will question her and warn her not to engage in prostitution. (5) She must produce a birth certificate for identification. Driver's licenses are not acceptable. (6) She must then see a doctor for a medical checkup (specifically, a checkup for venereal disease). (7) She must show proof of enrollment in a certified massage school. (8) She must take 70 hours of schooling that are to be concluded within 90 days. Schooling averages $250 for 70 hours.

These ordinances assure proper training, but authorities generally treat the masseuse as a legalized prostitute. "They made me feel like a whore while trying to get licensed. The medical check doesn't do any good. They don't care if I have infectious sores on my hands or tb. They simply want to assure that I won't give vd to my customers. Now what does that imply?"

Most full-time masseuses work eight to twelve hours per day, five to six days per week. The hours are long and tedious when the masseuse is busy; boring, when she is not. Many masseuses work twelve hours per day or more without overtime pay. They are usually paid on a commission basis that averages 40 percent (between $3 and $5) per massage. Very few get paid for sitting around waiting for a customer to come in.

One parlor gives $1.25 per hour plus commission. We found one higher class parlor paying its girls $2.50 an hour or $5 a massage, whichever was greater on a weekly basis.

Few businesses can maintain themselves financially without a regular clientele. As one masseuse put it, "If you're giving straight massages you might as well be on welfare." "You couldn't make it in this business without giving locals." Low pay forces the girls to cater to customers' wishes in hopes of getting a tip. If the customer is satisfied, he may become a regular, which makes the masseuse's rate of pay less sporadic. When a masseuse moves to another parlor, she may advertise in an underground paper so her regular customers will know where to find her. "Looking for Katie from N.Y.? I've moved to El Gato. Come see me soon."

### The Massage Parlor

The physical layout of a massage parlor varies according to the type of customer and the amount of capital invested. Parlors range from dives to very plush operations. An owner who wishes to attract working-class customers looking for sex and thrills need make only a small investment. Homes in unincorporated areas and low-rent, downtown storefronts have been converted into blue-collar massage parlors with the addition of partitions, curtains, a couch, a chair, massage tables, and linen. Advertising is a necessity. Ads need only show a seminude girl with the caption, "Your complete satisfaction on request."

A few higher class parlors cater to wealthier businessmen and financially influential people, yet offer much the same services. These parlors advertise subtly, preferring to attract a select clientele. Customers are provided such comforts as plush carpets, soft couches, clean linen, piped-in music, and soft lighting. All of this may demand a few thousand dollars extra, but as one manager said, "You wouldn't want to pay for a massage in a filthy place, would you?" Almost all parlors feature saunas and showers; the latter is required by law. Some even have their own laundry room for a constant supply of fresh linen.

**Occupational Precautions**

Masseuses must have a basic knowledge of solicitation laws. Women who engage in sexual acts must be certain that the customer does the soliciting. A mere hint for a tip could be distorted to infer solicitation. The question, "Is there anything else you'd like me to massage?" is far more suggestive than, "Is there anything you'd like massaged again?" Little word games such as these become crucial in a courtroom.

Since few owners stay on the premises during business hours, the masseuses must sniff out undercover policemen. Some are incredibly adept, cataloging a large variety of data before continuing with anything illegal. General appearance, mannerisms, tone of voice, type of language, overconfidence, or excessive nervousness—all are studied carefully. The masseuse may direct conversation in an attempt to discover any contradictions.

If a customer says he is a student, yet does not know when finals are, calls the school by the wrong name, and does not know any teachers in his department, he is obviously a liar and possibly an undercover policeman. One masseuse told us, "This dude came in and everything was cool until he told me he was in the real estate business. I asked him to help me with a problem involving the sale of an inherited home with depreciation value conflicts. He stuttered and stammered on that one. Shit, he didn't even know what a tax write-off was! We both laughed about it and he was pretty embarrassed. Needless to say he didn't get anything extra from me, tip or no tip!"

The one-to-one nature of the masseuse-customer relationship adds to the legal difficulties of both parties. One masseuse told me, "It doesn't matter what goes òn in that room. When they're assigned to bust you they're gonna bust you. Those cops will get up on the witness stand and lie through their teeth. It's your word against his and who do you think a jury is going to believe—the cop or the masseuse?" Some parlors have gone as far as installing tape recorders to protect them against undercover policemen in court. Even when who solicited whom is clear, a jury is likely to frown on a masseuse who performed a lewd act.

Handling phone calls is an art in itself. As a rule, one girl in a parlor will handle most of the calls. Crank calls are common, be they from genuine perverts, women trying to antagonize the masseuses, or policemen involved in harassment. Some girls have an incredible memory for phone voices: "There's this one cop who calls now and then. Once he asked if he could bite my panties. He said he'd give me $50 if I'd wear them for a week after that. He gets real pissed when we say something like 'Aw Fred, cut it out. Why don't you come on in and we'll talk about it.'"

Another caller asked, "How much does straight sex cost?" The masseuse replied, "Tenderness, sincerity, loving care, and another person." This caller wanted and expected either a straight dollars and cents answer or a flat rejection. Instead, he received an answer that forced him to think. Such answers arouse curiosity, which is the main commodity that a customer brings with him into a parlor. One masseuse even turned several gutter-level, obscene phone callers into regular customers.

**Locals**

Of all the legal questions involved in the massage profession, one stands out above them all: Is it legal for a man to enter a place of business, pay a fee, and eventually have his penis massaged in such a manner as to result in an ejaculation? On one side of this controversy are the enforcers of the law who are arresting girls right and left for soliciting to commit a lewd act. On the other side, of course, are the owners, masseuses, and customers. Lewd or not, locals are popular. We asked one masseuse, "What percentage of customers ask for locals?" She replied, "I kept track of that once. While working at this one parlor I did over 500 massages and only four guys *didn't* ask for a local."

Owners use a variety of methods to isolate themselves from the illegal activities in their parlors. Most owners never mention anything against the law to their employees. Some have even gone as far as filing the business in someone else's name. They still collect the profits while their dupe receives all the pressure.

One owner was asked if massages in his parlor included locals. "It was always up to the girl's discretion." We asked if masseuses ever told him about it. "I didn't want to know about it! I knew about it in the beginning and that just got me into trouble. I might as well have been running a whorehouse with all the problems I had."

As might be expected, a brothel has a higher profit ratio than a semistraight massage parlor. A parlor owner generally wants his girls to accommodate customers to the greatest degree possible. Owners protect themselves in two ways. First, if the owner knows that the employee is a prostitute, he will tell her openly not to ball the customers, while knowing all along that she will. He can always say that he knew nothing of what was going on. Second, the owner may give his total consent to the illicit activities. At the same time he will demand that the masseuse sign a contract asserting that she will *not* engage in anything sexually illegal. With this paper signed, as one owner said, "The girls are free to fuck like a bunny! It's very difficult for the cops to convict an owner on that. Almost impossible."

### Personality

Masseuses come from nearly all walks of life and all types of economic and social backgrounds. We met women who were from fourteen to sixty-four years old, with the majority being in their twenties. There are women in the profession with fifth-grade educations as well as several graduate students from nearby universities. There is simply no quality or characteristic that typifies the average masseuse.

Most find the work boring and react accordingly. Most customers, regardless of age, background, or personality are interested basically in receiving sexual pleasure. Some want to talk about personal problems.

Susan N. said, "It gets boring after awhile. The minute someones comes in, you know what that sexist, male chauvinist wants and you know that you'll get hassled for not giving him *everything* he wants. It gets to be a drag real quick. Now, when someone comes in who isn't after sex, he's unusual and your curiosity perks up. He's new and refreshing and you want to talk to him. And he talks back, not about what he can get out of you, but what's in your mind. Imagine! Someone, especially a customer, who's interested in you as a person, not as a body with a pair of tits and a cunt. We meet so many men that are sex-hungry that mental relationships become latent, stuffed away in a closet until someone comes around and asks what's on your mind."

How do masseuses handle grabby customers? One woman who believed that a relaxed, sensual atmosphere should be maintained at all costs, said she merely treated such a man like a baby: "I take his hands, fold them across his chest, and say: "Now, now! Let's be a good little boy. We don't want to ruin everything by being grabby now, do we?" That usually makes him laugh and get embarrassed, and I never have any trouble with him after that." What if he persists? "I'd probably act insulted and leave the room. I'd never do him any physical harm."

Another masseuse handles things differently. "It's all a personality thing. I was having a bad day once and this dude really capped it off. He paid $30 for a half and half (consisting of a regular massage followed by the customer massaging the masseuse) and didn't even wait for his turn to massage me when he reached for my snatch. I grabbed his hand and bent his finger back 'til it really hurt. I said, 'Goodbye, this massage is over,' and left the room." We asked, "Didn't your actions ruin the atmosphere of the massage?" "As far as I'm concerned *he* ruined the massage. I'm up to here with these people who think they can get away with anything just because they paid their money."

While most masseuses can readily justify their own actions, we found many have a low opinion of other masseuses, particularly those in other parlors. They are quick to label another masseuse "a whore" but reluctant to turn the same scrutiny on themselves.

One masseuse told us: "I couldn't figure out what was going on at the first place I worked. I was twice as pretty and built better than the other girls but they were getting all the customers. I found out later that most of them were turning tricks. Hey man! Those whores even have rooms rented by the month at the motel across the street!"

Many masseuses share society's contemptuous view of the massage game. They accept society's tendency to label as undesirable any incomprehensible area of behavior. While masseuses understand and accept their own behavior, they lack objectivity to pass judgment on their peers. This negative feeling toward other masseuses eventually becomes a self-judgment.

Women who remain in the profession go to great lengths to protect themselves from the prostitute image. We asked two masseuses about this. "How do you reply to inquiries about your occupation?" Sue L.: "I say I work in an office." Linda P.: "I usually tell them, but I get a lot of hassle. I find some guys will avoid me, where others think I'm really loose and will lay them that night if they take me out. Some think I'm a nymphomaniac. Then if I don't go to bed with them, they accuse me of being a lesbian." Sue L.: "Either way they want to look down on you. I'm searching for a house to live in now. If I was to tell the owner about my occupation, it would be all over." Linda P.: "Either that or he'd want to screw you for the rent!"

We found the rate of lesbianism among masseuses to be low if not nonexistent. Though many express contempt for men (as customers), we found very few bisexuals by admission or accusation from other employees. Most masseuses in these parlors are married, or have boyfriends, and do not demonstrate any desire to massage women or engage in sexual activities with them. There were no male homosexual massage parlors in our area of observation.

### Owners

The principal factor in determining massage-parlor working conditions is the boss. There is a distinct difference between owners who rely on the parlor for their sole support and owners to whom it is just another business venture. Because a massage parlor is primarily a small business—one can be opened for as little as $2,000—most owners fall into the former category. This results in a high level of exploitation and the general opinion among masseuses that an owner is little better than a pimp. As one masseuse told us, "It basically takes a pimp mentality to be an owner. They usually don't like to work and enjoy making money off other people's labor." Personality conflicts occur often between employer and employee. Several bosses have made deductions from paychecks (for arrest insurance, vacation pay, savings) while having no intention of ever returning it or using it for its set purpose. Masseuses have been fired for everything from rejecting a boss's sexual advances to changing the station on the parlor radio. One boss lives with two of his masseuses. As might be expected, they do his housework, laundry, and cooking. Once a boss bails a masseuse out of jail, their relationship often changes. Some bosses use this to pressure a girl to do topless or nude massages. Others demand longer hours or personal sexual favors. One boss was accused of addicting his employees to amphetamines in order to exert control. A masseuse's husband said that the pills separated him from his wife.

> It was some sort of speed that made her horny. She got it from her boss/boyfriend who likes to make sure that his chicks have lots of energy. He started giving the stuff to her a little bit at a time to make her work those long hours. After awhile she demanded more, and got it. That's why she started making so much money and couldn't stand to be fucked by me when she got home. The speed wore off and all she could do was doze off until he would give her some more at work the next day. A year later when I last saw her, she had his kid and was still fucked up on those pills; it was her whole life, those pills and the job.

There are many other tales of conflict between masseuses and bosses. This relationship is the main reason that many masseuses become transients in their own profession. The turnover of employees is large in nearly every parlor and the search for a better boss is widespread.

That search, it must be noted, is not always in vain. We have found several owners who carry on honest, trusting relationships with their employees. One owner keeps out of the bookkeeping entirely, believing explicitly that the masseuses are telling him the truth about the volume of business. Another takes his girls who cannot massage (for legal or medical reasons) and puts them to work in his office until they can massage again. The only thing that these types of owners have in common is the fact that, for them, the massage business is a sideline. They receive the main portion of their income from another source and they can afford to be honest, trusting, and nonexploitative.

## Getting Started

One massage parlor existed in this community from 1960 to 1970. In 1970 the second parlor opened. Two more opened in the first six months of 1971. Masseuses in the fourth parlor gave locals more freely than employees of the other parlors. Soon the fourth parlor began to attract hordes of customers. Among the preboom customers were men with capital who recognized a profitable business when they saw one. Three of these men opened parlors of their own within the following year.

One of the early owners explains how he got started.

> A friend of mine, kind of a wilder sort, had been going to —'s place for years when one day she whipped him off. It was one of the greatest experiences of his life and he got all excited about opening a parlor. He was in it to play around and I was always looking for an easy buck, so he talked me into it.
>
> There were only three other places in town and we were the first to have young, attractive masseuses. We brought in some really great stuff. Our parlor was running the others out of business by sheer quality! Our only real competitor opened the following month. They started right in with blow jobs and fucking the customers and that's when the other owners started screaming bloody murder.

From the end of 1971 to the present a new parlor has opened every two months. The peak has not been reached, and many owners are feeling the pinch of a glutted market.

Owners do not have nearly as many problems getting licensed as a masseuse. The prospective owner has but four requirements to meet. (1) He must pay a $50 fee to cover the cost of investigating his background. (2) He must not have been convicted of a sexual offense. (3) He must get a business license. (4) He must be fingerprinted and photographed by the police department.

The police department and city hall have thirty days to accept or reject the application. Instances of an applicant being rejected are rare. Most businessmen have their affairs in order before they apply.

The owner usually hires a manager to keep the place open on a regular basis, watch the girls, and act as a bouncer when necessary. A business will often fail when the girls alone are responsible for keeping regular business hours. Katherine L. said, "I was supposed to open the place up at 10:00 but I'd hardly ever get there before 11:30. If I didn't get a customer or a phone call in an hour or two, I'd split. What's the sense in staying open if there's no business?"

The manager is often a silent partner or unemployed friend of the owner. Since most owners depend on their parlor for their bread and butter, they often watch the manager as diligently as the manager is supposed to watch the masseuses.

### Recruitment

Attractive, intelligent, and personable girls are in great demand as employees. Even with an overcrowded market, a new parlor can still succeed if the quality of the girls hired is high. Thus, recruiting strategies and techniques have become increasingly important.

A straight newspaper ad can bring in dozens of applicants. This method requires a great deal of screening, but can be productive if the owner knows what he is looking for.

An excellent way to find masseuses is to have a good employee solicit her friends and acquaintances for the job. This eliminates a sizable amount of guesswork and research on prospective employees. Having friends work together adds to the relaxed environment of a parlor.

Scouting has been a successful method. Each parlor has at least one masseuse with considerably more charisma than the others. Many owners will send a friend to a parlor to seek out this employee. If she proves to be a capable masseuse, and is dissatisfied with her present job situation, she may accept a better offer from another parlor.

A recommendation from a customer or especially an ex-owner has been known to bear fruit. Many masseuses leave the profession because of long hours, low pay, or personality conflicts with an owner. An informed owner may make a better offer to attract a disgruntled masseuse back into the business.

### Owners' Problems

The owner of a massage parlor must also deal with his landlord. Some wealthy owners get around the landlord problem by buying the building that houses their parlor. Others are not so fortunate and find that a paranoid landlord can cramp their style. We asked an ex-owner about the person who recently purchased his parlor. Would he be a successful owner?

> I think he'll get buried! I sat down with this guy for three hours and told him every hassle, every detail about the business as I knew it and all he could do was stare at Mary's big tits. He's obviously not in it for the money, so he won't make much. Oh, he could draw $100, maybe $200 a week, but it'll be very difficult for him to make a pile of money without really opening up. If he does that, the landlord will boot him out of the building. He doesn't want a whorehouse operating there.

In several cases the police have attempted to stop the transfer of ownership. They can legally reject an application only if their investigation reveals contradiction in the applicant's background. The head of the local vice squad tried to block one transfer by slowing down the bureaucratic processes. The present owner eventually had to go to his superiors and threaten a law suit against the city. The processes were suddenly speeded up and the transfer approved!

Business pressures have forced owners to go to great lengths in order to protect themselves. One owner likes to go into a parlor where he is a silent partner and test the masseuses. He plays the role of undercover cop in an attempt to discover how far his unknowing employees will go. Another owner has a mirror on the end of a stick to check on his masseuses. The massage rooms are separated by eight-foot partitions and watching a masseuse in action is easy with his little gadget. Other owners, especially those with respected positions in the community, endeavor to make friends in the police department. As one masseuse told us, "———always knew when a bust was coming 'cause he was in with all those people. He would either leave town or just cool it for a couple of weeks." After a parlor is busted, even if the owner was not directly involved, he may be asked to make an appearance at the police station. Upon arriving there, days or even weeks after the bust, he may suddenly find himself under arrest. A long list of charges may be thrown at him which, more often than not, are drastically reduced after an extended period of court dates, public embarrassment, and harassment.

As a precaution, most parlors maintain a brief file on their customers. This serves to inform a masseuse of the preferences of regular customers as well as the identities of undercover policemen. Most of these files are kept on a first-name basis only. One highly respected parlor went further, however. Barbara C. said, "Before a customer could get even a local, he had to submit three things: a valid I.D., a business card, which was stapled to his card in the file, and a current credit card. In the future, then, we could just check his card before the massage and we would know how far we could go with him." Another parlor has a steady clientele of a dozen influential people who have agreed to testify that they were never solicited at that parlor.

The higher class owners have themselves pretty well covered. This has forced the small-time owners to organize a Massage Parlor Association. Roughly half of the parlor owners in town are dues-paying members of this organization. While its original purpose was to fight city ordinances while they were in the process of being legislated, a police crackdown around this time forced the association to divert its funds from public relations (offense) to legal fees (defense). This severely weakened the affiliation and caused much internal feuding. Half of the members ran reasonably legitimate parlors while the other half operated parlors of the whorehouse variety. Illegitimate parlors were busted first and the legitimate owners resented pumping money into the legal defense of prostitutes. The association showed early signs of being a significant force on the local massage scene. At this point, however, the burden of defending the few has rendered it virtually powerless.

One owner presented his view of the situation:

> It's weird. The laws are supposedly there to prevent prostitution, yet they actually encourage it. An owner is better off in the long run to open a whorehouse and make a big pile of money in a hurry. That way he can afford good lawyers and hire girls who don't care about morals charges. Chances are you're gonna get busted regardless of what goes on in your place. If society and the law treat a masseuse as a whore, she's likely to become one. Treat a legitimate parlor as a whorehouse and it's likely to become one. It sounds paradoxical, but that's the way it is.

### Customers

In our research we were able to determine that there is no such thing as a "typical" masseuse. Customers, on the other hand, fit several general categories. Most of our conclusions concerning customers are necessarily based primarily on what the masseuses told us about them and upon our impressions of customers as they entered the parlors we frequented. The largest group consists of white men over the age of thirty-five. (In over six months of hanging around the parlors and talking to masseuses, we heard of only two black customers.) As a rule they are white-collar businessmen. Curiosity and boredom with a daily routine are the two outstanding characteristics of the average customer. Many are simply starving for attention, and this need may be the chief reason for the success of the parlors. Where else can a person enter a business establishment, pay a fee, and for the next hour have an attractive girl pay attention to him and cater to his pleasure?

The second largest category of customers is composed of transients who have little to call their own. Sandy R. said, "We get a lot of transients through here. We get a lot of traveling salesmen, but more often it's a guy who just moved to the area and doesn't know anybody. He'll come in maybe once a week for three or four months, then less frequently as he begins to meet people and make some friends. Most of them drop in now and then to say hi. A lot of them admit that we kept them from going crazy while they were going through their changes."

The word *changes* refers to much more than a shift in geographical location. A sizable number of men will frequent a parlor when their personal lives are taking turns that they cannot comprehend. Cheryl T. told us, "Lately we've been getting a lot of young married guys. They've been married for, oh, two to five years and can't understand why their sex lives have gone stale. I try to rap to them about communication, you know, get 'em to tune into their old ladies. All they need, as far as I can see, is some confidence and a desire to work things out." Another side of this category consists of men whose wives have already left them. "I've had three customers who came home from work to find a 'Dear John' letter in a half-empty house. They all thought things were fine up until then. I couldn't believe they could be so out of touch with reality. I mean, if a guy's wife finally up and split physically, she'd probably left mentally a long time ago."

The final group of customers includes those men who, by current social standards, are physically or mentally unattractive. Men with deformities are frequent visitors to the parlors. These men may be too ashamed and withdrawn to approach females in everyday situations and find relief in being able to pay money for the attention they receive. A considerably larger group is composed of sexual deviants. Approximately half of the parlors employ one or two masseuses to service these men. What they receive comes under the general heading of a *dominant* massage. A dominant costs at least twice as much as a normal massage and large tips are commonplace.

What does a dominant massage consist of? Paula B. explained, "Well, since they pay more, it's usually whatever they want. Basically they want to be treated like a piece of shit. I had one guy who had me do nothing but cuss at him for a half hour. Man, I threw out every obscenity I could think of and he tipped me well for it. It really wore me out." Another masseuse related this story: "This guy about forty-five came with five pairs of high-heeled shoes. He had me put on each pair during the course of the massage. To cap it off he had me tie his hands with a bra he brought in, pull down the nylon panties he was wearing, and spank him with one of the spiked heels." Another masseuse had a customer with an invalid wife who, he said, treated him like a dog. "He wanted to play the role for real. He brought in his own leash, had me put it on him, and lead him around the room. I kicked him a few times and told him what a bad dog he was. He really got off on that."

Surprisingly, many customers come into a parlor just to talk. They are content with taking off their clothes and relating pieces of their private lives to a masseuse. "A lot of guys are just getting over the hangup of being nude and alone with a girl. We get things said to us that a customer would never dream of saying to someone he knows. Some things they say are just plain gross, but, more often we get dudes who rap about their personal relationships, homosexual tendencies, or their sexual hang-ups. I guess they figure they're never gonna see us again if that's the way they want it." Discretion is a valuable commodity to all customers.

It is difficult to go shoplifting in a massage parlor, yet some men still manage to make off with a free thrill now and then. One owner told us:

> Sure, we have our share of rip-offs. One guy ripped us off for five massages in a two-week period. The girls would usually collect after the massage in hopes of getting a tip. Well, this dude slipped out the front door twice and the back door twice. We were laying for him the fifth time, but he somehow managed to crawl out the bathroom window. Another guy came in and asked if he could take the girls' measurements. This one girl, who's a bit naive, said sure. So he breaks out his tape measure and measures her, copping a free feel here and there. He then asked for some kleenex and disappeared behind the bamboo curtain. The girl wondered where he went when she heard the thumping noise from behind the curtain. She looked and there he was, jacking off right in the parlor!

Incidents of exhibitionism are not foreign to masseuses. They occasionally become the objects of voyeurs exposing themselves. Janet H. said, "I remember this one guy, though he wasn't a customer. He came up to the parlor window, looked in, and saw me behind the desk talking on the telephone. Right in the middle of downtown, he whipped out his cock and started jacking off; rubbing it against the window and all. It wasn't long before he came and shot sperm all over the window. I happened to be talking to the police at the time and told them to come get this weirdo, but he was finished and gone before I knew it."

Rates for massages vary according to the parlor, clientele, and volume of business. We found prices from a $4 "special" to the popular "half and half" for $30. Customers are often fooled by the money factor. Is the sauna counted as part of the hour-long massage? Masseuses have been known to stick undesirable customers in the sauna for longer than usual in order to avoid giving him his money's worth. Seven dollars looks very economical in an advertisement, but is that for an hour or a half hour? Some parlors are notorious for skimping on the massage and getting down to what the customer really came for.

We found that one parlor employed a "blow-job (fellatio) specialist." It was said that there was not a single guy she could not get to come in less than three minutes flat. Volume was so high at this parlor, that on busy evenings she might perform the oral sex act up to twenty times. It was her sole function there. She absorbed the responsibility for anything illegal and the owner only had to cover for one girl.

Typical rates for the average parlor are $10 to $15 for an hour's massage. A masseuse at one of the looser parlors explained their policy: "It's $15 for an hour-long massage including a local. An extra $5 will get my top off and $5 more takes my bottom off. For $10 more he can bathe with me for a half hour. [This is a rare practice.] Anything after that is negotiable between me and the customer. I have to soak him for $35 before negotiating a blow job or a lay." It is nearly impossible for an owner, a landlord, a policeman, or a researcher to determine which parlors are engaged in illegal activities and which are not. A whorehouse today may be a health spa tomorrow, according to a number of variables. Financially though, if a parlor is a front for a house of prostitution, oral sex will cost between $30 or $40 and complete sexual intercourse between $40 and $60.

**Law Enforcement**

The law governing prostitution and solicitation in this community reads as follows:

> It shall be unlawful for any person to keep or carry on or become an inmate of, or a visitor to, or to in any way contribute to the support of any house of ill fame or prostitution, or to induce, or attempt to induce by any solicitation, prostitution to be carried on in any house, room, or place or to solicit by word, act, gesture, sign, or otherwise, any person for the purpose of prostitution.

Compared to the type of crime that proliferates in a large metropolitan county, the massage business—prostitution or no prostitution—is in reality a miniscule problem. Control of the businesses rests more with the legislative branch than the sheriff's department. Several parlors in the area were recently closed because laws were enacted that the parlor owners could not possibly comply with. One such law states that the owner of a massage parlor must be a licensed masseur. Few, if any, owners—be they enterprising businessmen or pimps—qualify as masseurs. The owners can scream and file suits against the county, but, during the period of litigation, the padlocks of the sheriff's department remain securely on the parlor doors.

As far as we could discover, the massage business in the nearest major city is under the control of an organized crime syndicate. The authorities in this city do not seem to be too concerned about the proliferation of parlors. Because their ownership is centralized, competition and sensationalism in advertising are virtually nonexistent. New competitors are forced to run wide-open parlors that dealt with swiftly and decisively by the syndicate. Rumors of payoffs proliferate to no one's surprise or concern.

This makes the smaller suburban areas ripe for the massage business. These cities do not possess the capital to fund a well-staffed vice squad. Investigation, arrests, and court proceedings have proved to be a heavy financial burden. The most recent raids in this community saw five masseuses arrested on charges of solicitation to commit a lewd act. One manager estimated that this raid will ultimately cost the city $30,000. This is a high price to pay for putting five masseuses out of business for a day or two despite favorable publicity for the police.

**Sisterhood Really Is Powerful**

We have painted a rather dismal picture of the life of a masseuse.
Her hours are long, the pay low, the employer is pressured, and he,
in turn, pressures her. She is constantly confronted with the fact
that, in society's eyes, she is a deviant.

Is there any hope for a better life? The answer is yes. We found
one unique parlor within the community. The masseuses were directly involved in virtually every area of setting up their working environment. The girls work seven hours per shift and the pay is comparatively high at $2.50 per hour. The owner of this parlor is well off
financially. We have determined, however, that this fact plays a
minor role in the total make up of the parlor.

There are many reasons for the parlor's overall success. The people involved took great care in preparing their establishment. The
owner thoroughly investigated the other parlors in the community.
The types of women in the work force, the physical layout of the
parlor, the types of customers catered to, and, most important, the
amount of capital invested and returned, all were considered before
the first girl was even approached for employment. Most of the girls
eventually hired came from another parlor in town. They had band-
ed together in a "sisterhood" as an intellectual reaction to the oppressive situation in that parlor. They shared two basic ideals. One
was a sincere desire to understand the psychological nature of their
profession. The second was an important realization: that the owner
needs the masseuses much more than they need him.

What is a sisterhood of masseuses? How did it form? How did it
(or could it) affect the life and working conditions of a masseuse?

> When I started being a masseuse I knew what the hustling
> game was. When I started working at The Palace all of the girls
> there were just finding out where they were at. They were either
> at the stage of being used or not knowing what they were doing.
> I met Sherry and could really relate to her and then I started
> relating to the other chicks. When you work at a bar, you have
> to handle about thirty to fifty men at a time, there are just
> masses of people out there. When you work at a massage par-
> lor it's like one to one with the guys and the group was the girls.
> So I started being able to relate to the girls and it was really
> good for my head. Sherry was writing a paper for one of her
> classes in college that really caused us to start thinking about
> different psychologies we applied in that room and what we had
> going for us. When we started really wording it, verbalizing it,
> and thinking about it, we started rapping to the other chicks
> about it. I was into reading Tarot cards real heavy then, so I

brought that into work with me and that became another way
to teach people to reflect on themselves, and look inside themselves. More and more the whole place started becoming like a
trip. Look around you and see what your environment's really
like and what's motivating you to do things and what kind of
control you have.

The best part about it was that it didn't get cannabalistic like
most group-therapy gigs do. Because we had a common cause,
we had a common ground where the "other" was the customer.
You had your own private life so you didn't have to confront
your personal life with the other people out there, you know,
society. And when you can pit the girls against that, they start
taking what they have learned in their experiences with the customers and start applying it into their own personal life. You
avoid the direct confrontation that a group therapy has, where
you are attacking your own personal life constantly. That's
what made it good. It was like getting a group sanity together
that really got us closer and closer, and the girls got to know
each other better and we spent a lot of time with each other.
Which is something I never did on any other job I had been in.
I had always totally dissociated myself from the people I
worked with. I never wanted them to know what my personal
home life was like because people would usually use it as a
weapon. Every time a new girl got hired we had to bring her
into the sisterhood. That's where we ran into trouble with the
boss because all of a sudden his neat plan of keeping everyone
alienated wasn't working anymore. He couldn't quite figure
out why it wasn't!

We asked the masseuse another question: "The final break with
The Palace was actually over vacation pay, right?"

Yeah, but that was after we already had decided to quit. It
simply came to [the point] that we had a sisterhood going and a
guy had offered us a job—what are we staying here for? The
vacation pay was owed to us and that was a crisis that initiated
it. Now we're going to test our strength, we're going to stand
up to him and see if our sisterhood really works, and it did! It
was a test of strength and we met him on his ground and we
won. All the girls who heard about it had that as an example.
You don't have to let him push you around . . . if you get organized. The enemy isn't the other girls or the customers. The
enemy is whoever is trying to make you feel ashamed or guilty
. . . because it's really *good* to be a sensual person; that gives
people pleasure. But you can't turn that against yourself if you
have these secret guilts and secret doubts and that's where the

strength of the sisterhood is. Most of the girls I've seen working in other massage parlors aren't proud of their work and that's because they accept the way other people look at it. . . instead of seeing it as a calling. Rather than seeing a massage parlor as a kind of sanctuary that can bring about change, they look at it the way the customers look at it when *they* come in there, and it drags them down. That's where they keep all the girls working for them, in all the bars, all the massage parlors, and anything that has to do with men-women relationships. Instead of the girls looking at themselves as people who offer solace, and that's being a good thing in society, they see themselves as being degraded.

Although one masseuse told us that working in a massage parlor absolutely kills your sex drive, the members of the sisterhood disagreed. "She's talking about her own bitter experience." We noted that the sensual level of the parlor was very high. It was obvious that the masseuses were not getting burned out by their work.

That's because we don't have a boss that sucks our energies. The girl you talked to is how a lot of girls can end up because when she goes in the room, she goes in there alone. . . . When I go in there, I'm not alone; all my sisters are with me. Anything he says to me he says to all of us. Several of my customers had come in very upset that their wives were starting to express Women's Lib ideas. I try to make them see why their wives were unhappy and why I was unhappy when I led that kind of life. You aren't supposed to relate to people intelligently, to be independent, or to be able to take care of yourself, and he's got all the sexual liberties. So if you want to do anything you have to sneak off and lie about it and feel like a criminal. More and more guys come with some remark like, "Well, are you married?" and I'll say, "Yes," and that will really stun them. "Why, your husband will let you work here?" "Let you," that phrase, "allows you!" I happen to know that my husband is proud of what I'm doing. More people should make other people feel better and my husband feels that way about it, too. What I do here is no threat to him. . . . The young guys who are in their early twenties have been asking us for advice and they go home and take what they learn from us back to their wives. It surprises me that more and more young guys come in now than a year ago, maybe because we have a nice place.

We responded strongly to this liberated masseuse. "Your place *is* nice. The atmosphere is very warm and friendly. Walk into another parlor in town—and we've been to most of them—and they make you feel like a chauvinist pervert of some kind." There is one basic reason that this liberated parlor is a success. The masseuses are simply not mind hungry. They have thought about what they are doing. They are on top of all the games. Here are the principles of Women's Liberation in a place where they are totally unexpected. These women have met the male chauvinist on his home ground, making the massage parlor a creative environment—a place for self-realization—rather than sexual exploitation.

# 12

# Swinging in Wedlock

Charles Palson
and Rebecca Palson

Since the latter 1960s, an increasing number of middle-class couples have turned to mate swapping or *swinging* as an alternative to strictly monogamous marriage. That is, married couples (or unmarried couples with an apparently stable relationship) willingly and knowingly relinquish sexual rights to their own mates so that others may temporarily enjoy these rights. This phenomenon, which is fairly recent in its openness and proportions, provides an opportunity of testing, on a large scale, the traditional theories about the consequences of extramarital sexual activity. It has often been assumed that sexual infidelity, where all the concerned parties know of it, results to some degree in jealousy. The intensity of jealousy is thought to increase in proportion to the amount of real or imagined emotional involvement on the part of the unfaithful member of the couple. Conversely, the more "purely physical" the infidelity, the less likely that there will be any jealousy. Thus it is often hypothesized that where marital stability coexists with infidelity, the character of the extramarital involvement is relatively depersonalized.

In the film *Bob and Carol and Ted and Alice,* Bob finds Carol, his wife, entertaining another man in their bedroom. Although he had previously told her that he was having an affair, and they had agreed in principle that she, too, could have affairs, he is obviously shaken by the reality. Nervously trying to reassure himself, he asks, "Well, it's just *sex,* isn't it? I mean, you don't *love* him?" In other words, Bob attempts to avoid feelings of jealousy by believing that Carol's affair involves only depersonalized sex in contrast to their own relationship of love.

In his book, *Group Sex,* Gilbert Bartell offers the same hypothesis about those people he calls *organization swingers:*

> They are terrified of the idea that involvement might take place. They take comfort from the fact that if they swing with a couple only once or at most twice, the chances of running into a marriage-threatening involvement are small.

These swingers, who can be described as organizational only in the sense that they tend to use swinger magazines or special swinging nightclubs to make their contacts, are mostly beginners who *may* act in ways that approximate Bartell's description. Near the end of the book, however, he mentions some couples he interviewed whom he calls *dropouts.* These people either had never desired depersonalized swinging or had passed through a depersonalized stage, but now preferred some degree of emotional involvement and long-term friendship from their swinging relationships. Bartell does not explain how these couples continue to keep stable relationships and can remain free of jealousy, but the fact that such couples exist indicates that depersonalization is not the only way to jealousy-free swinging.

Our involvement with the subject has been partly a personal one, and this requires some introductory explanation. In September 1969, we read an article about swinging and became fascinated by the questions it raised about sex and the American family. Did this practice signal the beginning of the breakup of the family? Or was it a way to inject new life into marriage as the authors of the article suggested? How do people go about swinging and why? We contemplated these and many other questions but, not knowing any swingers, we could arrive at only very limited answers. It seemed to us that the only way to find out what we wanted to know was to participate ourselves. In one way this seemed natural because anthropologists have traditionally lived with the people they have studied. But our curiosity about swinging at that time was more personal than professional, and we knew that ultimately our participation would have personal consequences, although we had no idea what their nature might be. We had to decide whether exploration of this particular unknown was worth the risk of changing the perfectly sound and gratifying relationship that we had built during the previous three-and-a-half years. Finally, our misgivings gave way to curiosity and we wrote off to some couples who advertised in a national swinger's magazine.

Although, like most beginners, we were excited about swinging, we were nervous, too. We did not know what swinging in reality was like or what "rules" there were, if any. In general, however, we found those first experiences not only enjoyable from a personal point of view, but stimulating intellectually. It was then that we decided to study swinging as anthropologists. But, like many anthropologists who use participant-observation as a method of study, we could never completely divorce ourselves from the personal aspects of our subject.

The method of participant-observation is sometimes criticized as being too subjective. In an area such as sex, where experiences are highly individual and personal, we feel that participant-observation can yield results even more thorough and disciplined than the more so-called objective methods. Most of our important insights into the nature of swinging could only have been found by actually experiencing some of the same things that our informants did. Had we not participated, we would not have known how to question them about many central aspects of their experience.

This chapter presents the results of our eighteen-month, participant-observation study of 136 swingers. We made our contacts in three ways. First, we reached couples through swinger magazines. These are magazines devoted almost exclusively to ads placed by swingers for the purpose of contacting other interested couples and/or singles. Many, although not all, of the couples we contacted in this way seemed to be beginners who had not yet found people with whom they were interested in forming long-term relationships. Second, we were introduced to couples through personal networks. Couples whom we knew would pass our name on to others, sometimes explicitly because they wanted our study to be a success. Third, some couples contacted us as a result of lectures or papers we presented, to volunteer themselves as informants. It should be noted that we did not investigate the swingers' bars, although secondhand reports from couples we met who had used them for making contacts seem to indicate that these couples did not significantly differ from those people who do not use the bars. Our informants came from Pennsylvania, New Jersey, New York, Massachusetts, Louisiana, California, Florida, and Illinois. They were mostly middle class, although ten could be classified as working class.

Usually we interviewed couples in very informal settings, and these interviews were often indistinguishable from ordinary conversation that swingers might have about themselves and their activities. After each session we would return home, discuss the conversation, and write notes on our observations. Later several couples volunteered to tape interviews, enabling us to check the accuracy of the field notes we had taken previously.

In spite of our efforts to find informants from as many different sources as possible, we can in no way guarantee the representativeness of our sample. It should be emphasized that statistics are practically useless in the study of swingers because of insurmountable sampling problems. We therefore avoided the statistical approach and instead focused the investigation on problems of a nonstatistical nature. The information we obtained enabled us to understand and describe the kinds of cultural symbols—a "symbolic calculus," if you will—that swingers must use to effectively navigate social situations with other swingers. This symbolic calculus organizes widely varying experiences into a coherent whole, enabling swingers to understand and evaluate each social situation in which they find themselves. They can thereby define the choices available to them and the desirability of each. Our research goal, then, was to describe the symbols that infuse meaning into the experiences of all the swingers that we contacted.

Unlike Bartell, we had no difficulty finding couples who either wanted to have or had succeeded in having some degree of emotional involvement and long-term friendship within a swinging context. In fact, many of them explained to us that depersonalization simply brought them no satisfaction. In observing such couples with their friends it was evident that they had formed close and enduring relationships. They host each other's children on weekends, celebrate birthdays together, take vacations together, and, in general, do what close friends usually do. It should be noted that there is no way of ascertaining the numbers of couples who have actually succeeded in finding close friends through swinging. In fact, they may be underrepresented because they tend to retreat into their own small circle of friends and dislike using swinger magazines to find other couples. Thus they are more difficult to contact.

In order to see how swingers are able to form such relationships it is necessary to understand not how they avoid jealousy, but how they deal with its causes. Insecurity and fear of being replaced are the major ingredients in any experience with jealousy. An effective defense against jealousy, then, would include a way to guarantee one's irreplaceability as a mate. If, for example, a wife knows that she is unlike any other woman her husband has ever met or ever will meet, and if they have a satisfying relationship in which they have invested much time and emotion, she can rest assured that no other relationship her husband has can threaten her. If, on the other hand, a woman feels that the continuance of her marital relationship depends on how well she cooks, cleans, and makes love, jealousy is more likely to occur, because she realizes that any number of women could fill the same role, perhaps better than she can.

Similarly, a man who feels that the continuance of his wife's loyalty depends on how well he provides financial security will be apt to feel more jealousy because many men could perform the same function. To one degree or another, many swingers naturally develop toward a more secure kind of marital relationship, a tendency we call *individuation*. Among the couples we contacted, individuation was achieved for the most part at a level that precluded jealousy. And we found that, to the extent that couples did not individuate, either jealousy occurred or swinging had to take other, less flexible forms in order to prevent it.

We found evidence of individuation in two areas. First, we found that patterns of behavior at gatherings of swingers who had passed the beginning stages were thoroughly pervaded by individuation. Second, we found that by following changes in a couple's attitudes toward themselves, both as individuals and as a couple and toward other swingers, a trend of increasing individuation could be observed.

### Individuating Behavior at Gatherings

When we first entered the swinging scene, we hypothesized that swinging must be characterized by a set of implicit and explicit rules or patterns of behavior. But every time we thought we had discovered a pattern, another encounter quickly invalidated it. We finally had to conclude that any particular swinging gathering is characterized by any one of a number of forms, whatever best suits the individuals involved. The ideal, as it is in nonswinging situations, is for the initiation of sexual interaction to appear to develop naturally—preferably in a nonverbal way. But with four or more people involved and all the signaling and cross-signaling of intentions that must take place, this ideal can only be approached in most cases. The initiation may begin with little or no socializing, much socializing with sex later on as a natural outgrowth of the good feelings thus created, or some mixture in between. Socializing is of the variety found at many types of nonswinging gatherings. The sexual interaction itself may be "open" where couples participate in the same room or "closet" where couples pair off in separate rooms. In open swinging, a "pretzel," "flesh pile," or "scene" may take place, all terms that signify groups of more than two people having sex with each other. Like Bartell, we found that females are much more like-

ly to participate in homosexuality—probably near 100 percent—
while very few men participate in homosexuality. Younger people
tend to be much more accepting about the latter.

All of this flexibility can be summed up by saying that swingers
consider an ideal gathering one in which everyone can express themselves as individuals *and* appreciate others for doing the same. If
even one person fails to have an enjoyable experience in these terms,
the gathering is that much less enjoyable for everyone.

An important consequence of this "do your own thing" ethic is
that sexual experiences are talked about as a primarily personal
matter. Conversely they are not evaluated according to general
standards. Thus one hears about "bad experiences" rather than
"bad swingers." This is not to say that swingers are not aware of
general sexual competence, but only that it is largely irrelevant to
their appreciation of other people. As one informant said:

> Technique is not that much. If she's all right, I don't care if
> she's technically terrible—if I think she's a beautiful person,
> she can't be that bad.

Beginners may make certain mistakes if they do not individuate.
They may, for example, take on the "social director" role. This kind
of person insists that a party become the materialization of his own
fantasies without regard for anyone else's wishes. This can make the
situation very uncomfortable for everyone else unless someone can
get him to stop. Or, a nervous beginner may feel compelled to look
around to find out what to do and, as a result, will imitate someone
else. This imitation can be disturbing to others for two reasons.
First, the imitator may not be enjoying himself. Second, he may be
competing with someone else by comparing the effects of the same
activity on their different partners. In either case, he is not involved
with perceiving and satisfying the individual needs of his own
partner. This would also be true in the case of the person who
regularly imitates his or her own previous behavior, making an
unchanging formula for interaction, no matter who he is with.
Swingers generally consider such behavior insensitive and/or insin-
cere.

### Modification of Attitudes

Beginners tend to approximate the popular stereotype of sex-
starved deviates. A fifty-year-old woman described one of her beginning experiences this way:

> It was one after another, and really, after a point it didn't make any difference *who* it was. It was just one great big prick after another. And I *never* experienced anything like that in my whole life. I have never had an experience like that with quite so many. I think in the course of three hours I must have had eleven or twelve men, and one greater than the next. It just kept on getting better every time. It snowballed.

The manner in which she describes her experience exemplifies the attitudes of both male and female beginners. They are not likely to develop a long-lasting friendship with one or a small number of couples, and they focus much more on sex than the personalities involved. Frequently, they will be more interested in larger parties where individual personality differences are blurred by the number of people.

Simple curiosity seems to be the reason for this attitude. As one beginner told us, "Sometimes, we get titillated with them as people, knowing in the long run that it won't work out." It seems that because the beginner has been prevented so often from satisfying his curiosity through sexual liaisons in "straight" life, an important goal of early swinging is to satisfy this curiosity about people in general. This goal is apt to take precedence over any other for quite some time. Thus, even if a couple sincerely hopes to find long-lasting friendships, their desire to "move on" is apt to win out at first.

Bartell has asserted that both personality shallowness and jealousy are always responsible for this focus on sex and the search for new faces. For the most part, neither of these factors is necessarily responsible. First, the very same couples who appear shallow in fact may develop friendships later on. Second, as we shall see below, some couples who focus almost exclusively on sex nevertheless experience jealousy and must take certain precautions. On the other hand, some swingers *do* couple-hop because of jealousy. For example, one couple disliked swinging with another couple more than once or twice because of the jealousy that arose each time. Very often only one member is jealous of the other's involvement but the jealousy will be hidden. Pride may prevent each from admitting jealousy for quite some time. Each partner may feel that to admit jealousy would be to admit a weakness and instead will feign disinterest in a particular couple to avoid another meeting.

This stage of swinging eventually stops in almost all cases we know of, probably because the superficial curiosity about people in general is satisfied. Women are usually responsible for the change, probably because they have been raised to reject superficial sexual relationships. Sometimes this is precipitated by a bad experience when, for example, a man is particularly rough or inconsiderate in some way. Sometimes a man will be the first to suggest a change because of erection problems that seem to be caused in some cases by a general lack of interest in superficial sexual contacts. In other words, once his general curiosity is satisfied, he can no longer sustain enough interest to be aroused.

The termination of the curiosity stage and the beginning of a stage of relative selectivity is characterized by increasing individuation of self and others. Among men this change manifests itself in the nature of fantasies that give interest to the sexual experience. The statement of one male informant exemplifies the change:

> Now, I don't fantasize much. There's too much reality to fantasize, too much sex and sex realities we've experienced. So there is not too much that I *can* fantasize with. I just remember the good times we've actually had.

Instead of fantasies being what one would wish to happen, they are instead a kind of reliving of pleasant past experiences with particular people. Also, some informants have noticed that where their previous fantasies had been impersonal, they eventually became tied to specific people with whom pleasant sexual experiences had been shared.

Increasing individuation is also noticeable in beginners' changing perceptions of certain problems that arise in swinging situations. Many male swingers have difficulty with erections at one time or another. Initially, this can be quite ego shattering. The reason for this trauma is not difficult to understand. Most Americans believe that the mere sight of a nude, sexually available woman should arouse a man almost instantly. A male who fails to be aroused may interpret this as a sign of his hitherto unknown impotency. But if he is not too discouraged by this first experience he may eventually find the real reasons. He may realize that he does not find some women attractive mentally and/or physically even though they are sexually available. He learns to recognize when he is being deliberately though subtly discouraged by a woman. He may discover that he dislikes certain situational factors. For example, he may find that he likes only open or only closet swinging or that he cannot relax sufficiently to perform after a hard day's work. Once a swinger realizes that his physical responses may very well be due to elements that inhere to the individual relationship rather than to an innate sexual inadequacy, he has arrived at a very different conception of sexual relationships. He is better able to see women as human beings to whom he may be attracted as personalities rather than as objects to be exploited for their sexual potential. In our terms, he can now more successfully individuate his relationships with women.

Women must cope with problems of a slightly different nature when they begin to swing. Their difficulties develop mostly because of their tendency to place decorum above the expression of their own individual desires in social situations. This tendency manifests itself from the time the husband suggests swinging. Many women seem to swing merely because their husbands want to rather than because of their own positive feelings on the matter. This should not be interpreted to mean that wives participate against their will, but only that as in most recreational activity, the male provides the initial impetus that she can then choose to go along with or reject. Her lack of positive initiative may express itself in the quality of her interaction. She is apt to swing with a man not because he manifests particular attributes that she appreciates, but because he lacks any traits that she finds outright objectionable. One woman describes one of her first experiences this way:

> As I recall, I did not find him particularly appealing, but he was nice, and that was OK. He actually embarrassed me a bit because he was so shy and such a kind of nonperson.

This is not to say that women do not enjoy their experiences once they begin participating. The same woman remarks about her first experience in this way:

> Somehow, it was the situation that made the demand. I got turned on, although I hadn't anticipated a thing up to that point. In fact, I still have a hard time accounting for my excitement that first time and the good time which I did actually have.

In fact, it sometimes happens at this stage that women become more enthusiastic about swinging than men, much to the latter's embarrassment.

Female enjoyment, however, seems to result from the same kind of psychology that is likely to propel them into swinging in the first place, the desire to please men. Hence, like her nonswinging counterparts, a woman in swinging will judge herself in terms of her desirability and her attractiveness to men much more than thinking about her own individuality in relation to others.

After swinging for awhile, however, her wish to be desired and to satisfy can no longer be as generalized because it becomes apparent that she is indeed desired by many men, and thus she has no need to prove it to herself. In order to make the experience meaningful, she arrives at a point where she feels that she must begin to actually refuse the advances of many men. This means that she must learn to define her own preferences more clearly and to learn to act on these preferences, an experience that many women rarely have because they have learned to rely on their husbands to make these kinds of decisions in social situations. In short, a woman learns to individuate both herself and others in the second stage of swinging.

Another change that swingers mention concerns their feelings toward their mates. They say that since they started swinging they communicate better than they did before. Such couples, who previously had a stable but uninteresting or stale marriage ("like brother and sister without the blood"), say that swinging has recreated the romantic feelings they once had for each other. These feelings seem to find concrete expression in an increasing satisfaction with the sexual aspects of the marital relationship, if not in an actual increase in sexual intercourse. This is almost always experienced by older couples in terms of feeling younger.

An explanation for this change, again, involves the individuation process. Marriage can grow stale if a couple loses a sense of appreciation of each other's individuality. A husband may look too much like an ordinary husband, a wife like an ordinary wife. This can happen easily especially when a couple's circumstances (job, children, and so forth) necessitate a great deal of routinization of their life together. Such couples find in swinging the rare opportunity to escape from the routine roles that must be assumed in everyday life. In this setting individual differences receive attention and appreciation and, because of this, married couples can again see and appreciate their own distinct individuality, thus reactivating their romantic feelings for each other.

It is interesting to note that those couples who do not answer in this way almost always experience jealousy, not romanticization, as a result of swinging. This is the case with one couple we interviewed, each of whom insists that the other is "better than anyone else," although it was clear by their jealousy of each other that neither was entirely confident of this.

Individuation, then, pervades the swinging scene and plays an important role in minimizing jealousy. But it alone cannot guarantee the control of jealousy—because there is always the possibility that a person will appreciate and be equally attracted to two unique individuals. Clearly, individuation must be complemented with something more if the marriage is to be effectively distinguished from other extramarital relationships.

This "something else" is compatibility. Two individuals who perceive and appreciate each other's individuality may nevertheless make poor living mates unless they are compatible. Compatibility is a kind of superindividuation. It requires not only the perception and appreciation of uniqueness, but the inclusion of this in the solutions to any problems that confront the relationship. Each partner must have the willingness and the ability to consider his or her mate's needs, desires, and attitudes, when making the basic decisions that affect them both. This is viewed as something that people must work to achieve, as indicated by the phrase, "He failed in his marriage."

Unlike swinging, then, marriage requires a great deal of day-to-day giving and taking, and an emotional investment that increases with the years. Because such an investment is not given up easily, it provides another important safeguard against jealousy.

The dimension of marital compatibility often shows itself in swinging situations. If and when serious problems are encountered by one marriage partner, it is expected that the other partner will take primary responsibility for doing what is necessary. One couple, for example, was at a gathering, each sitting with their swinging partners. It was the first time they had ever tried pot, and the wife suddenly became hysterical. The man she was with quickly relinquished his place to her husband, who was expected to take primary responsibility for comforting his wife, although everyone was concerned about her. Another example can occur when a man has erection problems. If he is obviously miserable, it is considered wrong for his wife to ignore his condition, although we have heard of a few cases where this has happened. His wife may go to his side and they will decide to go home or she may simply act worried and less than completely enthusiastic, thus evincing some minimal concern for her husband. In other words, the married couple is still distinguished as the most compatible partners and remains therefore the primary problem-solving unit.

The importance of compatibility also shows up in certain situations where a couple decides that they must stop swinging. In several cases reported to us, couples who had been married two years or less found that swinging tended to disrupt their marital relationship. We ourselves encountered three couples who had been married for under one year and had not lived together before marriage. All three had difficulties as a result of swinging, and one is now divorced. These couples evidently had not had the time to build up the emotional investment so necessary to a compatible marriage.

It is clear, then, that to the degree that couples individuate and are compatible, jealousy presents no major problems. Conversely, when these conditions are not satisfied, disruptive jealousy can result.

There are, however, some interesting exceptions. For a few couples who seem to place little emphasis on individuation, marital compatibility is an issue that remains chronically unresolved. Compatibility for them is a quality to be constantly demonstrated rather than a fact of life to be more or less taken for granted. Hence, every give-and-take becomes an issue.

These couples focus on the mechanics of sexual competence rather than on personal relationships. These are the people who will talk about "good swingers" and "bad swingers" rather than good and bad experiences. One of these husbands once commented:

> Some people say there's no such thing as a good lay and a bad lay. But in my experience that just isn't true. I remember this one woman I went with for a long time. She was just a bad lay. No matter what I did, she was just lousy!

In other words, his bad lay is everyone's bad lay. One of his friends expressed it differently. He did not understand why some swingers were so concerned with compatibility; he felt it was the sex that was important—and simply "having a good time."

Because they do not consider individuation important, these couples tend to approximate most closely the popular stereotypes of swingers as desiring only "pure sex." Swinging for these couples is primarily a matter of sexual interaction. Consequently, they are chiefly interested in seeing how sexually competent a couple is before they decide whether or not to develop a friendship. Competence may be defined in any or all of a number of ways. Endurance, size of penis, foreplay competence—all may be used to assess competence during the actual sexual interaction whether it be a large open party or a smaller gathering.

It is clear, then, that such couples perceive sex in a way that individuators find uncongenial or even repugnant. When we first observed and interviewed them, we interpreted their behavior as the beginning stage of promiscuity that new couples may go through. But when we asked, we would find that they had been swinging frequently for a period of two years, much too long to be considered inexperienced. How, we asked ourselves, could such couples avoid jealousy, if they regularly evaluated sexual partners against a common standard? It seemed to us that a husband or wife in such a situation could conceivably be replaced some day by a "better lay," especially if the issue of marital compatibility remained somewhat unresolved. Yet these couples did not appear to experience any disruptive jealousy as a result of swinging. We found that they are able to accomplish this by instituting special, somewhat less flexible arrangements for swinging. First, they are invariably exclusive open swingers. That is, sexual interaction must take place in the same room. This tends to reduce any emotional involvement in one interaction. They think that closet swinging (swinging in separate rooms) is "no better than cheating." They clearly worry about the possibility of emotional infidelity more than individuators. An insistence on open swinging reduces the possibility of emotional involvement, and with it, the reason for jealousy. Second, they try to control the swinging situation as much as possible. So, for example, they are much more likely to insist on being hosts. And they also desire to state their sexual preferences ahead of time, thereby insuring that nothing very spontaneous and unpredictable can happen. Third, the women are more likely to desire female homosexuality and more aggressively so. This often results in the women experiencing more emotional involvement with each other than with the men, which is more acceptable because it does not threaten the marital relationship.

**Sexual Revolution?**
We are now at the point where we can answer some of the questions with which we began our research. Contrary to many who have assumed that any extramarital activity results in at least some jealousy and possibly even marital breakup, especially when there is emotional involvement, we have found that swinging often succeeds in solidifying a marriage. It does this by reromanticizing marriage, thereby making it tolerable, even enjoyable to be married. In a very important way, then, swinging is a conservative institution.

It is usually assumed that the present "sexual revolution" of which swinging is a part will continue. Bartell, reflecting this view, points out that an increasing number of people are becoming interested in swinging. Basing his prediction on a projection of present trends, he believes that swinging will probably grow in popularity and become in some way a permanent part of American culture. A similar view is expressed by James and Lynne Smith. Although they do not believe that it will become a universal form in marriage, they believe that eventually as many as fifteen to twenty-five percent of married couples will adopt swinging.

But predictions based on projection are inadequate because they do not consider the causal processes involved and therefore cannot account for future deviations. In other words, in order to predict increasing sexual freedom, one must first understand what caused it to appear in the first place.

Although we cannot at this time make rigorous scientific statements amenable to disciplined criticism, a glance at American history in this century reveals trends that suggest some tentative answers. Since the 1920s, greater sexual freedom has always been followed by periods of relatively greater sexual repression. The flappers of the 1920s were followed by the more conservative women of the 1930s and the freer women of World War II were followed by an era where women flocked back to conservative roles in the home. And finally, of course, we have the counterculture that expresses an unprecedented height of sexual freedom in this century. An important factor present in all of these periods seems to be the economic ebb and flow. Economic depressions and recessions have preceded all years of more conservative sexual norms. And it is probably no accident that the present summit of sexual freedom has taken place in the longest run of prosperity this country has ever experienced. With increased economic independence, women have gained sexual privileges more nearly equal to those of men. Even homosexuality has become more acceptable. Further evidence that economic ebbs and flows may directly affect sexual norms can be seen by comparing class differences in sexual behavior. For example, working-class attitudes toward sex tend to be more conservative than those of the middle and upper classes. In general it would seem that as economic resources become more plentiful so do acceptable alternative norms of sexual behavior.

If this is so, given the present decline of economic prosperity, we should find the numbers of acceptable alternative norms shrinking. One of the more obvious indications of this is the back-to-Jesus trend that is attracting increasing numbers of young people who would have formerly been drawn to the rock-drug counterculture.

It is possible, then, that swinging and sexual freedom in general is a function of factors that are beyond the immediate control of individuals. Such factors as investment flows, limited resources, fluctuations in world markets, and so forth, all events that seem isolated from the arena of intimacy that people carve out for themselves are in fact very much a part of their most personal relationships. These superstructural events are critical in that they regulate the resources at the disposal of groups of people, thereby limiting the alternatives available to any one individual in his social relations, including his sexual relations.

Given economic prosperity as a necessary condition for increasing sexual freedom, it is quite possible that with the economic difficulties this country is now facing, the number of available acceptable sexual alternatives will decline and swinging may all but disappear from the American scene.

### Five Types of Swinging Couples:
### The Eversearches, the Closefriends, the Snares,
### the Races, and the Successes

The following are composite case histories of five swinging couples. Although each case history is closely tied to one couple whom we knew fairly well, the case itself is more generalized to represent at least a few couples we have met. To check the accuracy of our perceptions of these different types of couples, we showed these case histories to five couples. All recognized other swinging couples whom they had also met.

Two problems present themselves here—the representativeness of the individual cases and the comprehensiveness of the five cases taken as a whole. In regard to the former, there is no way to know what proportion of swingers represent each case. In fact, to judge proportions from our sample might very well be misleading. This is because couples such as the Eversearches use swinging media and are therefore visible and easier to contact, while couples like the Closefriends are very difficult to locate because they stay within their own circle of close friends. Hence, even though the Eversearches probably represent a higher proportion of our sample, this in no way tells us about the actual proportion of Eversearch types. In regard to the question of comprehensiveness, these case histories are only meant to intuitively represent the possible range of types. Many couples may better be seen as a mixture of types, and some types of couples may not be represented at all.

### Jack and Jeanine Eversearch

Jack and Jeanine grew up in the same small town. They went to the same schools and the same church. In their sophomore year of high school they began to go steady. Just before she was to graduate, Jeanine became pregnant, to her dismay, and her parents, experiencing a similar reaction, finally decided on abortion. They wanted her to go to college, enlarge her experiences, and perhaps find some other marriage prospect than the rather placid Jack.

At college, however, the two continued to see each other frequently. Jeanine occasionally went out with other men, but never felt as

comfortable with them as she did with Jack. Jack never went out
with anyone but Jeanine, mainly because his shyness prevented him
from meeting other girls. It was predictable that the two would
marry the June they graduated.

Five years and two children later, Jack and Jeanine were living
much as they always had, in a new suburban home, close to their
families. Life had become a routine of barbecues and bridge parties
on weekends and children to get ready for school during the week,
marked by occasional special events like a church social or a ride in
the country. To all appearances, they seemed to have a model marriage.

But their marriage had actually changed, so gradually that the
shift was almost imperceptible. Like most married couples, they
had experienced a waning of sexual interest from time to time. But
in their case, the troughs had lengthened until sex had become a per-
functory gesture, something they did just because they were married. As Jeanine said, "We didn't fight, because there was nothing
to fight about. We just felt the inevitability of being together for the
rest of our lives—something like brother and sister without the
blood."

They had used the church before in a social way; they turned to it
now for inspiration. Their congregation had recently acquired a new
pastor, a sincere and intelligent man, whom almost everyone liked.

But the home situation continued to disintegrate. Jeanine, on her
own there most of the day, found the situation intolerable and decided to seek help from the pastor:

> I knew something was wrong but it was too vague to talk
> about very clearly. I just kept stammering about how . . .
> things weren't what they used to be. But I couldn't say exactly
> why. In fact, I was so fuzzy that I was afraid he'd misunder-
> stand me and that instead of advice I'd get a lecture about how
> God is the source of all meaning in life or something like that.
> So, when he started telling me about the problems that he and
> his wife had, I was quite surprised but also delighted.

They continued to meet friends, and it became apparent that the
pastor needed Jeanine for personal comfort and support as much as
she needed him. This led to an affair, which lasted until Jack came
home unexpectedly early from work one day three months later.

After the initial shock faded, Jack was left with a feeling of total
inadequacy:

> I guess I thought that if Jeanine wanted to sleep with some-
> one else, that meant I had disappointed her. I felt that my in-
> ability to rise in the company reflected on our marriage and on
> her choice of me as a husband—which didn't do my ego any
> good.

The episode proved fortunate, because it provided them with a
reason to talk about their problems, and with the channels of communication open once more, their marriage began to seem fulfilling
again. Their sexual interest in each other returned:

> We started doing things in bed that we'd always been curious
> about but had never bothered to try or had been too embar-
> rassed to mention. There were many nights when we couldn't
> wait to get into bed.

About a year after Jeanine's affair ended, they started discussing
the possibility of swinging. But when they thought of it seriously,
they realized that not one other couple they knew would be willing
partners. Jack had heard of swingers' magazines, gave the local
smut peddler a try, and brought one home.

They examined the magazine for hours, wondering about the people who had placed the ads and looking at the pictures. Finally, cau-
tion gave way to curiosity, and they answered four of the more conservative ads. Within a few weeks they had received encouraging
answers from all four.

Jack and Jeanine found their first swinging experience very
pleasant. They felt nervous at first when they were greeted at the
door by the other couple because they did not know what to expect.
Nevertheless, they enjoyed themselves enough to agree to swing
when it was suggested by their hosts. Having their fantasies and
desires come true in the bedroom was intensely pleasurable to them
both, and when they returned home they longed to share their ela-
tion with someone else, but could think of no one who would not be
shocked. So they called the other couple back and told *them* what a
good time they had had.

Encouraged by this first happy experience, the Eversearches
began to swing with practically every couple they could contact.
Lately, they have become more selective, but they still devote some
time to contacting and meeting new people.

Looking back, both feel that swinging has changed them. Before,
Jack had always gone along with the men he knew, accepting, at
least verbally, their values, attitudes, and behavior:

It bugs me now that I have to play some kind of he-man role all the time. I never used to notice it. You know how guys are always talking about this girl and how they would like to get her in bed? Well . . . I'm not interested in just sex any more—I mean, I want to have someone I like, not just a writhing body.

Jeanine feels similarly:

All of a sudden it seems I have more insight into everybody, into how they interact with each other. Maybe because we've met so many different kinds of people. And I have to be very careful that I don't express some of my liberal views. Sometimes, I really want to tell our nonswinging friends about our new life—but then I'm sure they wouldn't understand.

### Mike and Maryann Closefriend

Mike and Maryann are thirty and twenty-five years old and have been married five years. They originally met when Mike, then an advanced graduate student, gave a lecture about inner-city family structure to a group of volunteer social workers. Maryann was in the audience and asked several penetrating questions. After the talk, she approached him to find out more. They were immediately attracted to each other and started going out frequently. After about six months they rented an apartment together, and when Mike got his Ph.D. in social science a year later, they married and moved to the East Coast, where he had obtained a teaching post.

Their early life together seemed an experience of endless enjoyment. They went camping on weekends, took pottery classes, and were lucky in meeting several people whose outlook on life was similar to theirs, with whom they developed close relationships. These friends have helped not only in practical things, such as moving or house painting, but in emotional crises. When, for example, Mike and Maryann seemed to be on the verge of breaking up about two years ago, their friends helped to smooth things over by acting as amateur psychologists.

The Closefriends do not remember exactly how they started swinging. Mike says it was "just a natural consequence of our friendship—our feeling for our friends." They remember some nudity at their parties before they swung, mostly unplanned. People took off their clothes because of the heat or just because they felt more comfortable that way. Sometimes they engaged in sexual play of various kinds, and this led to intercourse as a natural part of these occasions. Sometimes just two people felt like swinging, and sometimes everyone. If the former was the case, people could just watch, or if the couple wanted privacy, they went to another room. And sometimes no one felt like swinging, and the subject was never brought up.

For the Closefriends, swinging seems to be a natural outgrowth of the way they approached marriage and friendship, and the way they feel about and relate to people in general. As Maryann puts it:

> I guess it has to do with our basic belief in the totality of sharing and the kind of dialogue that we have with each other. Our no-holds-barred, no secrets kind of relationship produces such a lovely kind of glow that we just naturally like to share it with our friends. Our having close relationships with people is actually like having a second marriage. Not that we would all want to live together, although that might be possible some day. Some of the men, for example, couldn't live with me—we would be incompatible—but that doesn't make us any less desirable to each other.

### Paul and Georgia Snare

When Paul met Georgia, he had been married about a year and was beginning to find his wife Serita both boring and demanding. A handsome young man, Paul had led an exciting life as a bachelor and found the daily routine of marriage very depressing:

> I felt awfully trapped. . . . It just got worse and worse until I couldn't see going home anymore. I bought a motorcycle and joined up with a bunch of guys pretty much like me. We'd ride around all night so we wouldn't have to go home to our old ladies.

Georgia was a salesgirl in the drugstore next door to the camera shop where Paul worked. He used to drop by daily for cigarettes and a chat, and they became friendly. Paul even made a few passes, but Georgia knew he already had a wife and refused his attention. Unused to this kind of treatment, Paul took her refusals as a challenge and became quite serious in his efforts to persuade her to go out with him. Finally, when Paul and Serita got a formal separation, Georgia accepted his invitations, and they began to date steadily.

Georgia became pregnant about three months before Paul's divorce was due to come through, so they were married the week after the decree became final. At first things went well. Georgia stayed home and took care of the small house in the suburbs that Paul had bought for her, and the marriage ran smoothly for about six months, until the baby came. Then Paul began to feel trapped again, "going to work every day, coming home to dinner, and going to bed. I didn't want it to happen again but it did."

Paul resorted to outside affairs, but found them unsatisfactory because they took too much time and money, and "it just wasn't worth all the lying." He suggested to Georgia the possibility of swinging with some friends of theirs, pointing out that he loved her but that "every man needs a bit of variety." Georgia initially thought the idea was crazy, but Paul persisted and finally persuaded her to try it.

Persuading their friends, however, was another matter. They did not want to come right out and proposition them, so they decided on seduction as the method of persuasion. They would "date" a couple each weekend, and go dancing to provide an excuse for body contact. Paul would get increasingly intimate with the wife, and if the husband followed his example, Georgia would accept his advances.

They decided their first couple would be their old friends, Bill and Jean. Everything went as planned for a while until Bill became suspicious and asked Paul to explain his attentions to Jean. When Paul did so, the couple became upset and left almost immediately.

Somewhat depressed by the loss of the friends, Paul and Georgia tried another couple they knew, but this time they enacted their plan more slowly. It took about six months, but it worked, and they continued to swing with the couple exclusively for about a year, until they discovered swinging magazines and began making new contacts through them.

Neither of the Snares have any problems with jealousy, and agree that this is because "we are so good in bed with each other that no one could really compete." From time to time Paul even brings home girls he has met; Georgia does not get jealous "just so long as he introduces them to me first and they do their thing in my house." For her part, Georgia has discovered that she likes women, too, and regularly brings home girls from a nearby homosexual bar. "Men," she says, "are good for sex, but it isn't in their nature to be able to give the kind of affection a woman needs." Georgia's activities do not worry Paul a bit:

> A woman couldn't provide the kind of support I do. They just don't know how to get along in the world without a man. A lot of these lesbians she meets are really irresponsible and would never be able to take care of the kid.

Swinging has affected Georgia's self-confidence as well as changing her sex habits. She now feels much more confident in social situations, a change that occurred after she began making her own choices about whom she would swing with. At first, she had let Paul make all the decisions:

> If he liked the woman, then I would swing with the man. But it got so I couldn't stand it anymore. I had to make it with so many creeps! I just got sick of it after a while. Paul kept getting the good deals and I never found anybody I liked. Finally, I just had to insist on my rights!

Paul agrees that this is good and points out that one swinger they know constantly forces his wife to swing with men she has no desire for, and as a result their marriage is slowly disintegrating. He credits swinging with saving his own marriage with Georgia and thinks that, had he known about it before, it could have saved his first marriage, too.

### Frank and Helen Race

Frank and Helen met at a well-known West Coast university where both were top-ranked graduate students in biochemistry. Both were from Jewish backgrounds, strongly oriented toward academic achievement.

Frank, largely because of his parents' urging, had excelled in high school, both academically and in extracurricular activities. After high school, he enlisted in the marines, was commissioned after OCS training and commanded one of the best units on his base. Ultimately, he became dissatisfied with the life of a marine officer and left to attend college, where he finished his bachelor degree in three years, graduated with honors, and went on to graduate school.

As a child, Helen had experienced much the same kind of pressure. Her father, an excellent musician, dominated the family and drove her endlessly. She began piano lessons at age four and remembers that he was always at her shoulder to scold her when she made a mistake. She was able to end music lessons only because she attended a college where no facilities were available, leaving her free to devote all her time to the study of biochemistry, which she much preferred.

Helen and Frank married during their third year of graduate school. It seemed a perfect match—two fine scholars with identical interests, who could work as a team. For the next four years they did work closely together on their respective Ph.D. dissertations, which were published and became well known in the field. Despite this success, however, they could not find jobs with prestige schools and had to take posts at a less well-known institution.

They settled into their professional lives, both publishing as much as possible in the hope of eventually gaining positions at a more prestigious university. They worked together closely, constantly seeking each other's help and proffering severe criticisms. If either published more than the other during the year, the "under-published" one would experience intense jealousy. Realizing this disruptive competition was a serious threat to their marriage, they sought help from a psychotherapist and from group-therapy sessions.

The most important thing Frank and Helen learned about themselves in therapy was that by making their relationship competitive they had forfeited their appreciation of each other as individuals. They also discovered another element in their lives, which Frank links directly to their decision to take up swinging:

> I told Helen that I missed terribly the experiences that other men had as kids. I was always too busy with school to ever have a good time dating. I only had a date once in high school, for the senior prom, and I had only had one girlfriend in college. I felt that a whole stage of my life was totally absent. I wanted to do those things that I had missed out on—then maybe I'd feel more able to cope with our problems. Much to my surprise, Helen felt she, too, had missed out.

Like the Eversearches, the Races met their first couple through an ad in a swinger publication. Their first meeting, however, was somewhat unpleasant. Frank felt jealous because he feared the man might be sexually better than he was. He did not tell Helen this, however, but simply refused to return, on the grounds that he had not enjoyed the woman. Helen suspected Frank was in fact jealous, and many arguments ensued.

The Races have been swinging for about three years and average one contact every two or three months, a rate of frequency considerably lower than usual. Both agree that they have a lot of difficulty with jealousy. If, for example, they meet a couple and Helen is very attracted to the man, Frank will invariably insist he does not find the woman desirable. They have come to realize that the one who exercises the veto is probably jealous of the good time the other has had or is about to have and thus insists on breaking off the threatening relationship. They also realize that swinging may not be the best way to use their leisure time—but somehow they cannot give up the hope that they may find the experiences they missed as young people.

### Glen and Andrea Success

Glen and Andrea were married shortly before the end of the war, immediately after Glen graduated with a Ph.D. in biology. Because he felt that teaching at a university would be financially limiting, he found a job with a medical-supply manufacturing company, which promised him a high-ranking executive position in the future. He has stayed with the company for nearly twenty years, rising to positions of increased responsibility.

Five years after he had begun work, Andrea and Glen were able to afford a luxurious suburban home. Well settled into their house and community, they started their family. Andrea enjoyed motherhood and raised her two boys and a girl as model children:

> There wasn't a thing we couldn't do. Glen and I traveled all over the states and Europe. We even went to Australia. We had bought ourselves a lovely house, we had a fine marriage and wonderful, healthy children. We had many fine friends, too.

Glen claims it was this unusual good luck that eventually turned them to swinging. About seven years ago, they began to feel they had achieved everything that people usually want and anything else would be anticlimactic:

> We knew one couple with whom we could talk about anything and everything, and we did! One conversation especially, I think, led to our considering swinging. We were talking about success and trying to define exactly what it meant. Andrea and I thought it was something like having all the money you need and a good marriage. They said that if that was true, then we already had everything we would ever want. . . . Later on, when I thought about what he'd said, I got a funny kind of hollow feeling. Forty-five, I said to myself, and at the end of the line.

In this state of mind Glen got the idea that swinging might be a way out. He and Andrea spent about a month discussing the possibility and finally decided to try it out. Their first meeting with another couple was disturbing for them both, but they continued to look for more satisfactory people. If the second meeting had been equally bad, they probably would have given up the whole idea. But it ended pleasantly in a friendship that lasted about three years.

At first they had to rely on contacts from the *National Enquirer,* but about a year after they started swinging, their local newspaper began running ads on the lines of, "Modern couple interested in meeting the same. Box 1023." About ten of these ads appeared during the brief period before the paper found out what they were for and ceased to accept any more. By then Glen and Andrea had contacted all the couples who had advertised. These people, in turn, knew other swingers whom they had either met through national publications or had initiated themselves. Soon a large network began to form.

Glen applied his organizational talents to the swinging scene and was soon arranging parties for couples he felt would be compatible, spending his own money to rent halls for get-togethers. Many couples started coming to him with their problems, and to help them out, he arranged for a doctor to direct group discussions dealing with typical swinging problems. He even contacted lawyers whom he knew personally to protect "his swingers," as he was beginning to call them, should they have any difficulties with the law. In fact, the Successes knew so many couples that other swingers began to rely on them as a kind of dating service that could arrange for either quiet evenings or major parties.

The Successes feel that in swinging they have finally found an activity that offers lasting interest and stimulation. Says Andrea:

> Glen and I have done everything—I don't just mean sex. Just doing things doesn't really appeal to us anymore. But swinging has managed to hold our attention for a long time. If you give me a choice between going to South America, nightclubbing, or swinging, I think swinging is the most satisfying and interesting.

Why? Glen says:

> I think it's because in swinging you can see people for who they really are—as individuals, without the masks they have to wear most of the time. In a way, I guess I never knew people before, and I'm amazed at the variety. Maybe that's why swinging holds my interest—everybody is different, a challenge to get to know.

# IV

# Deviant Life-Styles
# and the Path
# to Imprisonment

# Introduction

Many of the activities detailed in the previous part bring their participants to the attention of the police, not infrequently resulting in arrest, publicity, trial, and incarceration. In this section we focus on aspects of the complex interrelationships between those individuals participating in deviant life-styles and people assigned the task of enforcing public morality. The first two chapters examine in detail the subcultural context surrounding juvenile delinquency, analyzing the behaviors that most commonly bring American youth to the attention of the police. The final selection looks at the deviant life-styles within which public drunkenness occurs, the offense for which more adults are arrested in the United States than for all other causes combined. The authors emphasize the complex interrelationships existing among proscribed human behavior, the enforcement activities of the police and other members of the judicial system, and the feedback of the enforcement system into the subculture of deviance.

This part opens with a detailed description and analysis of leader-follower relationships among members of four urban gangs. These groups were all composed of lower-class whites and were all located in the same neighborhood of a single metropolitan area. As Miller demonstrates, gang leadership is a complex matter. In just these four groups the form of leadership ranged widely. One gang followed a decentralized form of leadership, a "multileader power balance," while the second was directed by a "weak" leader who mediated between rival factions in his gang. The leadership of another gang was collective and situational, a form of organization in which leadership is based on competence in whatever activity the group is involved in. The fourth group was undergoing a power struggle, and the rival claimants to the rights of leadership were each competitively recruiting followers from the same group.

Humans are extremely complex organisms, and their various associational forms reflect this complexity. Though to an outsider lower-class male gangs may appear unified in purpose and activity, when one gains detailed inside information the situation is quite different. Fundamentally contrasting and competing ideologies, for example, were held by the members of one of the gangs. This group was characterized by a split between members who were oriented toward crime and those who were oriented toward noncriminal activities. Their contrasting verbal positions did not represent fundamental differences in moral codes, however, since all gang members were involved in delinquent behaviors. Regardless of their ideological stance, they all felt the need to participate in criminal activities as part of their technique of attaining manhood.

Every subcultural membership in which people find themselves represents demands that others make on the individual to conform with the expectations worked out by members of that group. These expectations range widely in difficulty of compliance, and with its particular demands the lower-class subculture does not represent the easiest end of the spectrum of requirements. One of the keys to understanding this subculture is manhood. Manhood is far from being a status that is automatically conferred on males by virtue of age. Rather, it must be attained through successive and successful involvements in what are considered to be manly virtues. These expectations of virtue may well be in sharp conflict with the expectations held by others, especially with ones held by persons located in other parts of the social-class hierarchy. The resulting social conflict frequently marks the path to imprisonment.

Contrary to popular opinion, gangs are much more than merely a wild bunch of adolescents who band together for mutual involvement in antisocial activities, striking out blindly at social forces that they do not understand. The gang, whether oriented to legal or illegal behavior, is an intrinsic part of lower-class life. Gangs provide a proving ground for individual competence. They set limits for behavior, establish attitudes toward authority, and provide a major means for developing skills in dealing with others. Becoming a major mechanism for coping with the rigorous demands of life in the impoverished areas of our society, gang membership frequently takes over in the socialization process where the family leaves off.

Participation in gang delinquency, however, is by no means limited to the lower class, and the second selection contrasts a gang made up of lower-class youth with one composed of youth from the upper-middle class. Though delinquent acts were as common in one gang as in the other, the response to gang members by persons in position of authority differed considerably. Both the police and the teachers and administrators of the high school that members of both gangs attended reacted with consistent differences to these boys. Members of the upper-middle class gang were perceived as conforming citizens, as sort of young saints headed for good things in life, while the lower-class gang members were seen as roughnecks headed for serious trouble. And with the exceptions carefully documented in this chapter, these expectations came true. Members of the upper-middle-class gang became successful citizens, while members of the lower-class gang became increasingly involved in difficulties with law-enforcement agents. Human behavior is continuously shaped by its social context, and in this case the commitment to deviance depended greatly on a self-fulfilling prophecy based on differential community response to social-class membership. It is this process of differential control over community response, and the intricate interrelationships between control and response with self-images, that are the major issues of Chambliss's analysis. Seldom are we treated to such a penetrating analysis of such sharply contrasting situations that throw this process into such sharp relief.

External behaviors, those characteristics most readily visible to an observer, can play a critical role as police and authorities decide how they will react to persons involved in deviance. Just as this is the case in the relationships between societal authorities and lower- and middle-class youth, so it also operates in the surveillance of the activities of skid-row alcoholics. The drinking behavior of the alcoholics of skid row is certainly highly visible, and this frequently initiates negative contact with the police. But, additionally, to societal authorities, the life-style of these urban nomads represents negative values. Their appearance is disreputable, they have little money, they fail to own homes or to rent apartments in reputable areas of the city, they are tran-

sients, they pay few taxes, they "hang around doing nothing"—
these and other characteristics remove them from many of the
amenities offered the middle class in their interactions with the
police.

In their harrowing trek of ever-downward social mobility and
commitment to a deviant way of life, these men are finally
stripped of their last shreds of social respectability. The judicial
process condemns them to months in jail because they do not
possess the few dollars bail money it would cost to avoid a jail
sentence. The arrest, trial, and incarceration process lead to an
identity void that becomes filled with negative self-images.
Spradley concentrates on the judicial process as he examines
why these men permanently join the ranks of urban nomads, for
it is largely in jail that they learn the attitudes, values, and skills
necessary for survival within the skid-row subculture. The world
of the tramp becomes a viable alternative as these men become
enmeshed in a cycle of travel to other cities to avoid further arrest, seeking out the skid row when they arrive because they
know the expectations of life there and can find people willing to
accept them, being arrested because they live and drink in this
high area of police surveillance, and then traveling to yet another city to avoid further arrest.

# 13

# White Gangs

Walter B. Miller

If one thinks about street-corner gangs at all these days, it is probably in the roseate glow of *West Side Story,* itself the last flowering of a literary and journalistic concern that goes back at least to the late forties. Those were the days when it seemed that the streets of every city in the country had become dark battlefields where small armies of young men engaged their honor in terrible trials of combat, clashing fiercely and suddenly, then retiring to the warm succor of their girl cohorts. The forward to a 1958 collection of short stories, *The Young Punks,* captures a bit of the flavor:

> These are the stories behind today's terrifying headlines— about a strange new frightening cult that has grown up in our midst. Every writer whose work is included in this book tells the truth. These kids are tough. Here are knife-carrying killers, and thirteen-year-old street walkers who could give the most hardened call-girl lessons. These kids pride themselves on their "ethics": never go chicken, even if it means knifing your own friend in the back. Never rat on a guy who wears your gang colors, unless he rats on you first. Old men on crutches are fair game. If a chick plays you for a sucker, blacken her eyes and walk away fast.

Today, the one-time devotee of this sort of stuff might be excused for wondering where they went, the Amboy Dukes and all those other adolescent warriors and lovers who so excited his fancy a decade ago. The answer, as we shall see, is quite simple—nowhere.

The street gangs are still there, out on the corner where they always were.

The fact is that the urban, adolescent street gang is as old as the American city. Henry Adams, in his *Education,* describes in vivid detail the gang fights between the Northsiders and Southsiders on Boston Common in the 1840s. An observer in 1856 Brooklyn writes: "At any and all hours there are multitudes of boys . . . congregated on the corners of the streets, idle in their habits, dissolute in their conduct, profane and obscene in their conversation, gross and vulgar in their manners. If a female passes one of the groups, she is shocked by what she sees and hears. . . ." The Red Raiders of Boston have hung out on the same corner at least since the thirties; similarly, gang fighting between the Tops and Bottoms in West Philadelphia, which started in the thirties, is still continuing into the seventies.

Despite this historical continuity, each new generation tends to perceive the street gang as a new phenomenon generated by particular contemporary conditions and destined to vanish as these conditions vanish. Gangs from 1910 through the twenties were attributed to the cultural dislocations and community disorganization accompanying the mass immigration of foreigners; in the thirties to the enforced idleness and economic pressures produced by the Great Depression; in the fifties to the emotional disturbance of parents and children caused by the increased stresses and tensions of modern life. At present, the existence of gangs is widely attributed to a range of social injustices: racial discrimination, unequal educational and work opportunities, resentment over inequalities in the distribution of wealth and privilege in an affluent society, and the ineffective or oppressive policies of service agencies, such as the police and the schools.

There is also a fairly substantial school of thought that believes that the street gangs are disappearing or have already disappeared. In New York City, the stage of so many real and fictional gang dramas of the fifties and early sixties, *The New York Times* sounded their death knell as long ago as 1966. Very often, the passing of the gang is explained by the notion that young people in the slums have converted their gang-forming propensities into various substitute activities. They have been knocked out by narcotics, or they have been "politicized" in ways that consume their energies in radical or reform movements, or their members have become involved in "constructive" commercial activities, or enrolled in publicly financed education and/or work-training programs.

As has often been the case, these explanations are usually based on very shaky factual grounds and derived from rather parochial, not to say self-serving, perspectives. For street gangs are not only still widespread in United States cities, but some of them also appear to have again taken up "gang warfare" on a scale that is equal to or greater than the phenomenon that received so much attention from the media in the fifties.

In Chicago, street gangs operating in the classic formations of that city—War Lords, High Supremes, Cobra Stones—accounted for thirty-three killings and 252 injuries during the first six months of 1969. Philadelphia has experienced a wave of gang violence that has probably resulted in more murders in a shorter period of time than during any equivalent phase of the "fighting gang" era in New York City. Police estimate that about 80 gangs comprising about 5,000 members are "active" in the city, and that about 20 are engaged in combat. Social agencies put the total estimated number of gangs at 200, with about 80 in the "most hostile" category. Between October 1962 and December 1968, gang members were reportedly involved in 257 shootings, 250 stabbings, and 205 "rumbles." In the period between January 1968 and June 1969, 54 homicides and over 520 injuries were attributed to armed battles between gangs. Of the murder victims, all but eight were known to be affiliated with street gangs. The assailants ranged in age from 13 to 20, with 70 percent of them between 16 and 18 years old. Most of these gangs are designated by the name of the major corner where they hang out, the 12th and Poplar Streeters, or the 21 Ws (for 21st and Westmoreland). Others bear traditional names such as the Centaurs, Morroccos, and Pagans.

Gangs also continue to be active in Boston. In a single ninety-minute period on 10 May 1969, one of the two channels of the Boston Police radio reported thirty-eight incidents involving gangs, or one every two-and-a-half minutes. This included two gang fights. Simultaneous field observation in several white, lower-class neighborhoods turned up evidence that gangs were congregating at numerous street corners throughout the area.

Although most of these gangs are similar to the classic types to be described in what follows, as of recently the national press had virtually ignored the revival of gang violence [1969]. *Time* magazine did include a brief mention of "casual mayhem" in its June 27 issue, but none of the thirty-eight incidents in Boston on May 10 was reported even in the local papers. It seems most likely, however, that if all this had been going on in New York City, where most of the media have their headquarters, a spate of newspaper features, magazine articles, and television specials would have created the impression that the country was being engulfed by a "new" wave of gang warfare. Instead, most people seem to persist in the belief that the gangs have disappeared or that they have been radically transformed.

This anomalous situation is partly a consequence of the problem of defining what a gang is (and we shall offer a definition at the end of our discussion of two specific gangs), but it is also testimony to the fact that this enduring aspect of the lives of urban slum youth remains complex and poorly understood. It is hoped that the following examination of the Bandits and the Outlaws—both of Midcity— will clarify at least some of the many open questions about streetcorner gangs in American cities.

Midcity, which was the location of our ten-year gang-study project (1954-64), is not really a city at all, but a portion of a large one, here called Port City. Midcity is a predominantly lower-class community with a relatively high rate of crime, in which both criminal behavior and a characteristic set of conditions—low-skill occupations, little education, low-rent dwellings, and many others—appeared as relatively stable and persisting features of a developed way of life. How did street gangs fit into this picture?

In common with most major cities during this period, there were many gangs in Midcity, but they varied widely in size, sex composition, stability, and range of activities. There were about fifty Midcity street corners that served as hangouts for local adolescents. Fifteen of these were "major" corners, in that they were rallying points for the full range of a gang's membership, while the remaining thirty-five were "minor," meaning that in general fewer groups of smaller size habitually hung out there.

In all, for Midcity in this period, 3,650 out of 5,740, or 64 percent, of Midcity boys habitually hung out at a particular corner and could therefore be considered members of a particular gang. For girls, the figure is 1,125 out of 6,250, or 18 percent. These estimates also suggest that something like 35 percent of Midcity's boys, and 80 percent of its girls, did *not* hang out. What can be said about them? What made them different from the approximately 65 percent of the boys and 20 percent of the girls who did hang out?

Indirect evidence appears to show that the practice of hanging out with a gang was more prevalent among lower-status adolescents, and that many who were not known to hang out lived in middleclass or lower-class-I (the higher range of the lower class) areas. At the same time, however, it is evident that a fair proportion of higher-status youngsters also hung out. The question of status, and its relation to gang membership and gang behavior is very complex, but it should be borne in mind as we now take a closer look at the gangs we studied.

## The Bandit Neighborhood

Between the Civil War and World War II, the Bandit neighborhood was well-known throughout the city as a colorful and close-knit community of Irish laborers. Moving to a flat in one of its ubiquitous three-decker, frame tenements represented an important step up for the impoverished potato-famine immigrants who had initially settled in the crowded slums of central Port City. By 1810 and shortly after, the second generation of Irish settlers had produced a spirited and energetic group of athletes and politicos, some of whom achieved national prominence.

Those residents of the Bandit neighborhood who shared in some degree the drive, vitality, and capability of these famous men assumed steady and fairly remunerative positions in the political, legal, and civil service world of Port City, and left the neighborhood for residential areas whose green lawns and single houses represented for them what Midcity had represented for their fathers and grandfathers. Individuals who lacked these qualities remained in the Bandit neighborhood, and at the outset of World War II made up a stable and relatively homogeneous community of low-skilled Irish laborers.

The Bandit neighborhood was directly adjacent to Midcity's major shopping district, and was spotted with bars, poolrooms, and dance halls that served as meeting places for an active neighborhood social life. Within two blocks of the Bandits' hanging-out corner were the Old Erin and New Hibernia dance halls, and numerous drinking establishments bearing names such as the Shamrock, Murphy and Donoghue's, and the Emerald Bar and Grill.

A number of developments following World War II disrupted the physical and social shape of the Bandit community. A mammoth federally financed housing project sliced through and blocked off the existing network of streets and razed the regular rows of wooden tenements. The neighborhood's small manufacturing plants were progressively diminished by the growth of a few large establishments, and by the fifties the physical face of the neighborhood was dominated by three large and growing factories. As these plants expanded they bought off many of the properties that had not been taken by the housing project, demolished buildings, and converted them into acres of black-topped parking lots for their employees.

During this period, the parents of the Bandit corner-gang members stubbornly held on to the decreasing number of low-rent, deteriorating, private-dwelling units. Although the Bandits' major hanging corner was almost surrounded by the housing project, virtually none of the gang members lived there. For these families, residence in the housing project would have entailed a degree of financial stability and restrained behavior that they were unable or unwilling to assume, for the corner-gang members of the Bandit neighborhood were the scions of men and women who occupied the lowest social level in Midcity. For them low rent was a passion, freedom to drink and to behave drunkenly a sacred privilege, sporadic employment a fact of life, and the social-welfare and law-enforcement agencies of the state, partners of one's existence.

The Bandit corner was subject to field observation for about three years—from June 1954 to May 1957. Hanging out on the corner during this period were six distinct but related gang subdivisions. There were four male groups: The Brigands, aged approximately 18 to 21 at the start of the study period; the Senior Bandits, aged 16 to 18; the Junior Bandits, 14 to 16; and the Midget Bandits, 12 to 14. There were also two distinct female subdivisions: The Bandettes, 14 to 16; and the Little Bandettes, 12 to 14.

The physical and psychic center of the Bandit corner was Sam's Variety Store, the owner and sole employee of which was not Sam but Ben, his son. Ben's father had founded the store in the twenties, the heyday of the Irish laboring class in the Bandit neighborhood. When his father died, Ben took over the store, but did not change its name. Ben was a stocky, round-faced Jew in his middle fifties, who looked upon the whole of the Bandit neighborhood as his personal fief and bounden responsibility—a sacred legacy from his father. He knew everybody and was concerned with everybody; through his store passed a constant stream of customers and noncustomers of all ages and both sexes. In a space not much larger than that of a fair-sized bedroom Ben managed to crowd a phone booth, a juke box, a pinball machine, a space heater, counters, shelves and stock, and an assorted variety of patrons. During one fifteen-minute period on an average day Ben would supply $1.37 worth of groceries to eleven-year-old Carol Donovan and enter the sum on her mother's page in the "tab" book, agree to extend Mrs. Thebodeau's already extended credit until her A.D.C. check arrived, bandage and solace the three-year-old Negro girl who came crying to him with a cut forefinger, and shoo into the street a covey of Junior Bandits whose altercation over a pinball score was impeding customer traffic and augmenting an already substantial level of din.

Ben was a bachelor, and while he had adopted the whole of the Bandit neighborhood as his extended family, he had taken on the

200 adolescents who hung out on the Bandit corner as his most immediate sons and daughters. Ben knew the background and present circumstances of every Bandit, and followed their lives with intense interest and concern. Ben's corner-gang progeny were a fast-moving and mercurial lot, and he watched over their adventures and misadventures with a curious mixture of indignation, solicitude, disgust, and sympathy. Ben's outlook on the affairs of the world was never bland; he held and freely voiced strong opinions on a wide variety of issues, prominent among which was the behavior and misbehavior of the younger generation.

This particular concern was given ample scope for attention by the young Bandits who congregated in and around his store. Of all the gangs studied, the Bandits were the most consistently and determinedly criminal, and central to Ben's concerns was how each one stood with regard to "trouble." In this respect, developments were seldom meager. By the time they reached the age of 18, every one of the 32 active members of the Senior Bandits had appeared in court at least once, and some many times; 28 of the 32 boys had been committed to a correctional institution and 16 had spent at least one term in confinement.

Ben's stout arm swept the expanse of pavement that fronted his store. "I'll tell ya, I give up on these kids. In all the years I been here, I never seen a worse bunch. You know what they should do? They should put up a big platform with one of them stocks right out there, and as soon as a kid gets in trouble, into the stocks with 'im. Then they'd straighten out. The way it is now, the kid tells a sob story to some soft-hearted cop or social worker, and pretty soon he's back at the same old thing. See that guy just comin' over here? That's what I mean. He's hopeless. Mark my word, he's gonna end up in the electric chair."

The Senior Bandit who entered the store came directly to Ben. "Hey, Ben, I just quit my job at the shoe factory. They don't pay ya nothin', and they got some wise guy nephew of the owner who thinks he can kick everyone around. I just got fed up. I ain't gonna tell Ma for awhile, she'll be mad." Ben's concern was evident. "Digger, ya just gotta learn you can't keep actin' smart to every boss ya have. And $1.30 an hour ain't bad pay at all for a seventeen-year-old boy. Look, I'll lend ya ten bucks so ya can give five to ya Ma, and she won't know."

In their dealings with Ben, the Bandits, for their part, were in turn hostile and affectionate, cordial and sullen, open and reserved. They clearly regarded Ben's as "their" store. This meant, among other things, exclusive possession of the right to make trouble within its confines. At least three times during the observation period corner boys from outside neighborhoods entered the store obviously bent on stealing or creating a disturbance. On each occasion these outsiders were efficiently and forcefully removed by nearby Bandits, who then waxed indignant at the temerity of "outside" kids daring to consider Ben's as a target of illegal activity. One consequence, then, of Ben's seigneurial relationship to the Bandits was that his store was unusually well protected against theft, armed and otherwise, which presented a constant hazard to the small-store owner in Midcity.

On the other hand, the Bandits guarded jealously their own right to raise hell in Ben's. On one occasion, several Senior Bandits came into the store with a cache of pistol bullets and proceeded to empty the powder from one of the bullets onto the pinball machine and to ignite the powder. When Ben ordered them out they continued operations on the front sidewalk by wrapping gunpowder in newspaper and igniting it. Finally they set fire to a wad of paper containing two live bullets, which exploded and narrowly missed local residents sitting on nearby doorsteps.

Such behavior, while calculated to bedevil Ben and perhaps to retaliate for a recent scolding or ejection, posed no real threat to him or his store; the same boys during this period were actively engaged in serious thefts from similar stores in other neighborhoods. For the most part, the behavior of the Bandits in and around the store involved the characteristic activities of hanging out. In warm weather the Bandits sat outside the store on the sidewalk or doorstoops playing cards, gambling, drinking, and talking to one another and to the Bandettes. In cooler weather they moved into the store as the hour and space permitted, and there played the pinball machine for such cash payoffs as Ben saw fit to render, danced with the Bandettes to juke-box records, and engaged in general horseplay.

While Ben's was the Bandits' favorite hangout, they did frequent other hanging locales, mostly within a few blocks of the corner. Among these was a park directly adjacent to the housing project where the boys played football and baseball in season. At night the park provided a favored locale for activities such as beer drinking and lovemaking, neither of which particularly endeared them to the adult residents of the project, who not infrequently summoned the police to clear the park of late-night revellers. Other areas of congregation in the local neighborhood were a nearby delicatessen ("the Delly"), a pool hall, and the apartments of those Bandettes whose parents happened to be away. The Bandits also ran their own dances at the Old Erin and New Hibernia, but they had to conceal their identity as Bandits when renting these dance halls, since the proprietors had learned that the rental fees were scarcely sufficient to compensate for the chaos inevitably attending the conduct of a Bandit dance.

The Bandits were able to find other sources of entertainment in the central business district of Port City. While most of the Bandits and Bandettes were too young to gain admission to the numerous downtown cafés with their rock 'n' roll bands, they were able to find amusement in going to the movies (sneaking in whenever possible), playing the coin machines in the penny arcades, and shoplifting from the downtown department stores. Sometimes, as a kind of diversion, small groups of Bandits spent the day in town job hunting, with little serious intention of finding work.

One especially favored form of downtown entertainment was the court trial. Members of the Junior and Senior Bandits performed as on-stage participants in some 250 court trials during a four-year period. Most trials involving juveniles were conducted in nearby Midcity Court as private proceedings, but the older Bandits had adopted as routine procedure the practice of appealing their local court sentences to the Superior Court located in downtown Port City. When the appeal was successful, it was the occasion for as large a turnout of gang members as could be mustered, and the Bandits were a rapt and vitally interested audience. Afterward, the gang held long and animated discussions about the severity or leniency of the sentence and other, finer points of legal procedure. The hearings provided not only an absorbing form of free entertainment, but also invaluable knowledge about court functioning, appropriate defendant behavior, and the predilections of particular judges—knowledge that would serve the spectators well when their own turn to star inevitably arrived.

### The Senior Bandits
The Senior Bandits, the second oldest of the four male gang subdivisions hanging out on the Bandit corner, were under intensive observation for a period of 20 months. At the start of this period the boys ranged in age from 15 to 17 (average age 16.3) and at the end, 17 to 19 (average age 18.1). The core group of the Senior Bandits numbered 32 boys.

Most of the gang members were Catholic, the majority of Irish background; several were Italian or French Canadian, and a few were English or Scotch Protestants. The gang contained two sets of brothers and several cousins, and about one-third of the boys had relatives in other subdivisions. These included a brother in the Midgets, six brothers in the Juniors, and three in the Brigands.

The educational and occupational circumstances of the Senior Bandits were remarkably like those of their parents. Some seven years after the end of the intensive study period, when the average age of the Bandits was 25, 23 out of the 27 gang members whose occupations were known held jobs ordinarily classified in the bottom two occupational categories of the United States census. Twenty-one were classified as "laborer," holding jobs such as roofer, stock boy, and trucker's helper. Of 24 fathers whose occupations were known, 18, or 83 percent, held jobs in the same bottom two occupational categories as their sons; 17 were described as "laborer," holding jobs such as furniture mover and roofer. Fathers even held jobs of similar kinds and in similar proportions to those of their sons, for example, construction laborers: sons 30 percent, fathers 25 percent; factory laborers: sons 15 percent, fathers 21 percent. Clearly the Senior Bandits were not rising above their fathers' status. In fact, there were indications of a slight decline, even taking account of the younger age of the sons. Two of the boys' fathers held jobs in "public safety" services—one policeman and one fireman; another had worked for a time in the "white-collar" position of a salesclerk at Sears; a fourth had risen to the rank of Chief Petty Officer in the Merchant Marine. Four of the fathers, in other words, had attained relatively elevated positions, while the sons produced only one policeman.

The education of the Senior Bandits was consistent with their occupational status. Of 29 boys whose educational experience was known, 27 dropped out of school in the eighth, ninth, or tenth grades, having reached the age of 16. Two did complete high school, and one of these was reputed to have taken some posthigh-school training in a local technical school. None entered college. It should be remarked that this record occurred not in a backward rural community of the 1800s, nor in a black community, but in the 1950s in a predominantly white neighborhood of a metropolis that took pride in being one of the major educational centers of the world.

Since only two of the Senior Bandits were still in school during the study, almost all of the boys held full-time jobs at some time during the contact period. But despite financial needs, pressure from parents and parole officers and other incentives to get work, the Senior Bandits found jobs slowly, accepted them reluctantly, and quit them with little provocation.

The Senior Bandits were clearly the most criminal of the seven gangs we studied most closely. For example, by the time he had reached the age of 18, the average Senior Bandit had been charged with offenses in court an average of 7.6 times; this compared with an average rate of 2.7 for all five male gangs, and added up to a total of almost 250 separate charges for the gang as a whole. A year after our intensive contact with the group, 100 percent of the Senior Bandits had been arrested at least once, compared with an average arrest figure of 45 percent for all groups. During the 20-month contact period, just about half of the Senior Bandits were on probation or parole for some period of time.

## Law Violation, Cliques, and Leadership

To a greater degree than in any of the other gangs we studied, crime as an occupation and preoccupation played a central role in the lives of the Senior Bandits. Prominent among recurrent topics of discussion were thefts successfully executed, fights recently engaged in, and the current status of gang members who were in the process of passing through the successive stages of arrest, appearing in court, being sentenced, appealing, re-appealing, and so on. Although none of the crimes of the Senior Bandits merited front-page headlines when we were close to them, a number of their more colorful exploits did receive newspaper attention, and the stories were carefully clipped and left in Ben's store for circulation among the gang members. Newspaper citations functioned for the Senior Bandits somewhat as do press notices for actors; gang members who made the papers were elated and granted prestige; those who did not were often disappointed; participants and nonparticipants who failed to see the stories felt cheated.

The majority of their crimes were thefts. The Senior Bandits were thieves par excellence, and their thievery was imaginative, colorful, and varied. Most thefts were from stores. Included among these was a department-store theft of watches, jewelry, and clothing for use as family Christmas presents; a daylight raid on a supermarket for food and refreshments needed for a beach outing; a daytime burglary of an antique store, in which eight gang members, in the presence of the owner, stole a Samurai sword and French duelling pistols. The gang also engaged in car theft. One summer several Bandits stole a car to visit girlfriends who were working at a summer resort. Sixty miles north of Port City, hailed by police for exceeding speed limits, they raced away at speeds of up to 100 miles an hour, overturned the car, and were hospitalized for injuries. In another instance, Bandits stole a car in an effort to return a drunken companion to his home and avoid the police; when this car stalled they stole a second one parked in front of its owner's house; the

owner ran out and fired several shots at the thieves, which, however,
failed to forestall the theft.

The frequency of Senior Bandit crimes, along with the relative
seriousness of their offenses, resulted in a high rate of arrest and
confinement. During the contact period somewhat over forty percent of the gang members were confined in correctional institutions,
with terms averaging eleven months per boy. The average Senior
Bandit spent approximately one month out of four in a correctional
facility. This circumstance prompted one of the Bandettes to remark, "Ya know, them guys got a new place to hang—the reforma-
tory. That bunch is never together—one halfa them don't even know
the other half . . . ."

This appraisal, while based on fact, failed to recognize an important feature of gang relationships. With institutional confinement a
frequent and predictable event, the Senior Bandits employed a set of
devices to maintain a high degree of group solidarity. Lines of communication between corner and institution were kept open by
frequent visits by those on the outside, during which inmates were
brought food, money, and cigarettes as well as news of the neighborhood and other correctional facilities. One Midcity social
worker claimed that the institutionalized boys knew what was going
on in the neighborhood before most neighborhood residents. The
Bandits also developed well-established methods for arranging and
carrying out institutional escape by those gang members who were
so inclined. Details of escapes were arranged in the course of visits
and interinmate contacts; escapees were provided by fellow gang
members with equipment such as ropes to scale prison walls and
also with getaway cars. The homes of one's gang fellows were also
made available as hideouts. Given this set of arrangements, the Bandits carried out several highly successful escapes, and one succeeded
in executing the first escape in the history of a maximum security in-
stallation.

The means by which the Senior Bandits achieved group cohesion
in spite of recurrent incarcerations of key members merit further
consideration—both because they are of interest in their own right,
and because they illuminate important relationships between leadership, group structure, and the motivation of criminal behavior. Despite the assertion that "one halfa them guys don't know the other
half," the Senior Bandits were a solidaristic-associational unit, with
clear group boundaries and definite criteria for differentiating people who were "one of us" from those who were not. It was still said
of an accepted group member that "he hangs with us"—even when
the boy had been away from the corner in an institution for a year or

more. Incarcerated leaders, in particular, were referred to frequently and in terms of admiration and respect.

The system used by the Senior Bandits to maintain solidarity and reliable leadership arrangements incorporated three major devices: the diffusion of authority, anticipation of contingencies, and interchangeability of roles. The recurring absence from the corner of varying numbers of gang members inhibited the formation of a set of relatively stable cliques of the kind found in the other gangs we studied intensively. What was fairly stable, instead, was a set of "classes" of members, each of which could include different individuals at different times. The relative size of these classes was fairly constant, and a member of one class could move to another to take the place of a member who had been removed by institutionalization.

The four major classes of gang members could be called *key leaders, standby leaders, primary followers,* and *secondary followers.* During the intensive contact period the gang contained five key leaders—boys whose accomplishments had earned them the right to command; six standby leaders—boys prepared to step into leadership positions when key leaders were institutionalized; eight primary followers—boys who hung out regularly and who were the most dependable followers of current leaders; and thirteen secondary followers—boys who hung out less regularly and who tended to adapt their allegiances to particular leadership situations.

Predictably, given the dominant role of criminal activity among the Senior Bandits, leadership and followership were significantly related to criminal involvement. Each of the five key leaders had demonstrated unusual ability in criminal activity; in this respect the Senior Bandits differed from the other gangs, each of which included at least one leader whose position was based in whole or in part on a commitment to a law-abiding course of action. One of the Senior Bandits' key leaders was especially respected for his daring and adeptness in theft; another, who stole infrequently relative to other leaders, for his courage, stamina, and resourcefulness as a fighter. The other three leaders had proven themselves in both theft and fighting, with theft the more important basis of eminence.

Confinement statistics show that gang members who were closest to leadership positions were also the most active in crime. They also suggest, however, that maintaining a system of leadership on this basis poses special problems. The more criminally active a gang member, the greater the likelihood that he would be apprehended and removed from the neighborhood, thus substantially diminishing his opportunities to convert earned prestige into operative leadership. How was it possible, then, for the Senior Bandits to maintain effective leadership arrangements? They utilized a remarkably efficient system whose several features were ingenious and deftly contrived.

First, the recognition by the Bandits of five key leaders—a relatively large number for a gang of thirty-two members—served as a form of insurance against being left without leadership. It was most unlikely that all five would be incarcerated at the same time, particularly since collective crimes were generally executed by one or possibly two leaders along with several of their followers. During one relatively brief part of the contact period, four of the key leaders were confined simultaneously, but over the full period the average number confined at any one time was two. One Bandit key leader expressed his conviction that exclusive reliance on a single leader was unwise, "since we been hangin' out [at Ben's corner] we ain't had no leader. Other kids got a leader of the gang. Like up in Cornerville, they always got one kid who's the big boss . . . so far we ain't did that, and I don't think we ever will. We talk about 'Smiley and his boys,' or 'Digger and his clique,' and like that. . . ."

It is clear that for this Bandit the term *leader* carried the connotation of a single and all-powerful gang lord, which was not applicable to the diffuse and decentralized leadership arrangements of the Bandits. It is also significant that the gangs of Cornerville that he used as an example were Italian gangs whose rate of criminal involvement was relatively low. The "one big boss" type of leadership found in these gangs derives from the "Caesar" or "Il Duce" pattern so well established in Italian culture, and it was workable for Cornerville gangs because the gangs and their leaders were sufficiently law abiding and/or sufficiently capable of evading arrest as to make the removal of the leader an improbable event.

A second feature of Bandit leadership, the use of "standby" leaders, made possible a relatively stable balance among the several cliques. When the key leader of his clique was present in the area, the standby leader assumed a subordinate role and did not initiate action; if and when the key leader was committed to an institution, the standby was ready to assume leadership. He knew, however, that he was expected to relinquish this position on the return of the key leader. By this device each of the five major cliques was assured some form of leadership even when key leaders were absent, and could maintain its form, identity, and influence vis-à-vis other cliques.

A third device that enabled the gang to maintain a relatively stable leadership and clique structure involved the phenomenon of "optimal" criminal involvement. Since excellence in crime was the major basis of gang leadership, it might be expected that some who aspired to leadership would assume that there was a simple and direct relationship between crime and leadership: the more crime, the more prestige; the more prestige, the stronger the basis of authority. The flaw in this simple formula was in fact recognized by the actual key leaders: in striving for maximal criminal involvement, one also incurred the maximum risk of incarceration. But leadership involved more than gaining prestige through crime; one had to be personally involved with other gang members for sufficiently extended periods to exploit won prestige through wooing followers, initiating noncriminal as well as criminal activities, and effecting working relationships with other leaders. Newly returned key leaders as well as the less criminally active class of standby leaders tended to step up their involvement in criminal activity on assuming or reassuming leadership positions in order to solidify their positions, but they also tended to diminish such involvement once this was achieved.

One fairly evident weakness in so flexible and fluid a system of cliques and leadership was the danger that violent and possibly disruptive internal conflict might erupt among key leaders who were competing for followers, or standby leaders who were reluctant to relinquish their positions. There was, in fact, surprisingly little overt conflict of any kind among Bandit leaders. On their release from confinement, leaders were welcomed with enthusiasm and appropriate observances both by their followers and by other leaders. They took the center of the stage as they recounted to rapt listeners their institutional experiences, the circumstances of members still confined, and new developments in policies, personnel, and politics at the correctional school.

When they were together Bandit leaders dealt with one another gingerly, warily, and with evident respect. On one occasion a standby leader, who was less criminally active than the returning key leader, offered little resistance to being displaced, but did serve his replacement with the warning that a resumption of his former high rate of crime would soon result in commitment both of himself and his clique. On another occasion one of the toughest of the Senior Bandits (later sentenced to an extended term in an adult institution for ringleading a major prison riot), returned to the corner to find that another leader had taken over not only some of his key followers but his steady girlfriend as well. Instead of taking on his rival in an angry and perhaps violent confrontation, he reacted quite mildly, venting his hostility in the form of sarcastic teasing, calculated to needle but not to incite. In the place of a direct challenge, the newly returned key leader set about to regain his followers and his girl by actively throwing himself back into criminal activity. This course of action—competing for followers by successful performance in prestigious activities rather than by brute-force confrontation—was standard practice among the Senior Bandits.

## The Junior Bandits

The leadership system of the Junior Bandits was, if anything, even farther removed from the "one big boss" pattern than was the "multileader power-balance" system of the Seniors. An intricate arrangement of cliques and leadership enabled this subdivision of the gang to contain within it a variety of individuals and cliques with different and often conflicting orientations.

Leadership for particular activities was provided as the occasion arose by boys whose competence in that activity had been established. Leadership was thus flexible, shifting, and adaptable to changing group circumstances. Insofar as there was a measure of relatively concentrated authority, it was invested in a collectivity rather than an individual. The several "situational" leaders of the dominant clique constituted what was in effect a kind of ruling council, which arrived at its decisions through a process of extended collective discussion generally involving all concerned. All members who were to execute a plan of action thereby took part in the process by which it was developed.

A final feature of this system concerns the boy who was recognized as "the leader" of the Junior Bandits. When the gang formed a club to expedite involvement in athletic activities, he was chosen its president. Although he was an accepted member of the dominant clique, he did not, on the surface, seem to possess any particular qualifications for this position. He was mild mannered, unassertive, and consistently refused to take a definite stand on outstanding issues, let alone taking the initiative in implementing policy. He appeared to follow rather than to lead. One night when the leaders of the two subordinate factions became infuriated with one another in the course of a dispute, he trailed both boys around for several hours, begging them to calm down and reconcile their differences. On another occasion the gang was on the verge of splitting into irreconcilable factions over a financial issue. One group accused another of stealing club funds; the accusation was hotly denied; angry recriminations arose that swept in a variety of dissatisfactions with the club and its conduct. In the course of this melee, the leader of one faction, the "bad boys," complained bitterly about the refusal of the president to take sides or assume any initiative in resolving the dispute, and called for a new election. This was agreed to and the election was held—with the result that the "weak" president was reelected by a decisive majority, and was reinstated in office amidst emotional outbursts of acclaim and reaffirmation of the unity of the gang.

It was thus evident that the majority of gang members, despite temporary periods of anger over particular issues, recognized on some level the function performed by a "weak" leader. Given the fact that the gang included a set of cliques with differing orientations and conflicting notions, and a set of leaders whose authority was limited to specific areas, the maintenance of gang cohesion required some special mechanisms. One was the device of the "weak" leader. It is most unlikely that a forceful or dominant person could have controlled the sanctions that would enable him to coerce the strong-willed factions into compliance. The very fact that the "weak" leader refused to take sides and was noncommittal on key issues made him acceptable to the conflicting interests represented in the gang. Further, along with the boy's nonassertive demeanor went a real talent for mediation.

## The Outlaw Neighborhood

The Outlaw street corner was less than a mile from that of the Bandits, and like the Bandits, the Outlaws were white, Catholic, and predominantly Irish, with a few Italians and Irish-Italians. But their social status, in the middle range of the lower class, was sufficiently higher than that of the Bandits to be reflected in significant differences in both their gang and family life. The neighborhood environment also was quite different.

Still, the Outlaws hung out on a classic corner—complete with drug store, variety store, a neighborhood bar (Callahan's Bar and Grill), a pool hall, and several other small businesses such as a laundromat. The corner was within one block of a large park, a convenient locale for card games, lovemaking, and athletic practice. Most residents of the Outlaw neighborhood were oblivious to the deafening roar of the elevated train that periodically rattled the houses and stores of Midcity Avenue, which formed one street of the Outlaw corner. There was no housing project in the Outlaw neighborhood, and none of the Outlaws were project residents. Most of their families rented one level of one of the three-decker wooden tenements that were common in the area; a few owned their own homes.

In the mid-1950s, however, the Outlaw neighborhood underwent significant changes as Negroes began moving in. Most of the white residents, gradually and with reluctance, left their homes and moved out to the first fringe of Port City's residential suburbs, abandoning the area to the Negroes.

Prior to this time the Outlaw corner had been a hanging locale for many years. The Outlaw name and corner dated from at least the late twenties, and perhaps earlier. One local boy who was not an Outlaw observed disgruntledly that anyone who started a fight with an Outlaw would end up fighting son, father, and grandfather, since all were or had been members of the gang. A somewhat drunken and sentimental Outlaw, speaking at a farewell banquet for their field-worker, declared impassionedly that any infant born into an Outlaw family was destined from birth to wear the Outlaw jacket.

One consequence of the fact that Outlaws had hung out on the same corner for many years was that the group that congregated there during the thirty-month observation period included a full complement of age-graded subdivisions. Another consequence was that the subdivisions were closely connected by kinship. There were six clearly differentiated subdivisions on the corner: the Marauders, boys in their late teens and early twenties; the Senior Outlaws, boys between 16 and 18; the Junior Outlaws, 14 to 16; and the Midget Outlaws, 11 to 13. There were also two girls groups, the Outlawettes and the Little Outlawettes. The number of Outlaws in all subdivisions totaled slightly over 200 persons, ranging in age, approximately, from 10 to 25 years.

The cohesiveness of the Outlaws, during the 1950s, was enhanced in no small measure by an adult who, like Ben for the Bandits, played a central role in the Outlaws' lives. This was Rosa—the owner of the variety store that was their principal hangout—a stout, unmarried woman of about forty who was, in effect, the street-corner mother of all 200 Outlaws.

### The Junior Outlaws

The Junior Outlaws, numbering 24 active members, were the third oldest of the four male subdivisions on the Outlaw corner, ranging in age from 14 to 16. Consistent with their middle-range lower-class status, the boys' fathers were employed in such jobs as bricklayer, mechanic, chauffeur, milk deliveryman; but a small minority of these men had attained somewhat higher positions, one being the owner of a small electroplating shop and the other rising to the position of plant superintendent. The educational status of the Junior Outlaws was higher than that of the Bandit gangs, but lower than that of their older-brother gang, the Senior Outlaws.

With regard to law violations the Junior Outlaws, as one might expect from their status and age, were considerably less criminal than the lower-status Bandits, but considerably more so than the Senior Outlaws. They ranked third among the five male gangs in illegal involvement during the observation period (25 involvements per 10 boys per 10 months), which was well below the second-ranking Senior Bandits (54.2) and well above the fourth-ranking Negro Kings (13.9). Nevertheless, the two-and-a-half-year period during which we observed the Juniors was for them, as for other boys of their status and age group, a time of substantial increase in the frequency and seriousness of illegal behavior. An account of the events of this time provides some insight into the process by which age-related influences engender criminality. It also provides another variation on the issue, already discussed in the case of the Bandits, of the relation of leadership to criminality.

It is clear from the case of the Bandits that gang affairs were ordered not by autocratic gang lords, but rather through a subtle and intricate interplay between leadership and a set of elements such as personal competency, intragang divisions, and law violation. The case of the Junior Outlaws is particularly dramatic in this regard, since the observation period found them at the critical age when boys of this social-status level are faced with a serious decision—the amount of weight to be granted to law-violating behavior as a basis of prestige. Because there were in the Junior Outlaws two cliques, each of which was committed quite clearly to opposing alternatives, the interplay of the various elements over time emerges with some vividness, and echoes the classic morality play wherein forces of good and evil are locked in mortal combat over the souls of the uncommitted.

At the start of the observation period, the Juniors, thirteen-, fourteen-, and fifteen-year olds, looked and acted for the most part like "nice young kids." By the end of the period both their voices and general demeanor had undergone a striking change. Their appearance, as they hung out in front of Rosa's store, was that of rough corner boys, and the series of thefts, fights, and drinking bouts that had occurred during the intervening two-and-one-half years was the substance behind that appearance. When we first contacted them, the Juniors comprised three main cliques: seven boys associated primarily with a "good boy" who was quite explicitly oriented to law-abiding behavior; a second clique of seven boys associated with a "bad boy" who was just starting to pursue prestige through drinking and auto theft; and a third, less frequently congregating group, who took a relatively neutral position with respect to the issue of violative behavior.

The leader of the "good boy" clique played an active part in the law-abiding activities of the gang, and was elected president of the formal club organized by the Juniors. This club at first included members of all three cliques; however, one of the first acts of the club members, dominated by the "good boy" leader and his supporters, was to vote out of membership the leader of the "bad boy" clique. Nevertheless, the "bad boy" leader and his followers continued to hang out on the corner with the other Juniors, and from this vantage point attempted to gain influence over the uncommitted boys as well as members of the "good boy" clique. His efforts proved unsuccessful, however, since during this period athletic prowess served for the majority of the Juniors as a basis of greater prestige than criminal behavior. Disgruntled by this failure, the "bad boy" leader took his followers and moved to a new hanging corner, about two blocks away from the traditional one.

From there, a tangible symbol of the ideological split within the Juniors, the "bad boy" leader continued his campaign to wean away the followers of the "good boy" leader, trying to persuade them to leave the old corner for the new. At the same time, behavior at the "bad boy" corner became increasingly delinquent, with, among other things, much noisy drinking and thefts of nearby cars. These incidents produced complaints by local residents that resulted in several police raids on the corner, and served to increase the antagonism between what now had become hostile factions. Determined to assert their separateness, the "bad boy" faction began to drink and create disturbances in Rosa's store, became hostile to her when she censured them, and finally stayed away from the store altogether.

The antagonism between the two factions finally became sufficiently intense to bring about a most unusual circumstance—plans for an actual gang fight, a "jam" of the type characteristic of rival gangs. The time and place for the battle were agreed on. But no one from either side showed up. A second battle site was selected. Again the combatants failed to appear. From the point of view of intragang relations, both the plan for the gang fight and its failure to materialize were significant. The fact that a physical fight between members of the same subdivision was actually projected showed that factional hostility over the issue of law violation had reached an unusual degree of bitterness; the fact that the planned encounters did not in fact occur indicated a realization that actual physical combat might well lead to an irreversible split.

A reunification of the hostile factions did not take place for almost a year, however. During this time changes occurred in both

factions that had the net effect of blunting the sharpness of the ideological issue dividing them. Discouraged by his failure to win over
the majority of the Outlaws to the cause of law violation as a major
badge of prestige, the leader of the "bad boy" clique began to hang
out less frequently. At the same time, the eight "uncommitted"
members of the Junior Outlaws, now moving toward their middle
teens, began to gravitate toward the "bad boy" corner—attracted
by the excitement and risk of its activities. More of the Juniors than
ever before became involved in illegal drinking and petty theft. This
trend became sufficiently pronounced to draw in members of the
"good boy" clique, and the influence of the "good boy" leader
diminished to the point where he could count on the loyalty only of
his own brother and two other boys. In desperation, sensing the all-
but-irresistible appeal of illegality for his erstwhile followers, he
increased the tempo of his own delinquent behavior in a last-ditch
effort to win them back. All in vain. Even his own brother deserted
the regular Outlaw corner, although he did not go so far as to join
the "bad boys" on theirs.

Disillusioned, the "good boy" leader took a night job that sharply
curtailed the time he was able to devote to gang activities. Members
of the "bad boy" clique now began a series of maneuvers aimed at
gaining control of the formal club. Finally, about two months before the close of the thirty-month contact period, a core member of
the "bad boy" clique was elected to the club presidency. In effect,
the proponents of illegality as a major basis of prestige had won the
long struggle for dominance of the Junior Outlaws. But this achievement, while on the surface a clear victory for the "bad boy" faction,
was in fact a far more subtle process of mutual accommodation.

The actions of each of the opposing sides accorded quite directly
with their expressed convictions; each member of the "bad boy"
faction averaged about seventeen known illegal acts during the observation period, compared to a figure of about two per boy for the
"good boy" faction. However, in the face of these sharp differences
in both actions and sentiments respecting illegality, the two factions
shared important common orientations. Most important, they
shared the conviction that the issue of violative behavior as a basis
of prestige was a paramount one, and one that required a choice.
Moreover, both sides remained uncertain as to whether the choice
they made was the correct one.

The behavior of both factions provides evidence of a fundamental
ambivalence with respect to the "demanded" nature of delinquent
behavior. The gradual withdrawal of support by followers of the
"good boy" leader and the movement toward violative behavior of

the previously "neutral" clique attest to a compelling conviction that prestige gained through law-abiding endeavor alone could not, at this age, suffice. Even more significant was the criminal experience of the "good boy" leader. As the prime exponent of law-abiding behavior, he might have been expected to serve as an exemplar in this respect. In fact, the opposite was true; his rate of illegal involvement was the highest of all the boys in his clique, and had been so even before his abortive attempt to regain his followers by a final burst of delinquency. This circumstance probably derived from his realization that a leader acceptable to both factions (which he wanted to be) would have to show proficiency in activities recognized by both as conferring prestige.

### To Be a Man

It is equally clear, by the same token, that members of the "bad boy" faction were less than serenely confident in their commitment to law violation as an ideal. Once they had won power in the club they did not keep as their leader the boy who had been the dominant figure on the "bad boy" corner, and who was without question the most criminally active of the Junior Outlaws, but instead elected as president another boy who was also criminally active, but considerably less so. Moreover, in the presence of older gang members, Seniors and Marauders, the "bad boy" clique was far more subdued, less obstreperous, and far less ardent in their advocacy of crime as an ideal. There was little question that they were sensitive to and responsive to negative reactions by others to their behavior.

It is noteworthy that members of both factions adhered more firmly to the "law-violation" and "law-abiding" positions on the level of abstract ideology than on the level of actual practice. This would suggest that the existence of the opposing ideologies and their corresponding factions served important functions both for individual gang members and for the group as a whole. Being in the same orbit as the "bad boys" made it possible for the "good boys" to reap some of the rewards of violative behavior without undergoing its risks; the presence of the "good boys" imposed restraints on the "bad" that they themselves desired, and helped protect them from dangerous excesses. The behavior and ideals of the "good boys" satisfied for both factions that component of their basic orientation that said "violation of the law is wrong and should be punished"; the behavioral and ideal component of the "bad boys" said "one cannot earn manhood without some involvement in criminal activity."

It is instructive to compare the stress and turmoil attending the struggle for dominance of the Junior Outlaws with the leadership circumstances of the Senior Bandits. In this gang, older and of lower social status (lower-class-III), competition for leadership had little to do with a choice between law-abiding and law-violating philosophies, but rather with the issue of which of a number of competing leaders was *best* able to demonstrate prowess in illegal activity. This virtual absence of effective pressures against delinquency contrasts sharply with the situation of the Junior Outlaws. During the year-long struggle between its "good" and "bad" factions, the Juniors were exposed to constant pressures, both internal and external to the gang, to refrain from illegality. External sources included Rosa, whom the boys loved and respected; a local youth worker, whom they held in high esteem; their older-brother gangs, whose frequent admonitions to the "little kids" to "straighten out" and "keep clean" were attended with utmost seriousness. Within the gang itself the "good boy" leader served as a consistent and persuasive advocate of a law-abiding course of action. In addition, most of the boys' parents deplored their misbehavior and urged them to keep out of trouble.

In the face of all these pressures from persons of no small importance in the lives of the Juniors, the final triumph of the proponents of illegality, however tempered, assumes added significance. What was it that impelled the "bad boy" faction? There was a quality of defiance about much of their delinquency, as if they were saying: "We know perfectly well that what we are doing is regarded as wrong, legally and morally; we also know that it violates the wishes and standards of many whose good opinion we value; yet, if we are to sustain our self-respect and our honor as males we *must,* at this stage of our lives, engage in criminal behavior." In light of the experience of the Junior Outlaws, one can scarcely argue that their delinquency sprang from any inability to distinguish right from wrong, or out of any simple conformity to a set of parochial standards that just happened to differ from the legal code or the adult, middle-class mores. Their delinquent behavior was engendered by a highly complex interplay of forces, including, among other elements, the fact that they were males, were in the middle range of the lower class, and, of critical importance in the present instance, were moving through the age period when the attainment of manhood was of the utmost concern.

In the younger gang just discussed—the Junior Outlaws—leadership and clique structure reflected an intense struggle between advocates and opponents of law violation as a prime basis of prestige.

**The Senior Outlaws**

Leadership in the older Senior Outlaws reflected a resolution of the law-conformity versus law-violation conflict, but with different results. Although the gang was not under direct observation during their earlier adolescence, what we know of the Juniors, along with evidence that the Senior Outlaws themselves had been more criminal when younger, would suggest that the gang had in fact undergone a similar struggle, and that the proponents of conformity to the law had won.

In any case, the events of the observation period made it clear that the Senior Outlaws sought "rep" as a gang primarily through effective execution of legitimate enterprises such as athletics, dances, and other nonviolative activities. In line with this objective, they maintained a consistent concern with the "good name" of the gang and with "keeping out of trouble" in the face of constant and ubiquitous temptations. For example, they attempted (without much success) to establish friendly relations with the senior priest of their parish—in contrast with the Junior Outlaws, who were on very bad terms with the local church. At one point during the contact period when belligerent Bandits, claiming that the Outlaws had attacked one of the Midget Bandits, vowed to "wipe out every Outlaw jacket in Midcity," the Senior Outlaws were concerned not only with the threat of attack but also with the threat to their reputation. "That does it," said one boy, "I knew we'd get into something. There goes the good name of the Outlaws."

Leadership and clique arrangements in the Senior Outlaws reflected three conditions, each related in some way to the relatively low stress on criminal activity: the stability of gang membership (members were rarely removed from the area by institutional confinement), the absence of significant conflict over the prestige and criminality issue, and the importance placed on legitimate collective activities. The Senior Bandits were the most unified of the gangs we observed directly; there were no important cleavages or factions; even the distinction between more-active and less-active members was less pronounced than in the other gangs.

But as it was in the other gangs, leadership among the Senior Outlaws was collective and situational. There were four key leaders, each of whom assumed authority in his own sphere of competence. As witnessed in the case of the Bandit gangs, there was little overt competition among leaders; when differences arose between the leadership and the rank and file, the several leaders tended to support one another. In one significant respect, however, Outlaw leadership differed from that of the other gangs—authority was exercised more firmly and accepted more readily. Those in charge of collective enterprises generally issued commands after the manner of a tough army sergeant or work-gang boss. Although obedience to such commands was frequently less than flawless, the leadership style of Outlaw leaders approximated the "snap-to-it" approach of organizations that control firmer sanctions than do most corner gangs. Compared to the near chaotic behavior of their younger-brother gang, the organizational practices of the Seniors appeared as a model of efficiency. The "authoritarian" mode of leadership was particularly characteristic of one boy, whose prerogatives were somewhat more generalized than those of the other leaders. While he was far from an undisputed "boss," holding instead a kind of *primus inter pares* position, he was as close to a "boss" as anything found among the direct-observation gangs.

His special position derived from the fact that he showed superior capability in an unusually wide range of activities, and this permitted him wider authority than the other leaders. One might have expected, in a gang oriented predominantly to law-abiding activity, that this leader would serve as an exemplar of legitimacy and rank among the most law abiding. This was not the case. He was, in fact, one of the most criminal of the Senior Outlaws, being among the relatively few who had "done time." He was a hard drinker, an able street-fighter, a skilled football strategist and team leader, and an accomplished dancer and smooth ladies' man. His leadership position was based not on his capacity to best exemplify the law-abiding orientation of the gang, but on his capabilities in a variety of activities, violative and nonviolative. Thus, even in the gang most concerned with "keeping clean," excellence in crime still constituted one important basis of prestige. Competence as such rather than the legitimacy of one's activities provided the major basis of authority.

We still have to ask, however, why leadership among the Senior Outlaws was more forceful than in the other gangs. One reason emerges by comparison with the "weak leader" situation of the Junior Bandits. Younger and of lower social status, their factional conflict over the law-violation-and-prestige issue was sufficiently intense so that only a leader without an explicit commitment to either side could be acceptable to both. The Seniors, older and of higher status, had developed a good degree of intragang consensus on this issue, and showed little factionalism. They could thus accept a relatively strong leader without jeopardizing gang unity.

A second reason also involves differences in age and social status, but as these relate to the world of work. In contrast to the younger gangs, whose perspectives more directly revolved around the subculture of adolescence and its specific concerns, the Senior Outlaws at age nineteen were on the threshold of adult work, and some in fact were actively engaged in it. In contrast to the lower-status gangs whose orientation to gainful employment was not and never would be as "responsible" as that of the Outlaws, the activities of the Seniors as gang members more directly reflected and anticipated the requirements and conditions of the adult occupational roles they would soon assume.

Of considerable importance in the prospective occupational world of the Outlaws was, and is, the capacity to give and take orders in the execution of collective enterprises. Unlike the Bandits, few of whom would ever occupy other than subordinate positions, the Outlaws belonged to that sector of society which provides the men who exercise direct authority over groups of laborers or blue-collar workers. The self-executed collective activities of the gang—organized athletics, recreational projects, fund-raising activities—provided a training ground for the practice of organizational skills—planning organized enterprises, working together in their conduct, executing the directives of legitimate superiors. It also provided a training ground wherein those boys with the requisite talents could learn and practice the difficult art of exercising authority effectively over lower-class men. By the time they had reached the age of twenty, the leaders of the Outlaws had experienced in the gang many of the problems and responsibilities confronting the army sergeant, the police lieutenant, and the factory foreman.

The nature and techniques of leadership in the Senior Outlaws had relevance not only to their own gang but to the Junior Outlaws as well. Relations between the Junior and Senior Outlaws were the closest of all the intensive-contact gang subdivisions. The Seniors kept a close watch on their younger fellows, and served them in a variety of ways, as athletic coaches, advisers, mediators, and arbiters. The older gang followed the factional conflicts of the Juniors with close attention, and were not above intervening when conflict reached sufficient intensity or threatened their own interests. The dominant leader of the Seniors was particularly concerned with the behavior of the Juniors; at one point, lecturing them about their disorderly conduct in Rosa's store, he remarked, "I don't hang with you guys, but I know what you do. . . ." The Seniors did not, however, succeed in either preventing the near breakup of the Junior Outlaws or slowing their move toward law-breaking activities.

### The Prevalence of Gangs

The subtle and intricately contrived relations among cliques, leadership, and crime in the four subdivisions of the Bandits and

Outlaws reveal the gang as an ordered and adaptive form of association, and its members as able and rational human beings. The fascinating pattern of intergang variation within a basic framework illustrates vividly the compelling influences of differences in age and social status on crime, leadership, and other forms of behavior—even when these differences are surprisingly small. The experiences of Midcity gang members show that the gang serves the lower-class adolescent as a flexible and adaptable training instrument for imparting vital knowledge concerning the value of individual competence, the appropriate limits of law-violating behavior, the uses and abuses of authority, and the skills of interpersonal relations. From this perspective, the street gang appears not as a casual or transient manifestation that emerges intermittently in response to unique and passing social conditions, but rather as a stable associational form, coordinate with and complementary to the family, and as an intrinsic part of the way of life of the urban low-status community.

How then can one account for the widespread conception of gangs as somehow popping up and then disappearing again? One critical reason concerns the way one defines what a gang is. Many observers, both scholars and nonscholars, often use a sine qua non to sort out "real" gangs from near-gangs, pseudogangs, and nongangs. Among the more common of these criteria are: autocratic one-man leadership, some "absolute" degree of solidarity or stable membership, a predominant involvement in violent conflict with other gangs, claim to a rigidly defined turf, or participation in activities thought to pose a threat to other sectors of the community. Reaction to groups lacking the sine qua non is often expressed with a dismissive, "Oh, them. That's not a *gang*. That's just a bunch of kids out on the corner."

**On the Corner Again**

For many people there are no gangs if there is no gang warfare. It is that simple. For them, as for all who concentrate on the "threatening" nature of the gang, the phenomenon is defined in terms of the degree of "problem" it poses: A group whose "problematic" behavior is difficult to ignore is a gang; one less problematic is not. But what some people see as a problem may not appear so to others. In Philadelphia, for example, the police reckoned there were 80 gangs, of which 20 were at war; while social workers estimated there were 200 gangs, of which 80 were "most hostile." Obviously, the social workers' 80 "most hostile" gangs were the same as the 80 "gangs" of the police. The additional 120 groups defined as gangs by the social workers were seen as such because they were thought to be appropriate objects of social work; but to the police they were not sufficiently troublesome to require consistent police attention, and were not therefore defined as gangs.

In view of this sort of confusion, let me state our definition of what a gang is. *A gang is a group of urban adolescents who congregate recurrently at one or more nonresidential locales, with continued affiliation based on self-defined criteria of inclusion and exclusion.* Recruitment, customary places of assembly, and ranging areas are based in a specific territory, over some portion of which limited use and occupancy rights are claimed. Membership both in the gang as a whole and in its subgroups is determined on the basis of age. The group maintains a versatile repertoire of activities, with hanging out, mating, recreational, and illegal activity being of central importance; and it is internally differentiated on the basis of authority, prestige, personality, and clique-formation.

The main reason that people have consistently mistaken the prevalence of gangs is the widespread tendency to define them as gangs on the basis of the presence or absence of one or two characteristics that are thought to be essential to the "true" gang. Changes in the forms or frequencies or particular characteristics, such as leadership, involvement in fighting, or modes of organization, are seen not as normal variations over time and space, but rather as signs of the emergence or disappearance of the gangs themselves. Our work does not support this view; instead, our evidence indicates that the core characteristics of the gang vary continuously from place to place and from time to time without negating the existence of the gang. Gangs may be larger or smaller, named or nameless, modestly or extensively differentiated, more or less active in gang fighting, stronger or weaker in leadership, black, white, yellow, or brown, without affecting their identity as gangs. So long as groups of adolescents gather periodically outside the home, frequent a particular territory, restrict membership by age and other criteria, pursue a variety of activities, and maintain differences in authority and prestige—so long will the gang continue to exist as a basic associational form.

# 14

# The Saints and the Roughnecks

## William J. Chambliss

Eight promising young men—children of good, stable, white upper-middle-class families, active in school affairs, good precollege students—were some of the most delinquent boys at Hanibal High School. While community residents and parents knew that these boys occasionally sowed a few wild oats, they were totally unaware that sowing wild oats completely occupied the daily routine of these young men. The Saints were constantly occupied with truancy, drinking, wild driving, petty theft, and vandalism. Yet not one was officially arrested for any misdeed during the two years I observed them.

This record was particularly surprising in light of my observations during the same two years of another gang of Hanibal High School students, six lower-class white boys known as the Roughnecks. The Roughnecks were constantly in trouble with police and community even though their rate of delinquency was about equal with that of the Saints. What was the cause of this disparity? the result? The following consideration of the activities, social class, and community perceptions of both gangs may provide some answers.

### The Saints from Monday to Friday

The Saints' principal daily concern was with getting out of school as early as possible. The boys managed to get out of school with minimum danger that they would be accused of playing hookey through an elaborate procedure for obtaining "legitimate" release from class. The most common procedure was for one boy to obtain the release of another by fabricating a meeting of some committee, program, or recognized club. Charles might raise his hand in his 9:00 chemistry class and ask to be excused—a euphemism for going to the bathroom. Charles would go to Ed's math class and inform the teacher that Ed was needed for a 9:30 rehearsal of the drama club play. The math teacher would recognize Ed and Charles as "good students" involved in numerous school activities and would permit Ed to leave at 9:30. Charles would return to his class, and Ed would go to Tom's English class to obtain his release. Tom would engineer Charles's escape. The strategy would continue until as many of the Saints as possible were freed. After a stealthy trip to the car (which had been parked in a strategic spot), the boys were off for a day of fun.

Over the two years I observed the Saints, this pattern was repeated nearly every day. There were variations on the theme, but in one form or another, the boys used this procedure for getting out of class and then off the school grounds. Rarely did all eight of the Saints manage to leave school at the same time. The average number avoiding school on the days I observed them was five.

Having escaped from the concrete corridors, the boys usually went either to a pool hall on the other (lower-class) side of town or to a café in the suburbs. Both places were out of the way of people the boys were likely to know (family or school officials), and both provided a source of entertainment. The pool-hall entertainment was the generally rough atmosphere, the occasional hustler, the sometimes drunk proprietor, and, of course, the game of pool. The café's entertainment was provided by the owner. The boys would "accidentally" knock a glass on the floor or spill cola on the counter—not all the time, but enough to be sporting. They would also bend spoons, put salt in sugar bowls, and generally tease whoever was working in the café. The owner had opened the café recently and was dependent on the boys' business that was, in fact, substantial, since between the horsing around and the teasing they bought food and drinks.

**The Saints on Weekends**

On weekends the automobile was even more critical than during the week, for on weekends the Saints went to Big Town—a large city with a population of over a million twenty-five miles from Hanibal. Every Friday and Saturday night most of the Saints would meet between 8:00 and 8:30 and would go into Big Town. Big Town activities included drinking heavily in taverns or nightclubs, driving drunkenly through the streets, and committing acts of vandalism and playing pranks.

By midnight on Fridays and Saturdays the Saints were usually thoroughly high, and one or two of them were often so drunk they had to be carried to the cars. Then the boys drove around town, calling obscenities to women and girls; occasionally trying (unsuccessfully so far as I could tell) to pick girls up; and driving recklessly through red lights and at high speeds with their lights out. Occasionally they played "chicken." One boy would climb out the back window of the car and across the roof to the driver's side of the car while the car was moving at high speed (between forty and fifty miles an hour); then the driver would move over and the boy who had just crawled across the car roof would take the driver's seat.

Searching for "fair game" for a prank was the boys' principal activity after they left the tavern. The boys would drive alongside a foot patrolman and ask directions to some street. If the policeman leaned on the car in the course of answering the question, the driver would speed away, causing him to lose his balance. The Saints were careful to play this prank only in an area where they were not going to spend much time and where they could quickly disappear around a corner to avoid having their license plate number taken.

Construction sites and road repair areas were the special province of the Saints' mischief. A soon-to-be-repaired hole in the road inevitably invited the Saints to remove lanterns and wooden barricades and put them in the car, leaving the hole unprotected. The boys would find a safe vantage point and wait for an unsuspecting motorist to drive into the hole. Often, though not always, the boys would go up to the motorist and commiserate with him about the dreadful way the city protected its citizenry.

Leaving the scene of the open hole and the motorist, the boys would then go searching for an appropriate place to erect the stolen barricade. An "appropriate place" was often a spot on a highway near a curve in the road where the barricade would not be seen by an oncoming motorist. The boys would wait to watch an unsuspecting motorist attempt to stop and (usually) crash into the wooden barricade. With saintly bearing the boys might offer help and understanding.

A stolen lantern might well find its way onto the back of a police car or hang from a street lamp. Once a lantern served as a prop for a reenactment of the "midnight ride of Paul Revere" until the "play," which was taking place at 2 A.M. in the center of a main street of Big Town, was interrupted by a police car several block away. The boys ran, leaving the lanterns on the street, and managed to avoid being apprehended.

Abandoned houses, especially if they were located in out-of-the-way places, were fair game for destruction and spontaneous vandalism. The boys would break windows, remove furniture to the yard and tear it apart, urinate on the walls, and scrawl obscenities inside.

[Through all the pranks, drinking, and reckless driving the boys managed miraculously to avoid being stopped by police. Only twice in two years was I aware that they had been stopped by a Big City policeman. Once was for speeding (which they did every time they drove whether they were drunk or sober), and the driver managed to convince the policeman that it was simply an error. The second time they were stopped they had just left a nightclub and were walking through an alley. Aaron stopped to urinate and the boys began making obscene remarks. A foot patrolman came into the alley, lectured the boys, and sent them home. Before the boys got to the car one began talking in a loud voice again. The policeman, who had followed them down the alley, arrested this boy for disturbing the peace and took him to the police station where the other Saints gathered. After paying a $5 fine, and with the assurance that there would be no permanent record of the arrest, the boy was released.

The boys had a spirit of frivolity and fun about their escapades. They did not view what they were engaged in as "delinquency," though it surely was by any reasonable definition of that word. They simply viewed themselves as having a little fun and who, they would ask, was really hurt by it? The answer had to be no one, although this fact remains one of the most difficult things to explain about the gang's behavior. Unlikely though it seems, in two years of drinking, driving, carousing, and vandalism no one was seriously injured as a result of the Saints' activities.

### The Saints in School

The Saints were highly successful in school. The average grade for the group was B, with two of the boys having close to a straight A average. Almost all of the boys were popular and many of them held offices in the school. One of the boys was vice-president of the student body one year. Six of the boys played on athletic teams.

At the end of their senior year, the student body selected ten seniors for special recognition as the "school wheels"; four of the ten were Saints. Teachers and school officials saw no problem with any of these boys and anticipated that they would all "make something of themselves."

How the boys managed to maintain this impression is surprising in view of their actual behavior while in school. Their technique for covering truancy was so successful that teachers did not even realize that the boys were absent from school much of the time. Occasionally, of course, the system would backfire and then the boy was on his own. A boy who was caught would be most contrite, would plead guilty, and ask for mercy. He inevitably got the mercy he sought.

Cheating on examinations was rampant, even to the point of orally communicating answers to exams as well as looking at one another's papers. Since none of the group studied, and since they were primarily dependent on one another for help, it is surprising that grades were so high. Teachers contributed to the deception in their admitted inclination to give these boys (and presumably others like them) the benefit of the doubt. When asked how the boys did in school, and when pressed on specific examinations, teachers might admit that they were disappointed in John's performance, but would quickly add that they "knew that he was capable of doing better," so John was given a higher grade than he had actually earned. How often this happened is impossible to know. During the time that I observed the group, I never saw any of the boys take homework home. Teachers may have been "understanding" very regularly.

One exception to the gang's generally good performance was Jerry, who had a C average in his junior year, experienced disaster the next year, and failed to graduate. Jerry had always been a little more nonchalant than the others about the liberties he took in school. Rather than wait for someone to come get him from class, he would offer his own excuse and leave. Although he probably did not miss any more classes than most of the others in the group, he did not take the requisite pains to cover his absences. Jerry was the only Saint whom I ever heard talk back to a teacher. Although teachers often called him a "cut up" or a "smart kid," they never referred to him as a troublemaker or as a kid headed for trouble. It seems likely, then, that Jerry's failure his senior year and his mediocre performance his junior year were consequences of his not playing the game the proper way (possibly because he was disturbed by his parents' divorce). His teachers regarded him as "immature" and not quite ready to get out of high school.

### The Police and the Saints

The local police saw the Saints as good boys who were among the leaders of the youth in the community. Rarely, the boys might be stopped in town for speeding or for running a stop sign. When this happened the boys were always polite, contrite, and pled for mercy.

As it was in school, they received the mercy they asked for. None ever received a ticket or was taken into the precinct by the local police.

The situation in Big City, where the boys engaged in most of their delinquency, was only slightly different. The police there did not know the boys at all, although occasionally the boys were stopped by a patrolman. Once they were caught taking a lantern from a construction site. Another time they were stopped for running a stop sign, and on several occasions they were stopped for speeding. Their behavior was as before: contrite, polite, and penitent. The urban police, like the local police, accepted their demeanor as sincere. More important, the urban police were convinced that these were good boys just out for a lark.

### The Roughnecks

Hanibal townspeople never perceived the Saints' high level of delinquency. The Saints were good boys who just went in for an occasional prank. After all, they were well dressed, well mannered, and had nice cars. The Roughnecks were a different story. Although the two gangs of boys were the same age, and both groups engaged in an equal amount of wild-oat sowing, everyone agreed that the not-so-well-dressed, not-so-well-mannered, not-so-rich boys were heading for trouble. Townspeople would say, "You can see the gang members at the drugstore, night after night, leaning against the storefront (sometimes drunk), or slouching around inside buying Cokes, reading magazines, and probably stealing old Mr. Wall blind. When they are outside and girls walk by, even respectable girls, these boys make suggestive remarks. Sometimes their remarks are downright lewd."

From the community's viewpoint, the real indication that these kids were in for trouble was that they were constantly involved with the police. Some of them had been picked up for stealing, mostly small stuff, of course, "but still it's stealing small stuff that leads to big-time crimes." "Too bad," people said. "Too bad that these boys couldn't behave like the other kids in town; stay out of trouble, be polite to adults, and look to their future."

The community's impression of the degree to which this group of six boys (ranging in age from sixteen to nineteen) engaged in delinquency was somewhat distorted. In some ways the gang was more delinquent than the community thought; in other ways they were less.

The fighting activities of the group were fairly readily and accurately perceived by almost everyone. At least once a month, the boys would get into some sort of fight, although most fights were scraps between members of the group or involved only one member of the group and some peripheral hanger-on. Only three times in the period of observation did the group fight together: once against a gang from across town, once against two blacks, and once against a group of boys from another school. For the first two fights the group went out "looking for trouble"—and they found it both times. The third fight followed a football game and began spontaneously with an argument on the football field between one of the Roughnecks and a member of the opposition's football team.

Jack had a particular propensity for fighting and was involved in most of the brawls. He was a prime mover of the escalation of arguments into fights.

More serious than fighting, had the community been aware of it, was theft. Although almost everyone was aware that boys occasionally stole things, they did not realize the extent of the activity. Petty stealing was a frequent event for the Roughnecks. Sometimes they stole as a group and coordinated their efforts; other times they stole in pairs. Rarely did they steal alone.

The thefts ranged from very small things like paperback books, comics, and ballpoint pens to expensive items like watches. The nature of the thefts varied from time to time. The gang would go through a period of systematically shoplifting items from automobiles or school lockers. Types of thievery varied with the whim of the gang. Some forms of thievery were more profitable than others, but all thefts were for profit, not just thrills.

Roughnecks siphoned gasoline from cars as often as they had access to an automobile, which was not very often. Unlike the Saints, who owned their own cars, the Roughnecks would have to borrow their parents' cars, an event that occurred only eight or nine times a year. The boys claimed to have stolen cars for joy rides from time to time.

Ron committed the most serious of the group's offenses. With an unidentified associate the boy attempted to burglarize a gasoline station. Although this station had been robbed twice previously in the same month, Ron denied any involvement in either of the other thefts. When Ron and his accomplice approached the station, the owner was hiding in the bushes beside the station. He fired both barrels of a double-barreled shotgun at the boys. Ron was severely injured; the other boy ran away and was never caught. Though he remained in critical condition for several months, Ron finally recovered and served six months of the following year in reform school. Upon release from reform school, Ron was put back a grade in

school, and began running around with a different gang of boys. The
Roughnecks considered the new gang less delinquent than themselves, and during the following year Ron had no more trouble with
the police.

⌈The Roughnecks, then, engaged mainly in three types of delinquency: theft, drinking, and fighting. Although community
members perceived that this gang of kids was delinquent, they mis-
takenly believed that their illegal activities were primarily drinking,
fighting, and being a nuisance to passersby. Drinking was limited
among the gang members, although it did occur, and theft was
much more prevalent than anyone realized.

⌈Drinking would doubtless have been more prevalent had the boys
had ready access to liquor. Since they rarely had automobiles at
their disposal, they could not travel very far, and the bars in town
would not serve them. Most of the boys had little money, and this,
too, inhibited their purchase of alcohol. Their major source of
liquor was a local drunk who would buy them a fifth if they would
give him enough extra to buy himself a pint of whiskey or a bottle of
wine.

The community's perception of drinking as prevalent stemmed
from the fact that it was the most obvious delinquency the boys engaged in. When one of the boys had been drinking, even a casual observer seeing him on the corner would suspect that he was high.

There was a high level of mutual distrust and dislike between the
the Roughnecks and the police. The boys felt very strongly that the
police were unfair and corrupt. Some evidence existed that the boys
were correct in their perception.

The main source of the boys' dislike for the police undoubtedly
stemmed from the fact that the police would sporadically harass the
group. From the standpoint of the boys, these acts of occasional enforcement of the law were whimsical and uncalled for. It made no
sense to them, for example, that the police would come to the corner
occasionally and threaten them with arrest for loitering when the
night before the boys had been out siphoning gasoline from cars and
the police had been nowhere in sight. To the boys, the police were
stupid on the one hand, for not being where they should have been
and catching the boys in a serious offense, and unfair on the other
hand, for trumping up "loitering" charges against them.

From the viewpoint of the police, the situation was quite different. They knew, with all the confidence necessary to be a policeman, that these boys were engaged in criminal activities. They knew
this partly from occasionally catching them, mostly from circum-
stantial evidence ("the boys were around when those tires were

slashed"), and partly because the police shared the view of the community in general that this was a bad bunch of boys. The best the police could hope to do was to be sensitive to the fact that these boys were engaged in illegal acts and arrest them whenever there was some evidence that they had been involved. Whether or not the boys had in fact committed a particular act in a particular way was not especially important. The police had a broader view: their job was to stamp out these kids' crimes; the tactics were not as important as the end result.

Over the period that the group was under observation, each member was arrested at least once. Several of the boys were arrested a number of times and spent at least one night in jail. While most were never taken to court, two of the boys were sentenced to six months' incarceration in boys' schools.

### The Roughnecks in School

The Roughnecks' behavior in school was not particularly disruptive. During school hours they did not all hang around together, but tended instead to spend most of their time with one or two other members of the gang who were their special buddies. Although every member of the gang attempted to avoid school as much as possible, they were not particularly successful and most of them attended school with surprising regularity. They considered school a burden—something to be got through with a minimum of conflict. If they were "bugged" by a particular teacher, it could lead to trouble. One of the boys, Al, once threatened to beat up a teacher and, according to the other boys, the teacher hid under a desk to escape him.

Teachers saw the boys the way the general community did, as heading for trouble, as being uninterested in making something of themselves. Some were also seen as being incapable of meeting the academic standards of the school. Most of the teachers expressed concern for this group of boys and were willing to pass them despite poor performance, in the belief that failing them would only aggravate the problem.

The group of boys had a grade-point average just slightly above C. No one in the group failed either grade, and no one had better than a C average. They were very consistent in their achievement or, at least, the teachers were consistent in their perception of the boys' achievement.

Two of the boys were good football players. Herb was acknowledged to be the best player in the school and Jack was almost as good. Both boys were criticized for their failure to abide by training rules, for refusing to come to practice as often as they should, and for not playing their best during practice. What they lacked in sportsmanship they made up for in skill, apparently, and played every game no matter how poorly they had performed in practice or how many practice sessions they had missed.

## Two Questions

Why did the community, the school, and the police react to the Saints as though they were good, upstanding, nondelinquent youths with bright futures, but to the Roughnecks as though they were tough, young criminals who were headed for trouble? Why did the Roughnecks and the Saints in fact have quite different careers after high school—careers that, by and large, live up to the expectations of the community?

The most obvious explanation for the differences in the community's and law-enforcement agencies' reactions to the two gangs is that one group of boys was "more delinquent" than the other. Which group *was* more delinquent? The answer to this question will determine in part how we explain the differential responses to these groups by the members of the community and, particularly, by law-enforcement and school officials.

In sheer number of illegal acts, the Saints were the more delinquent. They were truant from school for at least part of the day almost every day of the week. In addition, their drinking and vandalism occurred with surprising regularity. The Roughnecks, in contrast, engaged sporadically in delinquent episodes. While these episodes were frequent, they certainly did not occur on a daily or even a weekly basis.

The difference in frequency of offenses was probably caused by the Roughnecks' inability to obtain liquor and to manipulate legitimate excuses from school. Since the Roughnecks had less money than the Saints, and teachers carefully supervised their school activities, the Roughnecks' hearts may have been as black as the Saints', but their misdeeds were not nearly as frequent.

There are really no clear-cut criteria by which to measure qualitative differences in antisocial behavior. The most important dimension of the difference is generally referred to as the "seriousness" of the offenses.

If seriousness encompasses the relative economic costs of delinquent acts, then some assessment can be made. The Roughnecks probably stole an average of about $5 worth of goods a week. Some weeks the figure was considerably higher, but these times must be balanced against long periods when almost nothing was stolen.

The Saints were more continuously engaged in delinquency but their acts were not for the most part costly to property. Only their vandalism and occasional theft of gasoline would so qualify. Perhaps once or twice a month they would siphon a tankful of gas. The other costly items were street signs, construction lanterns, and the like. All of these acts combined probably did not quite average $5 a week, partly because much of the stolen equipment was abandoned and presumably could be recovered. The difference in cost of stolen property between the two groups was trivial, but the Roughnecks probably had a slightly more expensive set of activities than did the Saints.

Another meaning of seriousness is the potential threat of physical harm to members of the community and to the boys themselves. The Roughnecks were more prone to physical violence; they not only welcomed an opportunity to fight; they went seeking it. In addition, they fought among themselves frequently. Although the fighting never included deadly weapons, it was still a menace, however minor, to the physical safety of those involved.

The Saints never fought. They avoided physical conflict both inside and outside the group. At the same time, though, the Saints frequently endangered their own and other people's lives. They did so almost every time they drove a car, especially if they had been drinking. Sober, their driving was risky; under the influence of alcohol it was horrendous. In addition, the Saints endangered the lives of others with their pranks. Street excavations left unmarked were a very serious hazard.

Evaluating the relative seriousness of the two gangs' activities is difficult. The community reacted as though the behavior of the Roughnecks was a problem, and they reacted as though the behavior of the Saints was not. But the members of the community were ignorant of the array of delinquent acts that characterized the Saints' behavior. Although concerned citizens were unaware of much of the Roughnecks' behavior as well, they were much better informed about the Roughnecks' involvement in delinquency than they were about the Saints'.

## Visibility

Differential treatment of the two gangs resulted in part because one gang was infinitely more visible than the other. This differential visibility was a direct function of the economic standing of the families. The Saints had access to automobiles and were able to remove themselves from the sight of the community. In as routine a decision as to where to go to have a milkshake after school, the Saints stayed away from the mainstream of community life. Lacking transportation, the Roughnecks could not make it to the edge of town. The center of town was the only practical place for them to meet since their homes were scattered throughout the town and any noncentral meeting place put an undue hardship on some members. Through necessity the Roughnecks congregated in a crowded area where everyone in the community passed frequently, including teachers and law-enforcement officers. They could easily see the Roughnecks hanging around the drugstore.

The Roughnecks, of course, made themselves even more visible by making remarks to passersby and by occasionally getting into fights on the corner. Meanwhile, just as regularly, the Saints were either at the café on one edge of town or in the pool hall at the other edge of town. Without any particular realization that they were making themselves inconspicuous, the Saints were able to hide their time wasting. Not only were they removed from the mainstream of traffic, but they also were almost always inside a building.

On their escapades the Saints were also relatively invisible, since they left Hanibal and traveled to Big City. Here, too, they were mobile, roaming the city, rarely going to the same area twice.

**Demeanor**

To the notion of visibility must be added the difference in the responses of group members to outside intervention with their activities. If one of the Saints was confronted with an accusing policeman, even if he felt he was truly innocent of a wrongdoing, his demeanor was apologetic and penitent. A Roughneck's attitude was almost the polar opposite. When confronted with a threatening adult authority, even one who tried to be pleasant, the Roughneck's hostility and disdain were clearly observable. Sometimes he might attempt to put up a veneer of respect, but it was thin and was not accepted as sincere by the authority.

School was no different from the community at large. The Saints could manipulate the system by feigning compliance with the school norms. The availability of cars at school meant that once free from the immediate sight of the teacher, the boys could disappear rapidly. And this escape was well-enough planned that no administrator or teacher was nearby when the boys left. A Roughneck who wished to escape for a few hours was in a bind. If it were possible to get free from class, downtown was still a mile away, and even if he arrived there, he was still very visible. Truancy for the Roughnecks meant almost certain detection, while the Saints enjoyed almost complete immunity from sanctions.

## Bias

Community members were not aware of the transgressions of the Saints. Even if the Saints had been less discreet, their favorite delinquencies would have been perceived as less serious than those of the Roughnecks.

In the eyes of the police and school officials, a boy who drinks in an alley and stands intoxicated on the street corner is committing a more serious offense than is a boy who drinks to inebriation in a nightclub or a tavern and drives around afterward in a car. Similarly, a boy who steals a wallet from a store will be viewed as having committed a more serious offense than a boy who steals a lantern from a construction site.

Perceptual bias also operates with respect to the demeanor of the boys in the two groups when they are confronted by adults. It is not simply that adults dislike the posture affected by boys of the Roughneck ilk; more important is the conviction that the posture adopted by the Roughnecks is an indication of their devotion and commitment to deviance as a way of life. The posture becomes a cue, just as the type of the offense is a cue, to the degree to which the known transgressions are indicators of the youths' potential for other problems.

Visibility, demeanor, and bias are surface variables that explain the day-to-day operations of the police. Why do these surface variables operate as they do? Why did the police choose to disregard the Saints' delinquencies while breathing down the backs of the Roughnecks?

The answer lies in the class structure of American society and the control of legal institutions by those at the top of the class structure. Obviously, no representative of the upper class drew up the operational chart for the police that led them to look in the ghettos and on street corners—which led them to see the demeanor of lower-class youth as troublesome and that of upper-middle-class youth as tolerable. Rather, the procedures simply developed from experience—experience with irate and influential upper-middle-class parents insisting that their son's vandalism was simply a prank and his drunkenness only a momentary "sowing of wild oats"—experience with cooperative or indifferent, powerless, lower-class parents who acquiesced to the laws' definition of their son's behavior.

## Adult Careers of the Saints and the Roughnecks

The community's confidence in the potential of the Saints and the Roughnecks apparently was justified. If anything, the community members underestimated the degree to which these youngsters would turn out "good" or "bad."

Seven of the eight members of the Saints went on to college immediately after high school. Five of the boys graduated from college in four years. The sixth one finished college after two years in the Army, and the seventh spent four years in the Air Force before returning to college and receiving a B.A. degree. Of these seven college graduates, three went on for advanced degrees. One finished law school and is now active in state politics, one finished medical school and is practicing near Hanibal, and one boy is now working for a Ph.D. The other four college graduates entered submanagerial, managerial, or executive training positions with larger firms.

The only Saint who did not complete college was Jerry. Jerry had failed to graduate from high school with the other Saints. During his second senior year, after the other Saints had gone on to college, Jerry began to hang around with what several teachers described as a "rough crowd"—the gang that was heir apparent to the Roughnecks. At the end of his second senior year, when he did graduate from high school, Jerry took a job as a used-car salesman, got married, and quickly had a child. Although he made several abortive attempts to go to college by attending night school, when I last saw him (ten years after high school) Jerry was unemployed and had been living on unemployment for almost a year. His wife worked as a waitress.

Some of the Roughnecks have lived up to community expectations. A number of them were headed for trouble. A few were not.

Jack and Herb were the athletes among the Roughnecks and their athletic prowess paid off handsomely. Both boys received unsolicited athletic scholarships to college. After Herb received his scholarship (near the end of his senior year), he apparently did an about-face. His demeanor became very similar to that of the Saints. Although he remained a member in good standing of the Roughnecks, he stopped participating in most activities and did not hang on the corner as often.

Jack did not change. If anything, he became more prone to fighting. He even made excuses for accepting the scholarship. He told the other gang members that the school had guaranteed him a C average if he would come to play football—an idea that seems far-fetched, even in this day of highly competitive recruiting.

During the summer after graduation from high school, Jack attempted suicide by jumping from a tall building. The jump would certainly have killed most people trying it, but Jack survived. He entered college in the fall and played four years of football. He and Herb graduated in four years, and both are teaching and coaching in high schools. They are married and have stable families. If anything, Jack appears to have a more pretigious position in the community than does Herb, though both are well respected and secure in their positions.

Two of the boys never finished high school. Tommy left at the end of his junior year and went to another state. That summer he was arrested and placed on probation on a manslaughter charge. Three years later he was arrested for murder; he pleaded guilty to second-degree murder and is serving a thirty-year sentence in the state penitentiary.

Al, the other boy who did not finish high school, also left the state in his senior year. He is serving a life sentence in a state penitentiary for first-degree murder.

Wes is a small-time gambler. He finished high school and "bummed around." After several years he made contact with a bookmaker who employed him as a runner. Later he acquired his own area and has been working it ever since. His position among the bookmakers is almost identical to the position he had in the gang; he is always around but no one is really aware of him. He makes no trouble and he does not get into any. Steady, reliable, capable of keeping his mouth closed, he plays the game by the rules, even though the game is an illegal one.

That leaves only Ron. Some of his former friends reported that they had heard he was "driving a truck up North," but no one could provide any concrete information.

### Reinforcement

The community responded to the Roughnecks as boys in trouble, and the boys agreed with that perception. Their pattern of deviancy was reinforced, and breaking away from it became increasingly unlikely. Once the boys acquired an image of themselves as deviants, they selected new friends who affirmed that self-image. As that self-conception became more firmly entrenched, they also became willing to try new and more extreme deviances. With their growing alienation came freer expression of disrespect and hostility for representatives of the legitimate society. This disrespect increased the community's negativism, perpetuating the entire process of commitment to deviance. Lack of a commitment to deviance works the same way. In either case, the process will perpetuate itself unless some event (like a scholarship to college or a sudden failure) external to the established relationship intervenes. For two of the Rough-

necks (Herb and Jack), receiving college athletic scholarships created new relations and culminated in a break with the established
pattern of deviance. In the case of one of the Saints (Jerry), his
parents' divorce and his failing to graduate from high school
changed some of his other relations. Being held back in school for a
year and losing his place among the Saints had sufficient impact on
Jerry to alter his self-image and virtually to assure that he would not
go on to college as his peers did. Although the experiments of life
can rarely be reversed, it seems likely in view of the behavior of the
other boys who did not enjoy this special treatment by the school
that Jerry, too, would have "become something" had he graduated
as anticipated. For Herb and Jack outside intervention worked to
their advantage; for Jerry it was his undoing.

Selective perception and labeling—finding, processing, and pun-
ishing some kinds of criminality and not others—means that visible,
poor, nonmobile, outspoken, undiplomatic "tough" kids will be noticed, whether their actions are seriously delinquent or not. Other
kids, who have established a reputation for being bright (even
though underachieving), disciplined, and involved in respectable activities, who are mobile and monied, will be invisible when they
deviate from sanctioned activities. They will sow their wild oats—
perhaps even wilder and thicker than their lower-class cohorts—but
they will not be noticed. When it is time to leave adolescence most
will follow the expected path, settling into the ways of the middle
class, remembering fondly the delinquent but unnoticed fling of
their youth. The Roughnecks and others like them may turn
around, too. It is more likely that their noticeable deviance will have
been so reinforced by police and community that their lives will be
effectively channeled into careers consistent with their adolescent
background.

# 15

# The Moral Career of a Bum

James P. Spradley

More arrests occur in the United States for public drunkenness than for any other crime; during 1965, of six million arrests, nearly two million were for this charge. The president's Commission on Law Enforcement and Administration of Justice has commented that this system of criminal justice "burdens police, clogs lower criminal courts, and crowds penal institutions throughout the United States," an observation borne out in Seattle, where seventy percent of all police man-hours are spent on this type of offense and eighty percent of the jail population throughout the year are the chronic alcoholic offenders.

Any person arrested for public drunkenness in Seattle may post a bail of $20 and be released in a few hours, and most who post bail do not appear in court, preferring to forfeit their bail. Some chronic offenders spend hundreds of dollars each year in this manner. Those people without sufficient funds to post bail must appear in Seattle Criminal Court, where it was reported that during 1967 nearly sixty-five percent of all cases were those charged with public drunkenness, or an average of about seventy persons per day. Ninety-seven percent of those appearing in court are found guilty and sentenced to serve time in the city jail for their crime.

The effect of this system upon the individual, especially people who cannot post bail, is often held to be partially therapeutic by many members of our society. On 17 June 1968 the Supreme Court of the United States ruled, in the case of *Powell vs Texas,* to uphold the laws that make public drunkenness an offense in every state of

305

the Union. One of the majority opinions stated the following reasons for this decision:

> Jailing of chronic alcoholics is definitely defended as therapeutic, and the claims of therapeutic value are not insubstantial. As appellees note, the alcoholics are removed from the streets, where in their intoxicated state they may be in physical danger, and are given food, clothing, and shelter until they "sober up" and thus at least regain their ability to keep from being run over by automobiles in the street.

Not everyone agrees with this modestly positive evaluation, however, least of all the drunks themselves. They know they are caught in a revolving door, and it is time to listen to their view of it. Consider the case of Mr. John Hallman, a long-time resident of Seattle: he was first arrested for public drunkenness in 1947 and two years later declared by the courts to be a "common drunkard"; during the 21-year period from 1947 to 1968, he was convicted over 100 times for this crime; he received many suspended sentences and posted $165 in bails that he forfeited; and there were 74 charges of public drunkenness during this period on which he was sentenced to jail. He was given a total of 5,340 days for these convictions, or *more than 14 years*. If he had posted $20 bail, it would have cost him $1,480. In this man's experience, then, a year of his life was worth only about $100! During 1966 he received two six-month sentences, which he could have avoided for only $40.

### Making the Bucket

Why do urban nomads encounter the police, get arrested, plead guilty, and do time in an almost never-ending cycle? They do, of course, violate local ordinances that prohibit drunkenness, drinking, begging, sleeping, and urinating in public. But what they do is much less significant than who they are. These men do their life sentences on the installment plan because they have been discredited and stigmatized by other Americans.

No man begins life as a bum, nor were these men socialized into the world of tramps as children. At one time in their adult life these men had a variety of respected identities—they were fathers, husbands, students, sons, employers, and employees. Many attended high schools; some went to college. One informant who had been a tramp for several years was a graduate of Harvard University. Others had owned businesses or worked at skilled trades. Nearly half of these men had once maintained a family.

The conception a man has of himself and his place in the world is, in part, socially constructed. Like the brick and mortar that go into creating a building, so the edifice of the human self is constructed, one building block at a time. While new dimensions of self-identity may be acquired throughout the life span, dramatic change in personality can occur only if these former identities are subjected to radical manipulation.

The revolving jail-house door is for the drunks "making the bucket"; it is a rite de passage, the actions, timing, and spatial ordering of which are intertwined in a complex array of symbolic meanings that ceremonially tell the urban nomad and those in his world who he is no longer and who he is becoming. We shall focus here upon the "stages of making the bucket," using the categories that tramps employ to order their experience throughout this rite and to anticipate and prepare for what is ahead.

## Stage 1: Street

One of the most important ways in which members of any society learn a new identity is through a process of being labeled by others, especially people who hold power over their lives. Not all labeling activity by others is significant of course, but when a man's concept of himself is shaken because of his own loss of control over doing those things that society considers important, he is especially vulnerable to the labels others use for him.

For the *urban nomads,* as I shall call them, the most significant "others" are the police. One man recalled, "That bull [policeman] said I was just a wino and a bum that wasn't worth being tossed in a shit ditch." The label of *tramp* was often used in a manner that implied the inferiority of such an identify. "Get going, you fuckin' tramp. Can't you hear your own name, ass-hole?" Many other discrediting labels such as "you wino son-of-a-bitch," "ding bat," "fucking dehorn," "drunken bum," "cocksucker," "Skid Road bastard," "fuckin' tramp," and "phony ass" were among those reported by my informants. Tramps are often threatened as well— "Shut up or we will put you in the pads and beat the shit out of you."

A man may also be stigmatized by the police by having other aspects of his identify thrown up before him as evidence that he is only a bum. There is, for example, a large population of Indians in the city of Seattle, and many find companionship in the Skid Road District and often get charged with being drunk in public. In many ways they are considered beneath all others. One man said, "That bull called me a fucked-up chief and stated that liquor rights should never have been given to these fuckin' Injuns." Another remembered an officer saying to him, "They didn't play cowboys and Indians long enough; they should have killed all of you bastards off."

Whatever the reasons for this labeling behavior, most tramps are aware that it goes on and come to the same conclusion as the man who stated, "In many cops' minds a drunk isn't human."

### Stage 2: Call Box

Personal and social identity are not only structured by the roles we play and the names we use, but also by objects of personal property. For the tramps, rings, watches, money, wallets, identification papers, address books, and clothing help to give form and structure to *who* one is, and their loss is significant. Although they may be robbed at any point during the entire ritual of making the bucket, the first fleecing often takes place at the call box.

When a man is arrested by a policeman on the beat, he is taken to the call box where a paddy wagon or police car is summoned to take him to jail. In the interim he undergoes a thorough search and may lose some of his belongings; in a sample of 100 men, twenty-three percent of the men indicated they had been robbed by a policeman while he was shaking them down at a call box.

Even if they make it to jail without being robbed their possessions are not safe. When the wagon takes them off to jail, they hope against the odds that their possessions will be in their property box when they are released, but as one man recalled, "They took a watch and ring from me in 1968 and told me it would be in my property at the jail. I never got them back."

In addition to being despoiled of his property, a man at the call box is almost always robbed of his autonomy at a deeper psychological level. His world has been invaded by someone with the authority to treat him in a manner designed to show him that he is utterly powerless, certainly not that he is innocent until proven guilty. The street corners on Skid Road have a different meaning to tramps than they do to others in American society. They are not merely dingy public places, they are the living rooms and private meeting places for urban nomads. A man who has recently arrived in town will hang around a street corner hoping to meet an old friend or find a new one. Therefore, when a man is required to place his hands over his head and allow an officer to invade his clothing and other domains of privacy, while at the same time threatening him, it is done in full view of other tramps.

### Stage 3: Paddy Wagon or Police Car

Although the drive to the jail may involve only a few blocks, a man does not always get there after he is picked up in the paddy wagon; twenty-three percent of the sample reported the police had stopped them or picked them up, taken their money or other property, and then let them go. Because they are not arrested on such occasions, this form of shakedown is considered to be an involuntary payoff to the police. Only six percent of the sample reported they had ever made a *voluntary* payoff. Some have stories such as this man's: "In 1968 they picked me up in a prowl car and took me down on Skid Road back in an alley and searched me, took my money, drove me around for awhile, and then let me out way down on Skid Road in a back alley. They drove off without returning my money."

It is almost impossible to verify these incidents by legal means, but enough tramps have experienced this official thievery for it to have become part of their general cultural knowledge. The strategies tramps use to make themselves invisible when they sleep are also used to protect their personal property. Like chamelions, they are careful to conceal any hint that they have valuable possessions. So men reported they would dress in old clothes "like a bum" in order to avoid becoming a candidate for jackrollers and thieves.

### Stage 4: Elevator

The elevator from the basement of the Public Safety Building to the sixth floor where the jail is located is especially dangerous for the tramp. He is entirely cut off from the view of everyone except the police—not even a disinterested passerby can influence what takes place. Although it is a short trip, the "bull" (cop) can easily push the stop button between floors. As the elevator slowly rises, the reality of imprisonment sweeps over the tramp with an immediacy that suffocates any self-assertive wishes he may still harbor. The two bulls at his side, like uniformed bars of a cell, cannot be seen as human beings to whom he can respond, for any reaction on his part other than a plastic passivity may be interpreted as resistance. The tramp may not himself have been worked over in the elevator, but he has certainly heard of it from his fellow urban nomads.

Although being clubbed or smashed against a wall symbolically reminds a man that his body, the most intimate dimension of his self-concept, is vulnerable, it also has another important meaning. Like a rehearsal before a dramatic performance, it forcefully instructs the tramp to play the part of a dependent and passive actor within the bucket. The longer a man has been in the world of tramps, the more he learns to respond as if he were an animal whose master had broken his will. Labels, threats, physical abuse, and thefts of property in themselves are difficult for any man to take, but more significant is the implicit message in these actions: they clearly identify for the tramp the people who hold power over his life then and during the coming months he may spend in jail. If he refuses to acknowledge his deferential role, further steps will be taken, as they were with the man who recalled:

> In 1967 he shook me down, took my wallet, looked in it, took $11. Put my wallet back and I said, "Since when do you look for a gun or a knife in a man's wallet?" He split my head, and it took four stitches.

**Stage 5: Booking**
When the elevator door opens, a man sees to his left the gun rack where the officers will deposit their weapons. Before him is a row of closely spaced steel bars that lurch into motion with the sound of a buzzer pressed from behind the booking desk. As the steel gate opens he is ushered across a waiting area of twenty or thirty feet in diameter to a high counter with several windows. For each man the officer fills out in quadruplicate a property record and booking sheet. Although there is space for the prisoner to sign and verify the property record, almost seventy percent of my informants indicated they were not usually allowed to do this, and ninety-eight percent of the sample indicated they had never received a receipt.

When I questioned tramps about thefts from their property boxes, forty percent reported their occurrence. One man recalled this story:

> I was in jail and had no money, and there was a fellow who owed me $12, and so I wrote and asked him for it and told him to send it registered letter. I got the letter, but the money wasn't in it. When I got out I didn't have no money in my property box. I said, "I've got a registered letter here saying I was sent $12. I'm not leaving until I get it." The bull said, "You don't have no money." The sergeant came by just then, asked what it was and looked at the letter, and went back to the property box and then came out and said, "Oh, here's your $12. It was in the wrong property box."

One factor of which tramps are most keenly aware in the entire ritual of making the bucket is that at every point they receive different kinds of treatment than those they refer to as "citizens" or "uptown tramps." A well-dressed man is seldom robbed, beaten, or cursed because he is likely to cause trouble.

The booking desk has one further significant effect on these men who are undergoing an identity change, and that is creating a record. This record becomes part of the court file on each man, and it is used to determine the severity of his sentence. Later it may be much more widely disseminated, as was noted in the study on the Seattle Police Department made by the International Association of Chiefs of Police in 1968. Any success at passing as an average citizen, whether it be for employment, housing, or friendship, may crumble when others discover his record. Although *he* may know that many of his arrests were simply due to his visibility in the Skid Road area, it is not easy to convince others that this was the case.

### Stage 6: Padded Drunk Tank

From the booking desk it is a short distance down a hallway to the padded drunk tank, so called because a thin layer of cork covers the floor, to cushion the men as they sleep off a drunk or await the next stage of the ritual. Most men have very few memories of this tank because they spend little time there, or they are too drunk to remember what transpired. Only one of my informants got a second (sober) glimpse of the padded drunk tank. A young merchant seaman, who was twenty-nine, had arrived in Seattle and was arrested several times. While waiting for his appearance in court, the following incident occurred:

> I was in the cement drunk tank with about forty guys. They had some visitors coming through the jail, and they took several of us out of the cement drunk tank and gave us each two blankets and put us in the padded drunk tank. It had a rubber floor. They brought us in food, they heaped our trays with stew for dinner at 4:30, and the visitors came through and everything looked great.

Tramps are aware of such subterfuge, and it is one of the reasons they believe no one can discover their plight and that you "can't change City Hall."

### Stage 7: Mug and Print Room

Any man who has made the bucket more than once knows that here is the watershed at which the poor are separated from the not so poor. After a man is sober enough to be processed in this room, he also is sober enough to post a bail of $20, and then walk out of the jail a free man. He has bought his way out for $20. He has purchased a clean slate, a new sense of self, an *immediate* opportunity to assert himself and release all the pent-up hostility he may have felt toward the system—all for only $20. And he can continue bailing himself out forever if he has the resources or friends who will pay. But what does this say to the man who sees others post their bail, who tries to phone a friend or bondsman for the needed money, only to fail and enter the drunk tank with the knowledge that he could have been free if he had not been poor—a poverty that may have been incurred only a few hours earlier at the hands of his captors?

## Stage 8: Cement Drunk Tank

Events have moved rapidly for the tramp who has gone through the first stages of the ritual. From the street to the call box, into a paddy wagon, and up the elevator, through the booking-desk process, and on into the padded drunk tank for a few hours of sleep. X-rays and pictures follow in quick succession. And then suddenly, as the heavy door closes on the cement drunk tank, time seems to wind backwards.

The cement drunk tank is not a comfortable place to spend several days, and 90 percent of my sample reported having spent two or more days there. There are no bunks in this room—meant to hold about 35 men—and only one toilet and washbasin. Only 3 percent of the sample reported ever receiving a blanket. The lights are left on 24 hours a day, and there is nothing resembling privacy; but the most abhorrent part of this experience is the crowding, which makes it impossible for a man to protect himself from being contaminated by others. One man described these conditions in graphic terms:

> That's all right if you're a young fellow, you can take it. It's miserable, but you can take it. Sometimes, I don't know what the reason for it is, it doesn't make sense for you at all, but I've been in there when there is standing room only, in one of those concrete cells, for two or three days. There's barely room to sit down. You certainly can't lie down without putting your face in someone's dirty socks or something like that. And this is when there are two or three other tanks available that are completely empty. There's no reason why they don't take half of them and put them in another one, except they don't want to bother to clean it up.

In fact, the physical discomfort in itself is not unbearable; after all, tramps have slept on cold hard cement before without a blanket.

But now they have lost control of their lives, and as they lie there waiting for court, the drunk tank reminds them of this as nothing else could.

A man's most immediate needs are often for cigarettes, food, and information about the state of his property. He has lost the control over all of these items. Although food is served three times a day, it is never enough. If he has been able to smuggle some money into the drunk tank in his clothing, he can pay a "trusty" fifty cents or a dollar to "hustle" him a cup of coffee or get something from his property, but he can never depend on this. The trusties often steal, but the men cannot complain to the bulls, since it is against the rules to have money. Moreover, the bulls will often not even protect them against other prisoners in the drunk tank. One man recalled:

> I remember about three years ago I was working in a logging camp and had just come to town, and I ended up in the drunk tank. I woke up, and I caught some guy trying to steal my shoes in the drunk tank. He was taking them off my feet, see, so we got into it, and he had two or three buddies in the drunk tank, and I started hollering for the bull, the jailer, and they put the finger on me, see, that I started it. I tried to tell the jailer that the son-of-a-bitch was trying to steal my shoes. I'd sobered up by that time, and that big jailer, he says "You come out here." He took me over into an empty tank, and I knew what was coming then. He slammed the door shut, and he walks up to me and says, "You think you're pretty tough, huh?" I seen it coming, you know, and held my breath, and he hit me in the guts as hard as he could. He didn't even knock me down. I just stepped back two or three feet, and he kind of looked at me, you know, and that was it. He didn't knock me down the first time, so he left me alone, and I said, "What in hell did you do that for?" He didn't answer me, but if I had swung on him, which I could have done, well then they'd have brought in two or three more, you know, and really whipped my ass."

Even though he is already in the drunk tank, in principle a man may still contact a bondsman, attorney, employer, or friend who will help get him out of jail. But to contact the outside, he must of course use the phone. Eighty-five percent of my informants said they had been permitted to make one phone call, but the man who has no regular employment, family, or permanent address finds the privilege of a single telephone call next to useless. He may need to contact several people until he finds one who will bail him out, get his money, pay for his room, get his clothing, or assist him in some other way.

**Stage 9: Court Docket**

Time drags its feet in the drunk tank. The hours creep by, turning slowly into days and nights to be endured. The men think about food, count the hours until they will appear in court, rack their brains for someone who could bail them out, swap experiences of other jails, listen eagerly to newcomers with word from outside, and wonder where they will travel when they are released. Uppermost in the minds of most men are thoughts of "beating their drunk charge."

The heavy door of the drunk tank opens at about 8:00 A.M. each morning, Monday through Friday, for the drunks to file out, walk down the hallway, through the main lobby past the booking desk, up the stairs, and through a maze of corridors to the court docket. This room is much like the cement drunk tank except that it is smaller and filled with rows of steel benches where the men await court. On most days, just before court begins, a counselor for the alcoholism treatment center appears to explain their program and how a person can qualify for it. Most men are sitting sleepily on the benches or lying on the floor, some still fighting the pains of a hangover or withdrawal from a long drunk. They move out, then, in groups of about twenty-five into the small area to the right and front of the judge's bench, barricaded from the rest of the courtroom by a railing. They are crowded into this cramped space and told where to stand by the officer, where they remain, lined up three deep, pressed together, holding their hats in their hands, heads down, waiting for the judge to speak.

**Stage 10: Courtroom**

> You men have all been charged with drinking is public, drunk in public, or begging which are in violation of the ordinances of the City of Seattle. The maximum penalty for these crimes is $500 fine and/or 180 days in jail. You have a right to plead guilty or not guilty. You have a right to consult a lawyer before you enter a plea of guilty or not guilty. If you want to consult a lawyer, you must pay for your own attorney. The court does not have provisions for this. If you wish a continuance, please indicate when you return to court. On a plea of guilty you waive your rights to appeal to a higher court. On a plea of not guilty your case will be continued for trial at a later date. Now return to the court docket and when you are called in you will enter a plea of guilty or not guilty. If you wish to make a statement you may do so.

The "rights spiel," as one man fondly dubbed it, takes less than a minute to complete. The group of men are then hurried back into the court docket to listen for their name again. When a man hears his name, he returns to the courtroom alone. He faces the judge's bench, separated by the railing and the prosecuting attorney for the City of Seattle, who says, "You have been charged with the crime of public drunkenness, how do you plead?" If a man enters a plea of guilty, and over ninety percent of them do so, the prosecutor reads his prior record to the judge who will sentence him according to a preset formula based on his record. A man may plead guilty or not guilty, ask for a continuance, make a statement, or request he be sent to the alcoholism treatment center.

The best way to beat a drunk charge is to have a good record, a strategy that has wide ramifications for the life-style of tramps. In some courts there is a single sentence for anyone guilty of public drunkenness, but in Seattle, as it is in many cities, there is a sliding scale determined by a man's past record. A first offender, who may only be new to that court or who simply may have been out of action for six months or more, will get two days suspended. An eight-time loser may get as much as ninety days.

Whenever tramps discuss previous experiences in jail and court, they explain them by making references to how many days they have "hanging" (the amount of time they know they will be sentenced to do). It is impossible to understand the actions a man takes, such as bailing out, asking for the treatment center, or pleading guilty, unless it is also known how many days he had hanging.

The judge apparently gives sentences of increasing magnitude, with an occasional major suspended sentence, for two reasons: to reduce the recurrence of a man's drinking sprees and help him regain his health. Tramps, however, know they are arrested for many reasons besides their drinking behavior; it is their life-style, only one feature of which involves drinking, that brings them into court. While the punishment of longer sentences may motivate some men to abstain from public drunkenness, it has a much more significant influence for most tramps: it motivates them to travel. In order to improve their record in court so as to reduce the amount of time they will do on their next conviction, tramps choose another alternative—leaving town. With each succeeding arrest in Seattle a person's record becomes more tarnished and the number of days he has hanging increases. But every tramp knows this slate could be completely erased by leaving town for six months.

The suspended sentence is an even more important stimulus to the mobility of tramps. When a tramp receives a suspended sentence of ninety days, he has escaped doing time, but only for the moment; back on the street he walks with the knowledge that he now has probably doubled the number of days he has hanging. If arrested again, he may serve the suspended and the new sentence consecutively.

After a long period of incarceration, a man feels like "moving on" as an end in itself; he wants to enjoy his freedom to the utmost. But tramps also travel from one place to another because they become marked men who are arrested over and over again for their very presence in the Skid Road District. There is an intimate relationship between mobility and other features of their life-style that involve drinking: alcoholic beverages function as a social lubricant at all levels of American society, but they fulfill this need in a special way for urban nomads. Nomadism creates a unique kind of loneliness and sense of isolation in an individual, and when he arrives alone in a new town he seeks to find others of his own kind to reduce such anxieties. Almost the only place where he can find acceptance, friendship, and sociability is on Skid Road and in the bars located there. Bars are categorized among tramps in a variety of ways, but especially in terms of what one may find there in the way of friends, female companionship, and work opportunities. For urban nomads, bars function as churches and clubs, employment agencies and dating centers, begging places, drinking and eating places, and flops. Most of all, they are a place to find friendship, even if it is only of a fleeting nature. In a Skid Road bar one is not restricted in his behavior; he can perform in ways appropriate to this subculture and know he will be accepted; he can find out important information about jail and court and employment that other tramps will freely give him. One tramp who wanted to control his drinking behavior clearly saw the relationship between mobility and drinking. As he was about to be released from the alcoholism treatment center he commented: "My biggest problem when I get out next week is traveling. When I get in a strange vicinity I head for a bar. If I want work, I go to a bar. That's where they come to hire a man." Skid Road and its bars, in addition to being a place to solidify new-found friendships with a drink, is also where most arrests for public drunkenness occur. And so we have come full circle: *urban nomads visit Skid Road and its bars because they travel; they are arrested because they live and drink in this area of town; and they travel because they are arrested.*

Some of the strategies used to beat a drunk charge are linked together. A man who requests a continuance does so in order to be able to bail out; similarly, a person who uses an alias does so to have a good record or escape the one he has created over the past months. As one informant stated, "If they have no previous arrest for a name, they usually give a kickout. You've got to beat them some way." But few men use this dodge because it is too risky:

> One Friday Sanders gave the name Johnson, for he had time hanging. They called for Johnson many times Friday, Saturday, and Sunday. Monday morning when they called Johnson for court the officer who knew him spotted Sanders and told him he ought to kick his teeth in. Sanders had forgot what name he'd used.

The most widely used way to beat a drunk charge is a passive one—plead guilty and hope for the best. Ninety-four percent of the sample reported they usually pleaded guilty to a drunk charge even when they felt sure they were not really drunk at the time of arrest. Nearly ninety-seven percent of the drunk cases heard in this court result in convictions. Tramps firmly believe that "you can't beat the charge," "you can't win the case," and it does not make any difference what you plead—"you are guilty anyway." Most men feel they actually have no other choice, and some believe they will get a lighter sentence.

Twenty-seven percent of the sample had, however, entered a plea of not guilty at one time or another, although only four men reported they had been acquitted. One stated, "The judge told me if I did not think I was guilty to plead not guilty, which I did. He moved my case ahead 30 days, and I spent 30 days in jail, was found guilty, and sentenced to 30 days." It is important to remember how these men feel about the drunk tank and the sense of isolation there. It is an almost unbearable thought to stand in court and know that if you plead not guilty you will return to that place. A man pleads guilty because he can be sentenced sooner and start "doing my time." The uncertainty of waiting for the outcome of trial and the fact that the days you wait for trial may be "dead time," not even counted as part of the sentence you finally receive, are perceived as punishments for entering an honest plea, and they provide sufficient motivation to enter a plea of guilty. One who pleads not guilty also runs the risk of offending the arresting officers who must take time to appear in court as witnesses. One man recalled: "If you plead not guilty you have the arresting cops against you, so you can't win anyway."

Finally, men plead guilty most of the time because they believe the courts are in collusion with the police against them. "All a cop has to do is say you were drunk—the judge never goes against a cop."

Tramps not only know the principles and rules of our legal system, they also know that the law-enforcement agencies violate these rules as far as they are concerned: they are assumed to be guilty rather than innocent; they are rewarded for pleading guilty even when they are innocent; they have no way to provide themselves with a defense attorney; and they are punished if they go against the system by pleading not guilty. The network of protections for the innocent is stripped away from the process of criminal justice for these men, and in its place is an overwhelming pressure coercing them into violating their own integrity by agreeing with the verdict of the system.

One option usually open to a man attempting to beat a drunk charge is to make a statement. Only sixteen percent of the sample reported they had ever asked to make a statement in court and not been allowed to do so. The tramp learns which factors influence the judge as he sentences a man to jail for public drunkenness, and the statement he makes will reflect these concerns.

Equal justice for all under the law is the maxim of this court, yet when we consider whom the judge sentences and who escapes, we must conclude that some men are more equal than others. The man who still has family responsibilities may talk of family ties in an effort to get a suspended sentence. He is aware that being a responsible family man is one of the things that separates urban nomads from the rest of society, and any indication that he is still trying to keep from being a bum will carry weight with the judge.

Many men indicate they have a job, but unless it is a rather permanent one or unless there are some other extenuating circumstances, they are still apt to get a sentence. The most effective kind of statement may be a promise to get out of town. In these cases, the men are offering the judge the only thing they have left in life—their mobility:

> *Prosecutor:* Mr. Brown, you have been charged with being drunk in public. How do you plead?
> *Mr. Brown:* Guilty.
> *Judge:* When were you released?
> *Mr. Brown:* Last Saturday morning. Could I have a break? I want to go pick apples. Last time, I got out of jail and walked around to where the bus to the apples was, and when I got to the bus I was waiting in line to get on, and the patrol car picked me up.

> *Judge:* Will you go pick apples if I give you an opportunity?
> *Mr. Brown:* Yes, I will.
> *Judge:* Thirty days suspended.

Such claims as, "I was asleep in my car," or, "I just got out of the hospital, and I've been taking pills. I had a couple drinks and fell asleep, but it was the pills that made me fall asleep," are commonly heard in court, but they do not often lead to a suspended sentence. At the least they offer a meager opportunity for a man to attempt to restore his damaged self-respect for having given in to the system and pleaded guilty.

During the past couple of years in Seattle, a new strategy for beating drunk charges has been added to the list: request the alcoholism treatment center. When the judge considers a man to be a good candidate, he then continues his case, waits for him to be psychologically and medically examined, and finally recommended by the treatment-center staff for acceptance. If he is acceptable, he will then be sentenced to the treatment center for a period of four months. Sometimes a man is anxious for treatment but does not indicate appropriate interest and goes to jail instead, as seen in the following case:

> *Prosecutor:* Mr. Pace, you have been charged with being drunk in public. How do you plead?
> *Mr. Pace:* Guilty.
> *Judge:* Do you have a drinking problem?
> *Mr. Pace:* We all have drinking problems, but I've worked on mine.
> *Judge:* Have you had any help?
> *Mr. Pace:* Yes, I went to Alcoholics Anonymous, but their rules are too stringent. They wouldn't allow working any night job or overtime. I talked to the probation officer, and he said try to take their advice.
> *Judge:* Do you want assistance, or do you want to continue as you are?
> *Mr. Pace:* It depends on how strong the treatment would be.
> *Judge:* We have a new treatment center but it's only for those who want help and will cooperate with the program. If you don't want to, you can go back to the city jail.
> *Mr. Pace:* Well, I would like to go if their program isn't too stringent.
> *Judge:* There can be no conditions on your going there. The sentence is thirty days in the Seattle city jail.

The treatment center is viewed by some men, however, as an easier place to do time than in jail, and in a sense they "beat their drunk charge" by going there. Very few tramps have become totally immune to the norms and values of American culture, and they often feel guilty, especially when they are arrested for a long drunk. Some men reported that the worst aspect of court was the way it intensified their feelings of shame and guilt without any opportunity to express this. One said, "It hurts my pride. It's degrading. You are on exhibition for everyone to see, not being able to express how sorry you really are for being drunk." In all these experiences—the public humiliation, the waiting, facing the judge without any means of defense, the physical discomfort involved—tramps feel that underlying the whole process they are looked upon by the officials of the society as objects to be manipulated, as something less than human. The worst thing about court is being "herded around like a bunch of cattle—dumb animals."

**Stage 11: Holding Tank**

Men who receive a sentence walk back into the seventh-floor section of the jail and are placed in the holding tank after the court session is completed. The trusty officer joins them there, and a decision is made regarding the future role they will have in jail: trusty or lockup. This decision is probably the most significant factor in determining whether a man does hard time or easy time, since trusties have many advantages that lockups do not. They are put in several different kinds of tanks that are unlocked during the day. Some have freedom to move throughout most of the jail, and others may even go outside to work. Their greater freedom allows them to watch TV at certain times, and, most important, they have access to food and other resources in and out of the jail. It is difficult to determine the reasons why an individual may not become a trusty, but often there are not enough jobs, or a man may be too old and sick, while another may have run away the last time he was a trusty.

**Stage 12: Delousing Tank**

The men spend several hours in the delousing tank, and most of them felt it was the worst part of the entire process of making the bucket. As soon as the assignments are made in the holding tank, all inmates, both trusties and lockups, are taken a few feet down the hall to be deloused. There are sixteen bunks in this tank with a small passageway between the bunks, a shower, and a toilet. The men are crowded in and ordered to strip off all of their clothing. The nakedness that the men must now endure is felt to be degrading in itself, but the men also feel they may be contaminated by each other. And their clothes, if not lousy before, certainly will be after the treatment they get.

> One machine with thirty men's clothes for delousing—some guys are better than looking at carnivals, wearing a couple of union suits, couple pair of pants. The clothes should be turned inside out where the seams show so the greybacks can't hide; some guys are filthy. If they're lousy and guys are so crowded together, everybody's contaminated. Them clothes should really be in that machine for maybe three hours so nobody gets lousy.

Many men reported that they felt very keenly about their clothing, and they are perfectly aware that the designation of bum is used for them largely because of their appearance. While they were in court, after lying in the drunk tank for several days, the state of their clothing caused them great embarrassment and concern. But all these feelings about clothes reflect the fact that as the self crumbles, men cling more desperately to the last vestige of any material objects that symbolize, in some sense, their personal identity and the world outside. Not only is the men's clothing stripped from their backs, but the best articles are also sometimes stolen by trusties, and almost everything comes out of the heating machine in worse shape than when they went in.

### Stages 13 and 14: Time Tank and Trusty Tank

For the lockup nothing so increases the amount of hard time a man does as much as hunger. One man said, "You can do hard time any place especially if there's poor grub or if you're sleeping on the steel," and almost everyone agreed that in Seattle jail the grub was poor indeed and everyone was continually hungry.

The experience of doing hard time as a trusty or lockup is related to many other facets of life in the bucket besides food, however. It results, in part, from failure to maintain a compliant attitude toward the social and physical environment, failure to live a day at a time, losses of personal property and jobs on the outside, and losses of clothing in the delousing process. In addition, a system of rewards and punishments within the jail contributes directly to the experience of doing hard or easy time.

While rewards are sought and favors are gratefully accepted from many policemen, the men are aware that they are granted only if one maintains a submissive attitude, and even at that, they are few and far between. The men are much more alert to the possibility of punishment, which may come in the form of withheld privileges, extra physical torment, or being busted. In jail men have the privilege of writing letters, making a phone call each week, getting out of their cell for a brief period of exercise, and using the money in their property to purchase candy and cigarettes through the weekly commissary. These privileges are not equally available to all men, and their withdrawal by the police is felt as a terrible loss.

The bulls may also punish more directly. The men usually refer to this as being put on "the bull's shit list" or having "a cop on your ass." One man recalled, "Even a trusty may do hard time if a cop is on your ass." Fifteen percent of the sample reported that they had been put on the bull's shit list for various reasons—"I refused to polish a cop's shoes," or "because I told them I was going to call the Civil Liberties Union about the sadistic treatment," or "by not calling him 'officer.'"

The final kind of punishment is being busted. Almost any person, whether lockup or trusty, can be busted to another less desirable place within the jail. There are six distinct places within the jail to which a man may be busted for misbehavior, for getting on the bull's shit list, or for some unknown reason: the trusty tank, time tank, padded cell, drunk tank, stand-up cell, and the hole. One man reported being busted to the drunk tank because he kept asking for medical treatment: "This is what I received to keep me quiet." Another said, "The nurse had this man busted on word from another trusty which was not true pertaining to his work in the dispensary, and he did thirty-five days there."

A few men will go to the drunk tank at their own request in order to do easy time. They want the extra food that men who are too ill and cannot eat will leave there for them, or they may want to avoid having to control their behavior carefully as they must when they are lockups or trusties. But no one goes voluntarily to the stand-up cell or the hole. Many men did not know of these places, but one man described the hole this way:

> There was a small Indian man who I knew, and he got in a fight with a bull at the booking desk. They cuffed his hands behind his back and worked him over and then put him in the hole and left him there for two days. He said he passed his time by doing pushups. They stripped him naked, he had no clothing, and the hole is a little concrete cell about six-foot square. There was no light, and he was fed bread and water.

But overarching the concrete results of the rewards and punish-

ment used to control the tramp's behavior are two other factors. A
man summed up one, the dread of loss:

> Well, one thing a man does not do in jail is talk unless he is
> spoken to. There is a constant fear of loss, because loss is a
> penalty. One way to penalize a man is simply to ignore him as
> he rattles the bars of his cage or the cell. For instance, a man
> might be going into DTs and need some medical attention, and
> so to attract attention of the guard he will shake the cell bars
> very loudly, because he is desperate for some kind of help, and
> he'll be penalized by simply ignoring him.

Second, it should be pointed out that most men felt there was a
great deal of unpredictability in the punishments they might receive.
Everything depended on the vagaries of the officers' moods and
especially which officer one encountered.

### Stage 15: The Street Again

Whether a man is a lockup or trusty the days do pass until the inmate is doing short time—only a few days remain on his sentence.
For some, the last few days are easy time, filled with the knowledge
and expectation of release. For others, as their minds become filled
with memories of the outside and they plan for the days ahead, it is
not so easy. But eventually the morning arrives when a man knows
he will be escorted from his cell, lay aside his identity as a lockup or
trusty, and become, if only for a few hours, a kickout. After being
discharged he walks to the elevator and rides quickly to the ground
floor, walks out of the building—a free man who will now take up
his life as an urban nomad in other scenes of that world.

But jail is perhaps the most important scene in that world. Here
the remaining shreds of respectable identity have been stripped
away as they became participants in the elaborate ritual of making
the bucket. Society, which has swept them out of sight and in the
process cut them off from their former selves, now views them as
bums or common drunkards. But in jail there has developed in these
men an identity vacuum, along with powerful motivations to fill it,
not only because of their material losses, but also because inactivity,
restraint, and oversensitivity to the staff create pressures to act, to
become, and to gain a new sense of personal identity and a new set
of values to replace what has been lost.

The novice who repeats this experience several times may first
seek to escape it by travel to a new town, but once there he usually
goes to Skid Road for ready acceptance. Sooner or later, for many

men, the world and culture of the tramp become a viable alternative to replace what has been lost in the ritual of making the bucket. In that culture he may still be alienated from the rest of society—but *not from himself* or others like him. He will find acceptance as well as adaptive strategies for survival as an urban nomad. But more important, something else has been going on simultaneously during the days in jail—he has been learning the attitudes, values, and skills that are required for survival in this new culture.

### Letters from the Tank

Mr. William R. Tanner, the writer of these letters and notes, was forty-nine at the time and unmarried. He arrived in Seattle in 1967 and stayed for less than a year, during which time he was arrested nine times for public drunkenness and served nearly 200 days in jail. The author has lost contact with Mr. Tanner, who may well be languishing in jail somewhere. His story is common to thousands of men, the urban nomads of America.

Somewhere in Seattle, 14 August 1967

Dear Jim,

In all sincerity (as far as I'm able to be so) I'll be happy to write my own thoughts and you can sift thru the garbage and use whatever you wish. My only desire is that it would perhaps help some other in this bedlam. My background is peculiar: I was born in Minnesota, December 15, 1918. Father was a miner, mother a housewife. My brother Wayne, eight years my senior, was class valedictorian, a West Point nominee, a salesman, and compulsive gambler. Died in 1951—second heart attack. My "namesake Tanner," or my father, died of TB somewhere when I was born. Mother remarried my stepfather. We were pretty tight; he said I was his true son. Several older people have as much as said so. I had a grand childhood. I now have a nephew and a sister-in-law who is remarried. I took my frustrations and self-anger out on her at my stepdad's funeral so thus far she has understandably refused to forgive. Thru a priest I found out that she does not wish to hear from me. Perhaps in fear that I may contaminate my nephew. I still expect to make amends if time will permit. I was tested by a psychologist a year ago in Minneapolis, the Minnesota Multiphasic Personality Inventory. He said I didn't belong in jail at all, my I.Q. was 131. He said I indicated that I liked people and said he wished I'd go back to college and get a degree in anything and get into social work.

Well, I was pinched last Friday and they threw me in the drunk tank where I stayed until court time this morning. . . . The general consensus amongst the jail population is that this is the hungriest jail in the country—even the southern jails give of quantity if not quality. All seems to revolve around the pleasure-pain process. But why penalize the homeless, tortured, the ill? I reiterate, and Jim you're aware that in truth, none of us were slapped for being exuberant, jocose, morose, bellicose, or comatose, but because of lack of a lousy $20 bail. My own stand is that booze has been with us as long as the "oldest profession." Since humanism is being back-seated (not without a struggle), money is what's respected! The good judge gave me a kickout. I'm now going to seek work and try once again to get a period of sobriety. . . . It's 2:00 P.M.—I just sold a pint of plasma for five skins. I thank you much for your friendship and interest.

49er Bill


Tank #709—Seattle City Jail, 15 August 1967

I entered a plea of guilty to the good judge—no other way to do it—and I'm on the steel for another 10 days. There's no chance of beating a drunk charge. . . .


Tank #709—Seattle City Jail, 29 August 1967

I was busted last Saturday and got 20 days this time. Walked out on Friday and back in on Saturday. Some towns in California pay $1 a day and smokes for work done by inmate. Most state pens pay a little and give a man "gate money." This bit of turning a man loose at 10:00 A.M. or later, stone-broke and hungry, with parting shots like, "See you tomorrow!" First you must hustle pad, food, minus carfare—too late to seek work . . . rough. It's always easy to spear drink or promote a jug of apple wine. In emaciated condition it's very easy to get loaded and then back to the "ballroom" and equal justice. Only it's not equal unless you got $20.

A lad of 71 was released Monday and is back today. Out for a day-and-a-half. Slept most of the time he was here, slightly deaf and senile. The judge should have his head examined. The man's harmless! So he got drunk . . . I suspected he probably got robbed too. Doesn't weigh 90 pounds. They let us walk ten minutes in the corridor tonight and I looked in on him—he was conked out on the ballroom floor with a hangover. . . .

Alcoholism Treatment Center, 4 October 1967

The program here isn't started yet—this place just opened up a couple weeks ago with the first patients. The program isn't doing any of us any good. Of course they feed us well and they're building us up, but 30 days is enough to do that. It's not necessary for them to keep us in as long as they're going to keep us out here. It will take a lot of money to get this program off the ground. It may never get off the ground.

Alcoholism Treatment Center—Seattle, 9 October 1967

We had a meeting this afternoon and a lot of patients were angry about there not being much of a program out here. Alcoholics Anonymous meetings, lectures, vitamins, and work—most of the time we work! Routine and monotonous though it's a lot better than the jail. I had planned to bring up some questions—even typed them out on paper, but didn't even ask them. When do we get out of here? When does the training program and treatment program begin and what does it consist of? Who is going to decide about our release? Several patients asked why we had to be in here for six months and they said we could get out earlier if we had a job and a place to stay. So I guess I'll have to wait it out. I work every day cleaning up one of the dormitories. I have to mop and wax the floors, clean the commodes and sinks and mirrors. It doesn't take all day—but it is supposed to be work therapy. If I have to do this very long I'll become a zombie. . . .

Holding Tank—Seattle City Jail, 3 November 1967

Jim, I'm back again. Released from the treatment center on October 30. It was done in a casual manner. Given a letter to the president of Local #6 for a job. They dropped me off at a half-way house for alcoholics at 5:00 P.M. The assistant manager said they weren't interested in the fact that I'd been at the treatment center, I had to get on their program. I couldn't work for two weeks, had to attend Alcoholics Anonymous meetings seven nights a week, be in by 11:00 P.M., and do work at the half-way house. I felt as if I'd been transferred from one institution to another. When he stated, "The door swings both ways," I swung out—blew cool—ready for a drunk. When I presented letter to Local #6, he said, "Oh yes, the alcoholism treatment center, quite a place. I'll put you on the list." Sounded like, "Don't call us, we'll call you!" When I said I could wax, burr, strip, he said, "Well, maybe I can get you on right now," and made a call and did. I never showed. Had a beer. While in the rest room had a bag with two pairs of slacks stolen, so off to the races. I don't know why I got drunk. I didn't intend to drink. It was really a combination of things. A long bus wait, plus the desire to drink. The pure fact is, I did hard time even at the treatment center. Hadn't made a dime, no smokes, and a sense of anxiety because I was broke. But, facilities like that are an improvement over jail in that they will restore the body at least with food and rest. The compulsion to drink—I would think the proper approach would be to try and find out what is lacking, what the person needs to help fill his needs. Myself, I had a small taste of sobriety in the five-and-a-half months I wasn't drinking. Haven't been happy drinking since. Maybe that is all anyone needs—plus the ability to remember past miseries caused by booze.

#709 City Jail—Seattle, Washington, 18 November 1967
Greetings! I trust you are still pursuing your studies of the inebriates with tenacity and dedication.
Now to get to the toils and travails of Tanner. I pleaded guilty Thursday (November 16)—was sentenced to 35 days. I handed the judge a Writ of Habeas Corpus directed to the Superior Court. Gave notice of intent to appeal and appeal bond set at $50. I don't have 50 cents. The bailiff told me my time does not start until after my appeal. Now, he must be wrong, or else I may languish here for a year waiting trial. The theory of "Equal Protection" is a myth. Possibly it is idiotic of me but I do feel more strongly than I can state that it is futile to jail a drunk—cruel and purposeless. I probably do not possess the ability, stamina, or wherewithal to successfully contest the sentence and I realize I do not possess even the minimal virtues but I am curious to see the outcome.

Tank#709—Seattle City Jail, 14 December 1967
Jim, do me a favor and call the ACLU for me. I was sentenced to 35 days on 11/16/67 on public drunk. Given credit for time served from 11/8/67 My time has been served the hard way—purely because I tried to exercise my rights. I'm sending this note with another inmate who is being transferred to the treatment center from the jail. Please explain to the ACLU attorney that I have no means of communication other than this. This is absolutely the rottenest set-up I've ever seen. Thanks a lot, Your Friend. . . .

Somewhere in Seattle, 19 December 1967
Again—your bewildered, dismayed, bemused, delerious, bedazzled, defunct scribe salutes you with some gossamerlike, misty caperings. Yesterday they took me to court and the judge said, "Well,

since your time is served, your case has been remanded from Superior Court to me." I said, "Your Honor, I served 40 days!" Judge said, "You will be released today." As I walked away a fat cop says, "Get back in there!" I told him the judge said I was released. "Oh no," he says, "It is the jailor who has to release you." I thought they were going to give me 35 more days. Like the sergeant said, "You broke your pick with us—don't expect any favors." I'm afraid I'm becoming paranoid. When I got out the letter you wrote me on December 8 with writing material and stamps was in my property!

I'm gradually trying to introduce myself to society and regain my civilian bearings. If you can trail me along this devious track, you've a much better acumen than I. After 30 days in jail you owe yourself a drunk.

10:00 A.M., "Hotel Flea-Bag-On-The-Sound," 20 December 1967

I will not even attempt to justify my "smart bastard" self-projection of yesterday. I think I have the drunk out of my system. It does seem, at least to me, that I do seem to be able to communicate (with some false bravado) when loaded, which same I seem to lack when sober. I finally got to bed last night—first time since release. Such fun being amongst people again, even though I'm still leaning on alcohol to lubricate my communicational office.

My only intention in this writ and appeal bit was purely to see what a person without a dime could do. I wish almost that I'd stayed in until January 9. But, let's face it—appearance and reality. The latter I've always dodged.

Tank #709—Seattle City Jail, 21 January 1968

My last day—kickout tomorrow A.M. I think I'd better get back to Minneapolis or anywhere. The alcoholic treatment center kills you with kindness and boredom. This place is a pressure chamber and then some. Audio system plays some taped melancholic crap either so low you can't hear the news or so loud you can't hear each other or think—a sort of brainwashing—torture. Understand ballroom is loaded. The circle continues, where she stops no one knows. . . .

Edgecliff Sanitarium, Spokane, Washington, 29 March 1968

. . . now a TB suspect. Have been on a marathon drunk. I was pinched in Seattle on March 10 and the good judge gave me 60 days suspended. Next time in his court I would have gotten that 60 plus additional so I blew town.

Division of Corrections, Minneapolis, Minnesota, 20 May 1968

Greetings! Heavy, heavy hangs the time. I must have an urge to seek self-punishment—But like a homing pigeon I returned here—knowing damn well I'd wind up here. Slightly mellow, I walked or ran a red light—Damn if I do not get accosted by the most dedicated cops (I use the term loosely).

I hope you're not getting the impression that I'm getting a father complex writing you (bugging you). I've already got a "mother" complex as far as institutions are concerned. Everything was going good. Had a job, pad, clothes, etc.

Perhaps I'd better volunteer for a cure or start a flood of writs to bug the judge or judges. I guess I'm involved with about three. . . .

**Methodological Note**

This study was carried out between July 1967 and August 1968 in Seattle, Washington. Data were gathered by participant-observation in an alcoholism treatment center, the Seattle Criminal court, and on Skid Road. A lengthy questionnaire was administered to a sample of 100 men who had been arrested in Seattle for public drunkenness. The core of the project was done using a recently developed method in ethnographic description known as *ethnoscience*. The goal of this approach is to discover how members of a particular society categorize, code, and otherwise define their experience. The discovery and testing procedures of ethnoscience were used to elicit many different terminological sets used by informants to organize their experiences with law-enforcement officials. The steps in the revolving-door experience described here were discovered by repeated use of the question frame, "What are the different stages of making the bucket?" A list of over one hundred verbs were gathered that the men used to identify what a police officer could do to a tramp at each stage of the process. In addition to the data presented here, a number of other category systems were investigated, including kinds of "tramps," "bulls," "time," and "trusties." A variety of card-sorting tasks were used with informants to establish both the taxonomic and componential definitions of these culturally shared systems. These methods were developed by anthropologists to enable them to discover the socially constructed system of meanings members of non-Western societies were using to organize their behavior.

No claim is made here that there are not other ways to define and evaluate the experiences of these men. A complete study of this pressing social problem requires a thorough study of all perspectives. It is to the credit of the Seattle city council that they have recently established a detoxification center in Seattle to replace the revolving door of the jail. The law-enforcement process for drunks in Seattle is not unique. Indeed, these men have similar experiences in almost every major city in the United States.

# V

# Response to Deviant Life-Styles: Accommodation or Condemnation

# Introduction

Each society stakes a claim for a unique identity and elaborately marks out physical and other symbolic boundaries that separate it from other societies.* As a society guards its identity and protects what it deems to be its virtues, it exerts social control over its members. The forms of social control range widely. They can consist of little more than looks and words directed against offenders of cultural expectations, or they can involve varying degrees of official sanctioning, some of which was covered in the immediately preceding section. Social control can also be escalated into immense proportions, and can ultimately include the mobilization of society's institutions in a concerted effort to eliminate that which is viewed as an internal danger threatening society's existence.

This part contrasts two opposing reactions directed toward people who live deviant life-styles: the first response is that of toleration and accommodation, and the second reaction is condemnation and persecution. A mosaic of contrasting and competing life-styles is well able to peacefully coexist within the same society, and even

---

*With their contrasting orientation to physical space, nomads may appear to be an exception to marking out physical boundaries. Nomads, however, are oriented primarily toward transportable physical boundaries, and their use characteristics of geographical regions also separate them from other societies, even from other nomadic groups in the same region. Certainly not all societies are as concerned about their geographical limits as are modern nation-states, many of which will even risk their existence by warfare in order to preserve or extend them. But all societies utilize physical markers of various sorts, as well as nonphysical symbols, in order to create and maintain a unique identity.

within the same small geographical area. In the initial essay, Becker and Horowitz analyze the atmosphere of toleration toward deviant life-styles that characterize the city of San Francisco. This city sharply contrasts with most areas of the United States, where the more typical orientation is that a deviant life-style eventually or automatically leads to worse things. In San Francisco, however, deviant life-styles tend to be looked at as isolated from other aspects of life.

Being rarely subjected to repression allows San Francisco deviants to live more openly. They are able to actively participate in commercial and civic affairs, and to do so without needing to conceal their deviant identity. A homosexual, for example, does not have to pass as a heterosexual in order to avoid being fired. Being able to maintain their deviant identity while actively participating in other walks of life within the framework of that identity breaks down many negative and constricting stereotypes of deviance. The loosening of stereotypical perceptions further lessens fear and increases toleration. Tolerance and accommodation are part of a two-way street, however, and to maintain the precarious balance, the deviants must give up some of their more openly scandalizing behaviors to about the same degree that the straighter citizens give up some of their activities of vigilance.

As the authors are careful to indicate, San Francisco has a history unmatched by any other American city. It has experienced unique historical events that have created a tendency for toleration of differences and a willingness to take the steps necessary to accommodate them. Yet the adjustment worked out in San Francisco is far from idyllic, and there are still occasional outbursts of repression. The lesson of San Francisco, however, is worth emphasizing: it is possible for straights and various groups living deviant life-styles to peacefully coexist, but what is necessary is that those people living deviant life-styles be willing to give up some of their liberty and the straight community be willing to accept the part they give up as a sufficient price for adjusting to their open presence.

But as Amsterdam, with its almost unbelievable accommodation to a vast array of deviant life-styles, is not theNetherlands, neither is San Francisco the United States. More typical responses to deviant life-styles in the United States center around more or less rigid efforts at social control. Frequently these social-control efforts take the repressive form of condemnation and persecution. If a deviant life-style does not differ too drastically from dominant expectations, the social reaction is usually quite mild. But if the deviant life-style is perceived as a threat to cherished cultural values, the reaction is likely to take a serious turn.

There is no difficulty in locating historical examples of repressive reaction to people who differ from dominant orientations to life. We do not have to go way back in history to find them, for instance, to the Romans and the early Christians, or even to more recent history with the Nazis and the European Jews. We can find much closer to home many examples of the mobilization of societal resources to combat and eliminate a social group perceived to be an internal danger. Societal reaction to hippies is one such example, the focus of the concluding essay.

Though the topical matter of Brown's chapter is hippies, that is not its main importance, for hippies in any organized, visible form were an ephemeral group that quickly passed from the social scene (though it is impossible to say what form they would have taken had they not been subjected to organized repressive reaction). The significance of this concluding selection, rather, is that drawing primarily from the example of societal repression directed against hippies, as well as utilizing earlier historical examples of persecution, the author analyzes the social processes that lead to organized persecution of deviants. Because repressive reaction is such a common response to deviance in the United States, and because repressive reactions, though directed against a small number of persons, threatens the freedom of each of us, an understanding of these principles is of critical importance for both an adequate sociological understanding of deviant life-styles and for the protection of our own constitutionally granted right to be different.

# 16

# The Culture of Civility

Howard S. Becker
and Irving Louis Horowitz

## Deviance and Democracy in "The City"

Deviants of many kinds live well in San Francisco—natives and tourists alike make that observation. The city's apparently casual and easygoing response to "sex, dope, and cheap thrills" (to crib the suppressed full title of Janis Joplin's famous album—itself a San Francisco product) astounds visitors from other parts of the country who can scarcely credit either what they see happining or the way natives stroll by those same events unconcerned.

Walking in the Tenderloin on a summer evening, a block from the Hilton, you hear a black whore cursing at a policeman: "I wasn't either blocking the sidewalk! Why don't you motherfucking fuzz mind your own goddamn business!" The visiting New Yorker expects to see her arrested, if not shot, but the cop smiles goodnaturedly and moves on, having got her back into the doorway where she is supposed to be.

You enter one of the famous rock ballrooms and, as you stand getting used to the noise and lights, someone puts a lit joint of marijuana in your hand. The tourist looks for someplace to hide, not wishing to be caught in the mass arrest he expects to follow. No need to worry. The police will not come in, knowing that if they do they will have to arrest people and create disorder.

Candidates for the city's Board of Supervisors make their pitch for the homosexual vote, estimated by some at 90,000. They will not be run out of town; the candidates' remarks are dutifully reported in the daily paper, as are the evaluations of them by representatives of S.I.R., the Society for Individual Rights.

337

The media report (tongue in cheek) the annual Halloween Drag Ball, for which hundreds of homosexuals turn out in full regalia at one of the city's major hotels, unharassed by police.

One sees long-haired, bearded hippies all over the city, not just in a few preserves set aside for them. Straight citizens do not react to their presence, either by gawking, hostility, or flight.

Nudie movies, frank enough to satisfy anyone's curiosity, are exhibited in what must be the largest number of specialty movie houses per capita in the country. Periodic police attempts to close them down (one of the few occasions when repression has been attempted) fail.

The items can be multiplied indefinitely, and their multiplicity demands explanation. Most cities in the United States refuse to let deviants indulge themselves publicly, let alone tolerate candidates who seek their bloc votes. Quite the contrary. Other cities, New York and Chicago being good examples, would see events like these as signs of serious trouble, omens of a real breakdown in law enforcement and deviance control, the forerunner of saturnalia and barbarian takeover. Because its politicians and police allow and can live with activities that would freak out their opposite numbers elsewhere, San Francisco is a natural experiment in the consequences of tolerating deviance. We can see from its example what results when we ignore the warnings of the custodians of conventional morality. We can see, too, what lessons can be learned about the conditions under which problems that perhaps lie deeper than matters of morals or life-style can be solved to the satisfaction of all the parties to them.

## A Culture of Civility

We can summarize this low-key approach to deviance in the phrase *a culture of civility*. What are its components, and how does it maintain itself?

San Francisco prides itself on its sophistication, on being the most European of American cities, on its picturesque cosmopolitanism. The picturesque quality, indeed the quaintness, rests in part on physical beauty. As the filling of the bay and the destruction of the skyline by high-rise buildings proceeds to destroy that beauty, the city has come to depend even more on the presence of undigested ethnic minorities. It is as though San Francisco did not wish its Italians, Chinese, or Russians to assimilate and become standard Americans, preferring instead to maintain a panoply of ethnic differences: religious, cultural, and culinary (especially culinary). A sophisticated, livable city, on this view, contains people, colonies, and societies of all kinds. Their differences create a mosaic of life-styles, the very difference of whose sight and smell give pleasure.

Like ethnic minorities, deviant minorities create enclaves whose differences add to the pleasure of city life. Natives enjoy the presence of hippies and take tourists to see their areas, just as they take them to see the gay area of Polk Street. Deviance, like difference, is a civic resource, enjoyed by tourist and resident alike.

To enjoy deviance instead of fearing it requires a surrender of some commonsense notions about the world. Most people assume, when they see someone engaging in proscribed activity, that there is worse to come. "Anyone who would do that [take dope, dress in women's clothes, sell his body, or whatever] would do anything" is the major premise of the syllogism. "If you break one law or convention, who knows where you'll stop." Common sense ignores the contrary cases around us everywhere: professional criminals often flourish a legionnaire's patriotism; housewives who are in every other respect conventional sometimes shoplift; homosexuals may be good family providers; some people, who habitually use the rings from poptop cans to work the parking meter, would not dream of taking dope, and vice versa. "Deviance," like conforming behavior, is highly selective. San Francisco's culture of civility, accepting that premise, assumes that if I know that you steal or take dope or peddle your ass, that is all I *know*. There may be more to know; then again, there may be nothing. The deviant may be perfectly decent in every other respect. We are often enjoined, in a generalization of therapeutic doctrine, to treat other people as individuals; that prescription comes nearer to being filled in San Francisco than in most places in the United States.

Because of that tolerance, deviants find it possible to live somewhat more openly in San Francisco than elsewhere. People do not try so hard to catch them at their deviant activities and are less likely to punish them when caught. Because they live more openly, what they do is more visible to straight members of the community. An established canon of social psychology tells us that we find it more difficult to maintain negative stereotypes when our personal experience belies them. We see more clearly and believe more deeply that hippies or homosexuals are not dangerous when we confront them on the street day after day or live alongside them and realize that beard plus long hair does not equal a drug-crazed maniac, that limp wrist plus lisp does not equal child molester.

When such notions become embodied in a culture of civility, the citizenry begins to sense that "everyone" feels that way. We cannot say at what critical point a population senses that sophistication about deviance is the norm, rather than a liberal fad. But San Francisco clearly has that critical mass. To come on as an antideviant, in a way that would probably win friends and influence voters in more parochial areas, risks being greeted by laughter and ridicule in San Francisco. Conservatives who believe in law and order are thus inclined to keep their beliefs to themselves. The more people keep moralistic notions to themselves, the more everyone believes that tolerance is widespread. The culture maintains itself by convincing the populace that it is indeed the culture.

It gets help from public pronouncements of civic officials, who enunciate what will be taken as the collective sentiment of the city. San Francisco officials occasionally angle for the conservative vote that disapproves licentiousness. But they more frequently take the side of liberty, if not license. When the police, several years ago, felt compelled to close the first of the "topless joints," the judge threw the case out. He reasoned that Supreme Court decisions required him to take into account contemporary community standards. In his judgment San Francisco was not a prudish community; the case was dismissed. The city's major paper, the *Chronicle,* approved. Few protested.

Similarly, when California's leading yahoo, Superintendent of Public Instruction Max Rafferty, threatened to revoke the teaching credentials of any San Francisco teacher who used the obscene materials listed in the standard high-school curriculum (Eldridge Cleaver's *Soul on Ice* and LeRoi Jones's *Dutchman*), the city did not remove the offending books from its curriculum. Instead, it successfully sued to have Rafferty enjoined from interfering in its operation.

In short, San Franciscans know that they are supposed to be sophisticated and let that knowledge guide their public actions, whatever their private feelings. According to another well-known law of social psychology, their private feelings often come to resemble their public actions, and they learn to delight in what frightens citizens of less civil cities.

We do not suggest that all kinds of deviation are tolerated endlessly. The police try, in San Francisco as elsewhere, to stamp out some vices and keep a ceiling on others. Some deviance frightens San Franciscans, too, because it seems to portend worse to come (most recently, users and purveyors of methedrine—"speed merchants" and "speed freaks"—whose drug use is popularly thought to result in violence and crime). But the line is drawn much farther over on the side of "toleration" in San Francisco than elsewhere. A vastly wider range of activities is publicly acceptable. Despite the wide range of visible freakiness, the citizenry takes it all in stride, without the fear and madness that permeates the conventional sectors of cities like Detroit, Chicago, New York, Washington, D.C., and similar centers of undaunted virtue.

## Madames and Unionists

How does a culture of civility arise? Here we can only speculate, and then fragmentarily, since so few cities in the United States have one that we cannot make the comparisons that might uncover the crucial conditions. San Francisco's history suggests a number of possibilities.

It has, for one thing, a Latin heritage. Always a major seaport, it has long tolerated the vice that caters to sailors typical of such ports. It grew at the time of the gold rush in an explosive way that burst through conventional social controls. It ceded to its ethnic minorities, particularly the Chinese, the right to engage in prostitution, gambling, and other activities. Wickedness and high living form part of the prized past every "tourist" city constructs for itself; some minor downtown streets in San Francisco, for instance, are named for famous madames of the gold rush era.

Perhaps more important, a major potential source of repressive action—the working class—is in San Francisco more libertarian and politically sophisticated than one might expect. Harry Bridges's longshoremen act as bellwethers. It should be remembered that San Francisco is one of the few major American cities ever to experience a general strike. The event still reverberates, and working people who might support repression of others know by personal experience that the policeman may not be their friend. Trade unionism has a left-wing, honest base that gives the city a working-class democracy and even eccentricity, rather than the customary pattern of authoritarianism.

Finally, San Francisco is a town of single people. Whatever actual proportion of the adult population is married, the city's culture is oriented toward and organized for single people. As a consequence, citizens worry less about what public deviance will do to their children, for they do not have any and do not intend to, or they move from the city when they do. (Since there are, of course, plenty of families in the city, it may be more accurate to say that there are fewer white, middle-class families, that being the stratum that would, if family-based, provide the greatest number of complaints about deviance. Black, Chicano, and Oriental populations ordinarily have enough to worry about without becoming guardians of public morality.)

## The Place to Live

San Francisco is known across the country as a haven for deviants. Good homosexuals hope to go to San Francisco to stay when they die, if not before. Indeed, one of the problems of deviant communities in San Francisco is coping with the periodic influx of a new generation of bohemians who have heard that it is the place to be: the beatnik migration of the late fifties and the hippie hordes of 1967. But those problems should not obscure what is more important: that there are stable communities of some size there to be disrupted. It is the stable homosexual community that promises politicians 90,000 votes and the stable bohemian communities of several vintages that provide both personnel and customers for some important local industries (developing, recording, and distributing rock music is now a business of sizable proportions).

Stable communities are stable because their members have found enough of what they want to stay where they are for a while. If where they were proved totally unsatisfying, they presumably would move elsewhere, unless restrained. But no one forces deviants to live in San Francisco. They stay there because it offers them, via the culture of civility, a place to live where they are not shunned as fearsome or disgusting, where agents of control (police and others) do not regard them as unfortunate excrescences to be excised at the first opportunity. Because they have a place to stay that does not harass them, they sink roots like more conventional citizens: find jobs, buy houses, make friends, vote and take part in political activities, and all the other things that solid citizens do.

Sinking roots stabilizes deviants' lives, as it does the lives of conventional citizens. They find less need to act in the erratic ways that deviants often behave elsewhere, less need to fulfill the prophecy that because they are deviant in one respect they will be deviant in other, more dangerous ways. San Francisco employers know that homosexuals make good employees. Why not? They are not likely to be blackmailed by enterprising hustlers. The police seldom haul them off to jail for little reason or beat them because they feel like pushing some "queers" around. Homosexuals fear none of this in San Francisco, or fear it much less than in most places, and so are less given to the overcompensatory "camping" that gets their fellows into trouble elsewhere.

Police and others do not harass deviants because they have found, though they may deny it for public relations purposes, that looking the other way is sometimes a good policy. It is easier, when a be-in is going on, to turn your back on the sight of open marijuana smoking than it is to charge into the crowd and try to arrest people who will destroy the evidence before you get there, give you a hard time, make a fool of you, and earn you a bad press—and have no conviction to show for it. At the same time, when you turn your back, nothing worse is likely to happen: no muggings, no thefts, no rapes, no riots. Police, more calculating than they seem, often choose to reach just this kind of accommodation with stable deviant communities.

The accommodation works in circular fashion. When deviants can live decent lives, they find it possible to behave decently. Furthermore, they acquire the kind of stake they are often denied elsewhere in the present and future structure of the community. That stake constrains them to behave in ways that will not outrage nondeviants, for they do not want to lose what they have. They thus curb their activities according to what they think the community will stand for.

The community in turn, and especially the police, will put up with more than they might otherwise, because they understand that nothing else is forthcoming, and because they find that what they are confronted with is not so bad after all. If homosexuals have a Halloween Drag Ball, the community discovers it can treat it as a good-natured joke; those people who are offended discover that they need not go near the Hilton while it is happening.

No doubt neither party to such a bargain gets quite what he would like. Straight members of the community presumably would prefer not to have whores walking the downtown streets, would prefer not to have gay bars operating openly. Deviants of all kinds presumably would prefer not to have to make any concessions to straight sensibilities. Each gives up something and gets something, and to that degree the arrangement becomes stable, the stability itself something both prize.

## Deviance and Democracy

What we have just described verges on the idyllic, Peace and Harmony in Camelot forever. Such a dream of perfection does not exist in San Francisco, though more deviants there have more of the advantages of such a bargain, perhaps, than in any other city in the United States. Nor is it clear that the system we described, even in its perfect form, would be such an idyll.

In San Francisco, as everywhere, the forces of decency and respectability draw the line somewhere and can be every bit as forceful and ruthless the other side of that line as the forces of decency and respectability anywhere else. When the Haight-Ashbury got "out of hand" with the overcrowded transiency of 1967, the city moved in the police Tactical Squad, the City Health Department, and all the other bureaucratic weapons usually used to roust deviants. They did it again with the growth of violence in that area associated with the use and sale of methedrine. In general, the city has responded with great toughness to those deviants it believes will not be satisfied with something "reasonable." In particular, political dissent has some-times been met with force, though San Francisco police have never indulged themselves on any large scale such as that which made Chicago police internationally detested.

The system has beauty only for those deviants who do not mind giving up some portion of their liberty, and then only if the portion they are willing to give up is the same as what the community wants given up. This no doubt is the reason an accommodative system works well with those whose deviant desires are narrowly cir-cumscribed, and may have less utility with those whose wants can be accommodated only at the expense of others who will not easily give up their privileges. In fact, current political difficulties clearly result from the breakdown of accommodation.

These considerations indicate the more general importance of San Francisco's experiment in tolerating and accommodating to the minor forms of deviance encompassed in sex, dope, and cheap thrills. How can a complex and differentiated society deal with vari-ety and dissent and simultaneously with its own urges for central-ized control? An accommodative relationship to difference, in which it is allowed to persist while it pays some minimal dues to the whole, is what San Francisco recommends to us, suggesting that the amount of the dues and the breadth of the license be set where both parties will, for the time being, stand still for it. The resulting work-ing arrangement will be at least temporarily stable and provide for all concerned a tranquility that permits one to go about his business unharmed that many will find attractive.

But is this no more than a clever trick, a way of buying off deviant populations with minor freedoms while still keeping them enslaved? Beneath the rhetoric, the analysis is the same. The more radical statement adds only that the people who accept such a bargain ought not to, presumably because they have, if they only knew it, deeper and more important interests and desires that remain unsat-isfied in the accommodative arrangement. So, of course, do people who hold them in check. Perhaps that is the ultimate lesson of San

Francisco: the price of civilization, civility, and living together peacefully is not getting everything you want.

## Limits of Accommodation

It is tempting to think that an accommodation based on civility and mutual interest provides a model for settling the conflicts now wracking our urban areas. Our analysis suggests that this is a possibility, but no more than that. Peace can occur through accommodation, the example of the potheads and pimps tells us, only under certain not so easily attained conditions. Those conditions may not be present in the ethnic and political problems our major cities, San Francisco among them, are now experiencing.

Accommodation requires, as a first condition, that the parties involved prize peace and stability enough to give up some of what they want so that others may have their desires satisfied as well. But people take that point of view only when the accommodation leaves them enough of a share to want no more. Some urban groups no longer believe that they are getting that necessary minimum, either because they have learned to interpret their situation in a new light or because they have lost some advantages they once had.

Members of black communities may be no worse off than ever, but they are considerably worse off than whites and know it. For a variety of historical reasons, and as a matter of simple justice, some of them no longer regard the little they have as sufficient reason to keep the peace. All the discussion about how many blacks feel this way (is it ten percent or fifty percent?) and how strongly they feel it (are they willing to fight?) is irrelevant to the main point: enough feel strongly enough to make a lot of trouble for the white community, thus changing the balance of costs to the whites and insisting on a new division of rights as the price of stability.

Some members of white communities probably are objectively worse off and may resent it sufficiently to give up peace and stability in an effort to raise the costs to others and thus minimize their losses. Many whites in civil-service positions, in the skilled trades, and in similar protected occupational positions have lost or are in danger of losing competitive job advantages as governments act to do something about the injustice that afflicts black communities. Without a general expansion of the economy, which is *not* what blacks demand, injustices inflicted on blacks can be remedied only by taking something away from more favorably situated whites. It may be possible to improve the education of poor black children, for instance, only by taking away some of the privileges of white teachers. It may be possible to give black youths a chance at apprenticeships in skilled trades only by removing the privileged access to those positions of the sons of present white union members. When whites lose those privileges, they may feel strongly enough to fracture the consensus of civility.

The deviant communities of San Francisco show us cases in which the parties involved agree in a way that leaves each enough. But that may only be possible when the interests to be accommodated involve morals and life-styles. When those interests include substantial economic prizes, major forms of privilege, and real political power, it may be that nothing less than a real-life assessment of relative intensities of desire and ability to inflict costs on others will suffice. That assessment takes place in the marketplace of conflict.

This suggests a second, more procedural condition for the achievement of urban peace through accommodation and civility. Mechanisms and procedures must exist by which the conflicting desires and resources for bargaining can be brought together to produce a temporarily stable working arrangement. The accommodations of enforcement officials and deviants typically occur in a host of minor bargaining situations. Hassles are settled by the people immediately involved, and settled "on their own merits"—which is to say, in a way that respects the strength of everyone's feelings and the amount of trouble each is prepared to make to have his way. The culture of civility works well because the myriad of separate local bargains respect and reflect what most of the involved parties want or are willing to settle for.

We do not allow ourselves this extreme degree of decentralized decision making with respect to many important problems (though many critics have suggested we should). Instead, we allow federal, state, or city bureaucracies to make general policies that inhibit local accommodation. While government might well intervene when circumstances make bargaining positions unequal, we know now that it is not ordinarily well equipped to reach accommodative agreements that will work at the grassroots. Unable to know what the people who inhabit local areas will want and settle for, officials turn to technocrats for solutions.

Thus, when we confront the problem of slums and urban renewal, we send for the planner and the bulldozer. But the lives of urban residents are not determined by the number or newness of buildings. The character of their relationships with one another and with the outside world does that. Planners and technocrats typically ignore those relationships, and their influence in shaping what people want, in constructing solutions. They define "slums" impersonally, using such impersonal criteria as density or deterioration, and fail to see how awakened group consciousness can turn a "slum" into a "ghetto," and a rise in moral repute turn a "ghetto" into a "neighborhood."

Too often, the search for "model cities" implies not so much a model as an ideology—a rationalistic vision of human interaction that implies a people whose consistency of behavior can nowhere be found. We already have "model cities": Brasilia at the bureaucratic end and Levittown at the residential end. And in both instances, the force of human impulses had to break through the web of formal models to make these places inhabitable. In Brasilia the rise of shantytown dwellings outside the federal buildings made the place "a city," whereas the Levittowners had to break the middle-class mode and pass through a generation of conformity before they could produce a decent living arrangement. To design a city in conformity to "community standards"—which turn out to be little more than the prejudices of building inspectors, housing designers, and absentee landlords—only reinforces patterns of frustration, violence, and antagonism that now characterize so many of America's large cities. To think that the dismal failure of large housing projects will be resolved by their dismal replacement of small housing projects is nonsense. Minibuildings are no more of a solution than maxibuildings are the problem.

In any event, centralized planning operating in this way does not produce a mechanism through which the mutual desires, claims, and threats of interested groups can sort themselves out and allow a modus vivendi, if one exists, to uncover itself. The centralized body makes bargains for everyone under its influence, without knowing their circumstances or wants, and so makes it impossible for the people involved to reach a stable accommodation. But centralized planning still remains a major solution proffered for urban problems of every kind.

Accommodations reached through the mechanism of old-fashioned city political machines work little better, for contemporary machines typically fail to encompass all the people whose interests are at stake. Richard Daley demonstrated that when the Chicago ghetto, supposedly solidly under his control, exploded and revealed some people his famed consensus had not included. Lyndon Johnson made the same discovery with respect to opponents of the Vietnam War. Insofar as centralized decision making does not work, and interested parties are not allowed to make bargains at the local level, accommodative stability cannot occur.

So the example of San Francisco's handling of moral deviance may not provide the blueprint one would like for settling urban problems generally. Its requirements include a day-to-day working agreement among parties on the value of compromise and a procedure by which their immediate interests can be openly communicated and effectively adjusted. Those requirements are difficult to meet. Yet it may be that they are capable of being met in more places than we think, that even some of the knottier racial and political problems contain possibilities of accommodation, no more visible to us than the casual tolerance of deviance in San Francisco was thinkable to some of our prudish forebears.

# 17

## The Condemnation and Persecution of Hippies

### Michael E. Brown

This chapter is about persecution and terror. It speaks of the hippie and the temptations of intimacy that the myth of hippie has made poignant, and it does this to discuss the institutionalization of repression in the United States.

When people are attacked as a group, they change. Individuals in the group may or may not change, but the organization and expression of their collective life will be transformed. When the members of a gathering believe that there is a grave danger imminent and that opportunities for escape are rapidly diminishing, the group loses its organizational quality. It becomes transformed in panic. This type of change can also occur outside a situation of strict urgency: When opportunities for mobility or access to needed resources are cut off, people may engage in desperate collective actions. In both cases, the conversion of social form occurs when members of a collectivity are about to be hopelessly locked into undesired and undesirable positions.

The process is not, however, automatic. The essential ingredient for conversion is social control exercised by external agents on the collectivity itself. The result can be benign, just as a panic mob can be converted into a crowd that makes an orderly exit from danger. Or it can be cruel.

The transformation of groups under pressure is of general interest; but there are special cases that are morally critical to any epoch. Such critical cases occur when pressure is persecution, and transformation is destruction. The growth of repressive mechanisms and institutions is a key concern in this time of administrative cruelty. Such is the justification for the present study.

## Social Control as Terror

Four aspects of repressive social control such as that experienced by hippies are important. First, the administration of control is suspicious. It projects a dangerous future and guards against it. It also refuses the risk of inadequate coverage by enlarging the controlled population to include all who might be active in any capacity. Control may or may not be administered with a heavy hand, but it is always a generalization applied to specific instances. It is a rule and thus ends by pulling many fringe innocents into its bailiwick; it creates as it destroys.

Second, the administration of control is a technical problem that, depending on its site and object, requires the combination of many different agencies that are ordinarily dissociated or mutually hostile. A conglomerate of educational, legal, social welfare, and police organizations is highly efficient. The German case demonstrates that. Even more important, it is virtually impossible to oppose control administered under the auspices of such a conglomerate since it includes the countervailing institutions ordinarily available. When this happens, control is not only efficient and widespread, but also legitimate, commanding a practical, moral, and ideological realm that is truly one-dimensional.

Third, as time passes, control is applied to a wider and wider range of details, ultimately blanketing its objects' lives. At that point, as Hilberg suggests in his *The Destruction of the European Jews,* the extermination of the forms of lives leads easily to the extermination of the lives themselves. The line between persecution and terror is thin. For the oppressed, life is purged of personal style as every act becomes inexpressive, part of the struggle for survival. The options of a life-style are eliminated at the same time that its proponents are locked into it.

Fourth, control is relentless. It develops momentum as organization accumulates, as audiences develop, and as unofficial collaborators assume the definition of tasks, expression, and ideology. This, according to W. A. Westley's "The Escalation of Violence Through Legitimation," is the culture of control. It not only limits the behaviors, styles, individuals, and groups toward whom it is directed, but it suppresses all unsanctioned efforts as well. As struggle itself is destroyed, motivation vanishes or is turned inward.

These are the effects of repressive control. We may contrast them with the criminal law, which merely prohibits the performance of specific acts (with the exception, of course, of the "crime without victims"—homosexuality, abortion, and drug use). Repression converts or destroys an entire social form, whether that form is embodied in a group, a style, or an idea. In this sense, it is terror.

These general principles are especially relevant to our understanding of tendencies that are ripening in the United States day by day. Stated in terms that magnify it so that it can be seen despite ourselves, this is the persecution of the hippies, a particularly vulnerable group of people who are the cultural wing of a way of life recently emerged from its quiet and individualisitic quarters. Theodore Roszak, describing the hippies in terms of their relationship to the culture and politics of dissent, notes that "the underlying unity of youthful dissent consists . . . in the effort of beat-hip bohemianism to work out the personality structure, the total life-style that follows from New Left social criticism." This life-style is currently bearing the brunt of the assault on what Roszak calls a *counterculture*; it is an assault that is becoming more concentrated and savage every day. There are lessons for the American future to be drawn from this story.

**Persecution**

Near Boulder, Colorado, a restaurant sign says, "Hippies not served here." Large billboards in upstate New York carry slogans like, "Keep America Clean: Take a Bath," and, "Keep America Clean: Get a Haircut." These would be as amusing as ethnic jokes if they did not represent a more systematic repression.

The street sweeps so common in San Francisco and Berkeley in 1968 and 1969 were one of the first lines of attack. People were brutally scattered by club-wielding policemen who first closed exits from the assaulted area and then began systematically to beat and arrest those who were trapped. This form of place terror, like surveillance in Negro areas and defoliation in Vietman, curbs freedom and forces people to fight or submit to minute inspection by hostile forces. There have also been one-shot neighborhood pogroms, such as the police assault on the Tompkins Square Park gathering in New York's Lower East Side on Memorial Day 1967: "Sadistic glee was written on the faces of several officers," wrote the *East Village Other*. Some women became hysterical. The police slugged Frank Wise, and dragged him off, handcuffed and bloody, crying, "My God, my God, where is this happening? Is this America?" The police also plowed into a group of hippies, yippies, and straights at the April 1968, "yip-in" at Grand Central Station. The brutality was as clear in this action as it had been in the Tompkins Square bust. In both cases, the major newspapers editorialized against the police tactics, and in the first the mayor apologized for the "free wielding of nightsticks." But by the summer of 1968, street sweeps and busts and the continuous presence of New York's Tactical Police Force had given the Lower East Side an ominous atmosphere. Arrests were regularly accompanied by beatings and charges of "resistance to arrest." It became clear that arrests rather than subsequent procedures were the way in which control was to be exercised. The summer lost its street theaters, the relaxed circulation of people in the neighborhood, and the easy park gatherings.

Official action legitimizes nonofficial action. Private citizens take up the cudgel of law and order newly freed from the boundaries of due process and respect. After Tompkins Square, rapes and assaults became common as local toughs assumed the role, with the police, of defender of the faith. In Cambridge, Massachusetts, following a virulent attack on hippies by the mayor, *Newsweek* reported that vigilantes attacked hippie neighborhoods in force.

Ultimately more damaging are the attacks on centers of security. Police raids on "hippie pads," crash pads, churches, and movement centers had become daily occurrences in New York and California in the late sixties. The usual excuses for raids are drugs, runaways, and housing violations, but many incidents of unlawful entry by police and the expressions of a more generalized hostility by the responsible officials suggests that something deeper is involved. The chief of police in San Francisco put it bluntly; quoted in *The New York Times Magazine* in May 1967, he said:

> Hippies are no asset to the community. These people do not have the courage to face the reality of life. They are trying to escape. Nobody should let their young children take part in this hippy thing.

The director of health for San Francisco gave teeth to this counsel when he sent a task force of inspectors on a door-to-door sweep of Haight-Ashbury—"a two-day blitz" that ended with a strange result, again according to the *Times*: Very few of the hippies were guilty of housing violations.

Harassment and calculated degradation have been two of the most effective devices for introducing uncertainty to the day-to-day lives of the hippies. Cambridge's mayor's attack on the "hipbos" (the suffix stands for body odor) included, said *Newsweek* of 30 October 1967, a raid on a "hippie pad" by the mayor and "a platoon of television cameramen." They "seized a pile of diaries and personal letters and flushed a partially clad girl from the closet." In Wyoming, the *Times* reported that two "pacifists" were "jailed and shaved" for hitchhiking. This is a fairly common hazard, though Wyoming officials are perhaps more sadistic than most. A young couple whom I interviewed were also arrested in Wyoming during the summer of 1968. They were placed in solitary confinement for a week during which they were not permitted to place phone calls and were not told when or whether they would be charged or released. These are not exceptional cases. During the summer of 1968, I interviewed young hitchhikers throughout the country; most of them had similar stories to tell.

In the East Village of New York, one hears countless stories of apartment destruction by police (occasionally reported in the newspapers), insults from the police when rapes or robberies are reported, and cruel speeches and even crueler bails set by judges for arrested hippies.

In the light of this, San Francisco writer Mark Harris's indictment of the hippies as paranoid seems peculiar. In the September 1967 issue of *The Atlantic,* he wrote,

> The most obvious failure of perception was the hippies' failure to discriminate among elements of the Establishment, whether in Haight-Ashbury or in San Francisco in general. Their paranoia was the paranoia of all youthful heretics. . . .

This is like the demand of some white liberals that Negroes acknowledge that they (the liberals) are not the power structure, or that black people must distinguish between the good and the bad whites despite the fact that the black experience of white people in the United States has been, as the president's Commission on Civil Disorder suggested, fairly monolithic and racist.

Most journalists reviewing the "hippie scene" with any sympathy at all seem to agree with *Newsweek* that "the hippies do seem natural prey for publicity-hungry politicians—if not overzealous police," and that they have been subjected to varieties of cruelty that ought to be intolerable. This tactic was later elaborated in the massive paramilitary assault on Berkeley residents and students during a demonstration in support of Telegraph Avenue's street people and their People's Park. The terror of police violence, a constant in the lives of street people everywhere, in California carries the additional threat of martial law under a still-active state of extreme emergency. The whole structure of repression was given legitimacy and reluctant support by University of California officials. Step by step, they became allies of Reagan's "dogs of war." Roger W. Heyns, chancellor of the Berkeley campus, found himself belatedly reasserting the university's property in the lot. It was the law and the rights of the university that trapped the chancellor in the network of control and performed the vital function of providing justification and legitimacy for Sheriff Madigan and the National Guard. Heyns said: "We will have to put up a fence to reestablish the conveniently forgotten fact that this field is indeed the university's, and to exclude unauthorized personnel from the site. . . . The fence will give us time to plan and consult. We tried to get this time some other way and failed—hence the fence." And hence "Bloody Thursday" and the new regime.

And what of the hippies? They have come far since those balmy days of 1966-67, days of flowers, streetcleaning, free stores, decoration, and love. Many have fled to the hills of northern California to join their brethren who had set up camps there several years ago. Others have fled to communes outside the large cities and in the Middlewest. After the Tompkins Square assault, many of the East Village hippies refused to follow the lead of people who were more political. They refused to develop organizations of defense and to accept a hostile relationship with the police and neighborhood. Instead, they discussed at meeting after meeting, how they could show their attackers love. Many of those spirits have fled; others have been beaten or jailed too many times; and still others have modified their outlook in ways that reflect the struggle. Guerrilla theater, Up Against the Wall Mother Fucker (U.A.W.M.F.), the yippies, the urban communes; these are some of the more recent manifestations of the alternative culture. One could see these trends growing in the demonstrations mounted by hippies against arrests of runaways or pot smokers, the community organizations, such as the ones that grew in Berkeley for self-defense and politics, and the beginnings of the will to fight back when trapped in street sweeps.

It is my impression that the hippie culture is growing as it recedes from the eye of the media [1969]. As a consequence of the destruction of their urban places, there has been a redistribution of types. The flower people have left for the hills and become more communal; individuals who remained in the city were better adapted to terror, secretive or confrontative. The hippie culture is one of the forms radicalism can take in this society. The youngsters, 5,000 of them, who came to Washington, D.C., to counterdemonstrate against the Nixon inaugural showed the growing amalgamation of the New Left and its cultural wing. The yippies who went to Chicago for guerrilla theater and learned about "pigs" were the multigenera-

tional expression of the new wave. A UAWMF drama, played at
Lincoln Center during the New York City garbage strike—they
carted garbage from the neglected Lower East Side and dumped it
at the spic 'n' span cultural center—reflected another interpretation
of the struggle, one that could include the politically militant as well
as the culturally defiant. Many hippies have gone underground—in
an older sense of the word. They have shaved their beards, cut their
hair, and taken straight jobs, like the secret Jews of Spain; but
unlike those Jews, they are consciously an underground, a resistance.

What is most interesting and, I believe, a direct effect of the persecution, is the enormous divergence of forms that are still recognizable by the outsider as hippie and are still experienced as a shared
identity. "The yippies," says Abbie Hoffman, "are like hippies,
only fiercer and more fun." The "hippie types" described in newspaper accounts of drug raids on colleges turn out, in many cases, to be
New Leftists.

The dimensions by which these various forms are classified are
quite conventional: religious-political, visible-secret, urban-hill,
communal-individualistic. As their struggle intensifies, there will be
more efforts for unity and more militant approaches to the society
that gave birth to a real alternative only to turn against it with a
mindless savagery. Yippie leader Jerry Rubin, in an "emergency letter to my brothers and sisters in the movement," summed it up:

> Huey Newton is in prison.
> Eldridge Cleaver is in exile.
> Oakland Seven are accused of conspiracy.
> Tim Leary is up for thirty years and how many of our
> brothers are in court and jail for getting high?
> [...]
> Camp activists are expelled and arrested.
> War resisters are behind bars.
> Add it up!

Rubin preambles his summary with:

> From the Bay Area to New York, we are suffering the
> greatest depression in our history. People are taking bitterness
> in their coffee instead of sugar. The hippie-yippie-S.D.S. move-
> ment is a "white nigger" movement. The American economy
> no longer needs young whites and blacks. We are waste materi-
> al. We fulfill our destiny in life by rejecting a system which
> rejects us.

He advocates organizing "massive mobilizations for the spring, nationally coordinated and very theatrical, taking place near courts, jails, and military stockades."

An article published in a Black Panther magazine is entitled "The Hippies Are Not Our Enemies." White radicals have also overcome their initial rejection of cultural radicals. Something clearly is happening, and it is being fed, finally, by youth, the artists, the politicos, and the realization, through struggle, that America is not beautiful.

## Some Historical Analogies

The persecution of the Jews destroyed both a particular social form and the individuals who qualified for the Jewish fate by reason of birth. Looking at the process in the aggregate, Hilberg describes it as a gradual coming together of a multitude of loose laws, institutions, and intentions, rather than a program born mature. The control conglomerate that resulted was a refined engine "whose devices," Hilberg writes, "not only trap a larger number of victims; they also require a greater degree of specialization, and with that division of labor, the moral burden too is fragmented among the participants. The perpetrator can now kill his victims without touching them, without hearing them, without seeing them. . . . This ever-growing capacity for destruction cannot be arrested anywhere." Ultimately, the persecution of the Jews was a mixture of piety, repression, and mobilization directed against people who were in the society but suddenly not of it.

The early Christians were also faced with a refined and elaborate administrative structure whose harsh measures were ultimately directed at their ways of life: their social forms and their spiritual claims. The rationale was, and is, that certain deviant behaviors endanger society. Therefore, officials are obligated to use whatever means of control or persuasion they consider necessary to strike these forms from the list of human possibilities. This is the classical administrative rationale for the suppression of alternative values and world views.

As options closed and Christians found the opportunities to lead and explore Christian lives rapidly struck down, Christian life itself had to become rigid, prematurely closed, and obsessed with survival.

The persecution of the early Christians presents analogies to the persecution of European Jews. The German assault affected the quality of Jewish organizations no less than it affected the lives of individual Jews, distorting communities long before it destroyed them. Hilberg documents some of the ways in which efforts to escape the oppression led on occasion to a subordination of energies to the problem of simply staying alive—of finding some social options within the racial castle. The escapist mentality that dominated the response to oppression and distorted relationships can be seen in some Jewish leaders in Vienna. They exchanged individuals for promises. This is what persecution and terror do. As options close and all parts of the life of the oppressed are touched by procedure, surveillance, and control, behavior is transformed. The oppressed rarely retaliate (especially where they have internalized the very ethic that rejects them), simply because nothing is left untouched by the persecution. No energy is available for hostility, and, in any case, it is impossible to know where to begin. Bravery is stoicism. One sings to the cell or gas chamber.

The persecution of hippies in the United States involves, regardless of the original intentions of the agencies concerned, an assault on a way of life, an assault no less concentrated for its immaturity and occasional ambivalence. Social, cultural, and political resources have been mobilized to bring a group of individuals into line and to prevent others from refusing to toe the line.

The attractiveness of the hippie forms and the pathos of their persecution have together brought into being an impressive array of defenders. Nevertheless theirs has been a defense of gestures, outside the realm of politics and social action essential to any real protection. It has been verbal, scholarly, and appreciative, with occasional expressions of horror at official actions and attitudes. But unfortunately the arena of conflict within which the hippies, willy-nilly, must try to survive is dominated not by the likes of Susan Sontag, but by the likes of Daniel Patrick Moynihan, whose apparent compassion for the hippies will probably never be translated into action. For even as he writes (in the *American Scholar,* Autumn 1967) that these youths are "trying to tell us something" and that they are one test of our "ability to survive," he rejects them firmly, and not a little *ex cathedra*, as a "truth gone astray." The hippie remains helpless and more affected by the repressive forces (who will probably quote Moynihan) than by his own creative capacity or the sympathizers who support him in the journals. As John Kifner reported in the *Times*, " 'This scene is not the same anymore,' said the tall, thin Negro called Gypsy. 'There are some very bad vibrations.' "

### Social Form and Cultural Heresy

But it's just another murder. A hippie being killed is just like a housewife being killed or a career girl being killed or a hood-

lum being killed. None of these people, notice, are persons;
they're labels. Who cares who Groovy was; if you know he was
a "hippie," then already you know more about him than he did
about himself.

See, it's hard to explain to a lot of you what a hippie is because a lot of you really think a hippie IS something. You don't
realize that the word is just a convenience picked up by the
press to personify a social change thing beginning to happen to
young people. (Paul William, "Label Dies—But Not Philosophy," *Open City,* Los Angeles, 17-23 November 1967)

Because the mass media have publicized the growth of a fairly
well-articulated hippie culture, it now bears the status of a social
form. Variously identified as "counterculture," "hippiedom,"
"youth," or "underground," the phenomenon centers on a philosophy of the present and takes the personal and public forms appropriate to that philosophy. Its values constitute a heresy in a society
that consecrates the values of competition, social manipulation, and
functionalism, a society that defines ethical quality by long-range
and general consequences, and that honors only those attitudes and
institutions that affirm the primacy of the future and large-scale
over the local and immediately present. It is a heresy in a society
that eschews the primary value of intimacy for the sake of impersonal service to large and enduring organizations, a society that is
essentialist rather than existentialist, a society that prizes biography
over interactive quality. It is a heresy in a country whose president
could be praised for crying, "Ask not what your country can do for
you, but what you can do for your country!" Most important, however, it is heresy in a society whose official values, principles of
operation, and officials themselves are threatened domestically and
abroad.

For these reasons the hippie is available for persecution. When official authority is threatened, social and political deviants are readily conjured up as demons requiring collective exorcism and thus a
reaffirmation of that authority. Where exorcism is the exclusive
province of government, the government's power is reinforced by
the adoption of a scapegoat. Deviant style and ideals make a group
vulnerable to exploitation as a scapegoat, but it is official action
that translates vulnerability into actionable heresy.

By contrast, recent political developments within black communities and the accommodations reached through bargaining with
various official agencies have placed the blacks alongside the Viet
Cong as an official enemy, but not as a scapegoat. As an enemy, the
black is not a symbol but a source of society's troubles. It is a pre-

ferable position. The hippie's threat lies in the lure of his way of life rather than in his political potential. His vulnerability as well as his proven capacity to develop a real alternative life permits his selection as scapegoat. A threatened officialdom is all too likely to take the final step that "brings on the judge." At the same time, by defining its attack as moderate, it reaffirms its moral superiority in the very field of hate it cultivates.

## A Plausible Force

We are speaking of that which claims the lives, totally or in part, of perhaps hundreds of thousands of people of all ages throughout the United States and elsewhere. The number is not inconsiderable.

The plausibility of the hippie culture and its charisma can be argued on several grounds. Their outlook derives from a profound mobilizing idea: Quality resides in the present. Therefore, one seeks the local in all its social detail—not indulgently and alone, but openly and creatively. Vulnerability and improvisation are principles of action, repudiating the "rational" hierarchy of plans and stages that defines, for the grounded culture, all events as incidents of passage and means to an indefinitely postponable end—as transition. The allocation of reality to the past and the future is rejected in favor of the present, and a present that is known and felt immediately, not judged by external standards. The long run is the result rather than the goal of the present. "Psychical distance," the orientation of the insulated tourist to whom the environment is something forever foreign or of the administrator for whom the world is an object of administration, is repudiated as a relational principle. It is replaced by a principal of absorption. In this, relationships are more like play, dance, or jazz. Intimacy derives from absorption, from spontaneous involvement, to use Erving Goffman's phrase, rather than from frequent contact or attraction, as social psychologists have long argued.

This vision of social reality makes assumptions about human nature. It sees man as only a part of a present that depends on all its parts. To be a "part" is not to play a stereotyped role or to plan one's behavior prior to entering the scene. It is to be of a momentum. Collaboration, the overt manifestation of absorption, is critical to any social arrangement because the present, as experience, is essentially social. Love and charisma are the reflected properties of the plausible whole that results from mutual absorption. "To swing" or "to groove" is to be of the scene rather than simply at or in the scene. "Rapping," an improvised, expansive, and collaborative conversational form, is an active embodiment of the more general ethos. Its craft is humor, devotion, trust, openness to events in the process of formation, and the capacity to be relevant. Identity is neither strictly personal nor something to be maintained, but something always to be discovered. The individual body is the origin of sounds and motions, but behavior, ideas, images, and reflective thought stem from interaction itself. Development is not of personalities but of situations that include many bodies but, in effect, one mind. Various activities, such as smoking marijuana, are disciplines that serve the function of bringing people together and making them deeply interesting to each other.

The development of an authentic counterculture, or, better, "alternative culture," has some striking implications. For one, information and stress are processed through what amounts to a new conceptual system—a culture that replaces, in the committed, the intrapersonal structures that Western personality theories have assumed to account for intrapersonal order. For example, in 1966, young hippies often turned against their friends and their experience after a bad acid trip. But that was the year during which "the hippie thing" was merely one constructive expression of dissent. It was not, at that point, an alternative culture. As a result, the imagery cued in by the trauma was the imagery of the superego, the distant and punitive authority of the Western family and its macrocosmic social system. Guilt, self-hatred, and the rejection of experience was the result. Many youngsters returned home filled with a humiliation that could be forgotten, or converted to a seedy and defensive hatred of the dangerously deviant. By 1968 the bad trip, while still an occasion for reconversion for some, had for others become something to be guarded against and coped with in a context of care and experienced guidance. The atmosphere of trust and new language of stress-inspired dependence rather than recoil as the initial stage of cure. One could "get high with a little help from my friends." Conscience was purged of "authority."

Although the ethos depends on personal contact, it is carried by underground media (hundreds of newspapers claiming hundreds of thousands of readers), rock music, and collective activities, artistic and political, that deliver and duplicate the message; and it is processed through a generational flow. It is no longer simply a constructive expression of dissent and thus attractive because it is a vital answer to a system that destroys vitality; it is culture, and the young are growing up under the wisdom of its older generations. The ethos is realized most fully in the small communes that dot the American urbscape and constitute an important counterinstitution of the hippies.

This complex of population, culture, social form, and ideology is both a reinforcing environment for individuals and a context for the growth and elaboration of the complex itself. In it, life not only begins, but it also goes on; and, indeed, it must go on for individuals who are committed to it. Abbie Hoffman's *Revolution for the Hell of It* assumes the autonomy of this cultural frame of reference. It assumes that the individual has entered and has burned his bridges.

As the heresy takes an official definition and as the institutions of persecution form, a they-mentality emerges in the language that expresses the relationship between the oppressor and the oppressed. For the oppressed, it distinguishes life from nonlife so that living can go on. The they-mentality of the oppressed temporarily relieves them of the struggle by acknowledging the threat, identifying its agent, and compressing both into a quasi-poetic image, a cliché that can accommodate absurdity. One young man said, while coming down from an amphetamine high: "I'm simply going to continue to do what I want until they stop me."

But persecution is also structured by the they-mentality of the persecutors. This mentality draws lines around its objects as it fits them conceptually for full-scale social action. The particular uses of the term *hippie* in the mass media—like "Jew," "Communist," "Black Muslim," or "Black Panther"—cultivates not only disapproval and rejection but also a climate of opinion capable of excluding hippies from the moral order altogether. This is one phase of a subtle process that begins by locating and isolating a group, tying it to the criminal, sinful, or obscene, developing and displaying referential symbols at a high level of abstraction that depersonalize and objectify the group, defining the stigmata by which members are to be known, and placing the symbols in the context of ideology and readiness for action.

At this point, the symbols come to define public issues and are, consequently, sources of strength. The maintenance of power—the next phase of the story—depends less on the instruction of reading and viewing publics than on the elaboration of the persecutory institutions that demonstrate and justify power. The relationship between institution and public ceases to be one of expression or extension (of a public to an institution) and becomes one of transaction or dominance (of a public with or by an institution). The total dynamic is similar to advertising or the growth of the military as domestic powers in America.

An explosion of hippie stories appeared in the mass media during the summer of 1967. Almost every large-circulation magazine featured articles on the hippie "fad" or "subculture." *Life's* "The Other Culture" set the tone. The theme was repeated in *The New York Times Magazine* 14 May 1967, where Hunter Thompson wrote that "The 'Hashbury' [Haight-Asbury in San Francisco] is the new capital of what is rapidly becoming a drug culture." *Time's* "wholly new subculture" was "a cult whose mystique derives essentially from the influences of hallucinogenic drugs." By fall, while maintaining the emphasis on drugs as the cornerstone of the culture, the articles had shifted from the culturological to a "national character" approach, reminiscent of the World War II anti-Japanese propaganda, as personal traits were piled into the body of the symbol and objectification began. The hippies were "acid heads," "generally dirty," and "visible, audible, and sometimes smellable young rebels."

As "hippie" and its associated terms ("long-haired," "bearded") accumulated pejorative connotation, they began to be useful concepts and were featured regularly in news headlines: for example, "Hippie Mother Held in Slaying of Son, 2" (*The New York Times,* 22 November 1967); "S Squad Hits Four Pads" (*San Francisco Chronicle,* 27 July 1967). The articles themselves solidified usage by dwelling on "hippie types," "wild drug parties," and "long-haired, bearded" youths (see, for example, *The New York Times* of 13 February 1968, 16 September 1968, and 3 November 1967).

This is a phenomenon that R. H. Turner and S. J. Surace described in 1956 in order to account for the role of media in the development of hostile consciousness toward Mexicans. The presentation of certain symbols can remove their referents from the constraints of the conventional moral order so that extralegal and extramoral action can be used against them. Political cartoonists have used the same device with less powerful results. To call Mexican Americans "zootsuiters" in Los Angeles in 1943, was to free hostility from the limits of the conventional, though fragile, antiracism required by liberal ideology. The result was a wave of brutal anti-Mexican assaults. Turner and Surace hypothesized that:

> To the degree, then, to which any symbol evokes only one consistent set of connotations throughout the community, only one general course of action with respect to that object will be indicated, and the union of diverse members of the community into an acting crowd will be facilitated. . .or it will be an audience prepared to accept novel forms of official action.

First the symbol, then the accumulation of hostile connotations, and finally the action-issue: Such a sequence appears in the news coverage of hippies from the beginning of 1967 to the present. The amount of coverage has decreased in the late sixties, but this seems less a result of sympathy or sophistication and more one of certainty: The issue is decided and certain truths can be taken for granted. As this public consciousness finds official representation in the formation of a control conglomerate, it heralds the final and institutional stage in the growth of repressive force, persecution, and terror.

The growth of this control conglomerate, the mark of any repressive system, depends on the development of new techniques and organizations. But its momentum requires an ideological head of steam. In the case of the hippie life, the ideological condemnation is based on several counts: that it is dangerous and irresponsible, subversive to authority, immoral, and psychopathological.

Commenting on the relationship between beliefs and the development of the persecutory institutions for witchcontrol in the sixteenth century, Trevor-Roper, in an essay on "Witches and Witchcraft," states:

> In a climate of fear, it is easy to see how this process could happen: how individual deviations could be associated with a central pattern. We have seen it happen in our own time. The "McCarthyite" experience of the United States in the 1950s was exactly comparable: Social fear, the fear of an incompatible system of society, was given intellectual form as a heretical ideology and suspect individuals were persecuted by reference to that heresy.

The same fear finds its ideological expression against the hippies in the statement of Dr. Stanley F. Yolles, director of the National Institute of Mental Health, that "alienation," which he called a major underlying cause of drug abuse, "was wider, deeper, and more diffuse now than it has been in any other period in American history." The rejection of dissent in the name of mental health rather than moral values or social or political interest is a modern characteristic. Dr. Yolles suggested that if urgent attention is not given the problem:

> there are serious dangers that large proportions of current and future generations will reach adulthood embittered toward the larger society, unequipped to take on parental, vocational, and other citizen roles, and involved in some form of socially deviant behavior. . . .

Dr. Seymour L. Halleck, director of student psychiatry at the University of Wisconsin, also tied the heresy to various sources of sin: affluence, lack of contact with adults, and an excess of freedom. Dr. Henry Brill, director of Pilgrim State Hospital on Long Island and a consultant on drug use to federal and state agencies, is quoted in *The New York Times*, 26 September 1967:

> It is my opinion that the unrestricted use of marijuana-type substances produces a significant amount of vagabondage, dependency, and psychiatric disability.

Drs. Yolles, Halleck, and Brill are probably fairly representative of psychiatric opinion. Psychiatry has long defined normality and health in terms of each other in a "scientific" avoidance of serious value questions. Psychiatrists agree in principle on several related points that could constitute a medical-rational foundation for the persecution of hippies: They define the normal and healthy individual as patient and instrumental. He plans for the long range and pursues his goals temperately and economically. He is an individual with a need for privacy and his contacts are moderate and respectful. He is stable in style and identity, reasonably competitive and optimistic. Finally, he accepts reality and participates in the social forms that constitute the givens of his life. Drug use, sexual pleasure, a repudiation of clear long-range goals, the insistence on intimacy and self-affirmation, distrust of official authority, and radical dissent are all part of the abnormality that colors the hippies "alienated" or "disturbed" or "neurotic."

This ideology characterizes the heresy in technical terms. Mental illness is a scientific and medical problem, and isolation and treatment are recommended. Youth, alienation, and drug use are the discrediting characteristics of people who are unqualified for due process, discussion, or conflict. The genius of the ideology has been to separate the phenomenon under review from consideration of law and value. In this way the mutual hostilities that ordinarily divide the various agencies of control are bypassed and the issue endowed with ethical and political neutrality. Haurek and Clark, in their "Variants of Integration of Social Control Agencies," described two opposing orientations among social control agencies, the authoritarian-punitive (the police, the courts) and the humanitarian-welfare (private agencies, social workers), with the latter holding the former in low esteem. The hippies have brought them together.

The designation of the hippie impulse as heresy on the grounds of psychopathology not only bypasses traditional enmity among various agencies of social control, but its corollaries also activate each agency. It is the eventual coordination of their efforts that constitutes the control conglomerate. I shall briefly discuss several of these corollaries before examining the impact of the conglomerate. Youth, danger, and disobedience are the major themes.

Dominating the study of adolescence is a general theory that propounds that the adolescent is a psychosexual type. Due to an awakening of the instincts after a time of relative quiescence, he is readily overwhelmed by them. Consequently, his behavior may be viewed as the working out of intense intrapsychic conflict—it is symptomatic or expressive rather than rational and realistic. He is idealistic, easily influenced, and magical. The idealism is the expression of a threatened superego; the susceptibility to influence is an attempt to find support for an identity in danger of diffusion; the magic, reflected in adolescent romance and its rituals, is an attempt to get a grip on a reality that shifts and turns too much for comfort. By virtue of his entrance into the youth culture, he joins in the collective expression of emotional immaturity. At heart, he is the youth of Golding's *Lord of the Flies*, a fledgling adult living out a transitional status. His idealism may be sentimentally touching, but in truth he is morally irresponsible and dangerous.

## Youth

As the idealism of the young is processed through the youth culture, it becomes radical ideology, and even radical practice. The attempts by parents and educators to break the youth culture by rejecting its symbols and limiting the opportunities for its expression (ranging from dress regulations in school to the censorship of youth music on the air) are justified as a response to the dangerous political implications of the ideology of developed and ingrown immaturity. That these same parents and educators find their efforts to conventionalize the youth culture (through moderate imitations of youthful dress and attempts to "get together with the kids") rejected encourages them further to see the young as hostile, unreasonable, and intransigent. The danger of extremism (the New Left and the hippies) animates their criticism, and all intrusions on the normal are read as pointing in that direction. The ensuing conflict between the wise and the unreasonable is called (largely by the wise) the *generation gap*.

From this it follows that radicalism is the peculiar propensity of the young and, as Christopher Jencks and David Riesman have pointed out in *The Academic Revolution*, of individuals who identify with the young. At its best it is not considered serious; at its worst it is the counterculture. The myth of the generation gap, a myth that is all the more strongly held as less and less evidence is found for it, reinforces this view by assuming that radicalism ends, or should end, when the gap is bridged—when the young grow older and wiser. While this lays the groundwork for tolerance, or more likely, forbearance, it is a tolerance limited to youthful radicalism. It also lays the groundwork for a more thorough rejection of the radicalism of the not-so-young and the "extreme."

Thus, the theory of youth classifies radicalism as immature and, when cultivated, dangerous or pathological. Alienation is the explanation used to account for the extension of youthful idealism and paranoia into the realm of the politically and culturally adult. Its wrongness is temporary and trivial. If it persists, it becomes a structural defect requiring capture and treatment rather than due process and argument.

**Danger**

Once a life-style and its practices are declared illegal, its proponents are by definition criminal and subversive. On the one hand, the very dangers presupposed by the legal proscriptions immediately become clear and present. The illegal life-style becomes the living demonstration of its alleged dangers. The ragged vagabondage of the hippie is proof that drugs and promiscuity are alienating, and the attempts to sleep in parks, to gather, and to roam are the new "violence" of which we have been reading. Crime certainly is crime, and the hippies commit crime by their very existence. The dangers are: (1) crime and the temptation to commit crime; (2) alienation and the temptation to drop out. The behaviors that, if unchecked, become imbedded in the personality of the suspectible are, among others, drug use (in particular marijuana), apparel deviance, dropping out (usually of school), sexual promiscuity, communal living, nudity, hair deviance, draft resistance, demonstrating against the feudal oligarchies in cities and colleges, gathering, roaming, doing strange art, and being psychedelic. Many of these are defused by campaigns of definition; they become topical and in fashion. To wear bell-bottom pants, long sideburns, flowers on your car, and beads, is, if done with taste and among the right people, stylish and eccentric rather than another step toward the brink or a way of lending aid and comfort to the enemy. The disintegration of a form by coopting only its parts is a familiar phenomenon. It is tearing an argument apart by confronting each proposition as if it had no context, treating a message like an intellectual game.

Drugs, communalism, gathering, roaming, resisting and demonstrating, and certain styles of hair have not been defused. In fact, the drug scene is the site of the greatest concentration of justificatory energy and the banner under which the agencies of the control conglomerate unite. That their use is so widespread through the straight society indicates the role of drugs as temptation. That drugs have been pinned so clearly (despite the fact that many hippies are nonusers) and so gladly to the hippies, engages the institutions of persecution in the task of destroying the hippie thing.

The antimarijuana lobby has postulated a complex of violence, mental illness, genetic damage, apathy, and alienation, all arising out of the ashes of smoked pot. The hypothesis justifies a set of laws and practices of great harshness and discrimination, and the president [Nixon] recently recommended that they be made even more so. The number of arrests for use, possession, or sale of marijuana has soared in recent years: Between 1964 and 1966 yearly arrests doubled, from 7,000 to 15,000. The United States Narcotics Commissioner attributed the problem to "certain groups" that give marijuana to young people, and to "false information" about the danger of the drug.

Drug raids ordinarily net "hippie-type youth," although lately news reports refer to "youths from good homes." The use of spies on campuses, one of the bases for the original protest demonstrations at Nanterre prior to the May revolution, has become common, with all its socially destructive implications. Extensive spy operations were behind many of the police raids of college and private-school campuses during 1967, 1968, and 1969. Among those hit were Long Island University's Southampton College (twice), State University College at Oswego, New York, the Hun School of Princeton, Bard College, Syracuse University, Stony Brook College, and Franconia College in New Hampshire; the list could go on.

It is the "certain groups" that the commissioner spoke of who bear the brunt of the condemnation and the harshest penalties. The laws themselves are peculiar enough, having been strengthened largely since the hippies became visible, but they are enforced with obvious discrimination. Teenagers arrested in a "good residential section" of Naugatuck, Connecticut, were treated gently by the circuit court judge:

> I suspect that many of these youngsters should not have been arrested. . . . I'm not going to have these youngsters bouncing around with these charges hanging over them.

They were later released and the charges dismissed. In contrast, after a "mass arrest" in which fifteen of the twenty-five arrested were charged with being in a place where they knew that others were smoking marijuana, Washington, D.C.'s Judge Halleck underscored his determination "to show these long-haired ne'er-do-wells that society will not tolerate their conduct" (*Washington Post*, 21 May 1967).

The incidents of arrest and the exuberance with which the laws are discriminatorily enforced are justified, although not explained, by the magnifying judgment of "danger." At a meeting of agents from seventy-four police departments in Connecticut and New York, Westchester County Sheriff John E. Hoy, "in a dramatic stage whisper," said, "It is a frightening situation, my friends. . . marijuana is creeping up on us."

One assistant district attorney stated that "the problem is staggering." A county executive agreed that "the use of marijuana is vicious," while a school superintendent argued that "marijuana is a plaguelike disease, slowly but surely strangling our young people." Harvard freshmen were warned against the "social influences" that surround drugs and one chief of police attributed drug use and social deviance to permissiveness in a slogan that has since become more common (*St. Louis Post-Dispatch*, 22 August 1968).

Bennett Berger has pointed out that the issue of danger is an ideological ploy (*Denver Post*, 19 April 1968): "The real issue of marijuana is ethical and political, touching the 'core of cultural values.'" *The New York Times* of 11 January 1968, reports, "Students and high-school and college officials agree that 'drug use has increased sharply since the intensive coverage given to drugs and the hippies last summer by the mass media.'" It is also supported by other attempts to tie drugs to heresy: *The New York Times* of 17 November 1968, notes a Veterans Administration course for doctors on the hippies that ties hippies, drugs, and alienation together and suggests that the search for potential victims might begin in the seventh or eighth grades.

The dynamic relationship among ideology, organization, and practice is revealed both in President Johnson's "Message on Crime to Insure Public Safety" (delivered to Congress on 7 February 1968) and in the gradual internationalizing of the persecution. The president recommended "strong new laws," an increase in the number of enforcement agents, and the centralization of federal enforcement machinery. At the same time, the United Nations Economic and Social Council considered a resolution asking that governments "deal effectively with publicity that advocates legalization or tolerance of the nonmedical use of cannabis as a harmless drug." The resolution was consistent with President Johnson's plan to have the Federal Government of the United States "maintain worldwide operations. . . to suppress the trade in illicit narcotics and marijuana." The reasons for the international campaign were clarified by a World Health Organization panel's affirmation of its intent to prevent the use or sale of marijuana because it is "a drug of dependence, producing health and social problems." At the same time that scientific researchers at Harvard and Boston universities were exonerating the substance, the penalties increased and the efforts to proscribe it reached international proportions. A number of countries, including Laos and Thailand, have barred hippies, and Mexico has made it difficult for those with long hair and "serious eyes" to cross its border.

**Disobedience**

The assumption that society is held together by formal law and authority implies in principle that the habit of obedience must be reinforced. The details of the hippie culture are, in relation to the grounded culture, disobedient. From that perspective, too, their values and ideology are also explicitly disobedient. The disobedience goes far beyond the forms of social organization and personal presentation to the conventional systems of healing, dietary practice, and environmental use. There is virtually no system of authority that is not thrown into question. Methodologically, the situationalism of pornography, guerrilla theater, and place conversion is not only profoundly subversive in itself; it turns the grounded culture around. By coating conventional behavioral norms with ridicule and obscenity, by tying radically different meanings to old routines, it challenges our sentiments. By raising the level of our self-consciousness it allows us to become moral in the areas we had allowed to degenerate into habit (apathy or gluttony). When the rock group, the Fugs, sings and dances "Group Grope" or any of their other songs devoted brutally to "love" and "taste," they pin our tender routines to a humiliating obscenity. We can no longer take our behavior and our intentions for granted. The confrontation enables us to disobey or to reconsider or to choose simply by forcing into consciousness the patterns of behavior and belief of which we have become victims. The confrontation is manly because it exposes both sides in an arena of conflict.

When questions are posed in ways that permit us to disengage ourselves from their meaning to our lives, we tolerate the questions as a moderate and decent form of dissent. And we congratulate ourselves for our tolerance. But when people refuse to know their place, and, what is worse, our place, and they insist on themselves openly and demand that we redecide our own lives, we are willing to have them knocked down. Consciousness permits disobedience. As a result, systems threatened from within often begin the work of reassertion by an attack on consciousness and chosen forms of life.

Youth, danger, and disobedience define the heresy in terms that activate the host of agencies that, together, comprise the control conglomerate. Each agency, wrote Trevor-Roper, was ready: "The engine of persecution was set up before its future victims were legally subject to it." The conglomerate has its target. But it is a potential of the social system as much as it is an actor. Trevor-Roper comments further that

> once we see the persecution of heresy as social intolerance, the intellectual difference between one heresy and another becomes less significant.

And the difference, one might add, between one persecutor and another becomes less significant. Someone it does not matter who tells Mr. Blue (in Tom Paxton's song): "What will it take to whip you into line?"

How have I ended here? The chapter is an analysis of the institutionalization of persecution and the relationship between the control conglomerate that is the advanced form of official persecution and the hippies as an alternative culture, the target of control. But an analysis must work with a vision if it is to move beyond analysis into action. The tragedy of America may be that it completed the technology of control before it developed compassion and tolerance. It never learned to tolerate history, and now it is finally capable of ending history by ending the change that political sociologists and undergroups understand. The struggle has always gone on in the mind. Only now, for this society, is it going on in the open among people. Only now is it beginning to shape lives rather than simply shaping individuals. Whether it is too late or not will be worked out in the attempts to transcend the one-dimensionality that Marcuse described. That the alternative culture is here seems difficult to doubt. Whether it becomes revolutionary fast enough to supersede an officialdom bent on its destruction may be an important part of the story of America.

As an exercise in overestimation, this essay proposes a methodological tool for going from analysis to action in areas that are too easily absorbed by a larger picture but that are at the same time too critical to be viewed outside the context of political action.

The analysis suggests several conclusions:

Control usually transcends itself both in its selection of targets and in its organization.

At some point in its development, control is readily institutionalized and finally institutional. The control conglomerate represents a new stage in social organization and is an authentic change-inducing force for social systems.

The hallmark of an advanced system of control (and the key to its beginning) is an ideology that unites otherwise highly differing agencies.

Persecution and terror go in our society. The hippies, as a genuine heresy, have engaged official opposition to a growing cultural-social-political tendency. The organization of control has both eliminated countervailing official forces and begun to place all deviance in the category of heresy. This pattern may soon become endemic to the society.

# Contributors

ROBERT LYNN ADAMS is associate professor of sociology at Chapman College in Orange, California. Coauthor of articles of marriage and mobility in church and sect and on conflict over charges of heresy in American Protestant seminaries, he is currently working on a book on conflict and change in Appalachia and also continuing the Jesus movement study.

NATALIE ALLON is assistant professor of sociology at Hofstra University. Her professional interests include the sociology of religion—currently a study of nuns—and what she terms the *sociology of the body*. A consultant to the National Association to Aid Fat Americans, Inc., she lists her hobbies as swimming and eating, in interchangeable order.

HOWARD S. BECKER is professor of sociology at Northwestern University. He is the author of *Outsiders, Sociological Work*, the editor of *The Other Side, Culture and Civility in San Francisco*, and *Campus Power Struggles*, and with others he is the author of *Boys in White* and editor of *Institutions and the Person*.

MICHAEL E. BROWN is an assistant professor of sociology at Queens College and regional secretary of the New University Conference. With Amy Goldman he coauthored *Collective Behavior: Unauthorized Social Action*, published by Goodyear Publishing Company. He is currently working on a book on the underground press. The study was sponsored by the Center for Movement Research, Department of Sociology, Queens College, Flushing, New York.

WILLIAM J. CHAMBLISS is a professor of sociology at the University of California at Santa Barbara. He is the author or editor of *Crime and the Legal Process; Criminal Law in Action; Law, Order, and Power; Whose Law, What Order?;* and *Problems of Industrial Society.*

JAMES P. DRISCOLL is a Ph.D. candidate at the University of California at Santa Barbara, where he is a lecturer in sociology. His areas of special interest are criminology, deviant behavior, and the sociology of law. Prior to his return to graduate school he was an advertising salesman, teamster, bartender, cab driver, longshoreman, and had his own printing business.

ROBERT JON FOX is a master's candidate in counseling psychology at Chapman College.

NATHAN L. GERRARD is professor and chairman of the Department of Sociology, Morris Harvey College, Charleston, West Virginia. He has maintained continuous and intimate contact with a serpent-handling church for the last seven years. His study was supported by the Wenner-Gren Foundation and the National Institute of Mental Health. His research interests include the cultural and social patterns of the "hollows," the communities of nonfarm rural poor in West Virginia.

JAMES M. HENSLIN is a professor of sociology at Southern Illinois University at Edwardsville. He has written *Introducing Sociology: Toward Understanding Life in Society* and among other books has edited *Down to Earth Sociology, Studies in the Sociology of Sex,* and *Introducing Sociology: Selected Readings.*

IRVING LOUIS HOROWITZ is professor of sociology and political science at Rutgers University, director of *Studies in Comparative International Development,* and editor-in-chief of *Transaction/Society.*

JOHN HORTON is an associate professor of sociology at the University of California at Los Angeles. In addition to his research on crime and the social structure, he has written in the areas of political sociology and sociological theory.

LAUD HUMPHREYS is a professor of sociology at Pitzer College. He is the author of *Tearoom Trade,* winner of the C. Wright Mills Award, and editor of *Out of the Closets.*

THOMAS KOCHMAN is associate professor in the Department of Linguistics at Northeastern Illinois State College. He is the author of *Rappin' and Stylin' Out,* a book focusing on communication styles among urban blacks.

STANFORD M. LYMAN is a professor of sociology in the Graduate Faculty of Political and Social Science at the New School for Social Research. He has written: *The Asian in the West; The Black American in Sociological Thought; Chinese Americas;* and with Marvin Scott has published *Sociology of the Absurd* and *The Drama of Social Reality.*

WALTER B. MILLER is an anthropologist associated with the Center for Criminal Justice at the Law School of Harvard University. He is the author of numerous articles and the coauthor of *The Mollusks of the Arid Southwest.*

CHARLES PALSON is a doctoral candidate in anthropology at the University of Chicago. At present he is teaching marriage and family relations at Immaculata College, Immaculata, Pennsylvania. He is national president of the Student Evaluation Project (S.T.E.P.), which publishes student evaluations of graduate departments of anthropology.

REBECCA PALSON has studied anthropology and art. Coauthor with her husband of several articles on the culture of sex and the structure of swingers' relationships, she is working with him on a book, *Friends and Lovers: A Study in the Use and Meaning of Sex.*

DAVID J. PITTMAN is chairman and professor of sociology at Washington University. He is the author of: *The Drug Scene in Great Britain; Alcoholism;* and *Society, Culture, and Drinking Patterns;* as well as the coauthor of *Revolving Door.*

MARILYN SALUTIN is a Ph.D. candidate at York University in Toronto. This chapter is based on her M.A. thesis done at York. She has written a forthcoming book about strippers and comics and her research experience. She is also a researcher at the Ontario Institute for Studies in Education.

JAMES P. SPRADLEY is an associate professor of anthropology at Macalester College, St. Paul, Minnesota. He is coeditor of the *Nacirema* and has written *Guests Never Leave Hungry,* the autobiography of a Kwakiutl Indian, as well as *You Owe Yourself a Drunk: An Ethnography of Urban Nomads.*

ALBERT J. VELARDE is doing graduate work at Northwestern University. He plans to earn a Ph.D. in sociology.

MARK WARLICK received a B.A. degree in philosophy from California State University at Hayward. His plans include further research, travel, and graduate school.

# Index

377